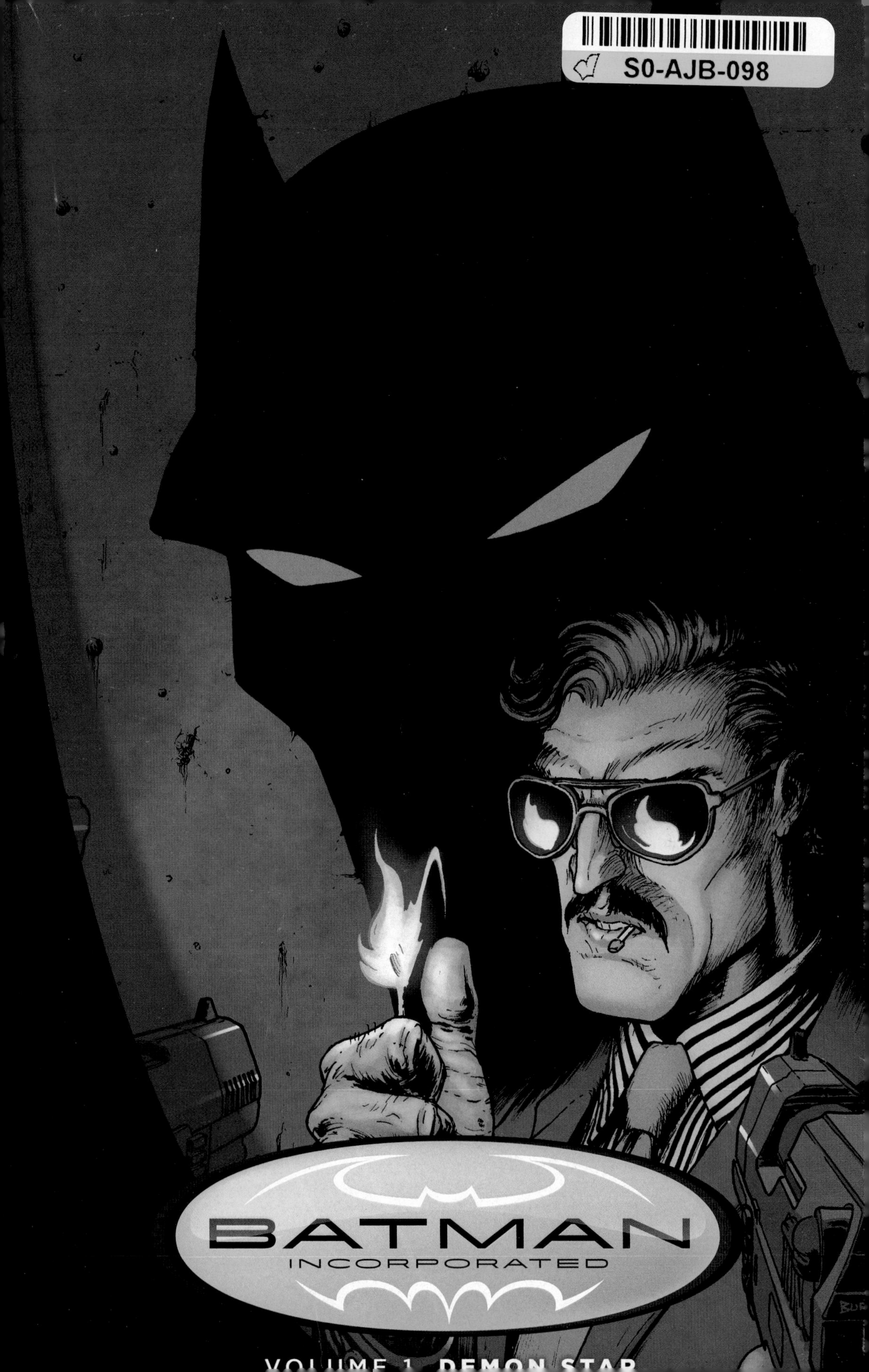
BATMAN
INCORPORATED
VOLUME 1 DEMON STAR

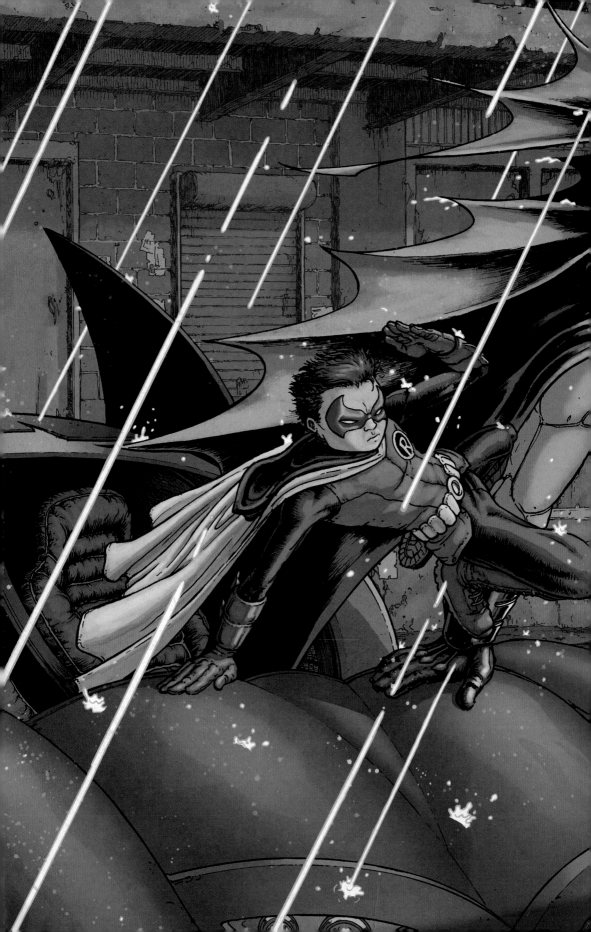

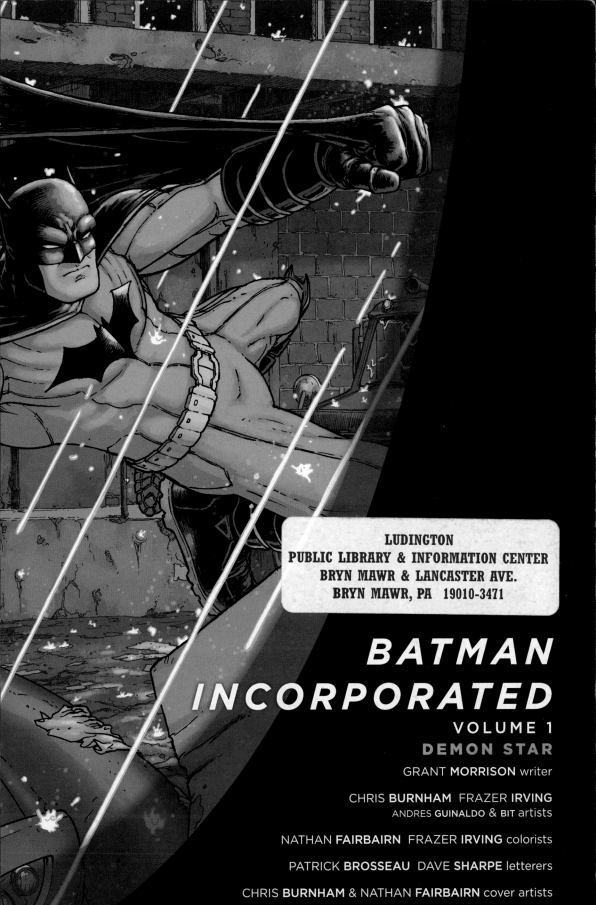

BATMAN INCORPORATED

VOLUME 1
DEMON STAR

GRANT **MORRISON** writer

CHRIS **BURNHAM**   FRAZER **IRVING**
ANDRES **GUINALDO** & **BIT** artists

NATHAN **FAIRBAIRN**   FRAZER **IRVING** colorists

PATRICK **BROSSEAU**   DAVE **SHARPE** letterers

CHRIS **BURNHAM** & NATHAN **FAIRBAIRN** cover artists

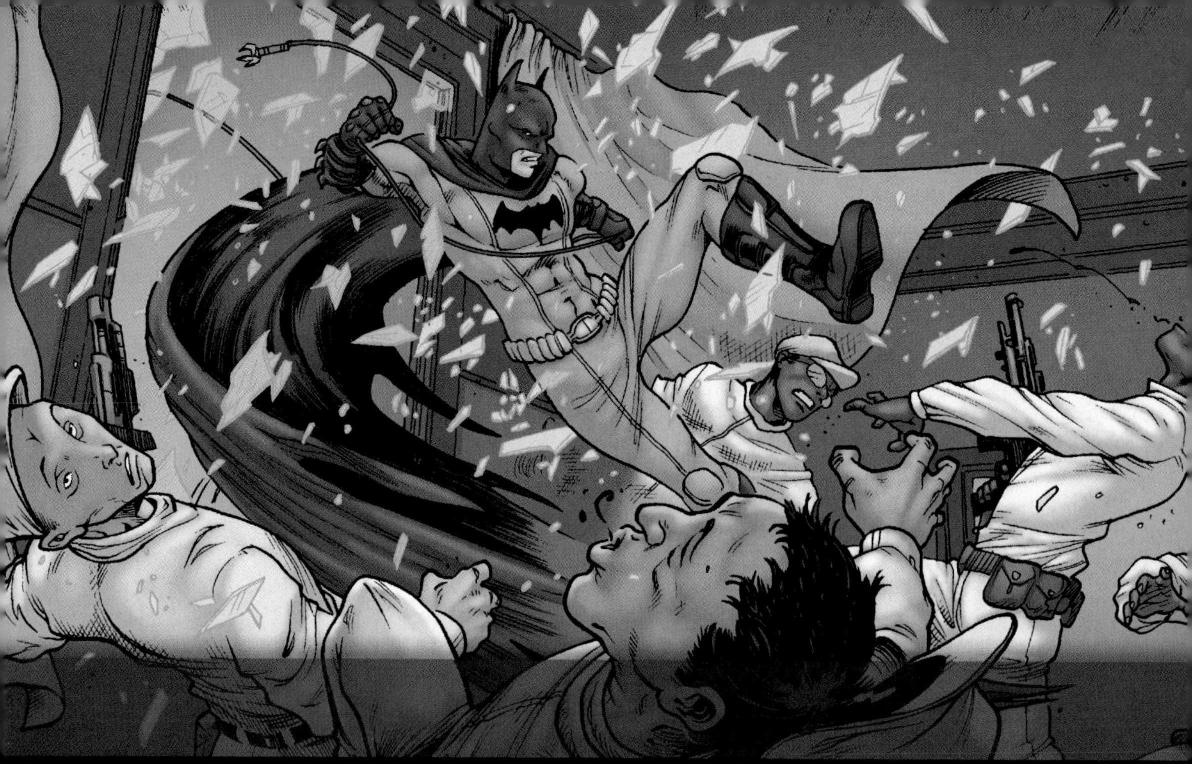

MIKE MARTS Editor - Original Series BRIAN SMITH Associate Editor - Original Series
RICKEY PURDIN Assistant Editor - Original Series PETER HAMBOUSSI Editor
ROBBIN BROSTERMAN Design Director - Books ROBBIE BIEDERMAN Publication Design

BOB HARRAS Senior VP - Editor-in-Chief, DC Comics

DIANE NELSON President DAN DIDIO and JIM LEE Co-Publishers
GEOFF JOHNS Chief Creative Officer
JOHN ROOD Executive VP - Sales, Marketing and Business Development
AMY GENKINS Senior VP - Business and Legal Affairs NAIRI GARDINER Senior VP - Finance
JEFF BOISON VP - Publishing Planning MARK CHIARELLO VP - Art Direction and Design
JOHN CUNNINGHAM VP - Marketing TERRI CUNNINGHAM VP - Editorial Administration
ALISON GILL Senior VP - Manufacturing and Operations HANK KANALZ Senior VP - Vertigo and Integrated Publishing
JAY KOGAN VP - Business and Legal Affairs, Publishing JACK MAHAN VP - Business Affairs, Talent
NICK NAPOLITANO VP - Manufacturing Administration SUE POHJA VP - Book Sales
COURTNEY SIMMONS Senior VP - Publicity BOB WAYNE Senior VP - Sales

BATMAN INCORPORATED VOLUME 1: DEMON STAR

DC Comics, 1700 Broadway, New York, NY 10019
A Warner Bros. Entertainment Company
Printed by RR Donnelley, Salem, VA, USA. 10/25/13. First Printing.

ISBN: 978-1-4012-4263-3

Library of Congress Cataloging-in-Publication Data

Morrison, Grant, author.
Batman, Incorporated. Volume 1, Demon Star / Grant Morrison, Chris Burnham.
pages cm
"Originally published in single magazine form in Batman, Incorporated 0-6."
ISBN 978-1-4012-3888-9
1. Graphic novels. I. Burnham, Chris, 1977- illustrator. II. Title. III. Title: Demon Star.
PN6728.B36M675 2013
741.5'973—dc23
2012050769

SUSTAINABLE FORESTRY INITIATIVE
Certified Chain of Custody
At Least 20% Certified Forest Content
www.sfiprogram.org
SFI-01042
APPLIES TO TEXT STOCK ONLY

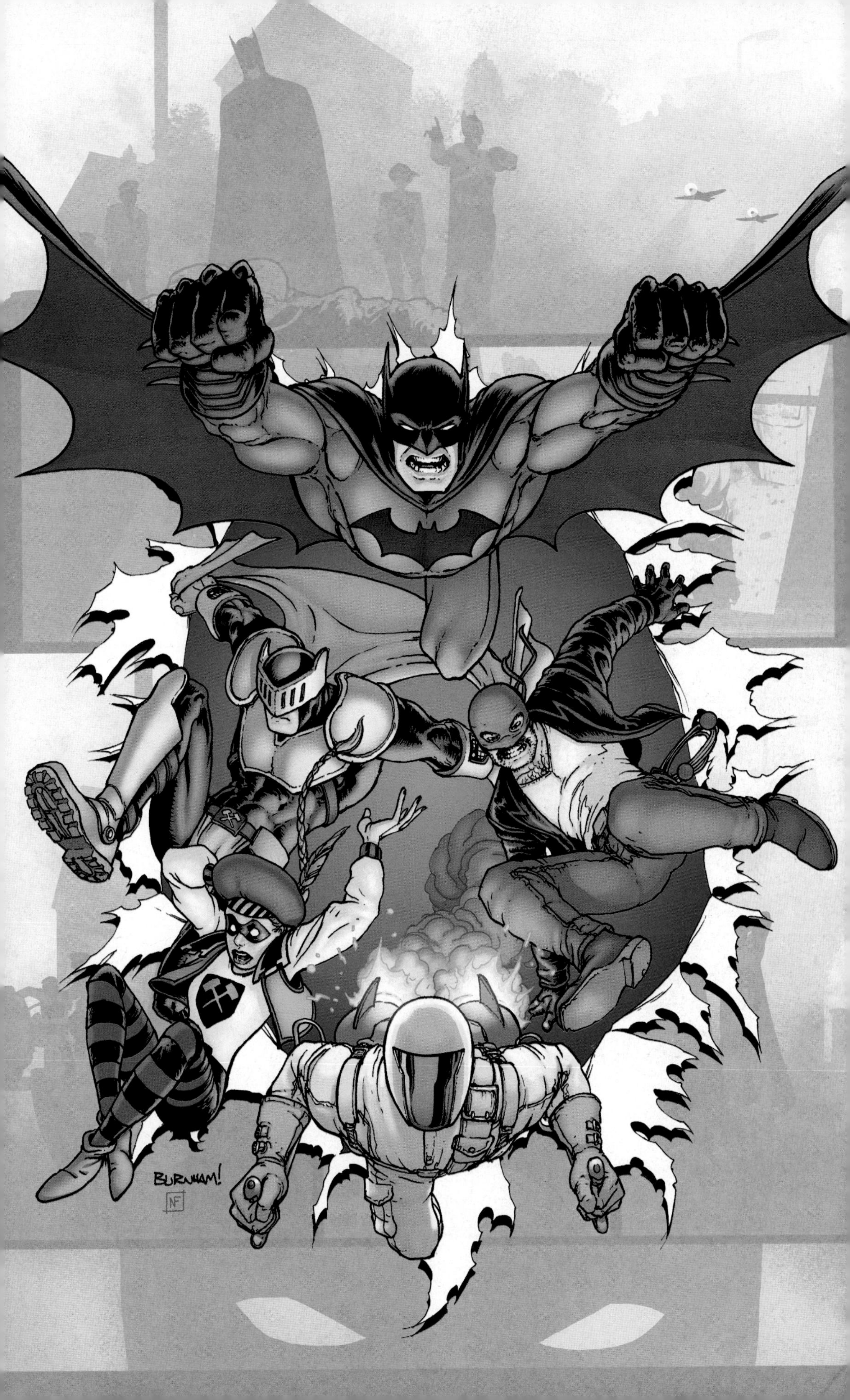
BURNHAM!
NF

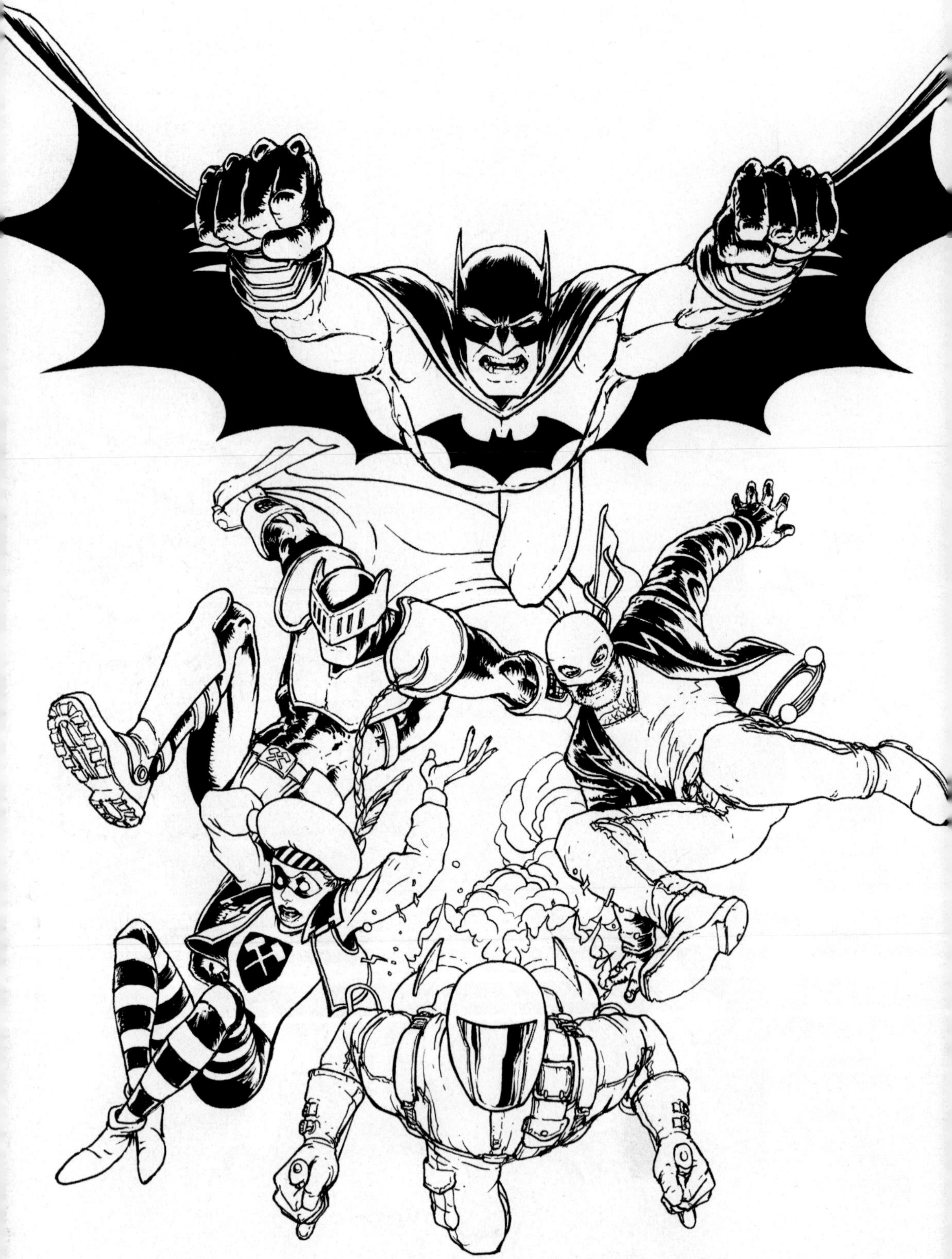

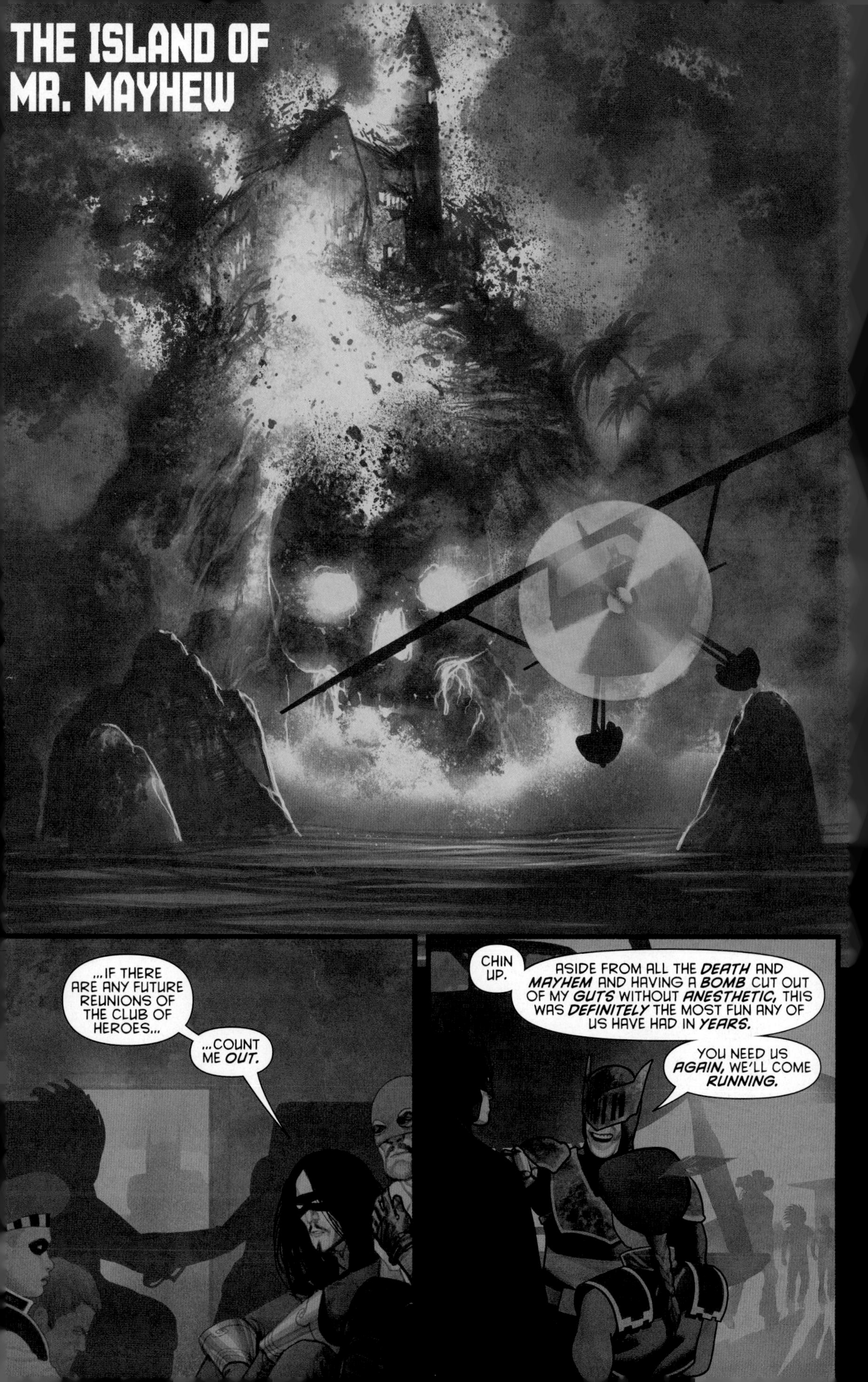

THE ISLAND OF MR. MAYHEW
...IF THERE ARE ANY FUTURE REUNIONS OF THE CLUB OF HEROES...
...COUNT ME *OUT.*
CHIN UP.
ASIDE FROM ALL THE *DEATH* AND *MAYHEM* AND HAVING A *BOMB* CUT OUT OF MY *GUTS* WITHOUT *ANESTHETIC,* THIS WAS *DEFINITELY* THE MOST FUN ANY OF US HAVE HAD IN *YEARS.*
YOU NEED US *AGAIN,* WE'LL COME *RUNNING.*

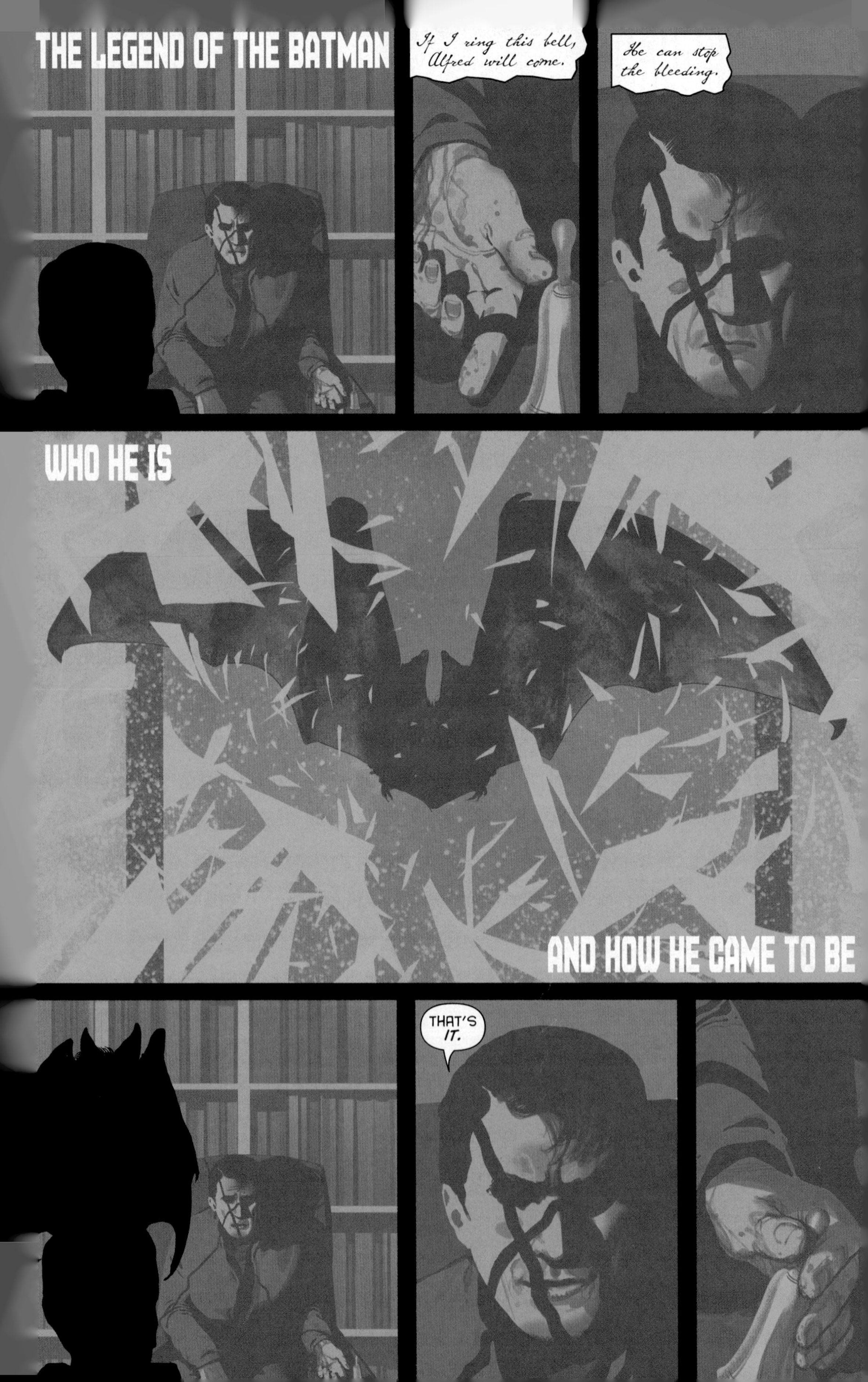
THE LEGEND OF THE BATMAN
If I ring this bell, Alfred will come.
He can stop the bleeding.
WHO HE IS
AND HOW HE CAME TO BE
THAT'S IT.

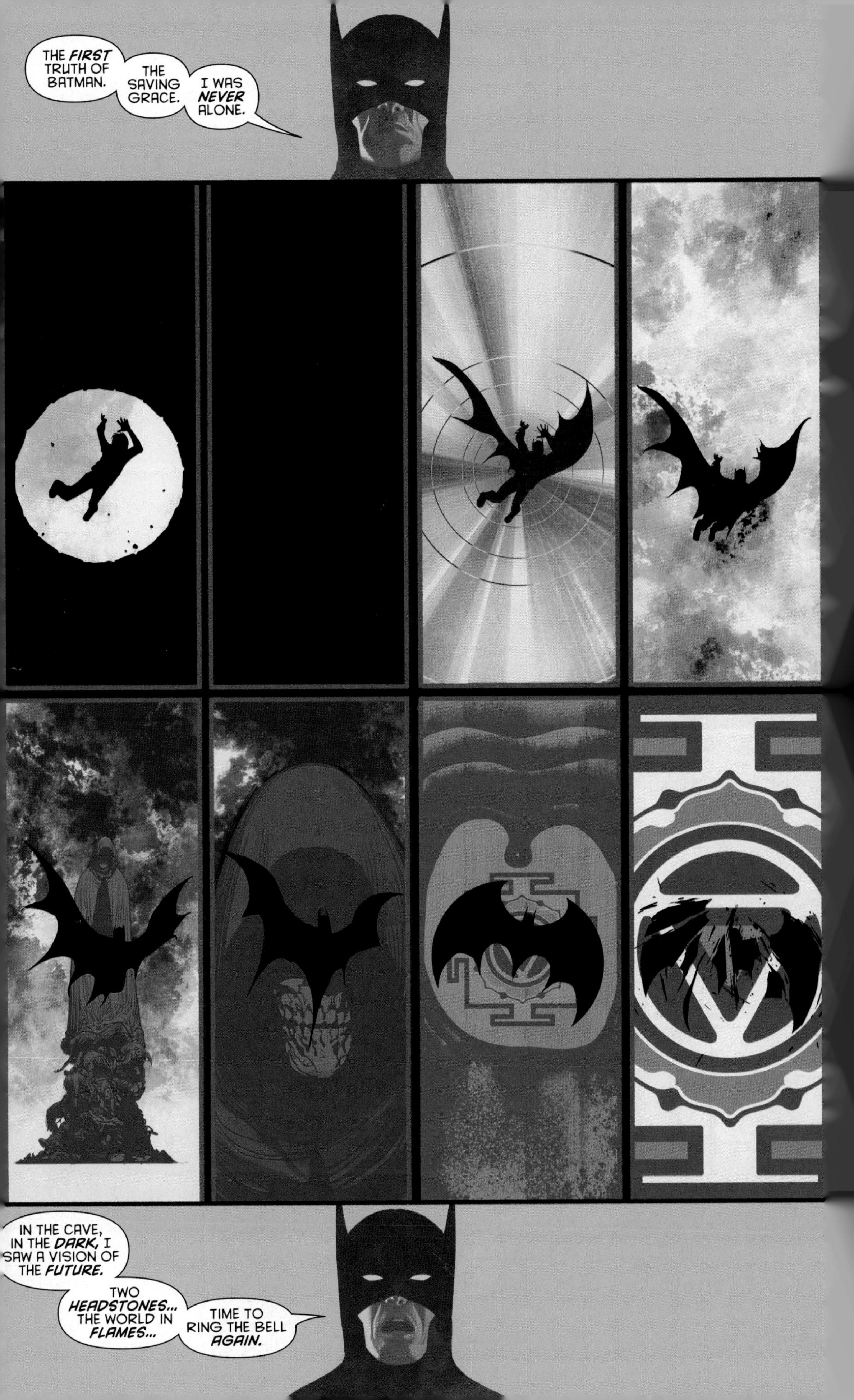
THE FIRST TRUTH OF BATMAN.
THE SAVING GRACE.
I WAS NEVER ALONE.
IN THE CAVE, IN THE DARK, I SAW A VISION OF THE FUTURE.
TWO HEADSTONES... THE WORLD IN FLAMES...
TIME TO RING THE BELL AGAIN.

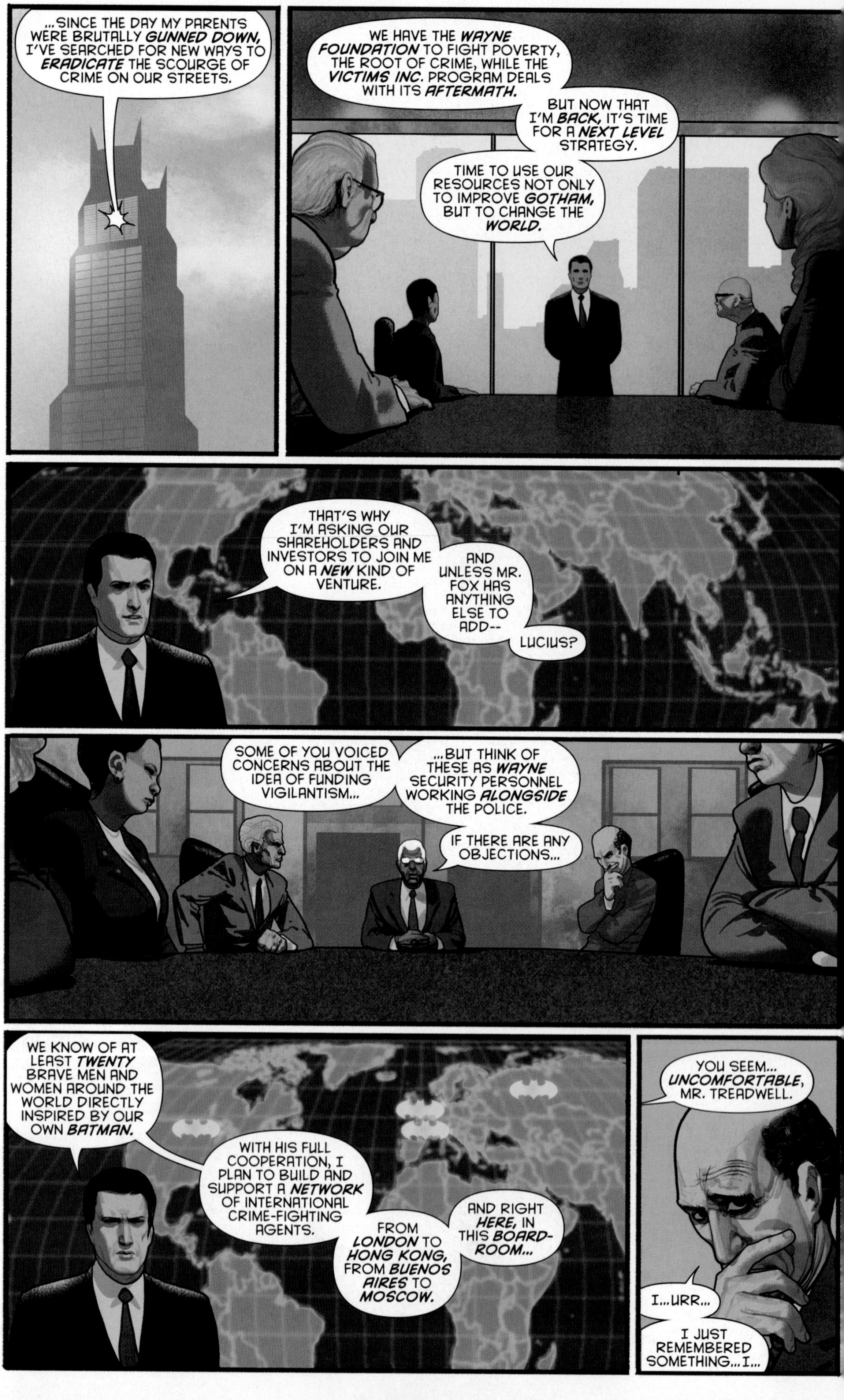
...SINCE THE DAY MY PARENTS WERE BRUTALLY GUNNED DOWN, I'VE SEARCHED FOR NEW WAYS TO ERADICATE THE SCOURGE OF CRIME ON OUR STREETS.
WE HAVE THE WAYNE FOUNDATION TO FIGHT POVERTY, THE ROOT OF CRIME, WHILE THE VICTIMS INC. PROGRAM DEALS WITH ITS AFTERMATH.
BUT NOW THAT I'M BACK, IT'S TIME FOR A NEXT LEVEL STRATEGY.
TIME TO USE OUR RESOURCES NOT ONLY TO IMPROVE GOTHAM, BUT TO CHANGE THE WORLD.
THAT'S WHY I'M ASKING OUR SHAREHOLDERS AND INVESTORS TO JOIN ME ON A NEW KIND OF VENTURE.
AND UNLESS MR. FOX HAS ANYTHING ELSE TO ADD--
LUCIUS?
SOME OF YOU VOICED CONCERNS ABOUT THE IDEA OF FUNDING VIGILANTISM...
...BUT THINK OF THESE AS WAYNE SECURITY PERSONNEL WORKING ALONGSIDE THE POLICE.
IF THERE ARE ANY OBJECTIONS...
WE KNOW OF AT LEAST TWENTY BRAVE MEN AND WOMEN AROUND THE WORLD DIRECTLY INSPIRED BY OUR OWN BATMAN.
WITH HIS FULL COOPERATION, I PLAN TO BUILD AND SUPPORT A NETWORK OF INTERNATIONAL CRIME-FIGHTING AGENTS.
FROM LONDON TO HONG KONG, FROM BUENOS AIRES TO MOSCOW.
AND RIGHT HERE, IN THIS BOARD-ROOM...
YOU SEEM... UNCOMFORTABLE, MR. TREADWELL.
I...URR...
I JUST REMEMBERED SOMETHING...I...

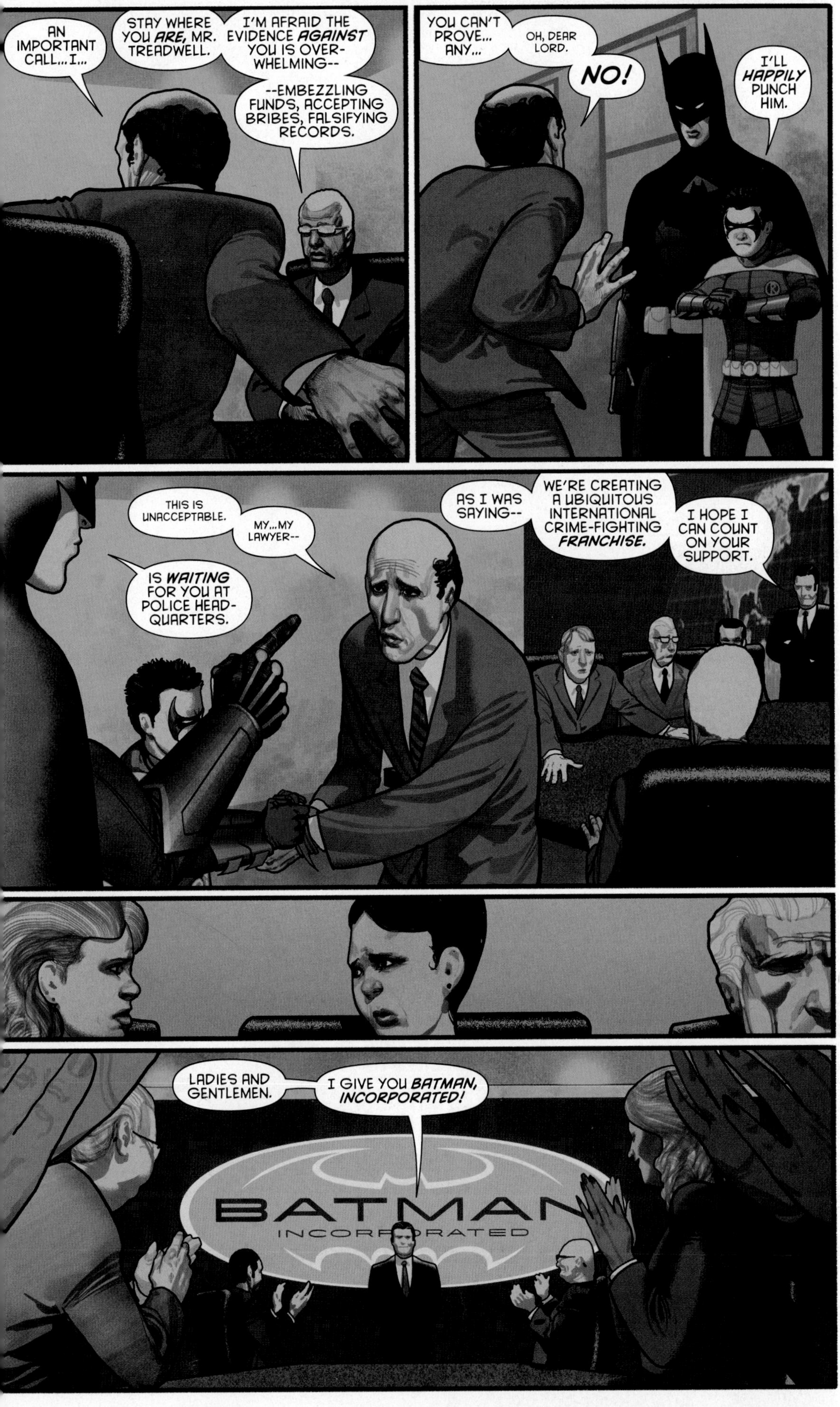
AN IMPORTANT CALL...I...
STAY WHERE YOU *ARE,* MR. TREADWELL.
I'M AFRAID THE EVIDENCE *AGAINST* YOU IS OVER-WHELMING--
--EMBEZZLING FUNDS, ACCEPTING BRIBES, FALSIFYING RECORDS.
YOU CAN'T PROVE... ANY...
OH, DEAR LORD.
NO!
I'LL *HAPPILY* PUNCH HIM.
THIS IS UNACCEPTABLE.
MY...MY LAWYER--
IS *WAITING* FOR YOU AT POLICE HEAD-QUARTERS.
AS I WAS SAYING--
WE'RE CREATING A UBIQUITOUS INTERNATIONAL CRIME-FIGHTING *FRANCHISE.*
I HOPE I CAN COUNT ON YOUR SUPPORT.
LADIES AND GENTLEMEN.
I GIVE YOU *BATMAN, INCORPORATED!*
BATMAN
INCORPORATED

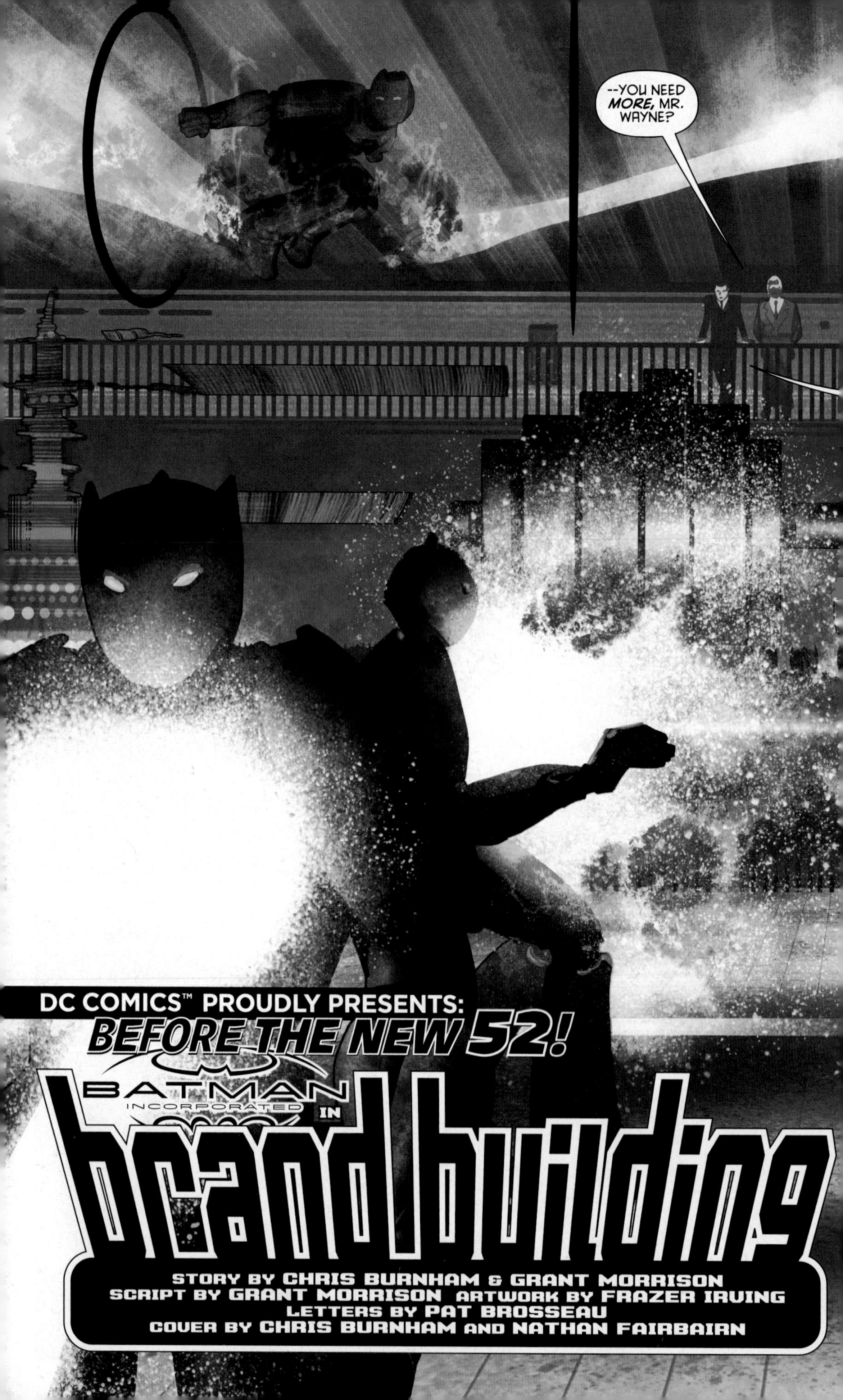

--YOU NEED MORE, MR. WAYNE?
DC COMICS™ PROUDLY PRESENTS:
BEFORE THE NEW 52!
BATMAN INCORPORATED IN
brandbuilding
STORY BY CHRIS BURNHAM & GRANT MORRISON
SCRIPT BY GRANT MORRISON ARTWORK BY FRAZER IRVING
LETTERS BY PAT BROSSEAU
COVER BY CHRIS BURNHAM AND NATHAN FAIRBAIRN

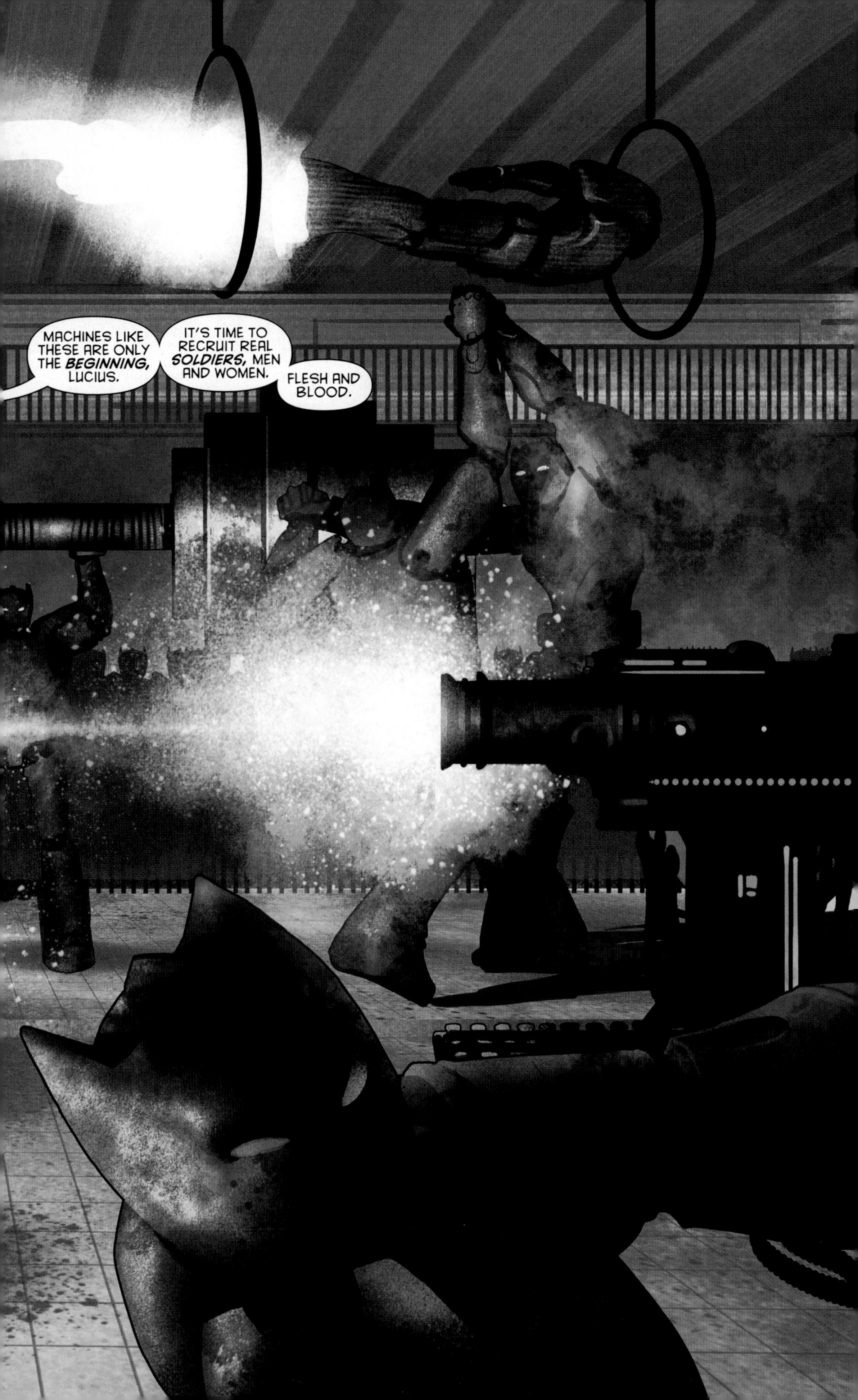
MACHINES LIKE THESE ARE ONLY THE BEGINNING, LUCIUS.
IT'S TIME TO RECRUIT REAL SOLDIERS, MEN AND WOMEN.
FLESH AND BLOOD.

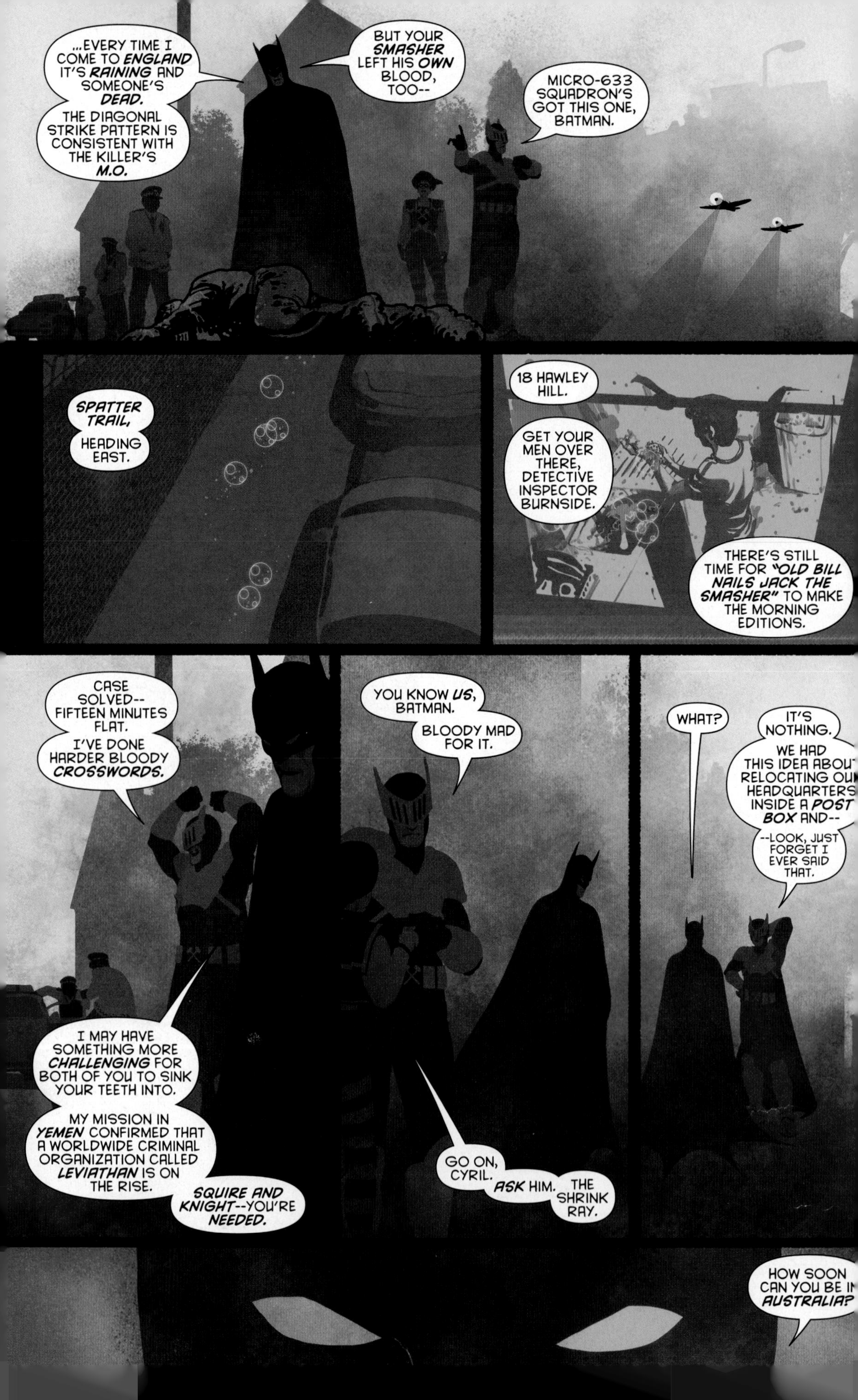

...EVERY TIME I COME TO ENGLAND IT'S RAINING AND SOMEONE'S DEAD.
THE DIAGONAL STRIKE PATTERN IS CONSISTENT WITH THE KILLER'S M.O.
BUT YOUR SMASHER LEFT HIS OWN BLOOD, TOO--
MICRO-633 SQUADRON'S GOT THIS ONE, BATMAN.
SPATTER TRAIL,
HEADING EAST.
18 HAWLEY HILL.
GET YOUR MEN OVER THERE, DETECTIVE INSPECTOR BURNSIDE.
THERE'S STILL TIME FOR "OLD BILL NAILS JACK THE SMASHER" TO MAKE THE MORNING EDITIONS.
CASE SOLVED-- FIFTEEN MINUTES FLAT.
I'VE DONE HARDER BLOODY CROSSWORDS.
I MAY HAVE SOMETHING MORE CHALLENGING FOR BOTH OF YOU TO SINK YOUR TEETH INTO.
MY MISSION IN YEMEN CONFIRMED THAT A WORLDWIDE CRIMINAL ORGANIZATION CALLED LEVIATHAN IS ON THE RISE.
SQUIRE AND KNIGHT--YOU'RE NEEDED.
YOU KNOW US, BATMAN.
BLOODY MAD FOR IT.
GO ON, CYRIL.
ASK HIM.
THE SHRINK RAY.
WHAT?
IT'S NOTHING.
WE HAD THIS IDEA ABOUT RELOCATING OU HEADQUARTERS INSIDE A POST BOX AND--
--LOOK, JUST FORGET I EVER SAID THAT.
HOW SOON CAN YOU BE I AUSTRALIA?

THAT'S YOU DONE, MATE. CRYSTAL CREATURE VS. CYCLOPS MAN.

IF THE GIRLS *DON'T* GO WILD, IT'S *YOUR* FAULT NOT MINE.

THE NIGHT'S NOT OVER *YET*, DARK RANGER.

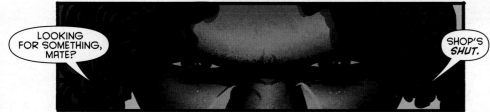

LOOKING FOR SOMETHING, MATE?

SHOP'S *SHUT.*

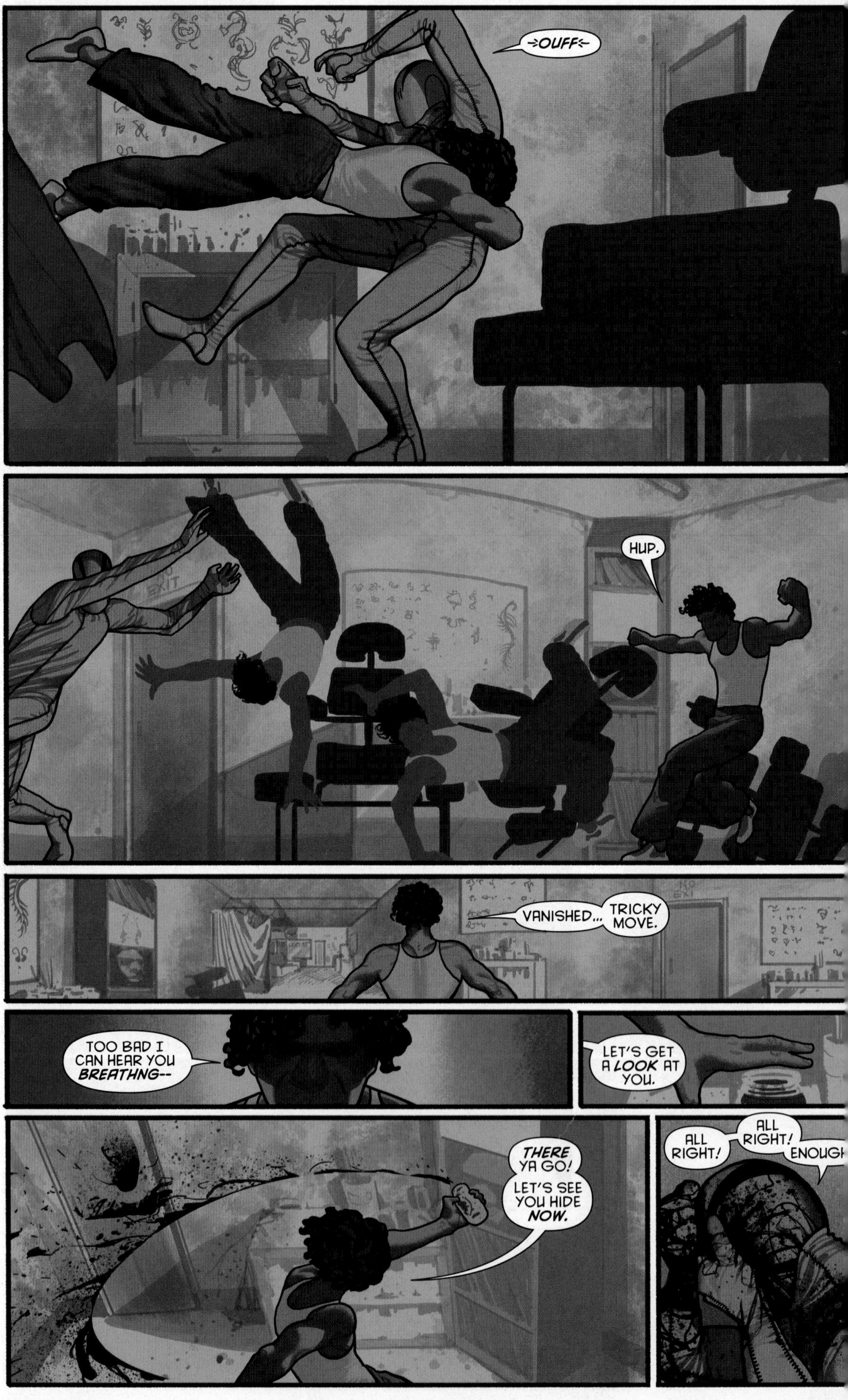

=OUFF=
HUP.
VANISHED...
TRICKY MOVE.
TOO BAD I CAN HEAR YOU BREATHNG--
LET'S GET A LOOK AT YOU.
THERE YA GO!
LET'S SEE YOU HIDE NOW.
ALL RIGHT!
ALL RIGHT!
ENOUGH

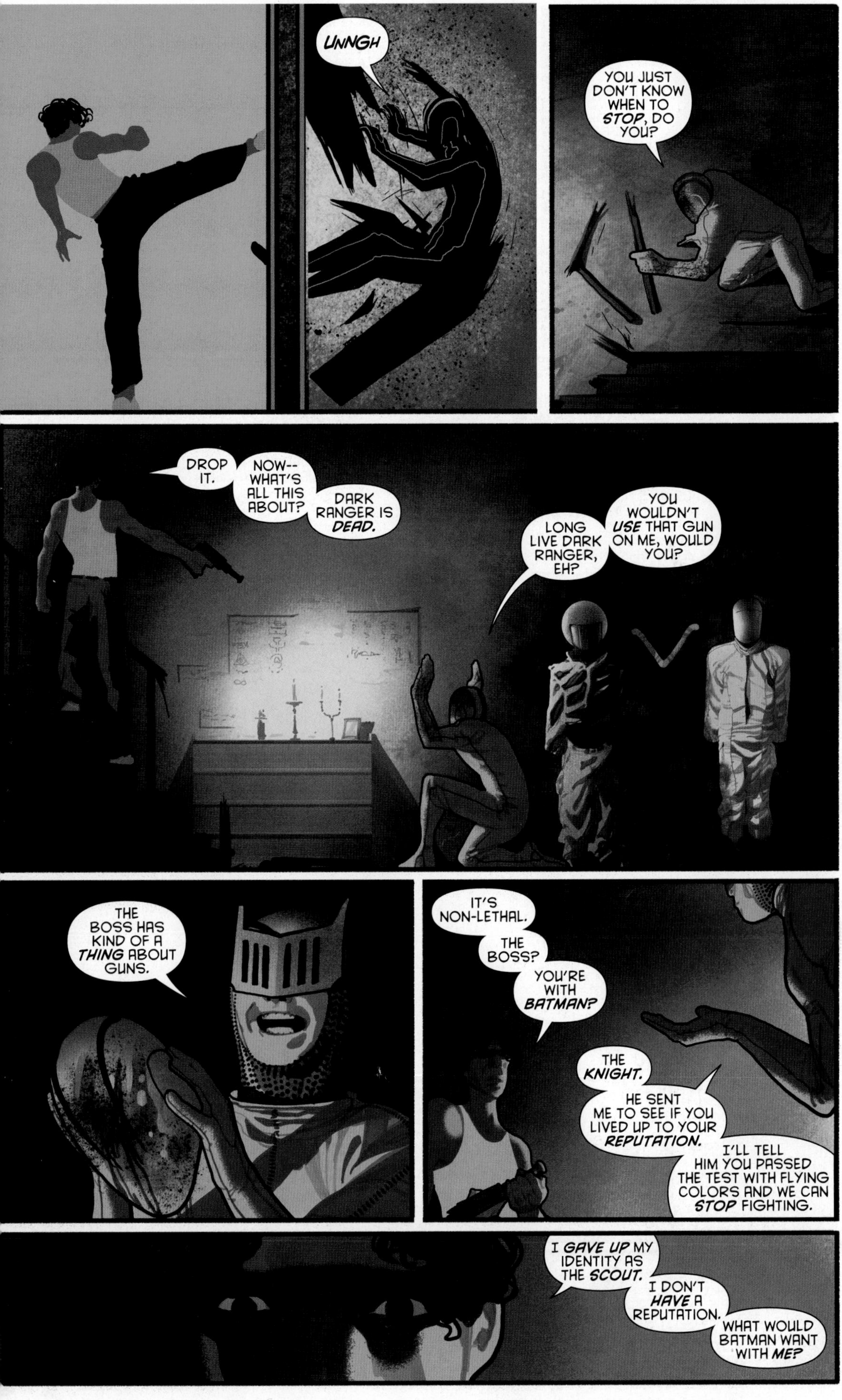
UNNGH
YOU JUST DON'T KNOW WHEN TO STOP, DO YOU?
DROP IT.
NOW-- WHAT'S ALL THIS ABOUT?
DARK RANGER IS DEAD.
LONG LIVE DARK RANGER, EH?
YOU WOULDN'T USE THAT GUN ON ME, WOULD YOU?
THE BOSS HAS KIND OF A THING ABOUT GUNS.
IT'S NON-LETHAL.
THE BOSS?
YOU'RE WITH BATMAN?
THE KNIGHT.
HE SENT ME TO SEE IF YOU LIVED UP TO YOUR REPUTATION.
I'LL TELL HIM YOU PASSED THE TEST WITH FLYING COLORS AND WE CAN STOP FIGHTING.
I GAVE UP MY IDENTITY AS THE SCOUT.
I DON'T HAVE A REPUTATION.
WHAT WOULD BATMAN WANT WITH ME?

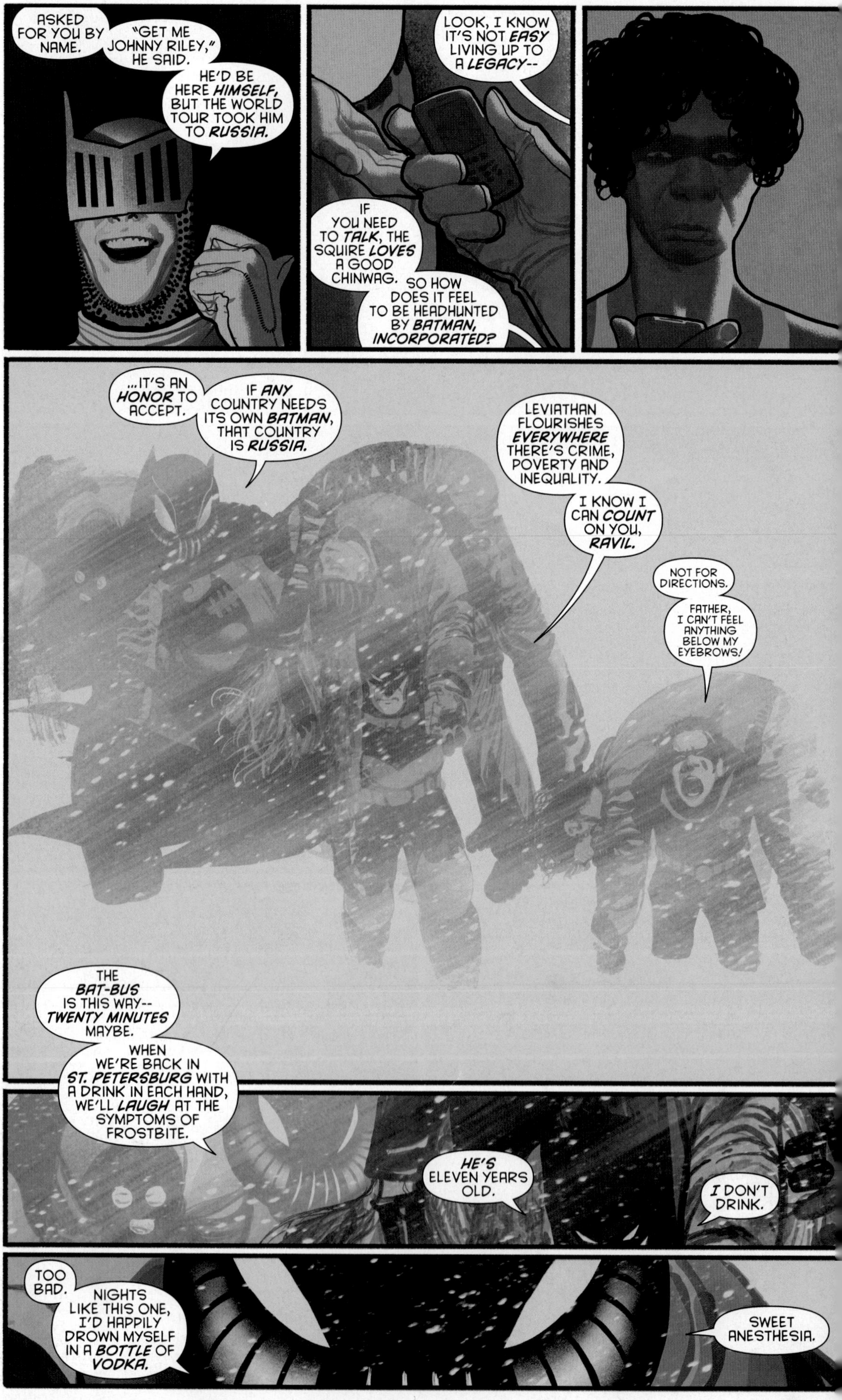
ASKED FOR YOU BY NAME.
"GET ME JOHNNY RILEY," HE SAID.
HE'D BE HERE HIMSELF, BUT THE WORLD TOUR TOOK HIM TO RUSSIA.
LOOK, I KNOW IT'S NOT EASY LIVING UP TO A LEGACY--
IF YOU NEED TO TALK, THE SQUIRE LOVES A GOOD CHINWAG.
SO HOW DOES IT FEEL TO BE HEADHUNTED BY BATMAN, INCORPORATED?
...IT'S AN HONOR TO ACCEPT.
IF ANY COUNTRY NEEDS ITS OWN BATMAN, THAT COUNTRY IS RUSSIA.
LEVIATHAN FLOURISHES EVERYWHERE THERE'S CRIME, POVERTY AND INEQUALITY.
I KNOW I CAN COUNT ON YOU, RAVIL.
NOT FOR DIRECTIONS.
FATHER, I CAN'T FEEL ANYTHING BELOW MY EYEBROWS!
THE BAT-BUS IS THIS WAY-- TWENTY MINUTES MAYBE.
WHEN WE'RE BACK IN ST. PETERSBURG WITH A DRINK IN EACH HAND, WE'LL LAUGH AT THE SYMPTOMS OF FROSTBITE.
HE'S ELEVEN YEARS OLD.
I DON'T DRINK.
TOO BAD.
NIGHTS LIKE THIS ONE, I'D HAPPILY DROWN MYSELF IN A BOTTLE OF VODKA.
SWEET ANESTHESIA.

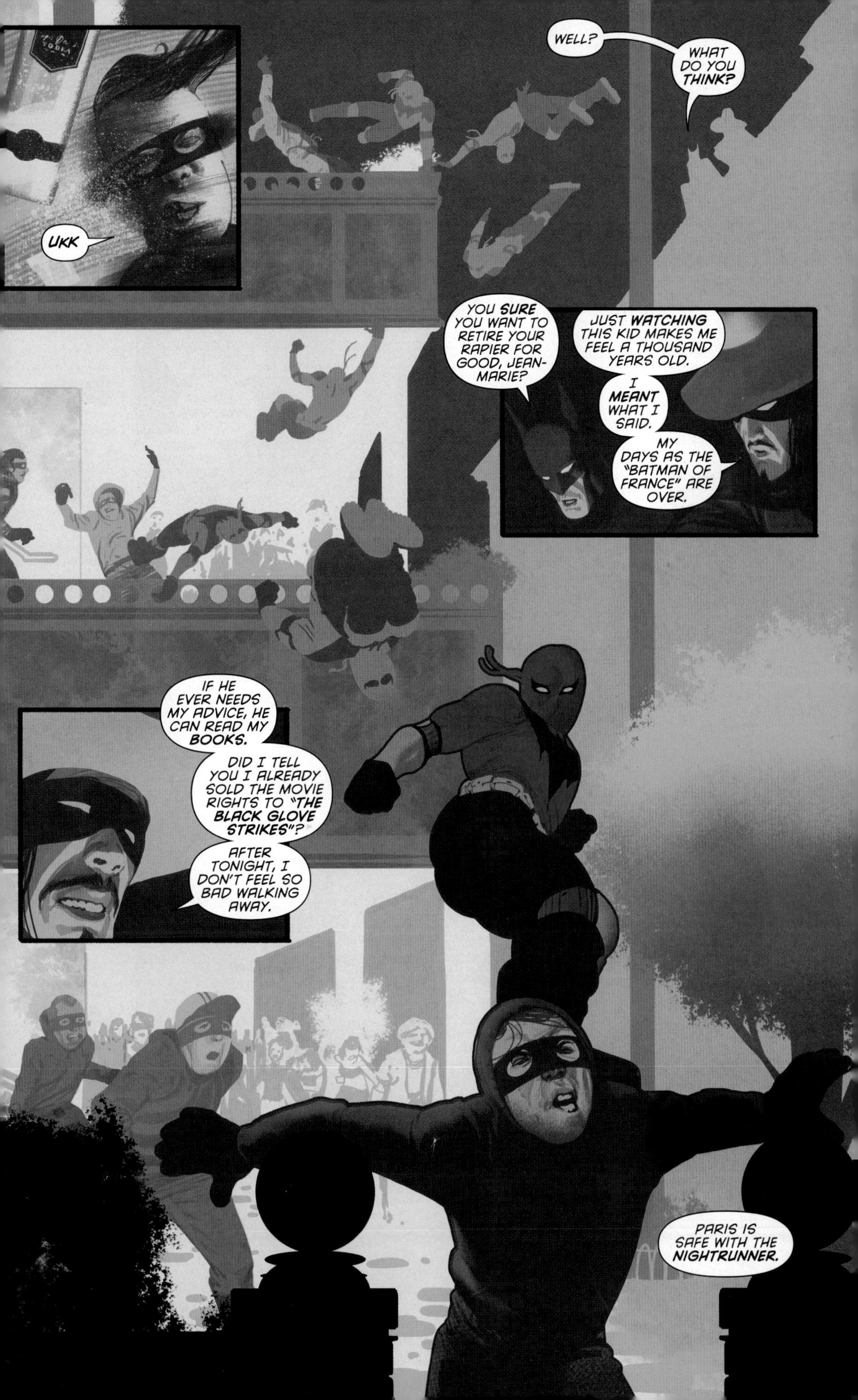
UKK
WELL?
WHAT DO YOU THINK?
YOU SURE YOU WANT TO RETIRE YOUR RAPIER FOR GOOD, JEAN-MARIE?
JUST WATCHING THIS KID MAKES ME FEEL A THOUSAND YEARS OLD.
I MEANT WHAT I SAID.
MY DAYS AS THE "BATMAN OF FRANCE" ARE OVER.
IF HE EVER NEEDS MY ADVICE, HE CAN READ MY BOOKS.
DID I TELL YOU I ALREADY SOLD THE MOVIE RIGHTS TO "THE BLACK GLOVE STRIKES"?
AFTER TONIGHT, I DON'T FEEL SO BAD WALKING AWAY.
PARIS IS SAFE WITH THE NIGHTRUNNER.

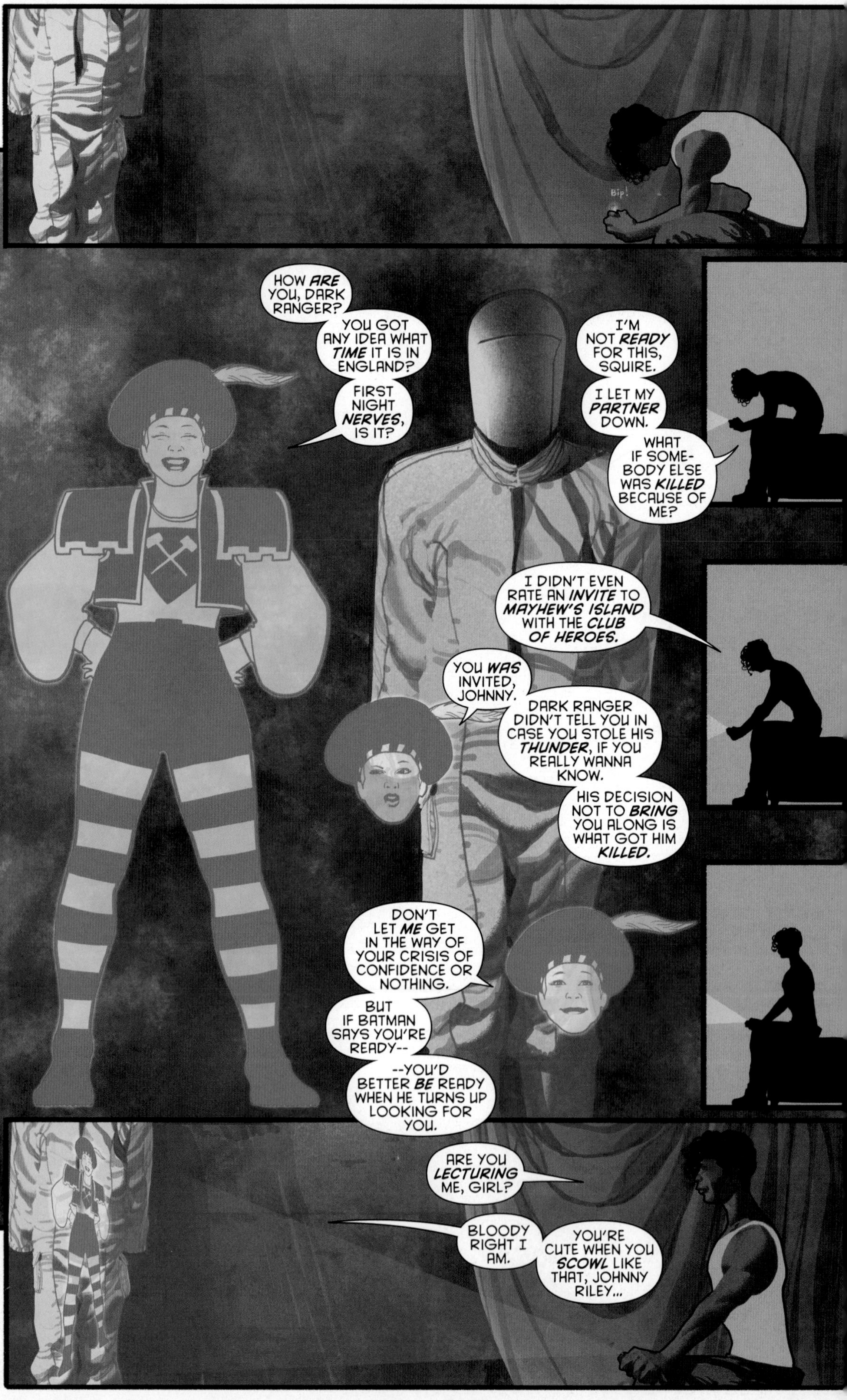
Bip!
HOW ARE YOU, DARK RANGER?
YOU GOT ANY IDEA WHAT TIME IT IS IN ENGLAND?
FIRST NIGHT NERVES, IS IT?
I'M NOT READY FOR THIS, SQUIRE.
I LET MY PARTNER DOWN.
WHAT IF SOMEBODY ELSE WAS KILLED BECAUSE OF ME?
I DIDN'T EVEN RATE AN INVITE TO MAYHEW'S ISLAND WITH THE CLUB OF HEROES.
YOU WAS INVITED, JOHNNY.
DARK RANGER DIDN'T TELL YOU IN CASE YOU STOLE HIS THUNDER, IF YOU REALLY WANNA KNOW.
HIS DECISION NOT TO BRING YOU ALONG IS WHAT GOT HIM KILLED.
DON'T LET ME GET IN THE WAY OF YOUR CRISIS OF CONFIDENCE OR NOTHING.
BUT IF BATMAN SAYS YOU'RE READY--
--YOU'D BETTER BE READY WHEN HE TURNS UP LOOKING FOR YOU.
ARE YOU LECTURING ME, GIRL?
BLOODY RIGHT I AM.
YOU'RE CUTE WHEN YOU SCOWL LIKE THAT, JOHNNY RILEY...

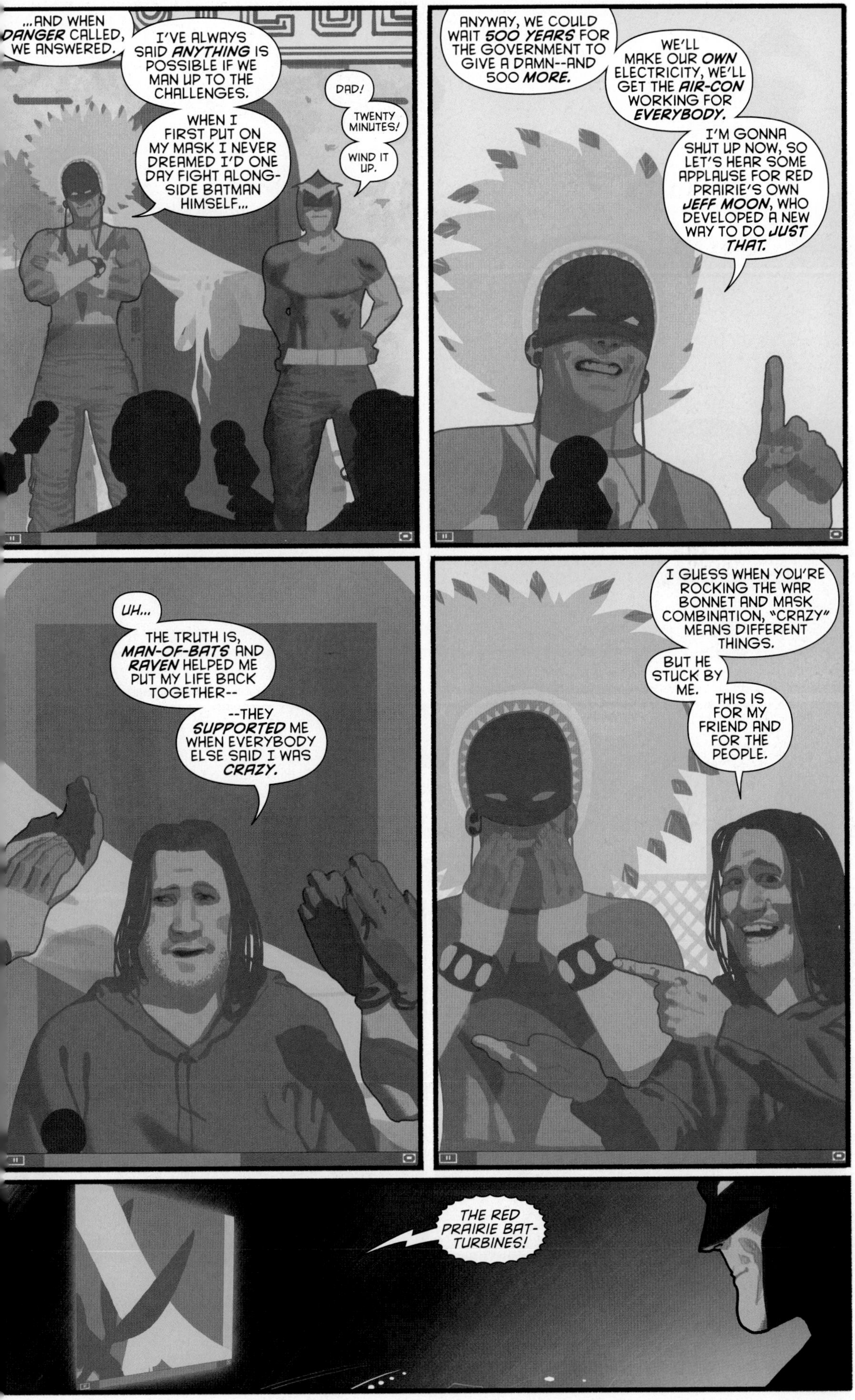
...AND WHEN DANGER CALLED, WE ANSWERED.
I'VE ALWAYS SAID ANYTHING IS POSSIBLE IF WE MAN UP TO THE CHALLENGES.
WHEN I FIRST PUT ON MY MASK I NEVER DREAMED I'D ONE DAY FIGHT ALONG-SIDE BATMAN HIMSELF...
DAD!
TWENTY MINUTES!
WIND IT UP.
ANYWAY, WE COULD WAIT 500 YEARS FOR THE GOVERNMENT TO GIVE A DAMN--AND 500 MORE.
WE'LL MAKE OUR OWN ELECTRICITY, WE'LL GET THE AIR-CON WORKING FOR EVERYBODY.
I'M GONNA SHUT UP NOW, SO LET'S HEAR SOME APPLAUSE FOR RED PRAIRIE'S OWN JEFF MOON, WHO DEVELOPED A NEW WAY TO DO JUST THAT.
UH...
THE TRUTH IS, MAN-OF-BATS AND RAVEN HELPED ME PUT MY LIFE BACK TOGETHER--
--THEY SUPPORTED ME WHEN EVERYBODY ELSE SAID I WAS CRAZY.
I GUESS WHEN YOU'RE ROCKING THE WAR BONNET AND MASK COMBINATION, "CRAZY" MEANS DIFFERENT THINGS.
BUT HE STUCK BY ME.
THIS IS FOR MY FRIEND AND FOR THE PEOPLE.
THE RED PRAIRIE BAT-TURBINES!

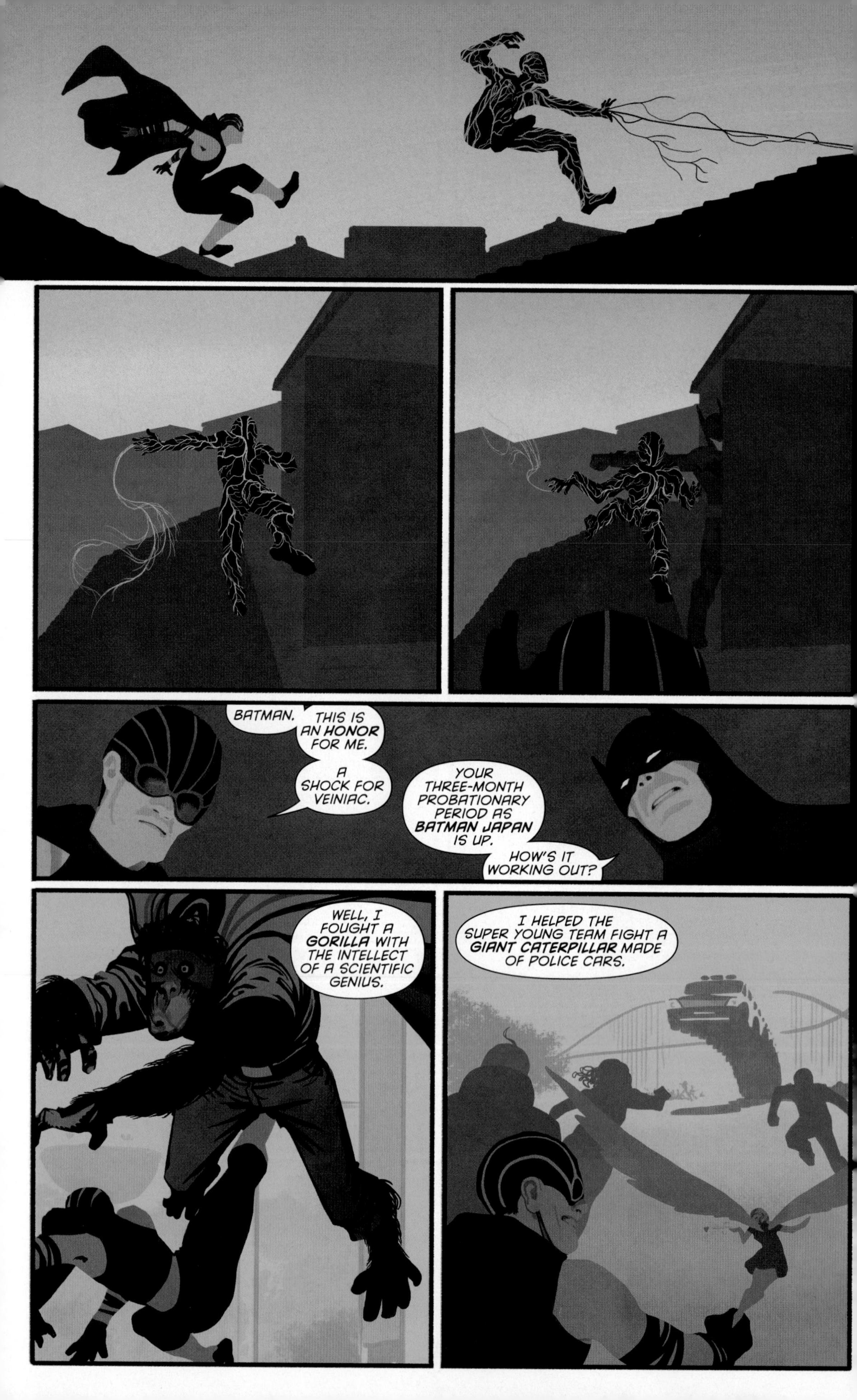
BATMAN.
THIS IS AN HONOR FOR ME.
A SHOCK FOR VEINIAC.
YOUR THREE-MONTH PROBATIONARY PERIOD AS BATMAN JAPAN IS UP.
HOW'S IT WORKING OUT?
WELL, I FOUGHT A GORILLA WITH THE INTELLECT OF A SCIENTIFIC GENIUS.
I HELPED THE SUPER YOUNG TEAM FIGHT A GIANT CATERPILLAR MADE OF POLICE CARS.

AND DOUBLEFACE!

I STILL HAVEN'T CAPTURED THAT ONE.

HIS FOUR EYES GIVE HIM UNBEATABLE SPATIAL AWARENESS.

AND HE'S IMMUNE TO STANDARD NERVE STRIKES. NEXT TIME, PACK X-RAY LENSES.

TO FIND THE USUAL WEAK POINTS, YOU MAY NEED TO LOOK IN UNLIKELY PLACES.

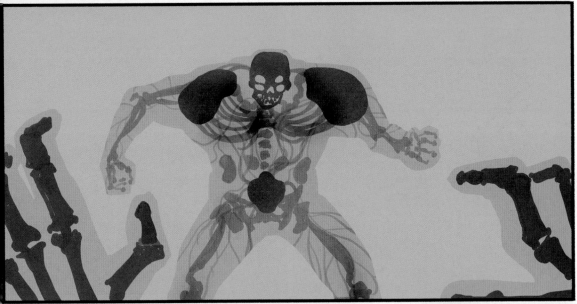

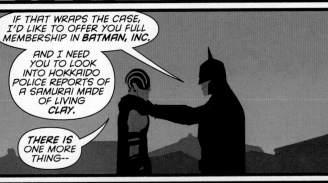

IF THAT WRAPS THE CASE, I'D LIKE TO OFFER YOU FULL MEMBERSHIP IN BATMAN, INC.

AND I NEED YOU TO LOOK INTO HOKKAIDO POLICE REPORTS OF A SAMURAI MADE OF LIVING CLAY.

THERE IS ONE MORE THING--

--I'M SWEET ON LOLITA CANARY OF THE YOUNG TEAM, BUT SHE'S ONLY THIS TALL.

I HEARD YOU MAY HAVE ACCESS TO A SHRINK RAY.

DON'T MAKE ME CHANGE MY MIND, JIRO.

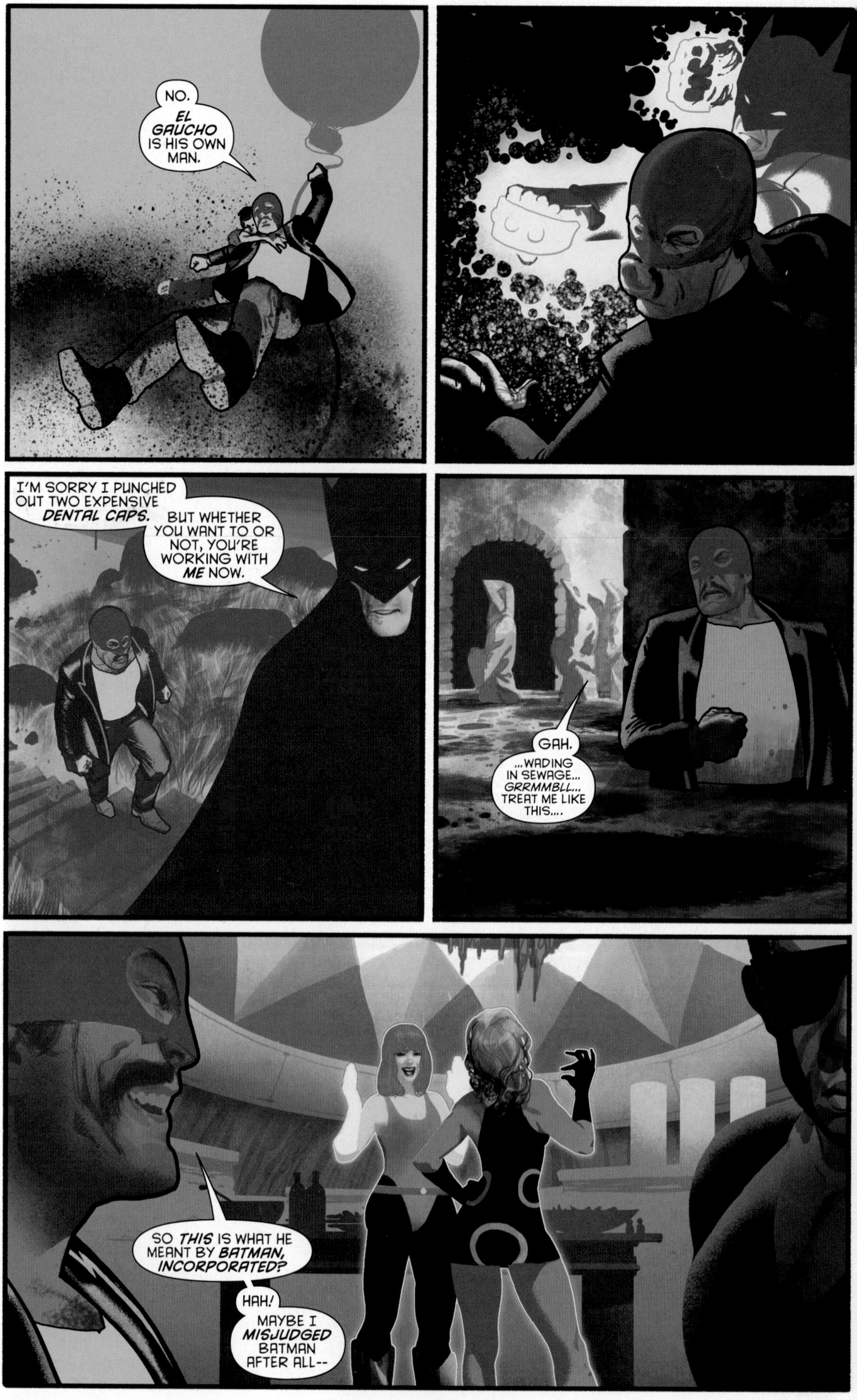
NO. EL GAUCHO IS HIS OWN MAN.
I'M SORRY I PUNCHED OUT TWO EXPENSIVE DENTAL CAPS.
BUT WHETHER YOU WANT TO OR NOT, YOU'RE WORKING WITH ME NOW.
GAH.
...WADING IN SEWAGE... GRRMMBLL... TREAT ME LIKE THIS....
SO THIS IS WHAT HE MEANT BY BATMAN, INCORPORATED?
HAH!
MAYBE I MISJUDGED BATMAN AFTER ALL--

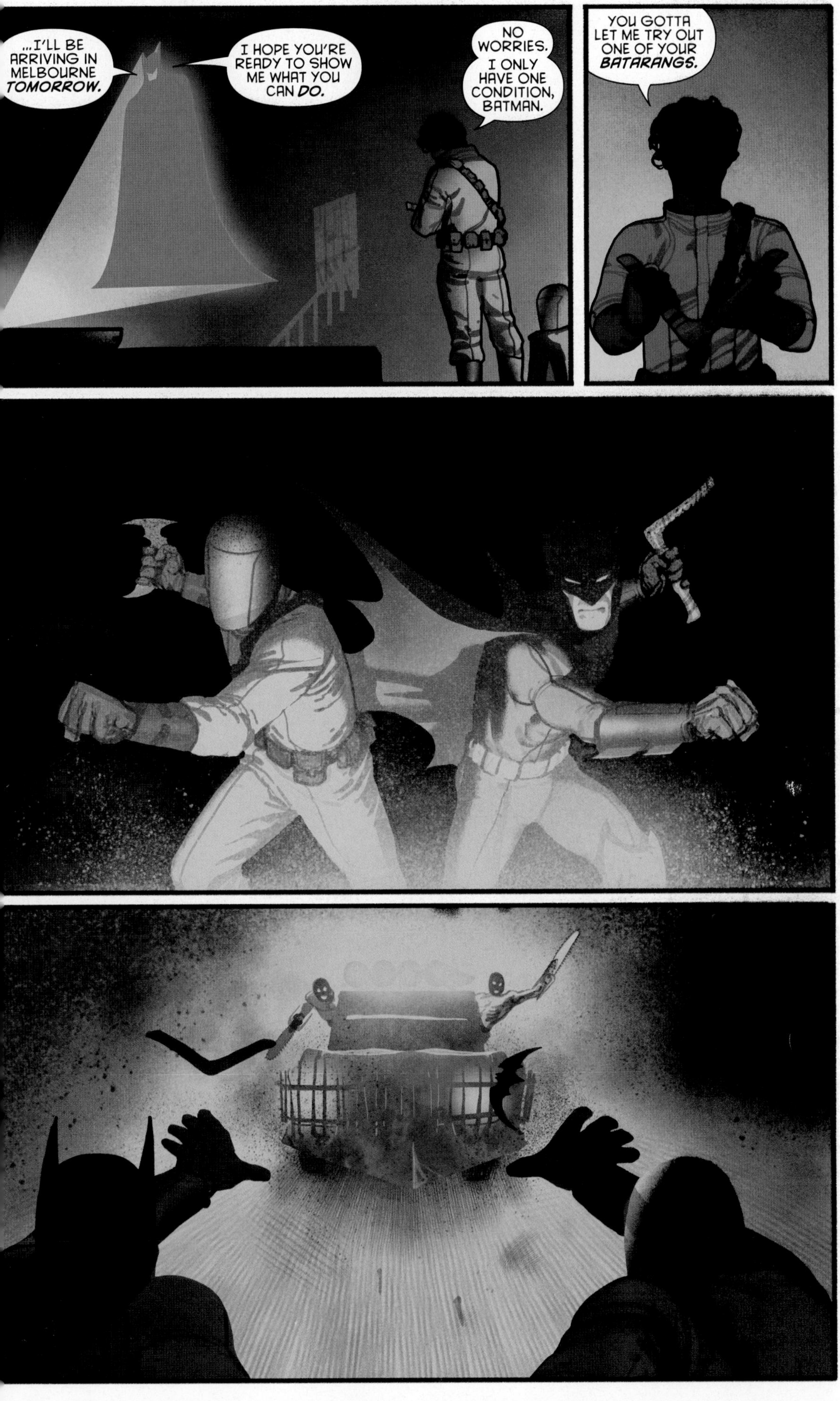
...I'LL BE ARRIVING IN MELBOURNE *TOMORROW.*
I HOPE YOU'RE READY TO SHOW ME WHAT YOU CAN *DO.*
NO WORRIES. I ONLY HAVE ONE CONDITION, BATMAN.
YOU GOTTA LET ME TRY OUT ONE OF YOUR *BATARANGS.*

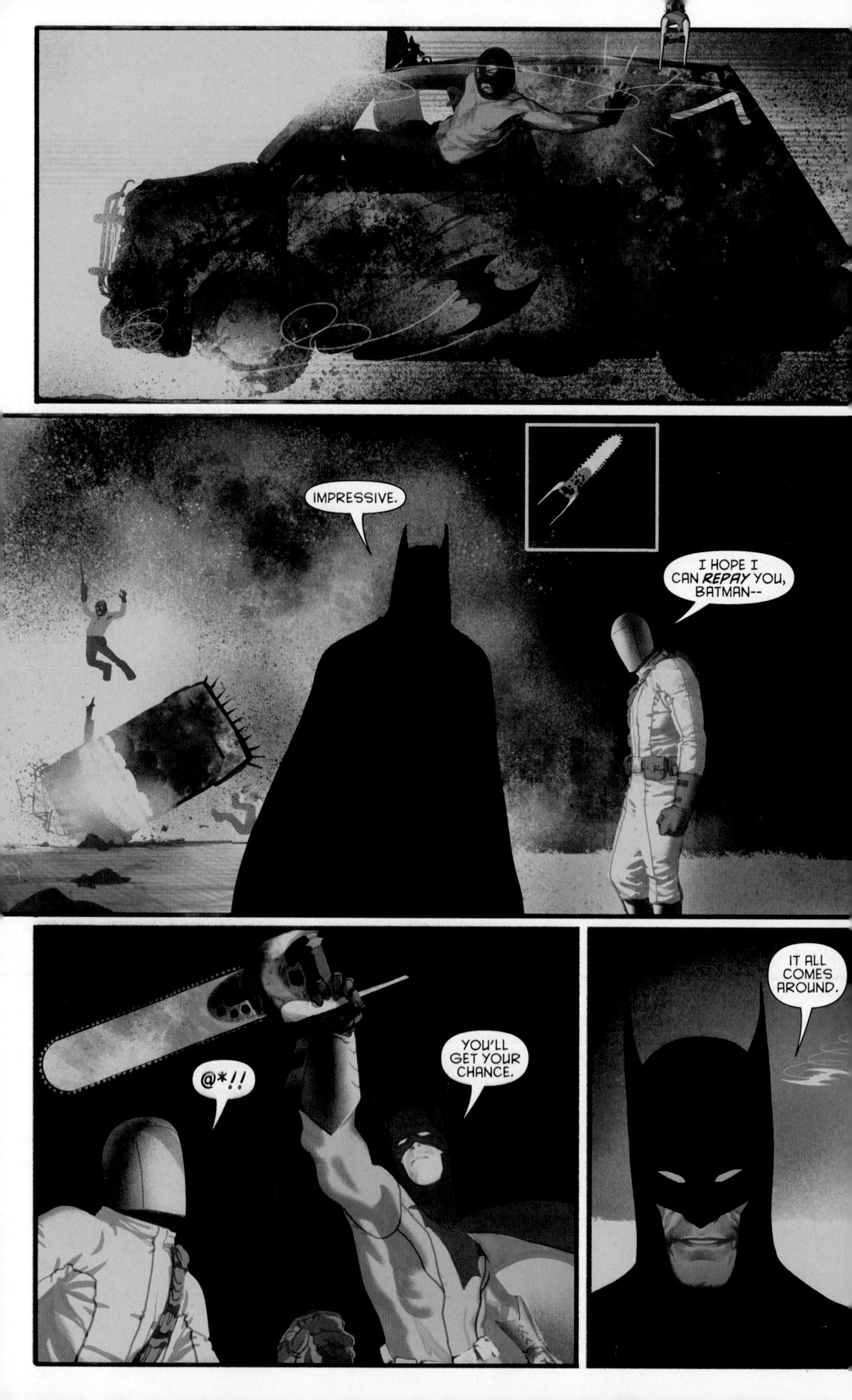
IMPRESSIVE.
I HOPE I CAN REPAY YOU, BATMAN--
@*!!
YOU'LL GET YOUR CHANCE.
IT ALL COMES AROUND.

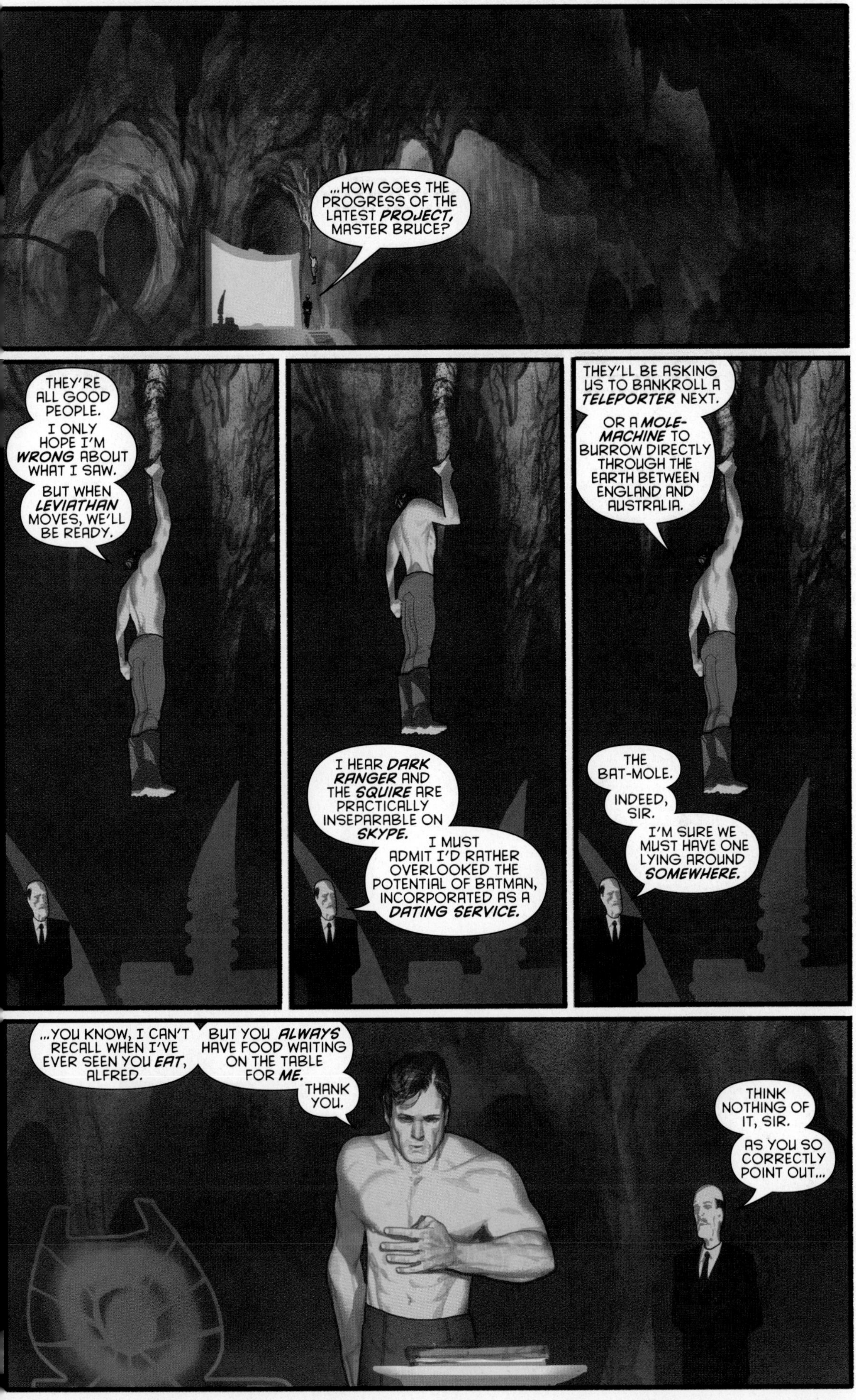
...HOW GOES THE PROGRESS OF THE LATEST PROJECT, MASTER BRUCE?
THEY'RE ALL GOOD PEOPLE.
I ONLY HOPE I'M WRONG ABOUT WHAT I SAW.
BUT WHEN LEVIATHAN MOVES, WE'LL BE READY.
I HEAR DARK RANGER AND THE SQUIRE ARE PRACTICALLY INSEPARABLE ON SKYPE.
I MUST ADMIT I'D RATHER OVERLOOKED THE POTENTIAL OF BATMAN, INCORPORATED AS A DATING SERVICE.
THEY'LL BE ASKING US TO BANKROLL A TELEPORTER NEXT.
OR A MOLE-MACHINE TO BURROW DIRECTLY THROUGH THE EARTH BETWEEN ENGLAND AND AUSTRALIA.
THE BAT-MOLE.
INDEED, SIR.
I'M SURE WE MUST HAVE ONE LYING AROUND SOMEWHERE.
...YOU KNOW, I CAN'T RECALL WHEN I'VE EVER SEEN YOU EAT, ALFRED.
BUT YOU ALWAYS HAVE FOOD WAITING ON THE TABLE FOR ME.
THANK YOU.
THINK NOTHING OF IT, SIR.
AS YOU SO CORRECTLY POINT OUT...

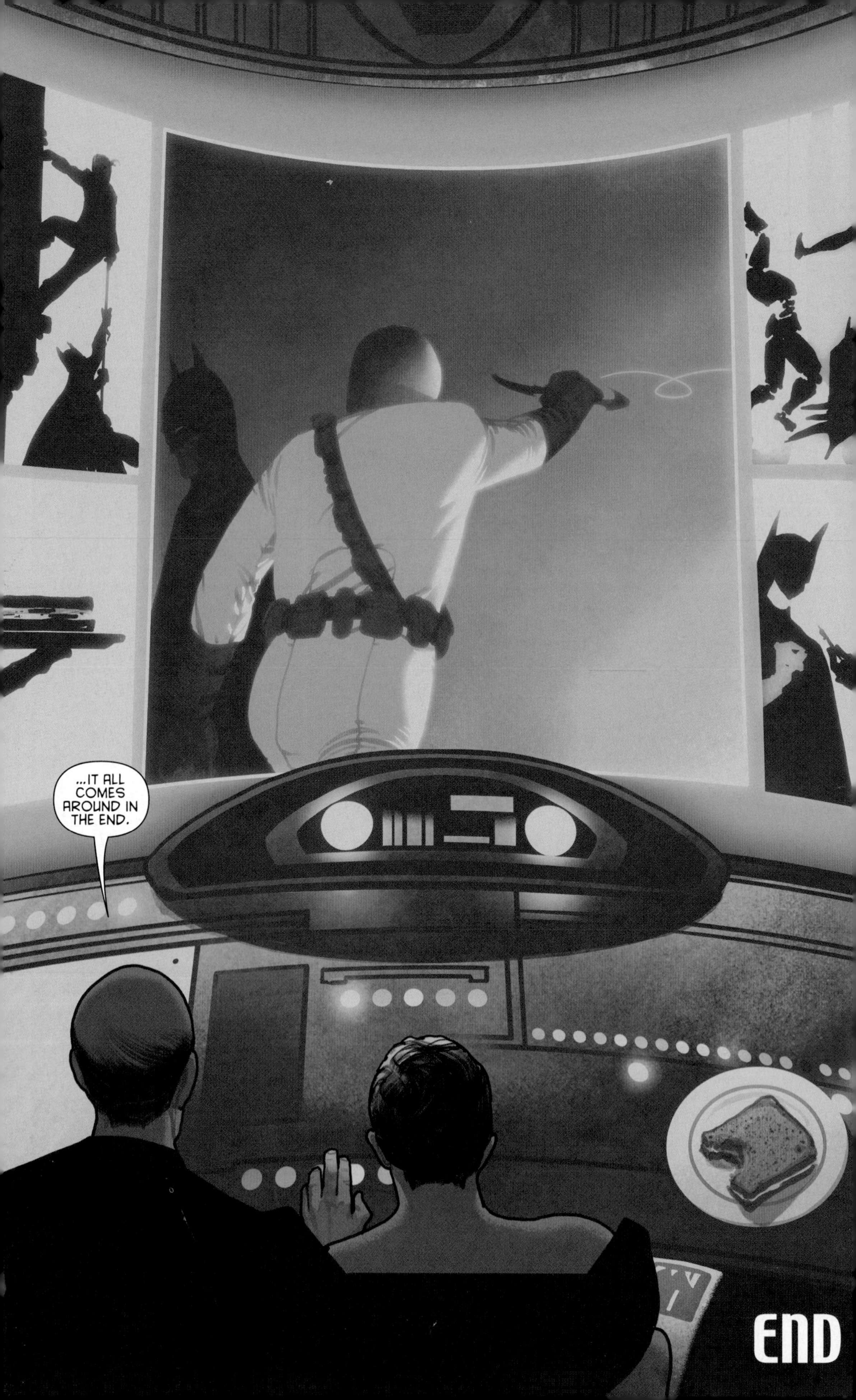
...IT ALL COMES AROUND IN THE END.
END

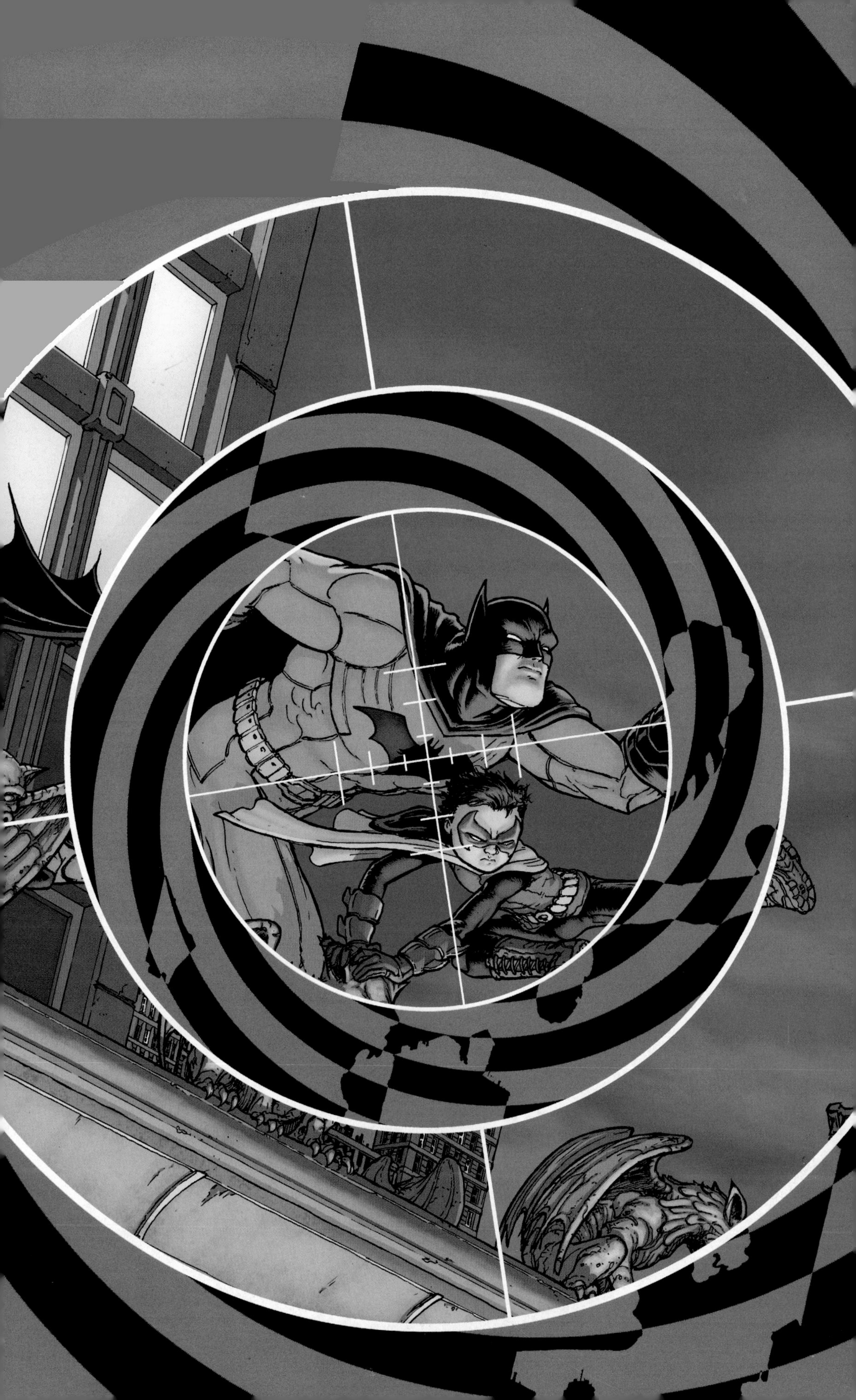

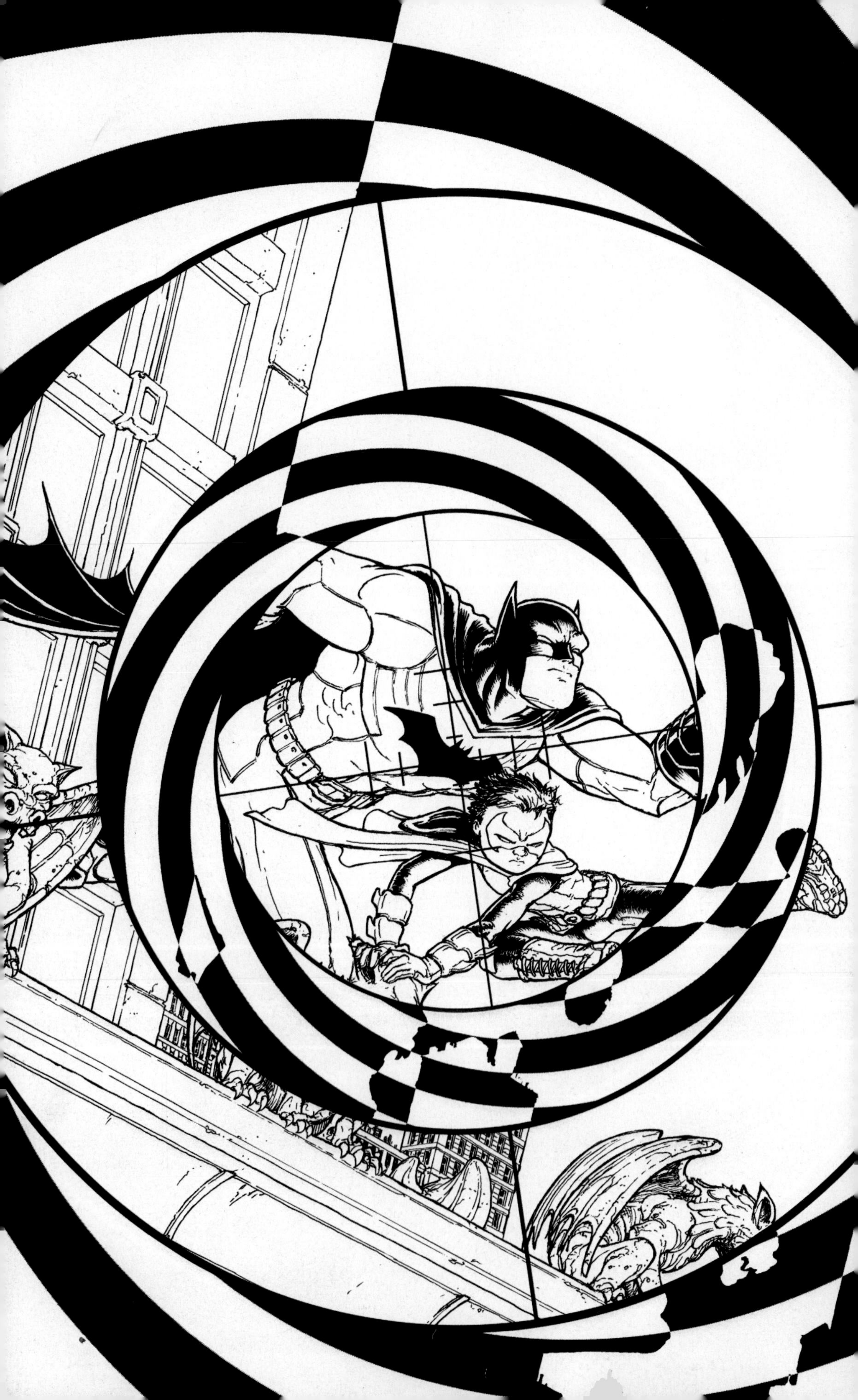

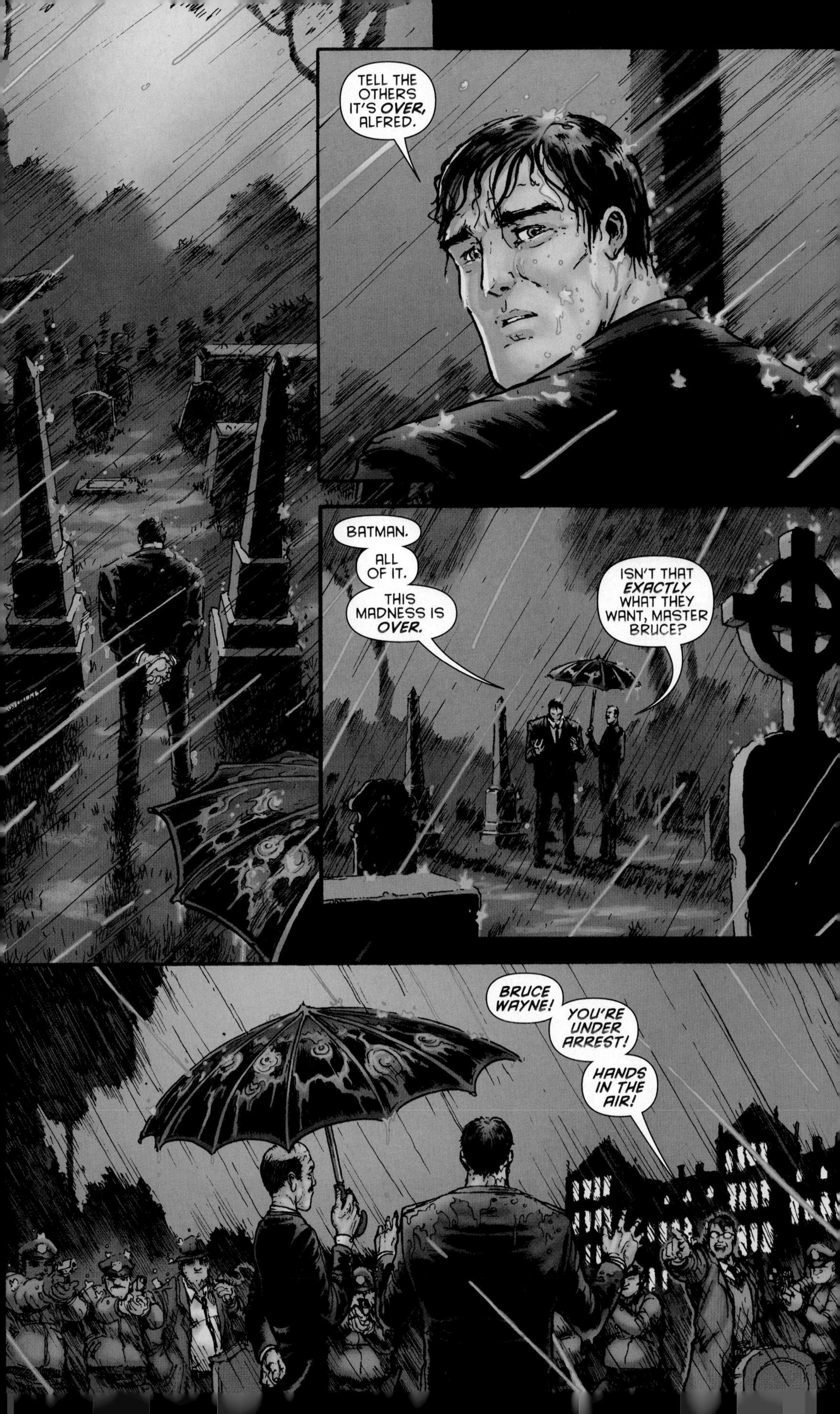
TELL THE OTHERS IT'S OVER, ALFRED.
BATMAN.
ALL OF IT.
THIS MADNESS IS OVER.
ISN'T THAT EXACTLY WHAT THEY WANT, MASTER BRUCE?
BRUCE WAYNE!
YOU'RE UNDER ARREST!
HANDS IN THE AIR!

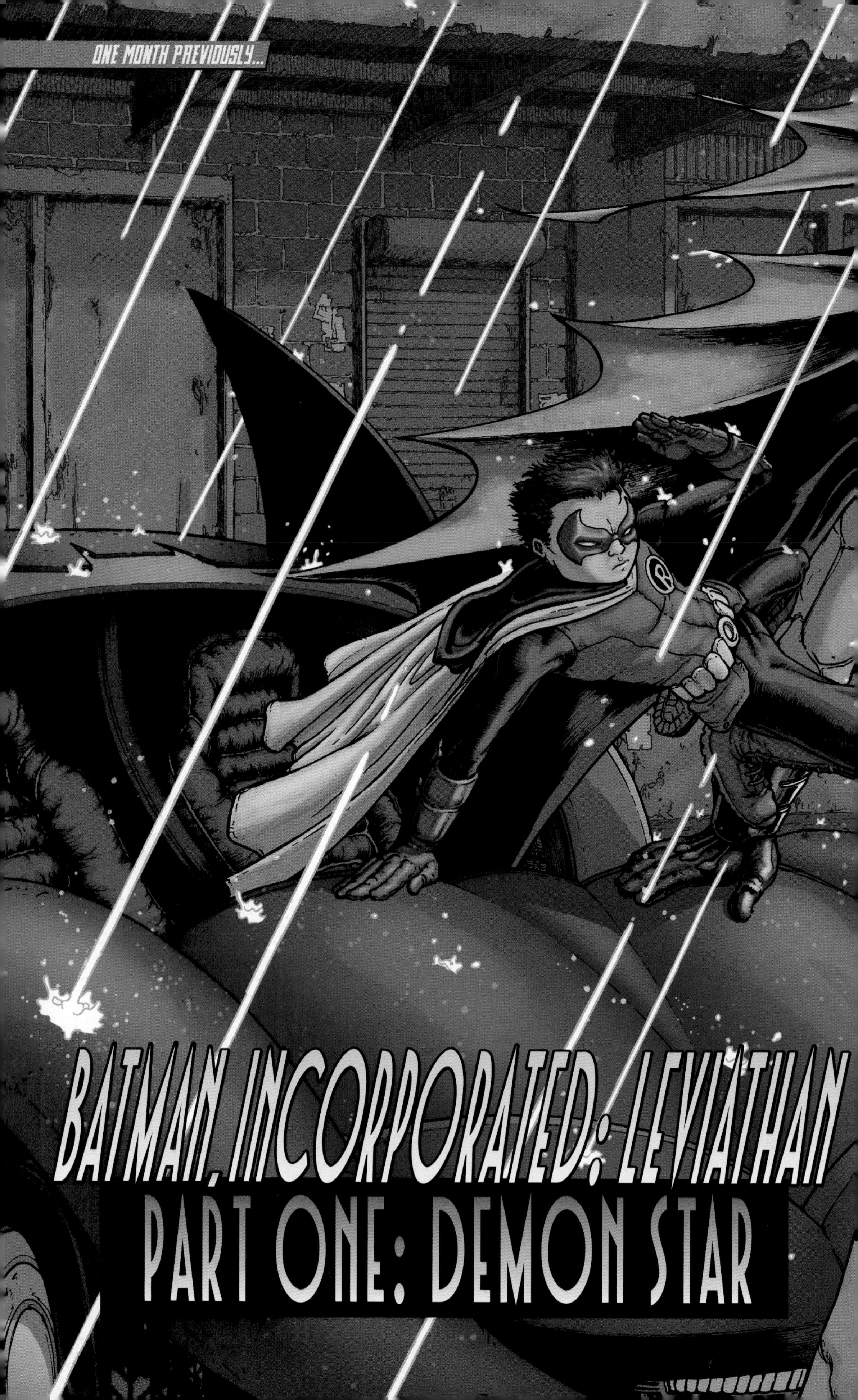
ONE MONTH PREVIOUSLY...
BATMAN, INCORPORATED: LEVIATHAN
PART ONE: DEMON STAR

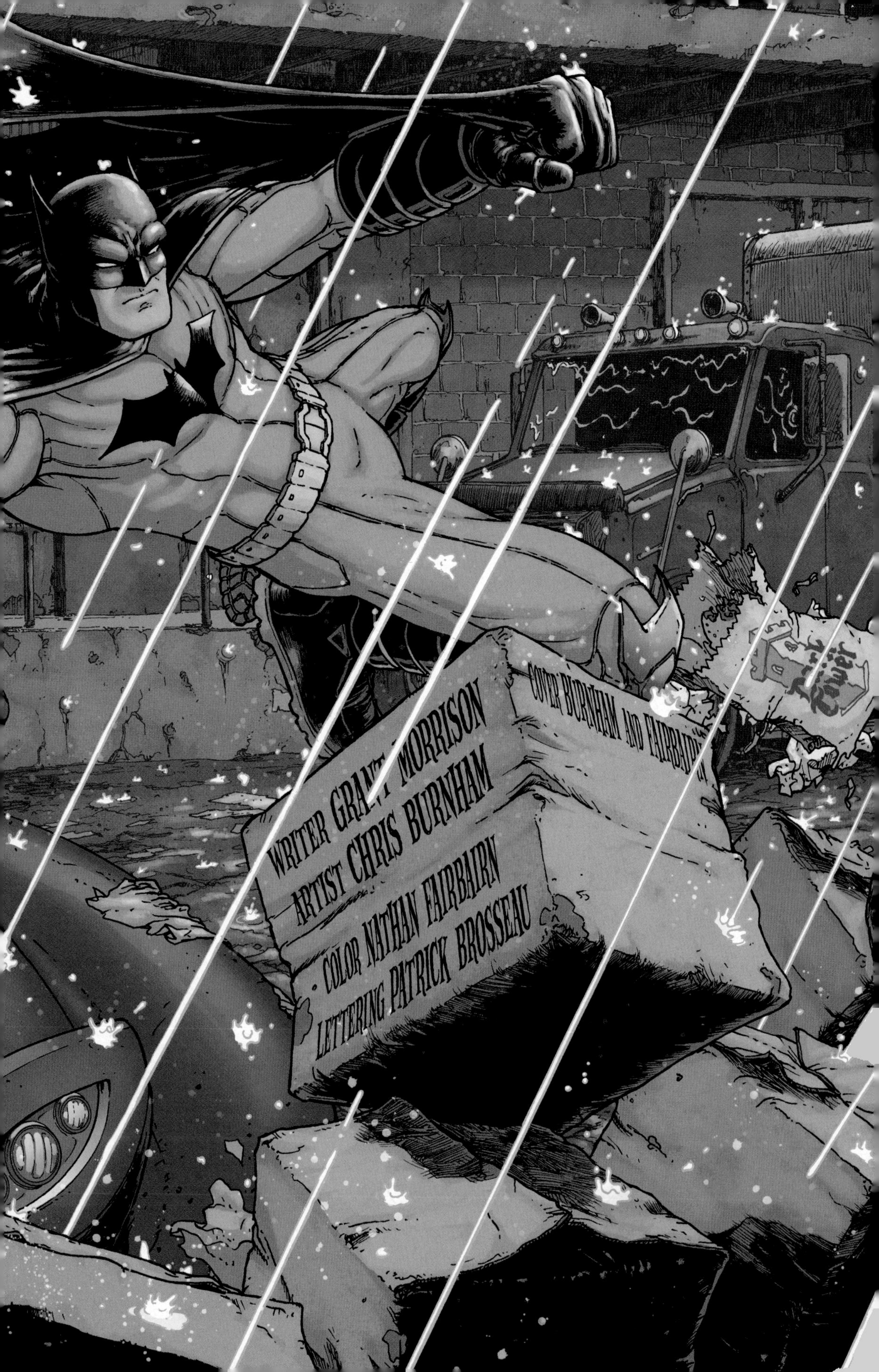
WRITER GRANT MORRISON
ARTIST CHRIS BURNHAM
COLOR NATHAN FAIRBAIRN
LETTERING PATRICK BROSSEAU
COVER BURNHAM AND FAIRBAIRN

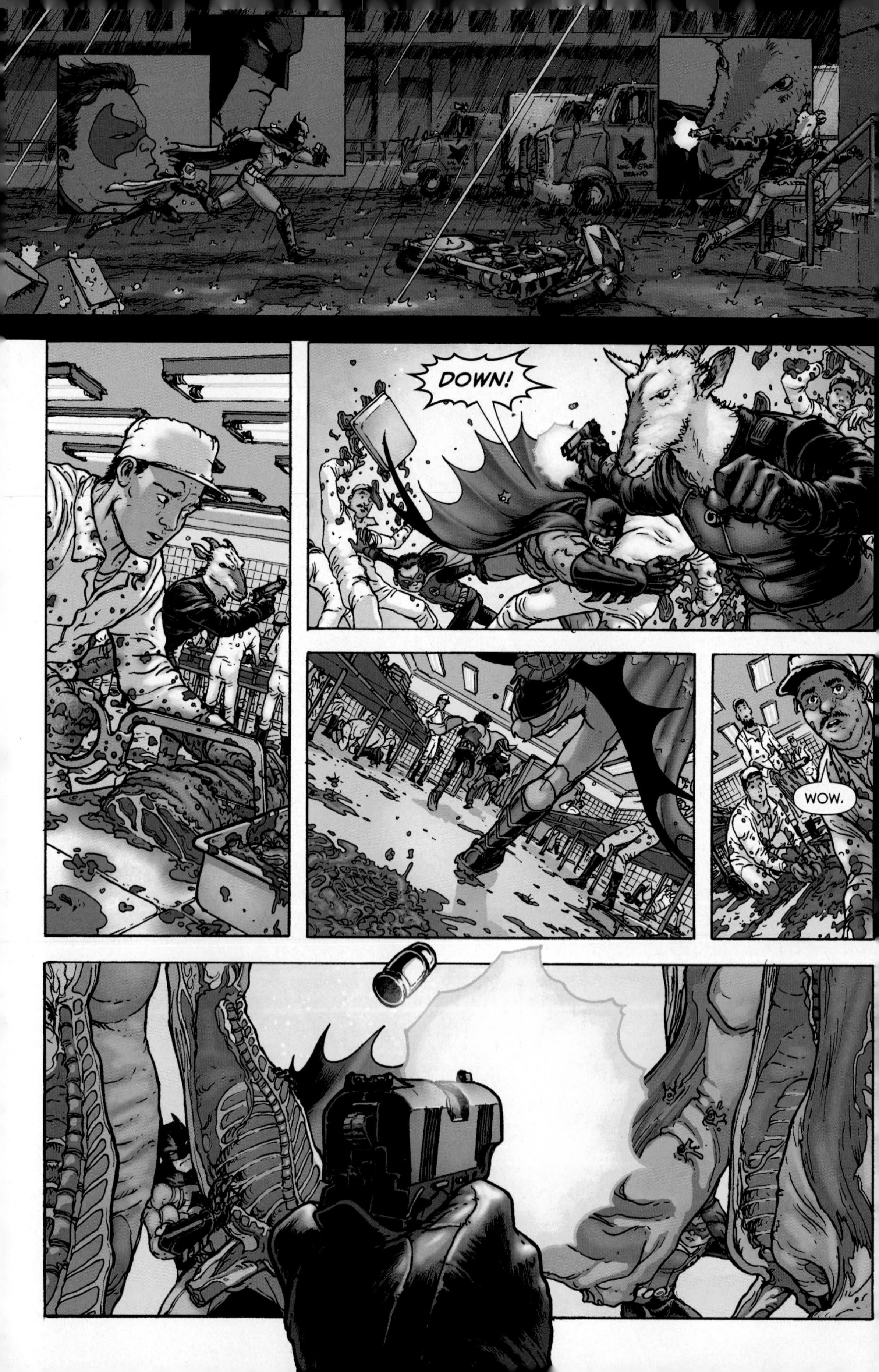
DOWN!
WOW.

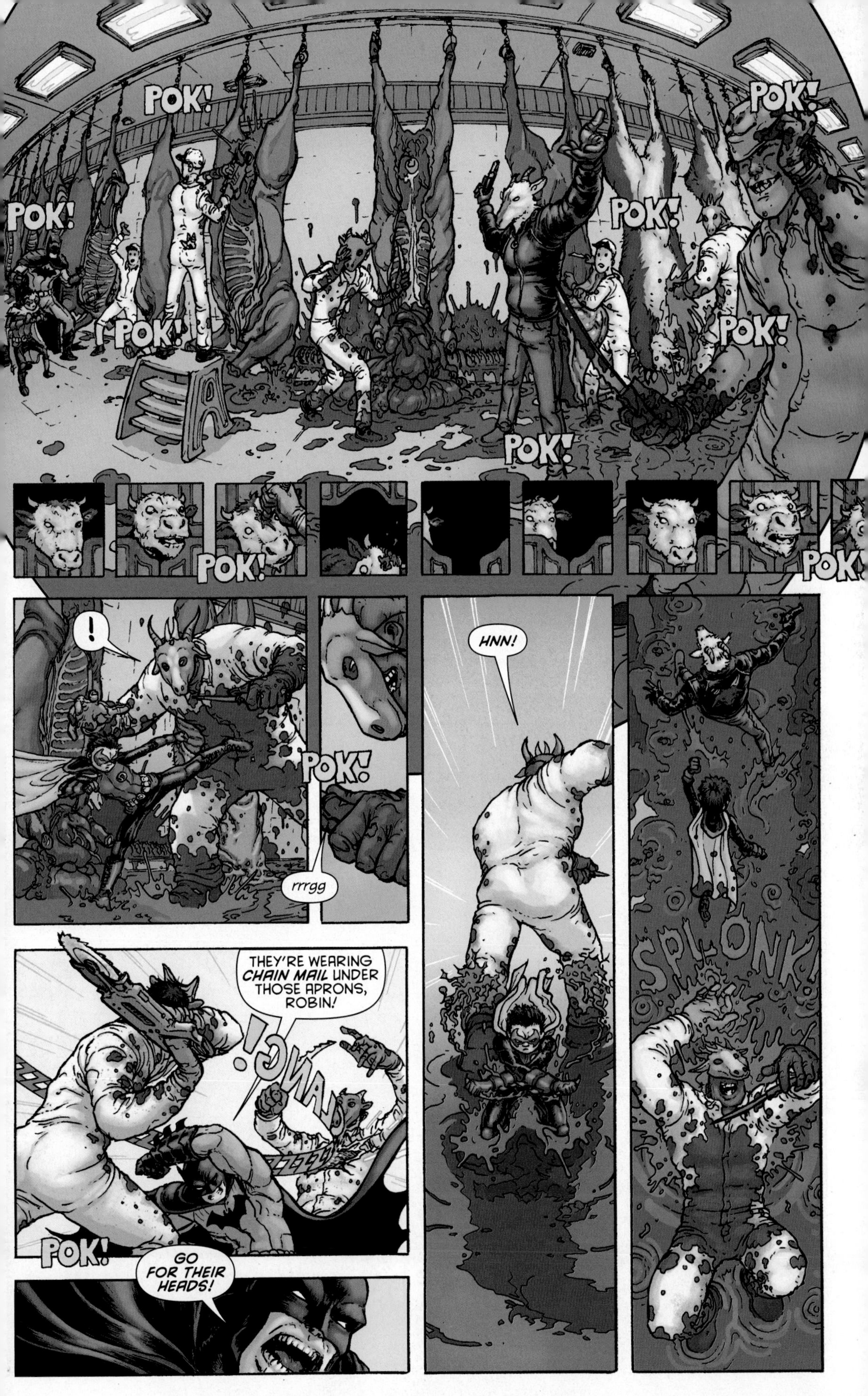
POK!
POK!
POK!
POK!
POK!
POK!
POK!
POK!
POK!
!
POK!
rrrgg
HNN!
SPLONK!
THEY'RE WEARING *CHAIN MAIL* UNDER THOSE APRONS, ROBIN!
POK!
GO FOR THEIR HEADS!

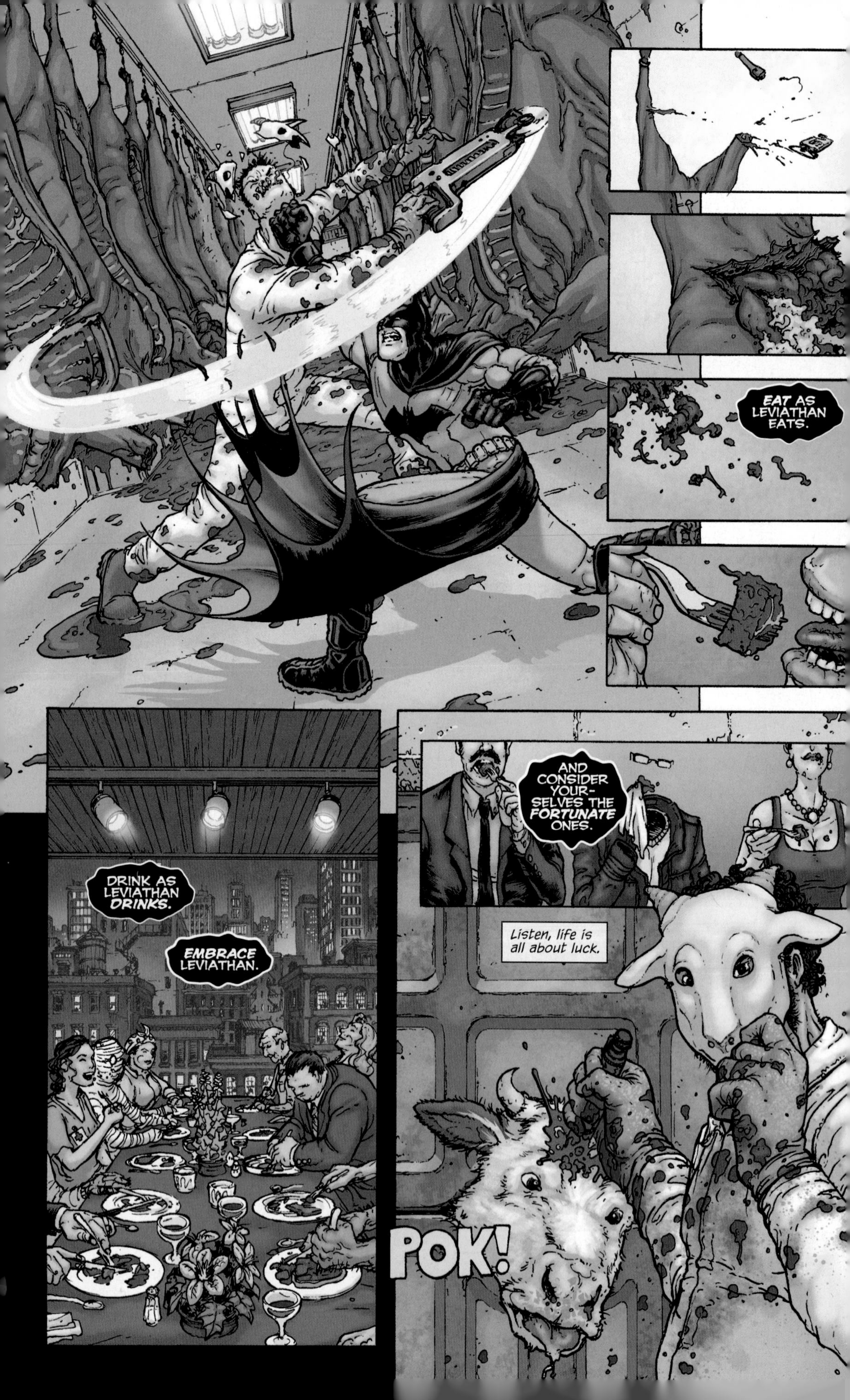

EAT AS LEVIATHAN EATS.
DRINK AS LEVIATHAN DRINKS.
EMBRACE LEVIATHAN.
AND CONSIDER YOURSELVES THE FORTUNATE ONES.
Listen, life is all about luck.
POK!

Some have it.

SPÁK

Some don't.

Sam Lucas was my best friend.

The kinda guy who was always there for me when I needed him.

Even when that meant acting as bait for the Caped Crusader.

TALK!

NOW!

SHOOT HIM...

kurkk

Sam's luck ran out when a hollowpoint rocket-bullet turned his ribcage to matchsticks.

IT WASN'T ME!

I DIDN'T DO IT

I still curse myself for being the rotten pal who fired that shell into the beating heart of a guy who'd been best man at my wedding.

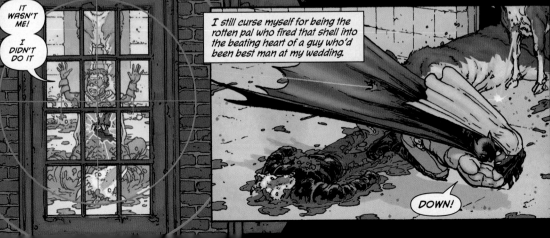

DOWN!

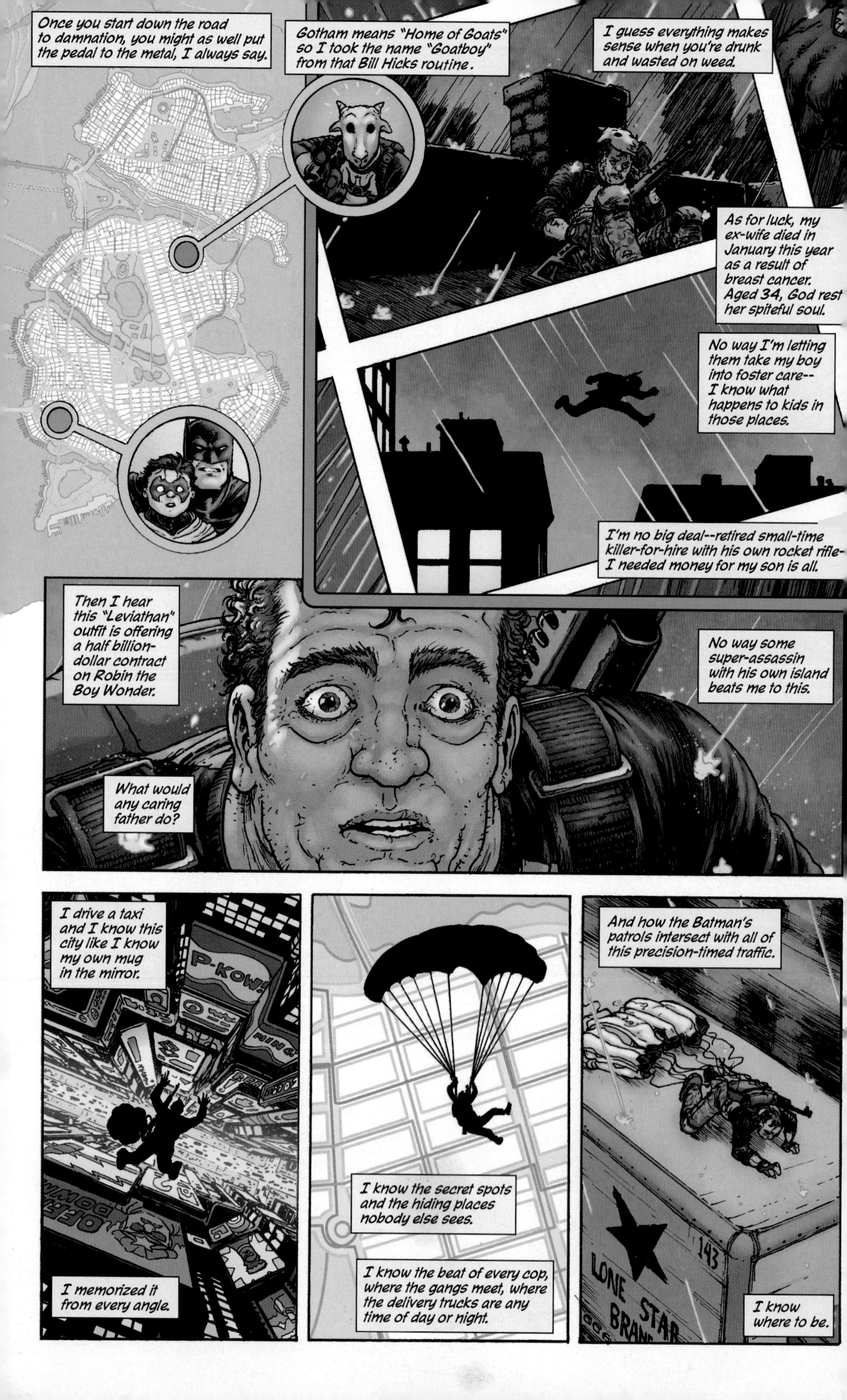

Once you start down the road to damnation, you might as well put the pedal to the metal, I always say.
Gotham means "Home of Goats" so I took the name "Goatboy" from that Bill Hicks routine.
I guess everything makes sense when you're drunk and wasted on weed.
As for luck, my ex-wife died in January this year as a result of breast cancer. Aged 34, God rest her spiteful soul.
No way I'm letting them take my boy into foster care--I know what happens to kids in those places.
I'm no big deal--retired small-time killer-for-hire with his own rocket rifle-I needed money for my son is all.
Then I hear this "Leviathan" outfit is offering a half billion-dollar contract on Robin the Boy Wonder.
No way some super-assassin with his own island beats me to this.
What would any caring father do?
I drive a taxi and I know this city like I know my own mug in the mirror.
P-KOW!
I memorized it from every angle.
I know the secret spots and the hiding places nobody else sees.
I know the beat of every cop, where the gangs meet, where the delivery trucks are any time of day or night.
And how the Batman's patrols intersect with all of this precision-timed traffic.
143
LONE STAR BRAN
I know where to be.

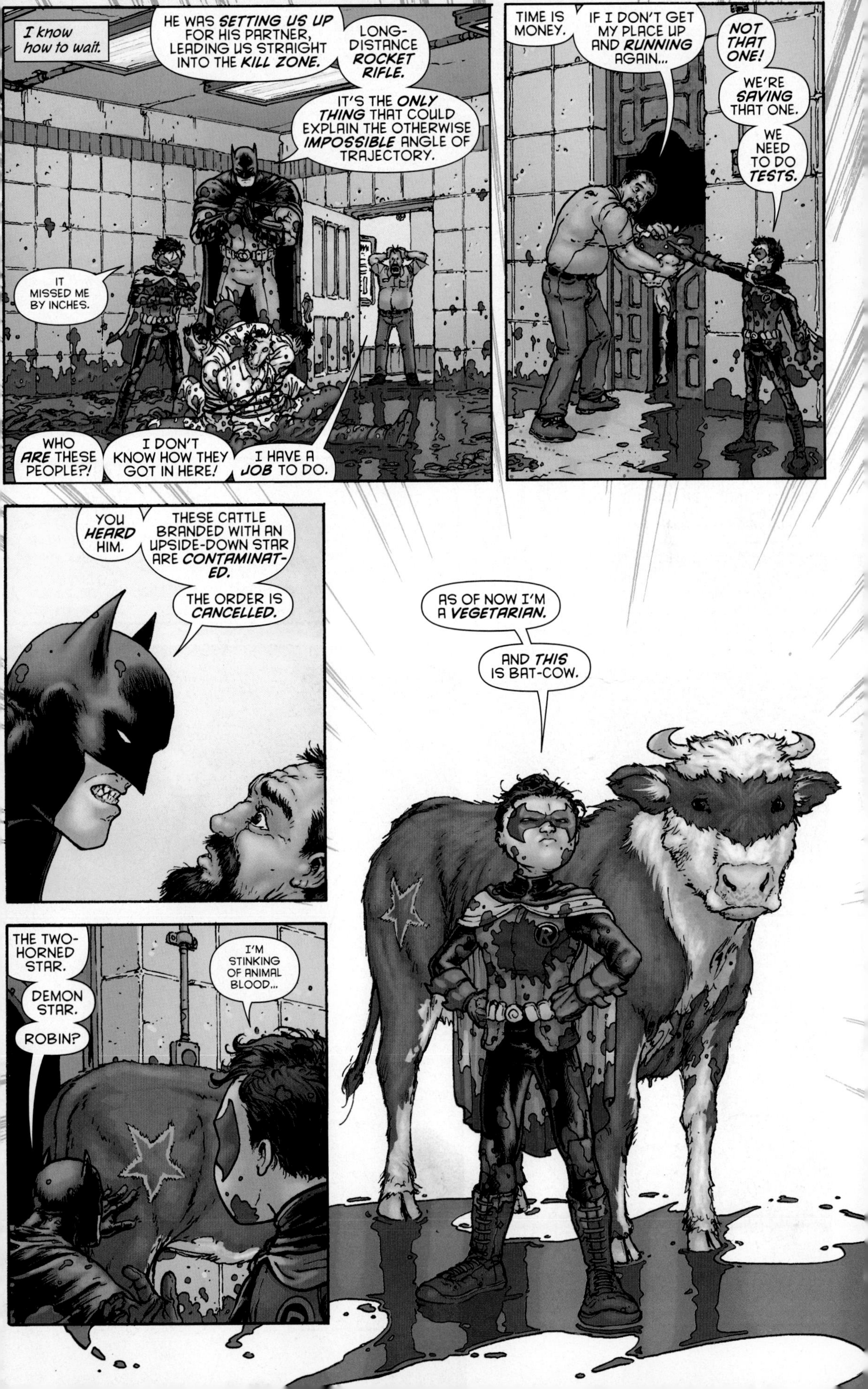
I know how to wait.
HE WAS SETTING US UP FOR HIS PARTNER, LEADING US STRAIGHT INTO THE KILL ZONE.
LONG-DISTANCE ROCKET RIFLE.
IT'S THE ONLY THING THAT COULD EXPLAIN THE OTHERWISE IMPOSSIBLE ANGLE OF TRAJECTORY.
IT MISSED ME BY INCHES.
WHO ARE THESE PEOPLE?!
I DON'T KNOW HOW THEY GOT IN HERE!
I HAVE A JOB TO DO.
TIME IS MONEY.
IF I DON'T GET MY PLACE UP AND RUNNING AGAIN...
NOT THAT ONE!
WE'RE SAVING THAT ONE.
WE NEED TO DO TESTS.
YOU HEARD HIM.
THESE CATTLE BRANDED WITH AN UPSIDE-DOWN STAR ARE CONTAMINATED.
THE ORDER IS CANCELLED.
THE TWO-HORNED STAR.
DEMON STAR.
ROBIN?
I'M STINKING OF ANIMAL BLOOD...
AS OF NOW I'M A VEGETARIAN.
AND THIS IS BAT-COW.

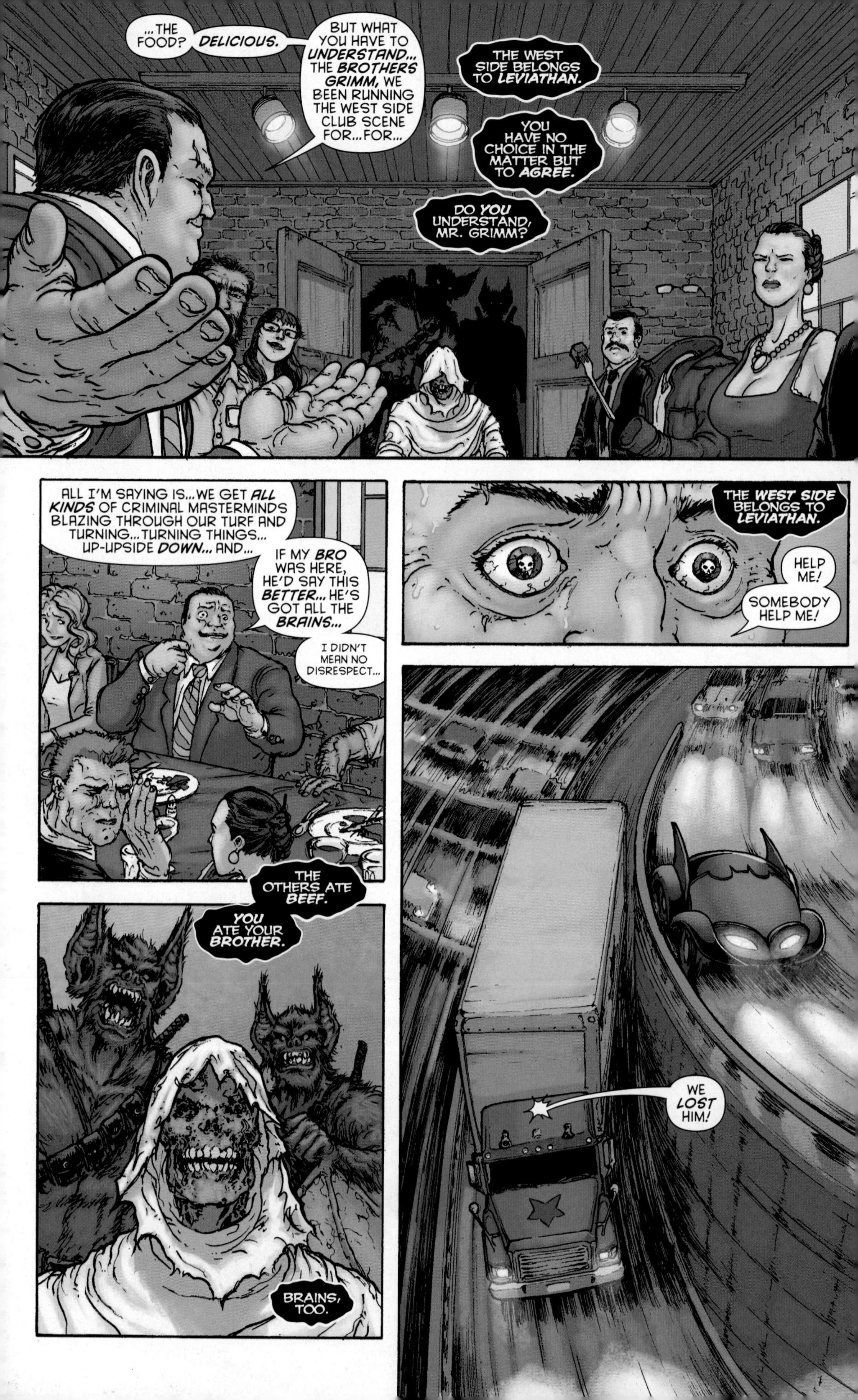
...THE FOOD? DELICIOUS.
BUT WHAT YOU HAVE TO UNDERSTAND... THE BROTHERS GRIMM, WE BEEN RUNNING THE WEST SIDE CLUB SCENE FOR...FOR...
THE WEST SIDE BELONGS TO LEVIATHAN.
YOU HAVE NO CHOICE IN THE MATTER BUT TO AGREE.
DO YOU UNDERSTAND, MR. GRIMM?
ALL I'M SAYING IS...WE GET ALL KINDS OF CRIMINAL MASTERMINDS BLAZING THROUGH OUR TURF AND TURNING...TURNING THINGS... UP-UPSIDE DOWN... AND...
IF MY BRO WAS HERE, HE'D SAY THIS BETTER... HE'S GOT ALL THE BRAINS...
I DIDN'T MEAN NO DISRESPECT...
THE OTHERS ATE BEEF.
YOU ATE YOUR BROTHER.
BRAINS, TOO.
THE WEST SIDE BELONGS TO LEVIATHAN.
HELP ME!
SOMEBODY HELP ME!
WE LOST HIM!

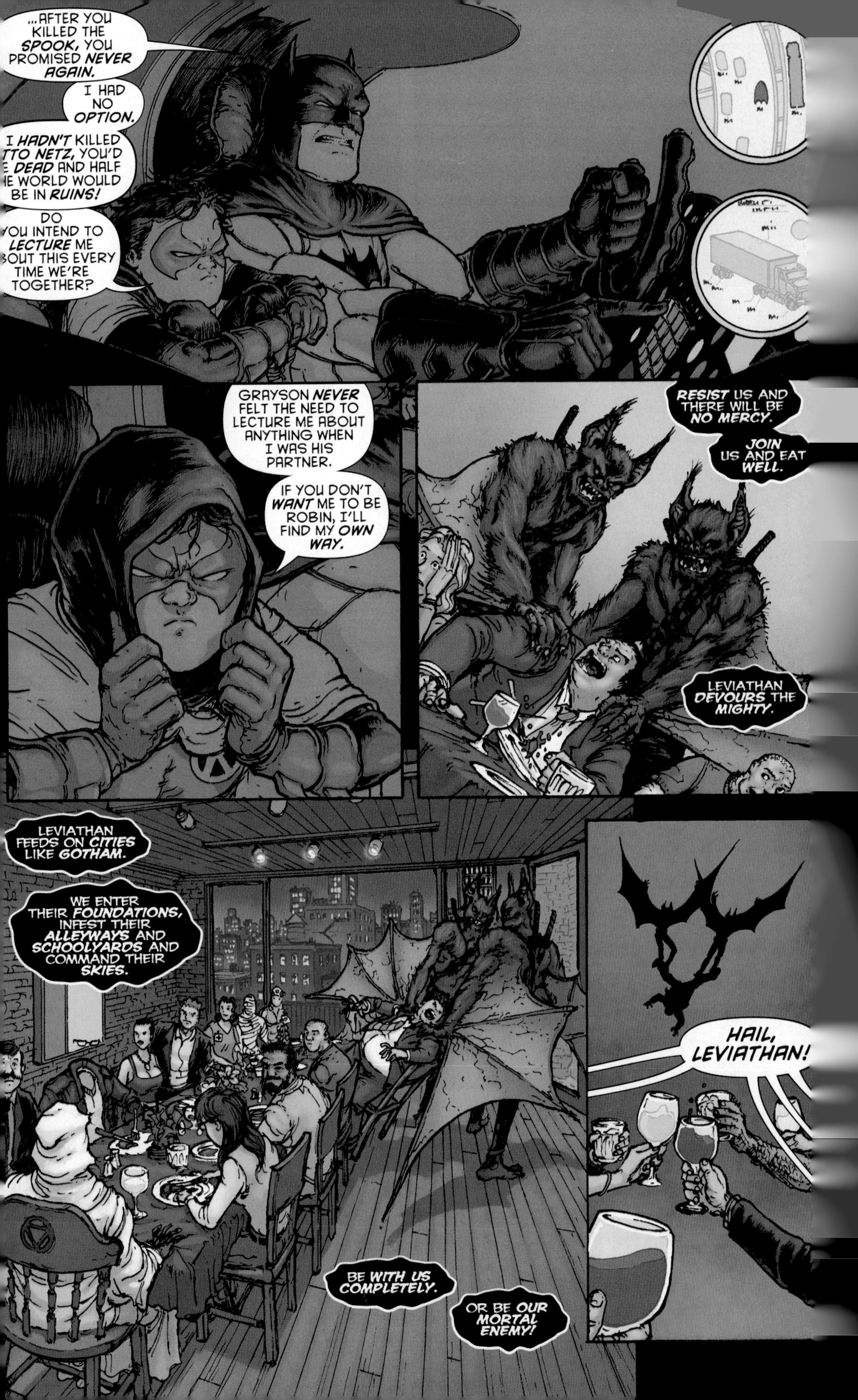
...AFTER YOU KILLED THE SPOOK, YOU PROMISED NEVER AGAIN.
I HAD NO OPTION.
I HADN'T KILLED TTO NETZ, YOU'D E DEAD AND HALF IE WORLD WOULD BE IN RUINS!
DO YOU INTEND TO LECTURE ME BOUT THIS EVERY TIME WE'RE TOGETHER?
GRAYSON NEVER FELT THE NEED TO LECTURE ME ABOUT ANYTHING WHEN I WAS HIS PARTNER.
IF YOU DON'T WANT ME TO BE ROBIN, I'LL FIND MY OWN WAY.
RESIST US AND THERE WILL BE NO MERCY.
JOIN US AND EAT WELL.
LEVIATHAN DEVOURS THE MIGHTY.
LEVIATHAN FEEDS ON CITIES LIKE GOTHAM.
WE ENTER THEIR FOUNDATIONS, INFEST THEIR ALLEYWAYS AND SCHOOLYARDS AND COMMAND THEIR SKIES.
BE WITH US COMPLETELY.
OR BE OUR MORTAL ENEMY!
HAIL, LEVIATHAN!

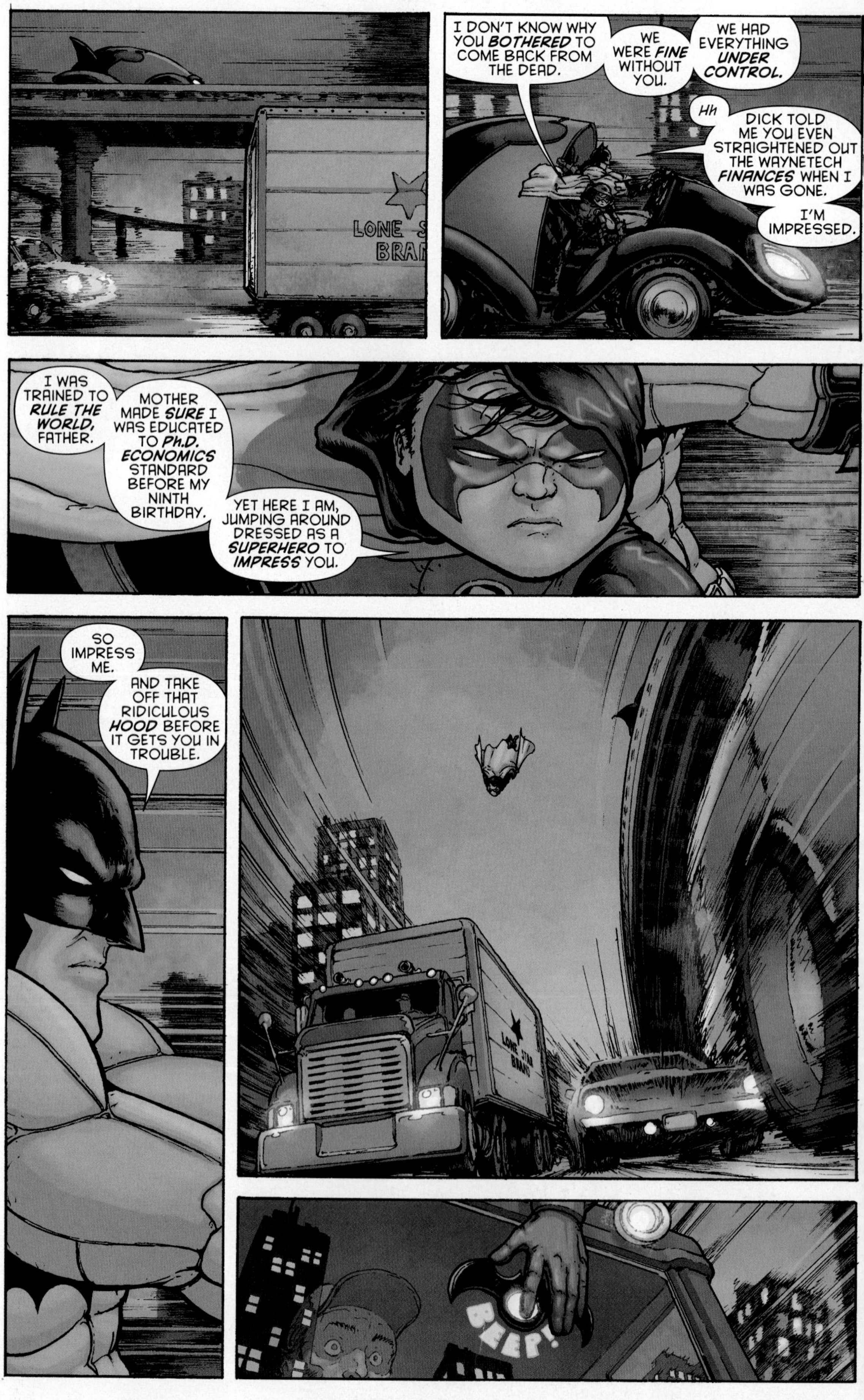
LONE S
BRA
I DON'T KNOW WHY YOU **BOTHERED** TO COME BACK FROM THE DEAD.
WE WERE **FINE** WITHOUT YOU.
WE HAD EVERYTHING **UNDER CONTROL.**
Hh
DICK TOLD ME YOU EVEN STRAIGHTENED OUT THE WAYNETECH **FINANCES** WHEN I WAS GONE.
I'M IMPRESSED.
I WAS TRAINED TO **RULE THE WORLD,** FATHER.
MOTHER MADE **SURE** I WAS EDUCATED TO **Ph.D. ECONOMICS** STANDARD BEFORE MY NINTH BIRTHDAY.
YET HERE I AM, JUMPING AROUND DRESSED AS A **SUPERHERO** TO **IMPRESS** YOU.
SO IMPRESS ME.
AND TAKE OFF THAT RIDICULOUS **HOOD** BEFORE IT GETS YOU IN TROUBLE.
BEEP!

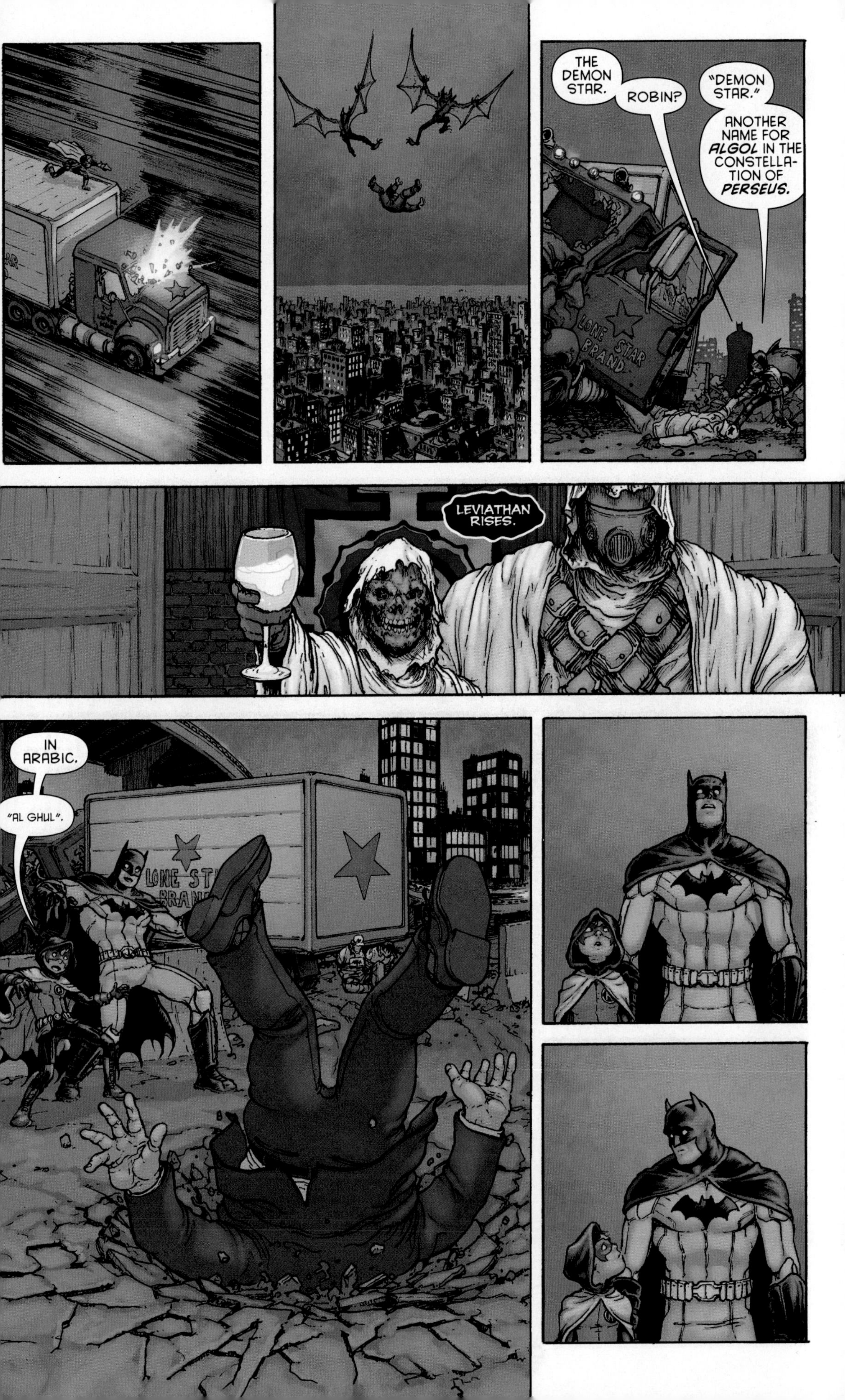

THE DEMON STAR.
ROBIN?
"DEMON STAR."
ANOTHER NAME FOR ALGOL IN THE CONSTELLATION OF PERSEUS.
LONE STAR BRAND
LEVIATHAN RISES.
IN ARABIC.
"AL GHUL".
LONE ST BRAN

SAN FRANCISCO.

ALL RIGHT, LUV?

JUST DROPPED IN TO SEE IF MY *PERV SUIT'S* TURNED UP.

THE OUTFIT YOU ORDERED IS *RIGHT HERE.*

♪

HM?

FANTASTIC.

BLOODY FANTASTIC.

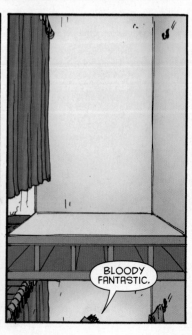

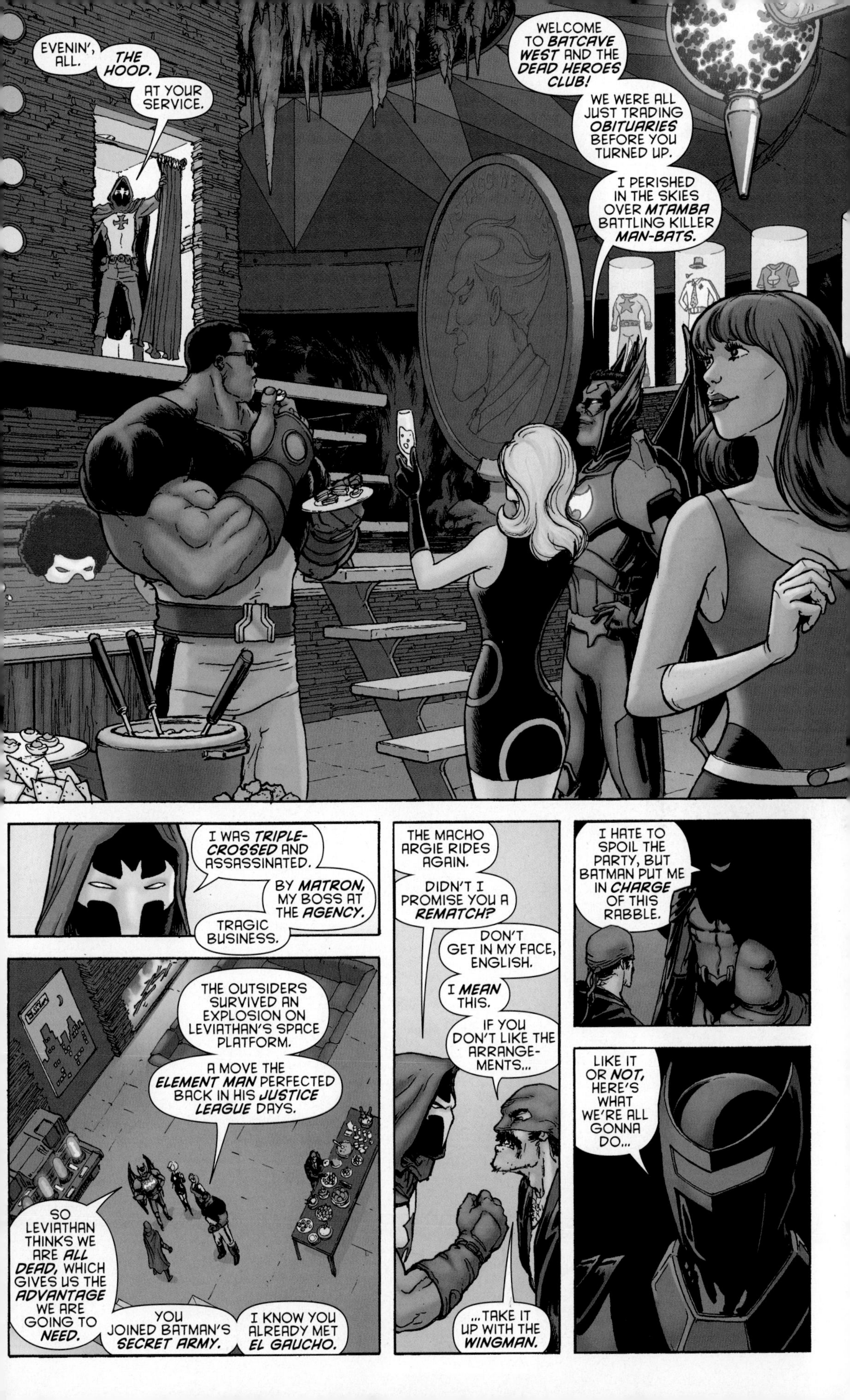
EVENIN', ALL.
THE HOOD.
AT YOUR SERVICE.
WELCOME TO BATCAVE WEST AND THE DEAD HEROES CLUB!
WE WERE ALL JUST TRADING OBITUARIES BEFORE YOU TURNED UP.
I PERISHED IN THE SKIES OVER MTAMBA BATTLING KILLER MAN-BATS.
I WAS TRIPLE-CROSSED AND ASSASSINATED.
BY MATRON, MY BOSS AT THE AGENCY.
TRAGIC BUSINESS.
THE OUTSIDERS SURVIVED AN EXPLOSION ON LEVIATHAN'S SPACE PLATFORM.
A MOVE THE ELEMENT MAN PERFECTED BACK IN HIS JUSTICE LEAGUE DAYS.
SO LEVIATHAN THINKS WE ARE ALL DEAD, WHICH GIVES US THE ADVANTAGE WE ARE GOING TO NEED.
YOU JOINED BATMAN'S SECRET ARMY.
I KNOW YOU ALREADY MET EL GAUCHO.
THE MACHO ARGIE RIDES AGAIN.
DIDN'T I PROMISE YOU A REMATCH?
DON'T GET IN MY FACE, ENGLISH.
I MEAN THIS.
IF YOU DON'T LIKE THE ARRANGE-MENTS...
...TAKE IT UP WITH THE WINGMAN.
I HATE TO SPOIL THE PARTY, BUT BATMAN PUT ME IN CHARGE OF THIS RABBLE.
LIKE IT OR NOT, HERE'S WHAT WE'RE ALL GONNA DO...

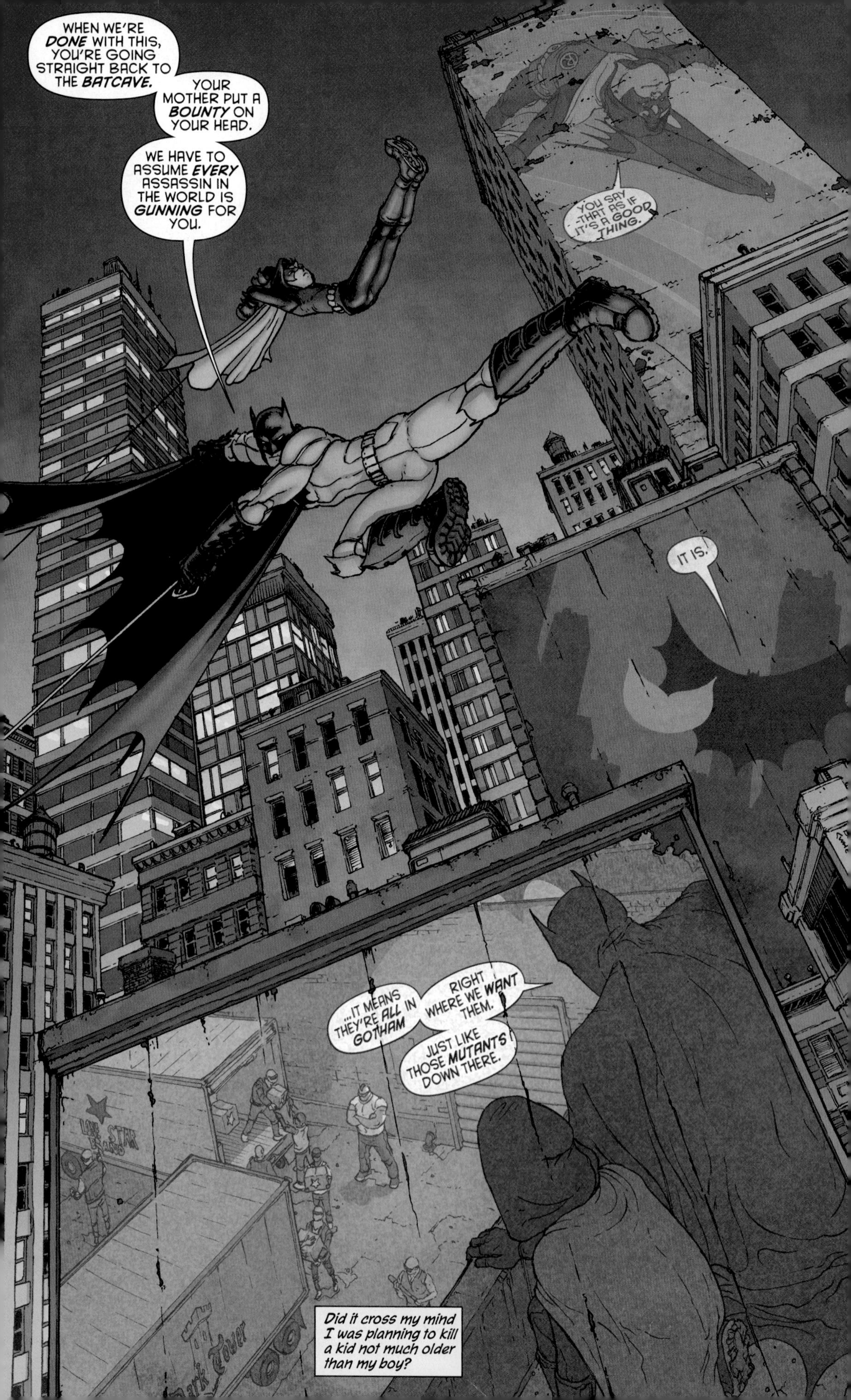
WHEN WE'RE DONE WITH THIS, YOU'RE GOING STRAIGHT BACK TO THE BATCAVE.
YOUR MOTHER PUT A BOUNTY ON YOUR HEAD.
WE HAVE TO ASSUME EVERY ASSASSIN IN THE WORLD IS GUNNING FOR YOU.
YOU SAY THAT AS IF IT'S A GOOD THING.
IT IS.
...IT MEANS THEY'RE ALL IN GOTHAM
RIGHT WHERE WE WANT THEM.
JUST LIKE THOSE MUTANTS DOWN THERE.
Did it cross my mind I was planning to kill a kid not much older than my boy?

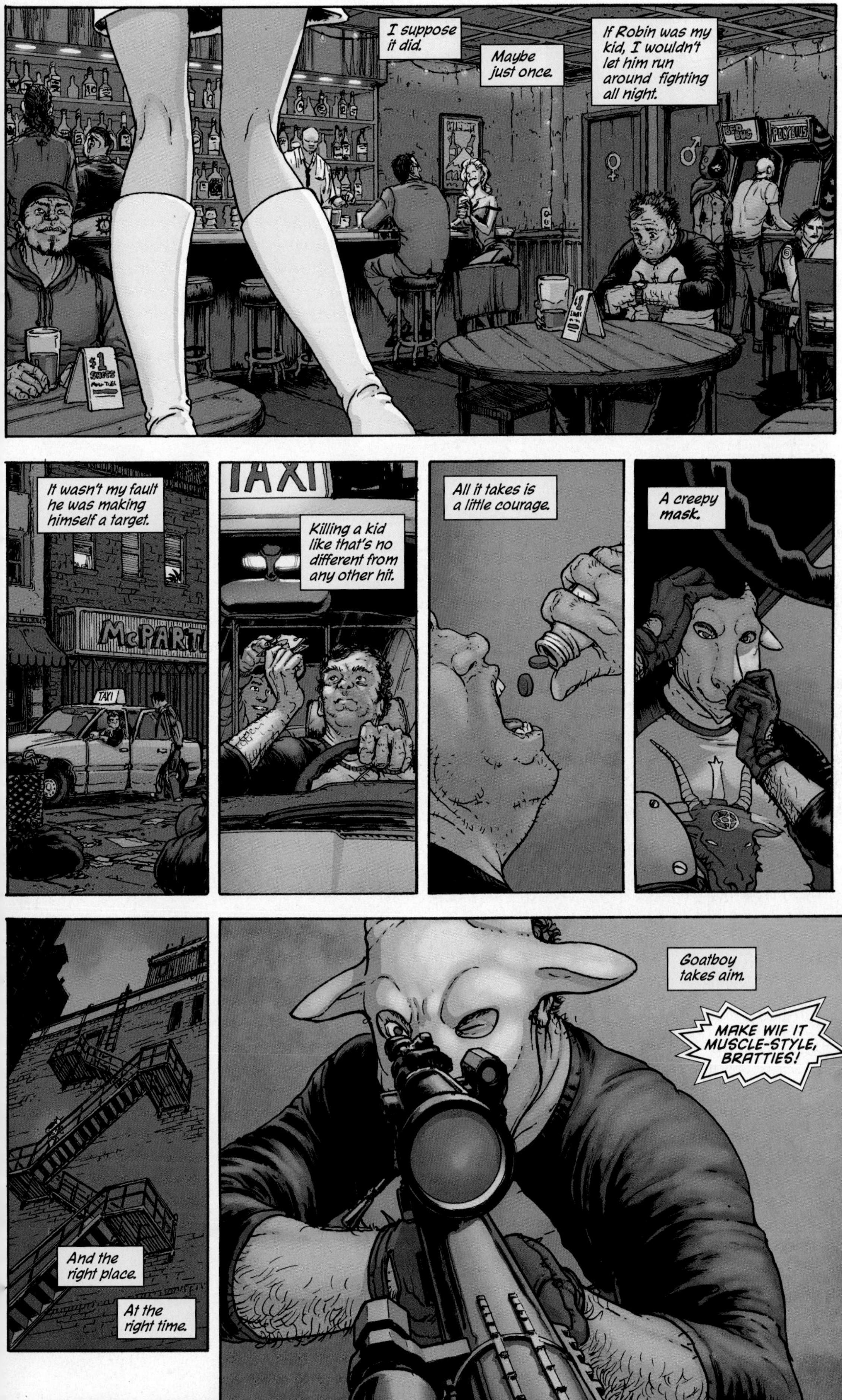
I suppose it did.
Maybe just once.
If Robin was my kid, I wouldn't let him run around fighting all night.
$1 SHOTS
It wasn't my fault he was making himself a target.
McPART
TAXI
Killing a kid like that's no different from any other hit.
All it takes is a little courage.
A creepy mask.
And the right place.
At the right time.
Goatboy takes aim.
MAKE WIF IT MUSCLE-STYLE, BRATTIES!

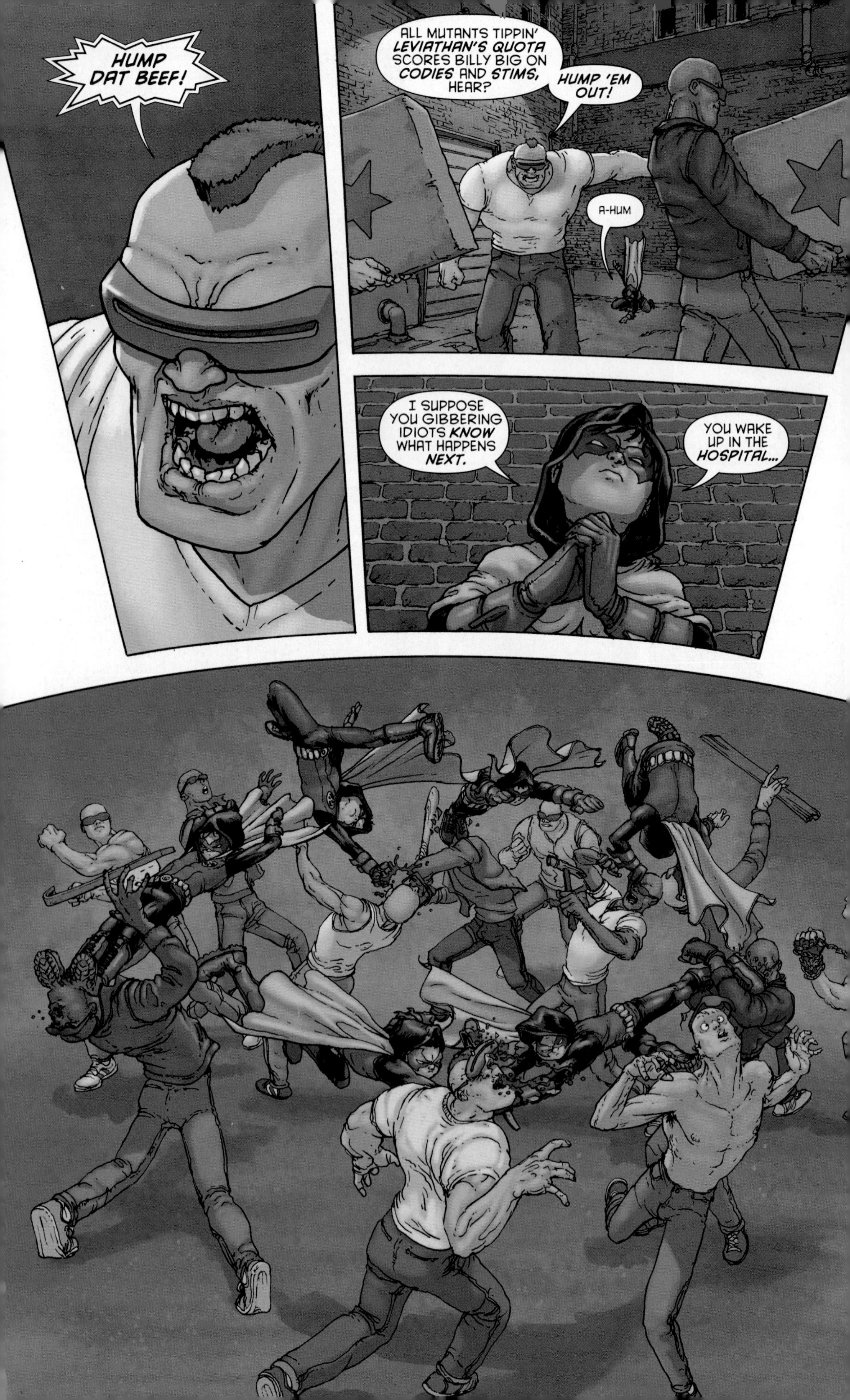
HUMP DAT BEEF!
ALL MUTANTS TIPPIN' LEVIATHAN'S QUOTA SCORES BILLY BIG ON CODIES AND STIMS, HEAR?
HUMP 'EM OUT!
A-HUM
I SUPPOSE YOU GIBBERING IDIOTS KNOW WHAT HAPPENS NEXT.
YOU WAKE UP IN THE HOSPITAL...

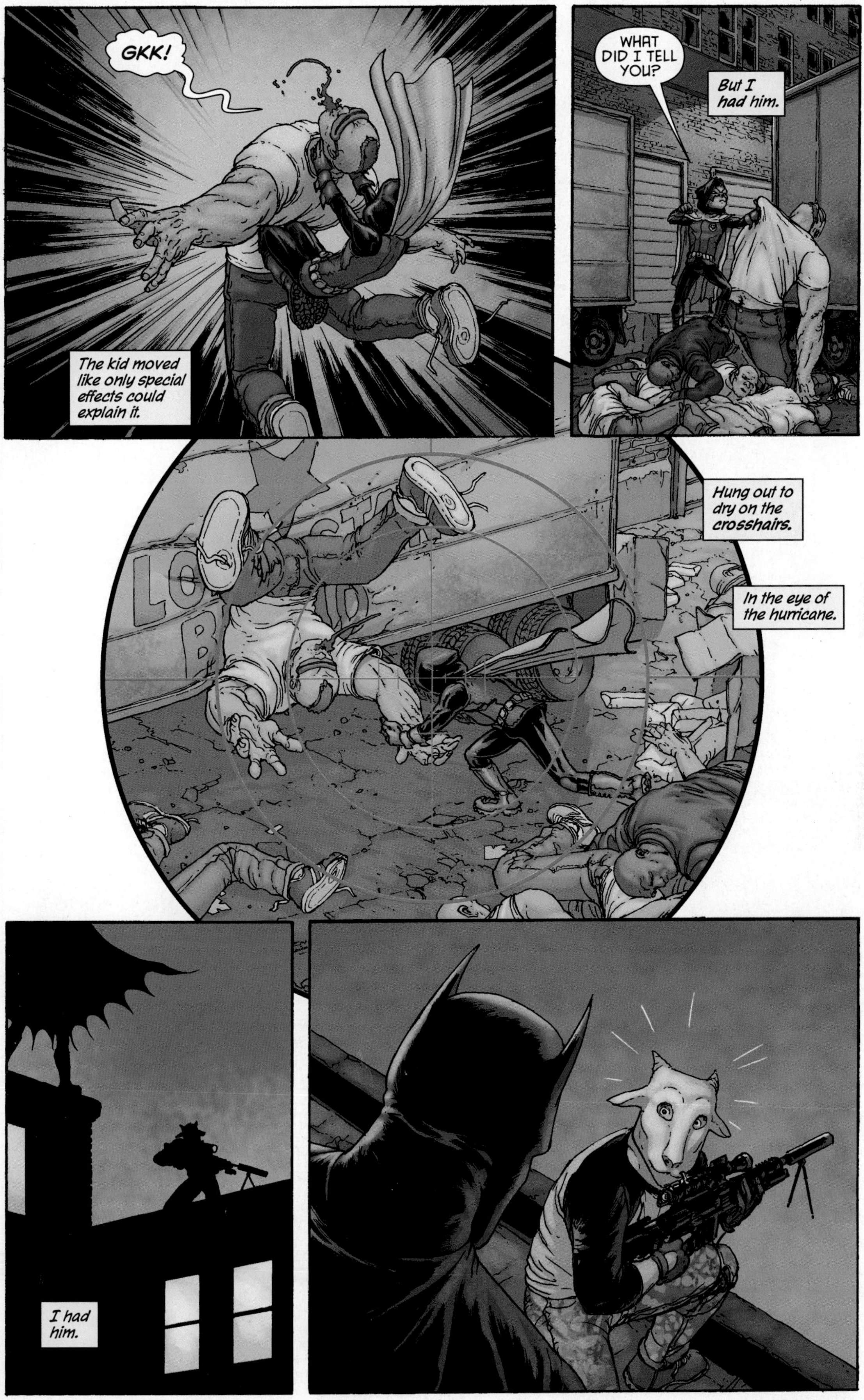
GKK!
The kid moved like only special effects could explain it.
WHAT DID I TELL YOU?
But I had him.
Hung out to dry on the crosshairs.
In the eye of the hurricane.
I had him.

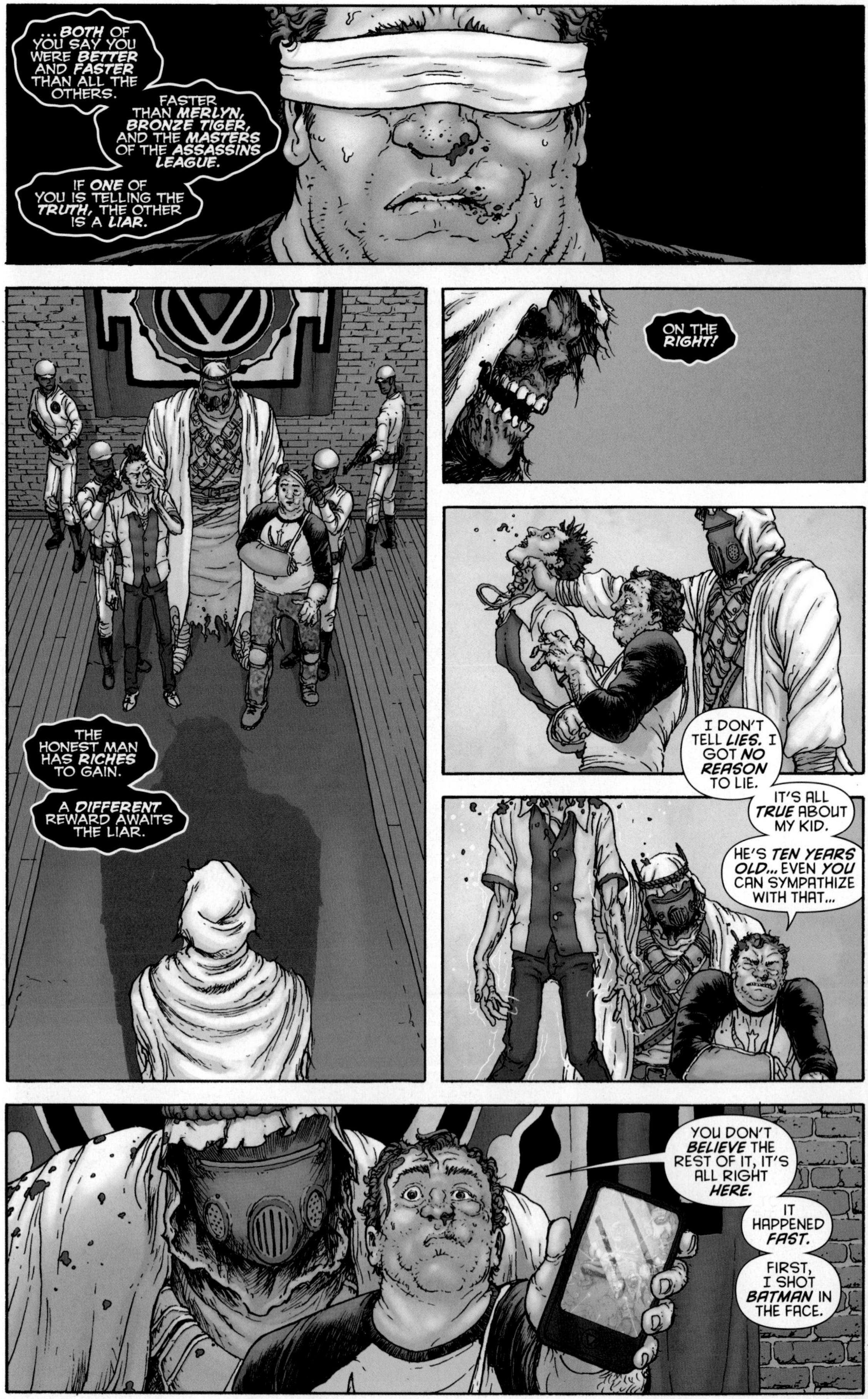
...BOTH OF YOU SAY YOU WERE BETTER AND FASTER THAN ALL THE OTHERS.
FASTER THAN MERLYN, BRONZE TIGER, AND THE MASTERS OF THE ASSASSINS LEAGUE.
IF ONE OF YOU IS TELLING THE TRUTH, THE OTHER IS A LIAR.
THE HONEST MAN HAS RICHES TO GAIN.
A DIFFERENT REWARD AWAITS THE LIAR.
ON THE RIGHT!
I DON'T TELL LIES. I GOT NO REASON TO LIE.
IT'S ALL TRUE ABOUT MY KID.
HE'S TEN YEARS OLD... EVEN YOU CAN SYMPATHIZE WITH THAT...
YOU DON'T BELIEVE THE REST OF IT, IT'S ALL RIGHT HERE.
IT HAPPENED FAST.
FIRST, I SHOT BATMAN IN THE FACE.

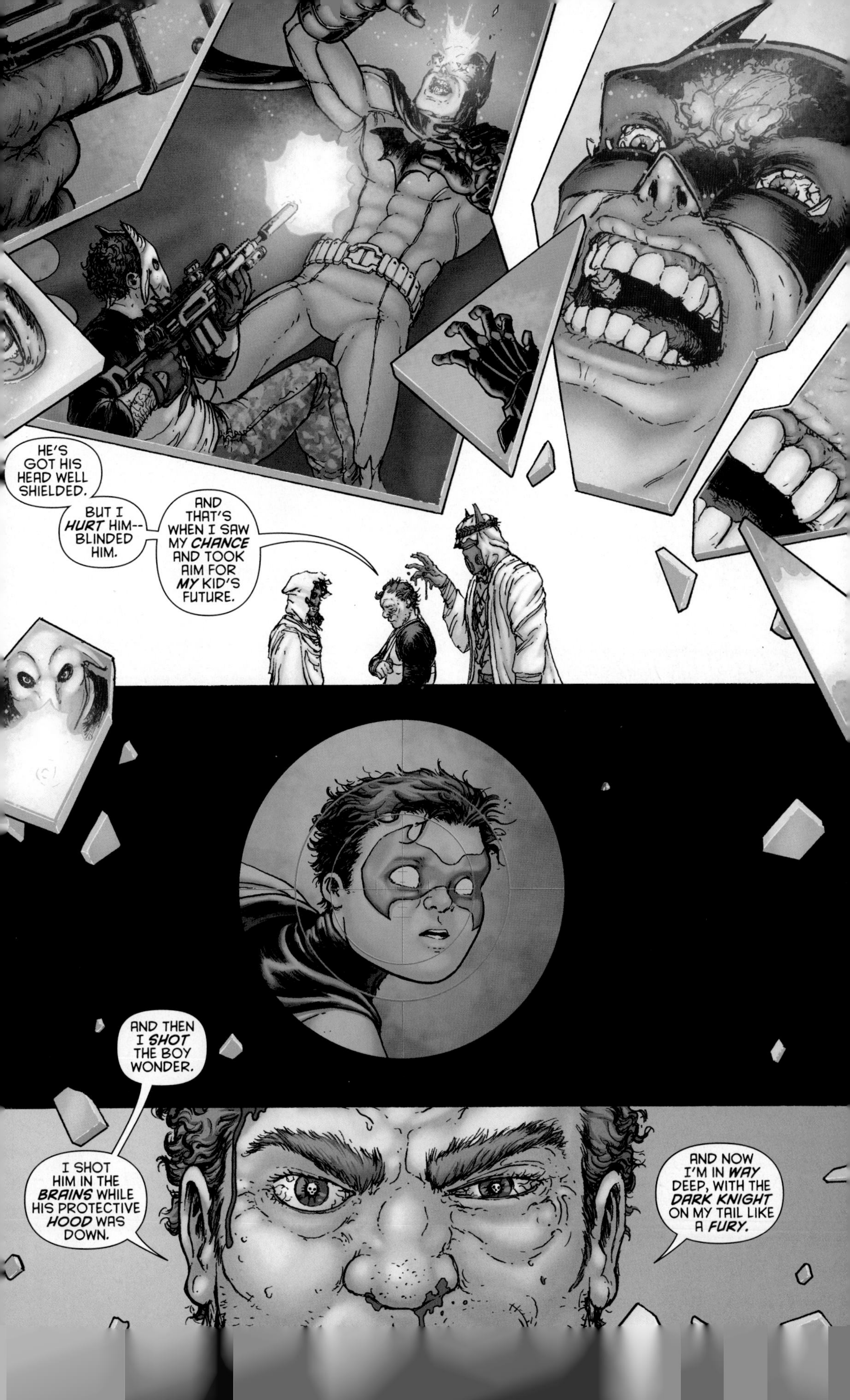

HE'S GOT HIS HEAD WELL SHIELDED.
BUT I HURT HIM-- BLINDED HIM.
AND THAT'S WHEN I SAW MY CHANCE AND TOOK AIM FOR MY KID'S FUTURE.
AND THEN I SHOT THE BOY WONDER.
I SHOT HIM IN THE BRAINS WHILE HIS PROTECTIVE HOOD WAS DOWN.
AND NOW I'M IN WAY DEEP, WITH THE DARK KNIGHT ON MY TAIL LIKE A FURY.

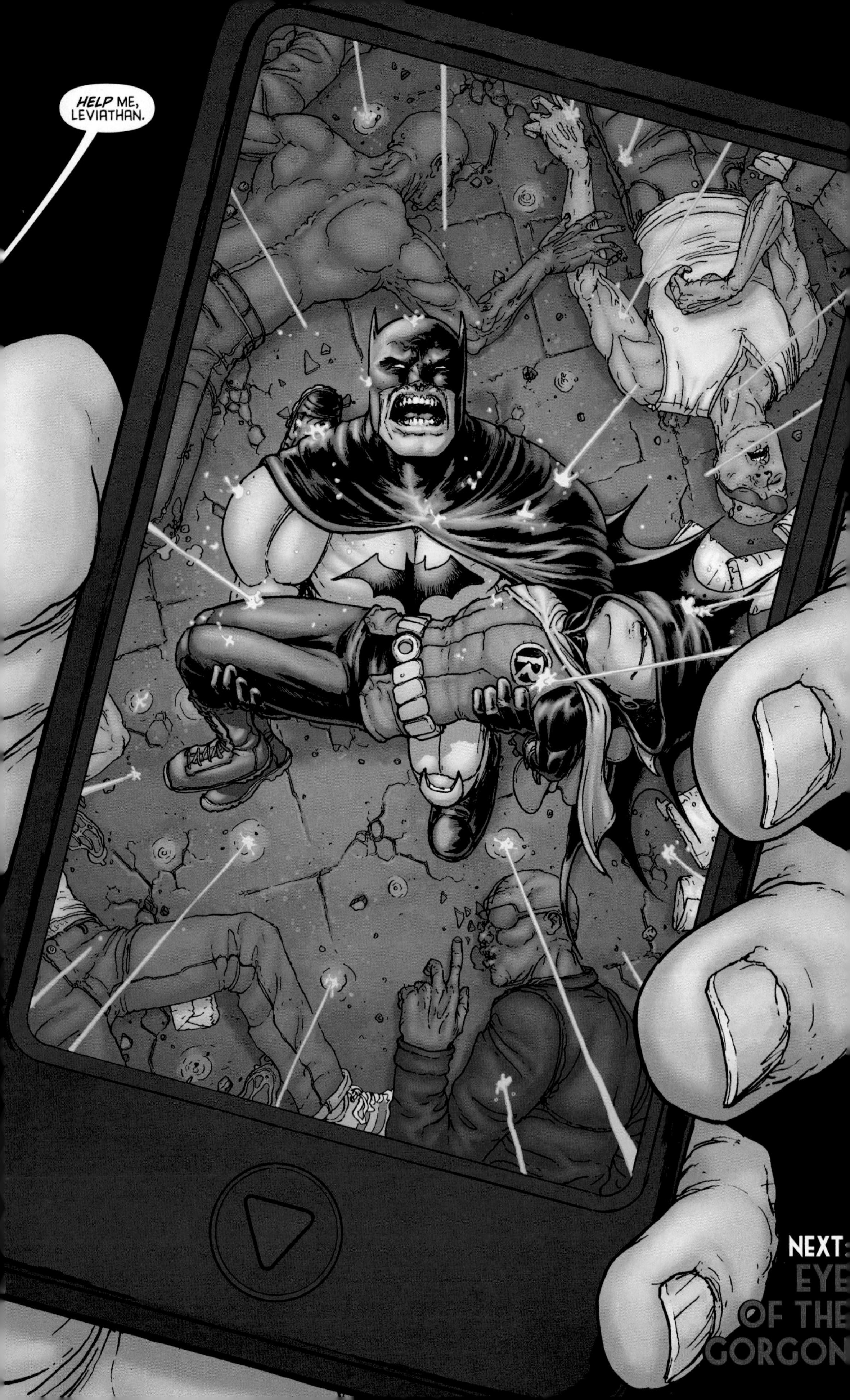
HELP ME, LEVIATHAN.
NEXT: EYE OF THE GORGON

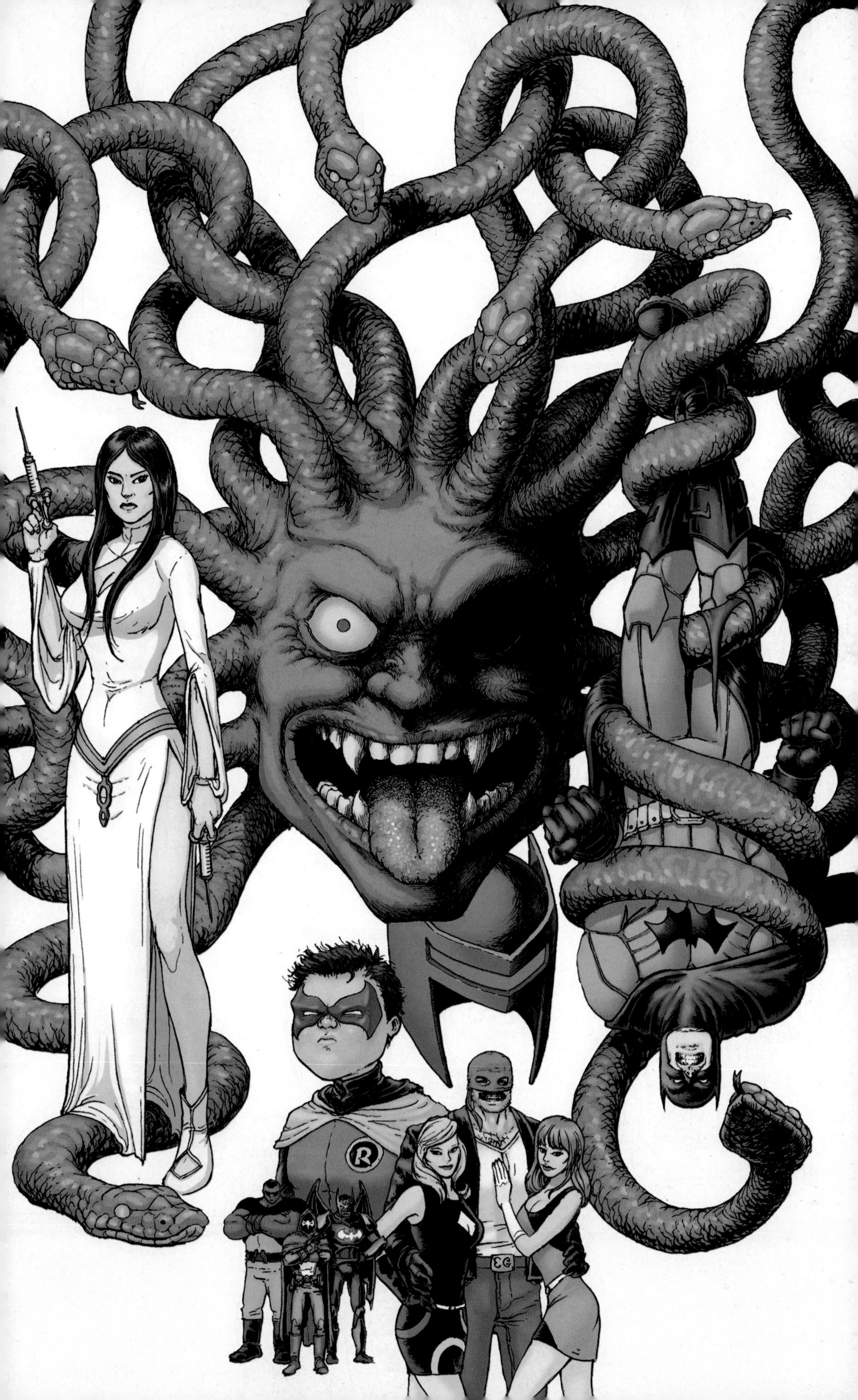

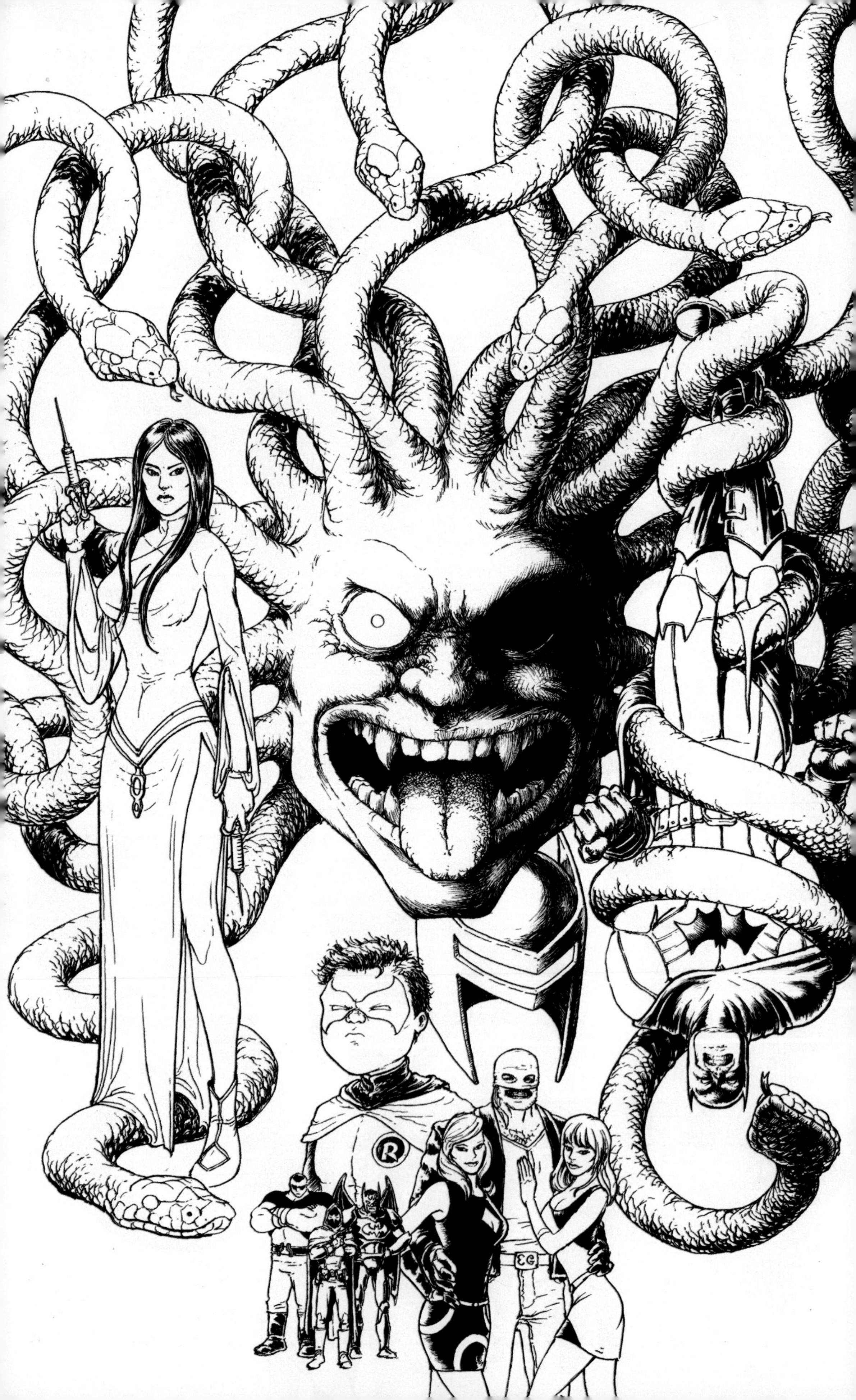

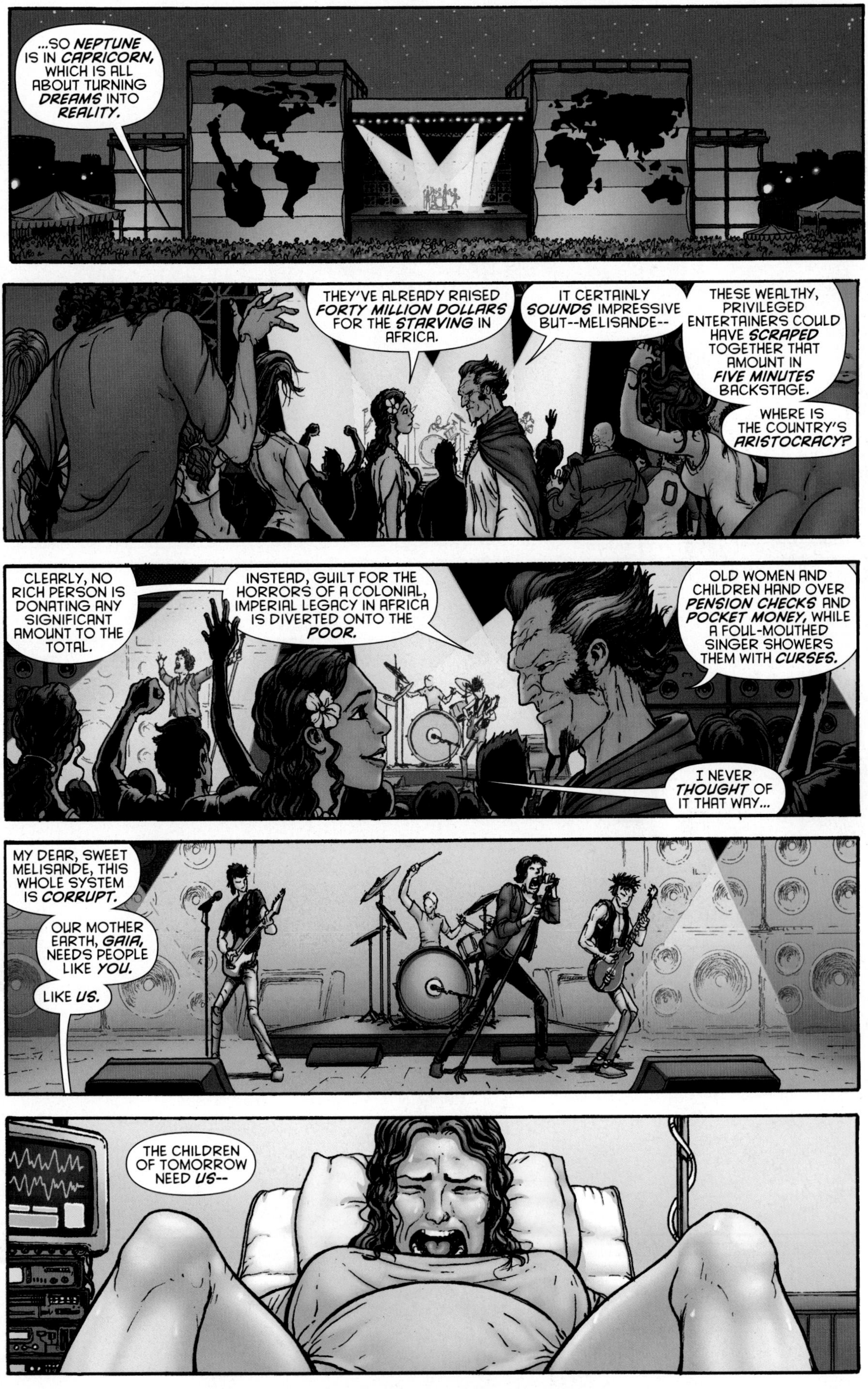
...SO NEPTUNE IS IN CAPRICORN, WHICH IS ALL ABOUT TURNING DREAMS INTO REALITY.
THEY'VE ALREADY RAISED FORTY MILLION DOLLARS FOR THE STARVING IN AFRICA.
IT CERTAINLY SOUNDS IMPRESSIVE BUT--MELISANDE--
THESE WEALTHY, PRIVILEGED ENTERTAINERS COULD HAVE SCRAPED TOGETHER THAT AMOUNT IN FIVE MINUTES BACKSTAGE.
WHERE IS THE COUNTRY'S ARISTOCRACY?
CLEARLY, NO RICH PERSON IS DONATING ANY SIGNIFICANT AMOUNT TO THE TOTAL.
INSTEAD, GUILT FOR THE HORRORS OF A COLONIAL, IMPERIAL LEGACY IN AFRICA IS DIVERTED ONTO THE POOR.
OLD WOMEN AND CHILDREN HAND OVER PENSION CHECKS AND POCKET MONEY, WHILE A FOUL-MOUTHED SINGER SHOWERS THEM WITH CURSES.
I NEVER THOUGHT OF IT THAT WAY...
MY DEAR, SWEET MELISANDE, THIS WHOLE SYSTEM IS CORRUPT.
OUR MOTHER EARTH, GAIA, NEEDS PEOPLE LIKE YOU.
LIKE US.
THE CHILDREN OF TOMORROW NEED US--

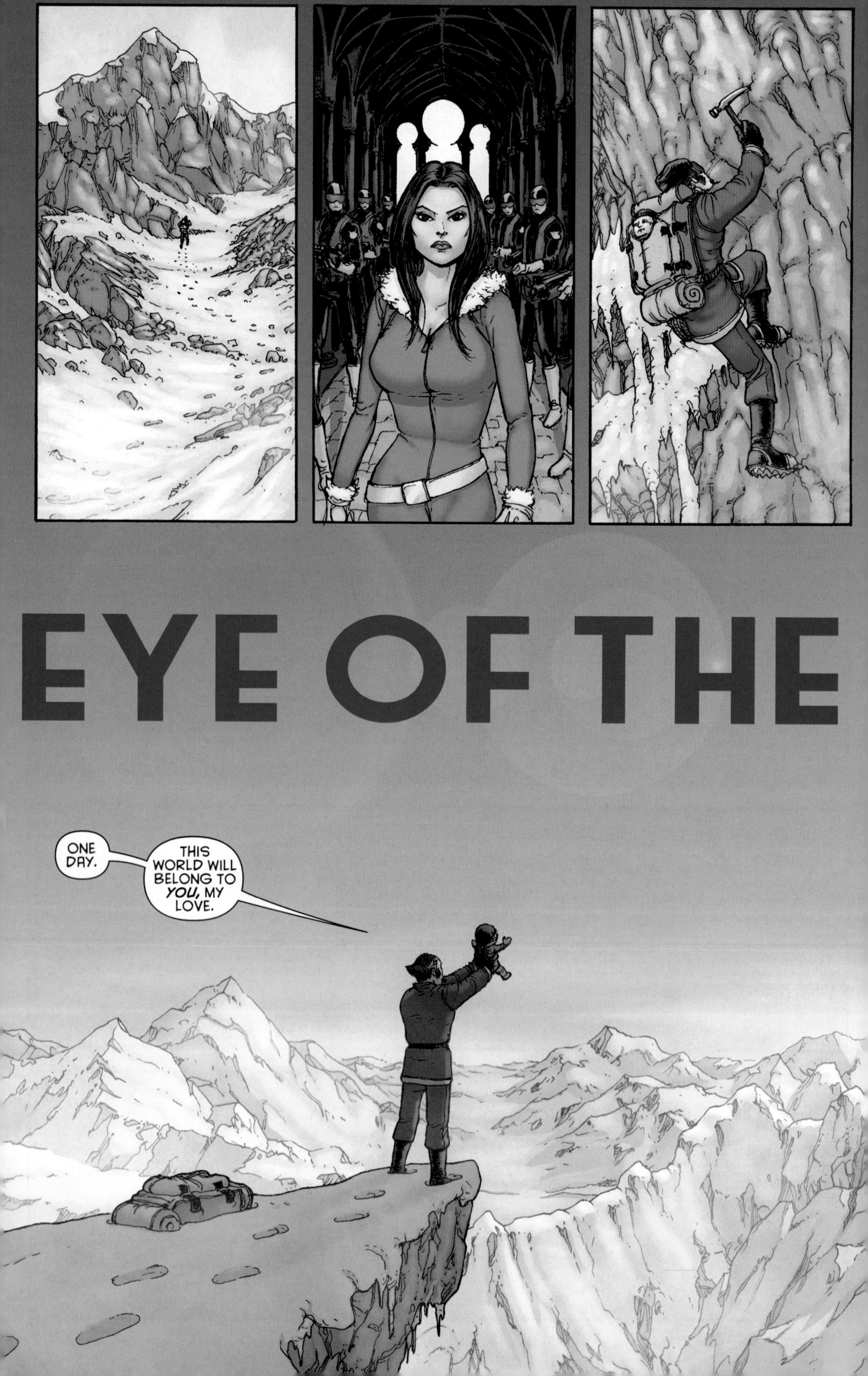
EYE OF THE
ONE DAY.
THIS WORLD WILL BELONG TO *YOU,* MY LOVE.

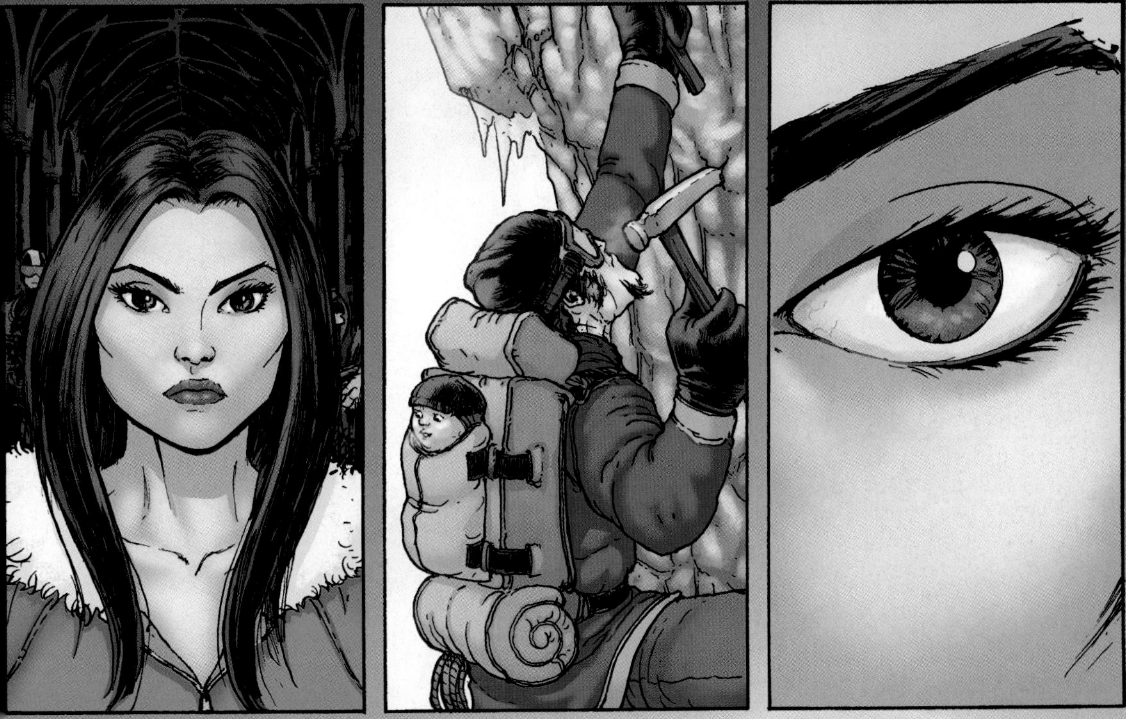

GORGON

WRITER GRANT MORRISON **ARTIST** CHRIS BURNHAM

COLOR NATHAN FAIRBAIRN **LETTERING** PATRICK BROSSEAU

COVER BURNHAM AND FAIRBAIRN

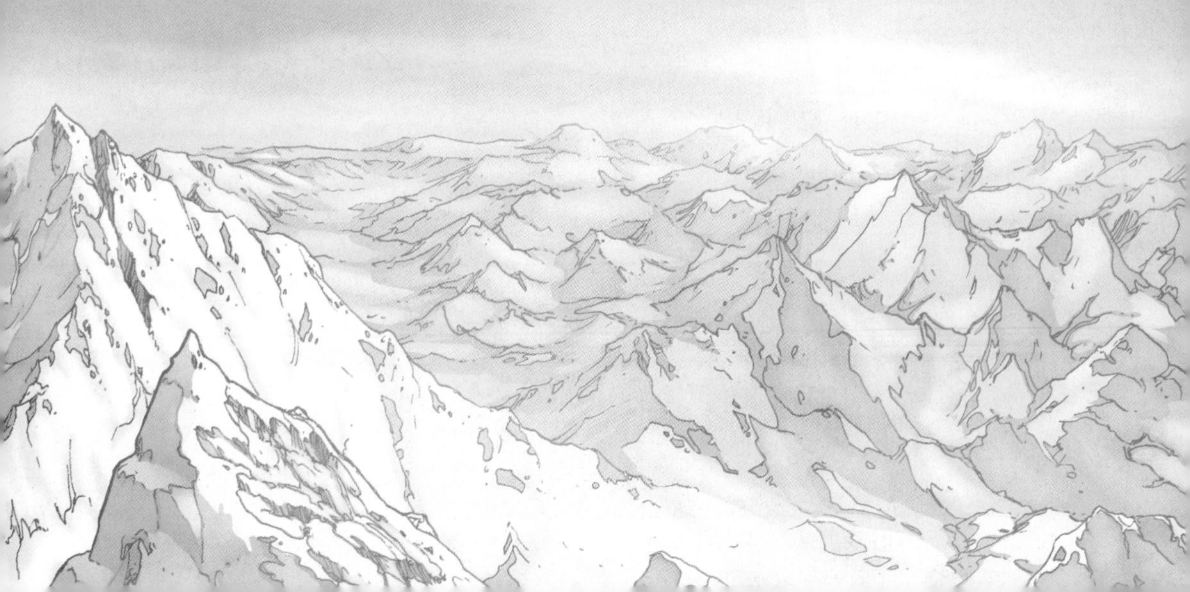

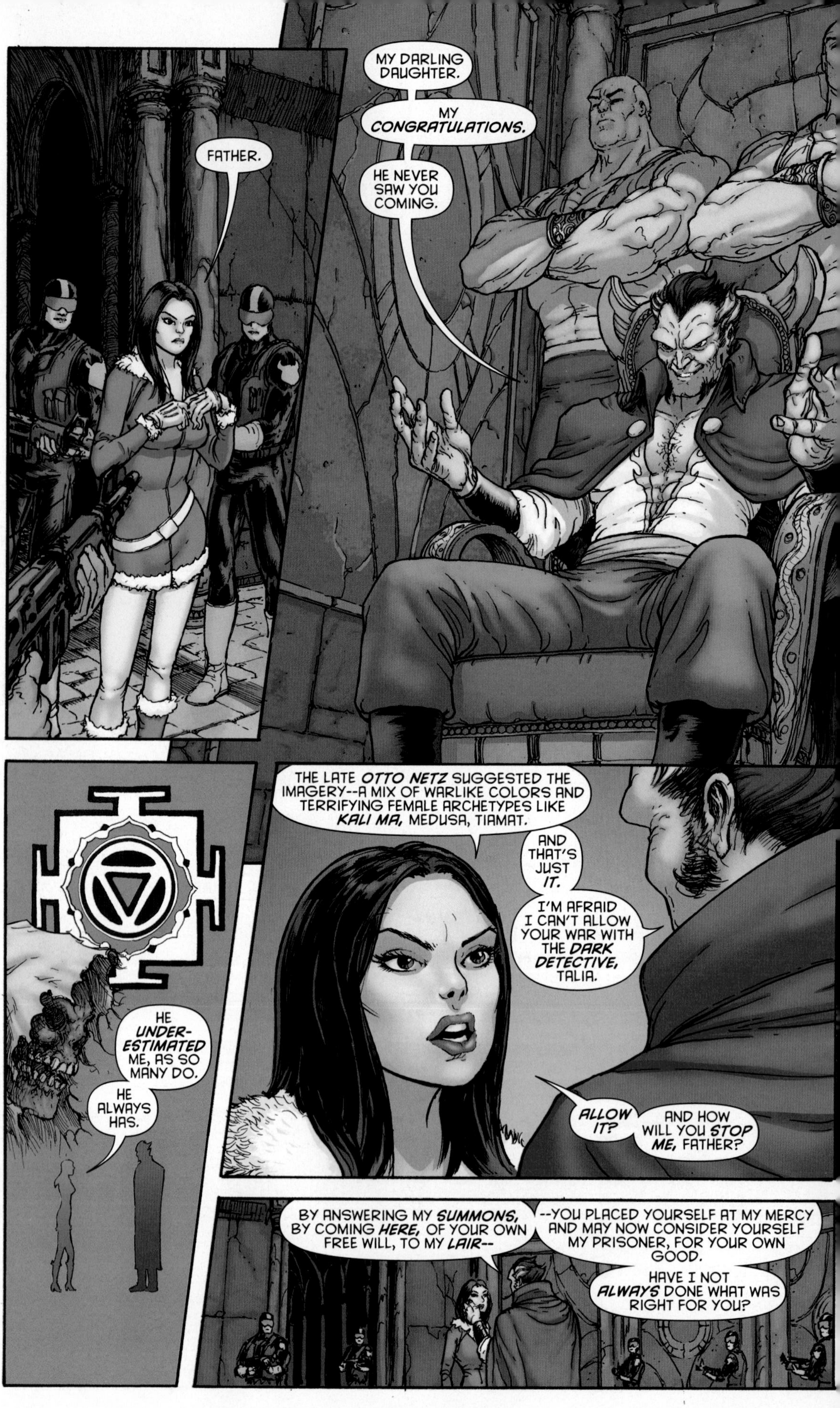
FATHER.
MY DARLING DAUGHTER.
MY CONGRATULATIONS.
HE NEVER SAW YOU COMING.
HE UNDER-ESTIMATED ME, AS SO MANY DO.
HE ALWAYS HAS.
THE LATE OTTO NETZ SUGGESTED THE IMAGERY--A MIX OF WARLIKE COLORS AND TERRIFYING FEMALE ARCHETYPES LIKE KALI MA, MEDUSA, TIAMAT.
AND THAT'S JUST IT.
I'M AFRAID I CAN'T ALLOW YOUR WAR WITH THE DARK DETECTIVE, TALIA.
ALLOW IT?
AND HOW WILL YOU STOP ME, FATHER?
BY ANSWERING MY SUMMONS, BY COMING HERE, OF YOUR OWN FREE WILL, TO MY LAIR--
--YOU PLACED YOURSELF AT MY MERCY AND MAY NOW CONSIDER YOURSELF MY PRISONER, FOR YOUR OWN GOOD.
HAVE I NOT ALWAYS DONE WHAT WAS RIGHT FOR YOU?

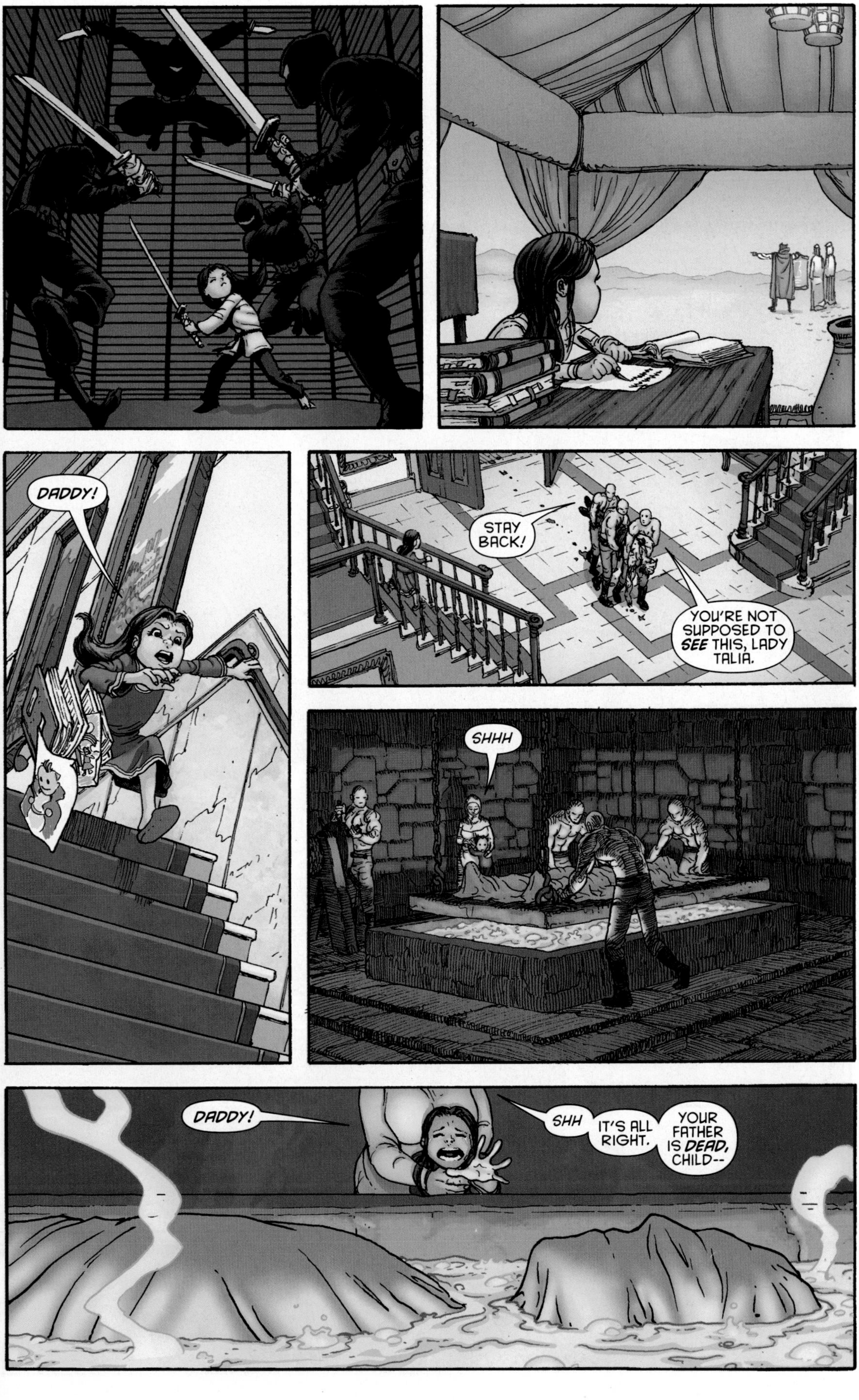
DADDY!
STAY BACK!
YOU'RE NOT SUPPOSED TO SEE THIS, LADY TALIA.
SHHH
DADDY!
SHH
IT'S ALL RIGHT.
YOUR FATHER IS DEAD, CHILD--

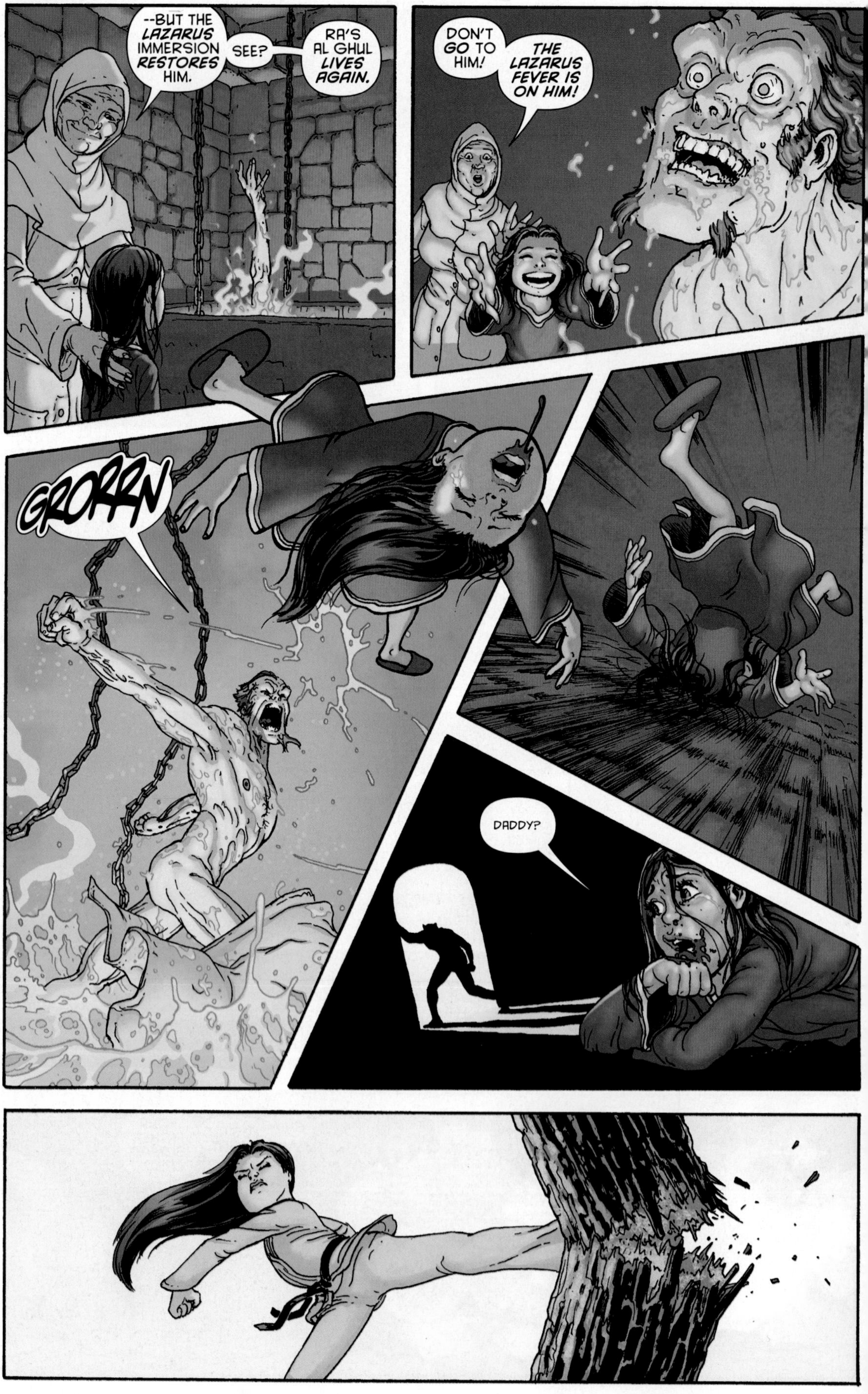
--BUT THE *LAZARUS* IMMERSION *RESTORES* HIM.
SEE?
RA'S AL GHUL *LIVES AGAIN.*
DON'T *GO* TO HIM!
THE LAZARUS FEVER IS ON HIM!
GRORRN
DADDY?

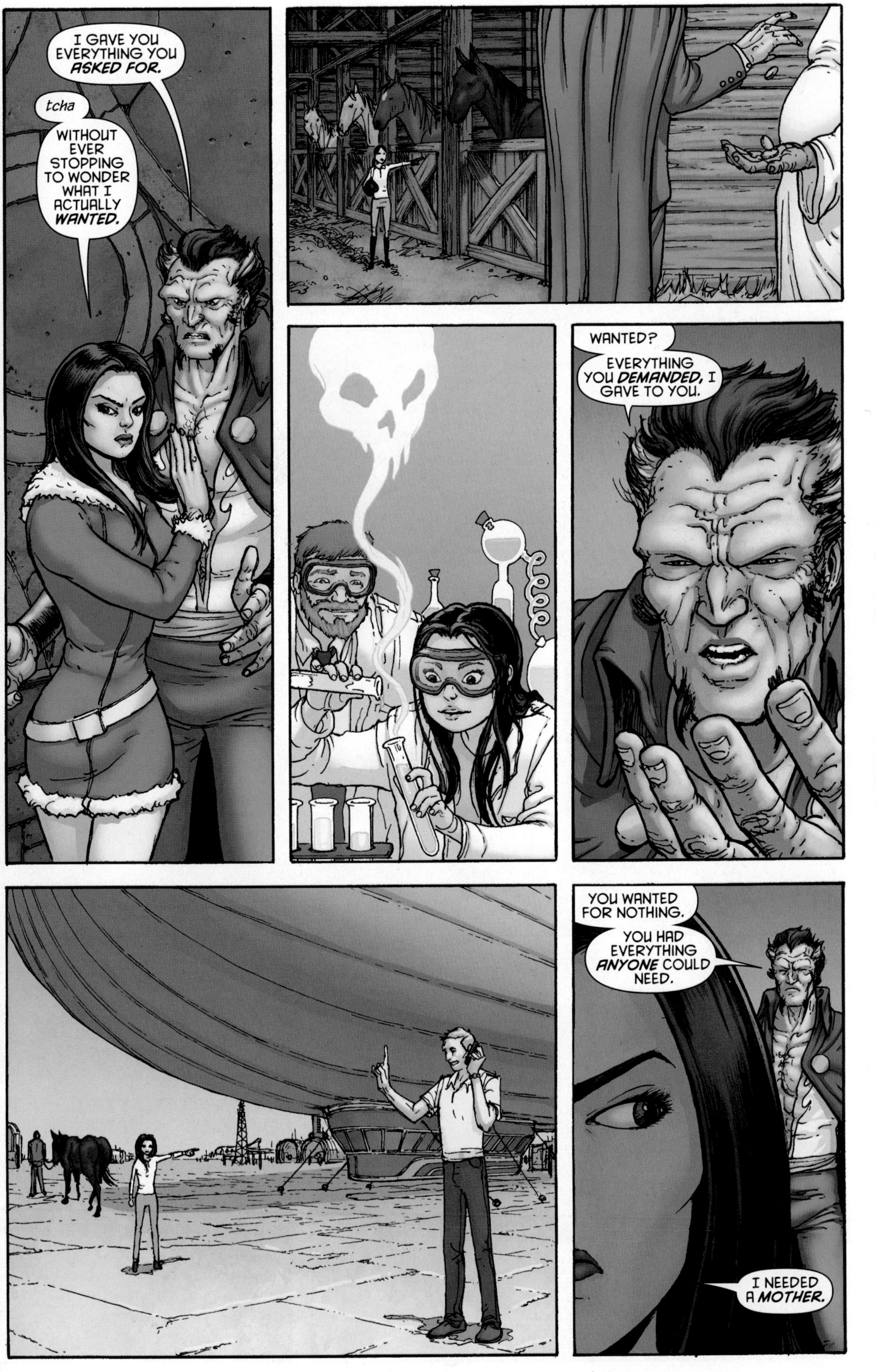
I GAVE YOU EVERYTHING YOU ASKED FOR.
tcha
WITHOUT EVER STOPPING TO WONDER WHAT I ACTUALLY WANTED.
WANTED?
EVERYTHING YOU DEMANDED, I GAVE TO YOU.
YOU WANTED FOR NOTHING.
YOU HAD EVERYTHING ANYONE COULD NEED.
I NEEDED A MOTHER.

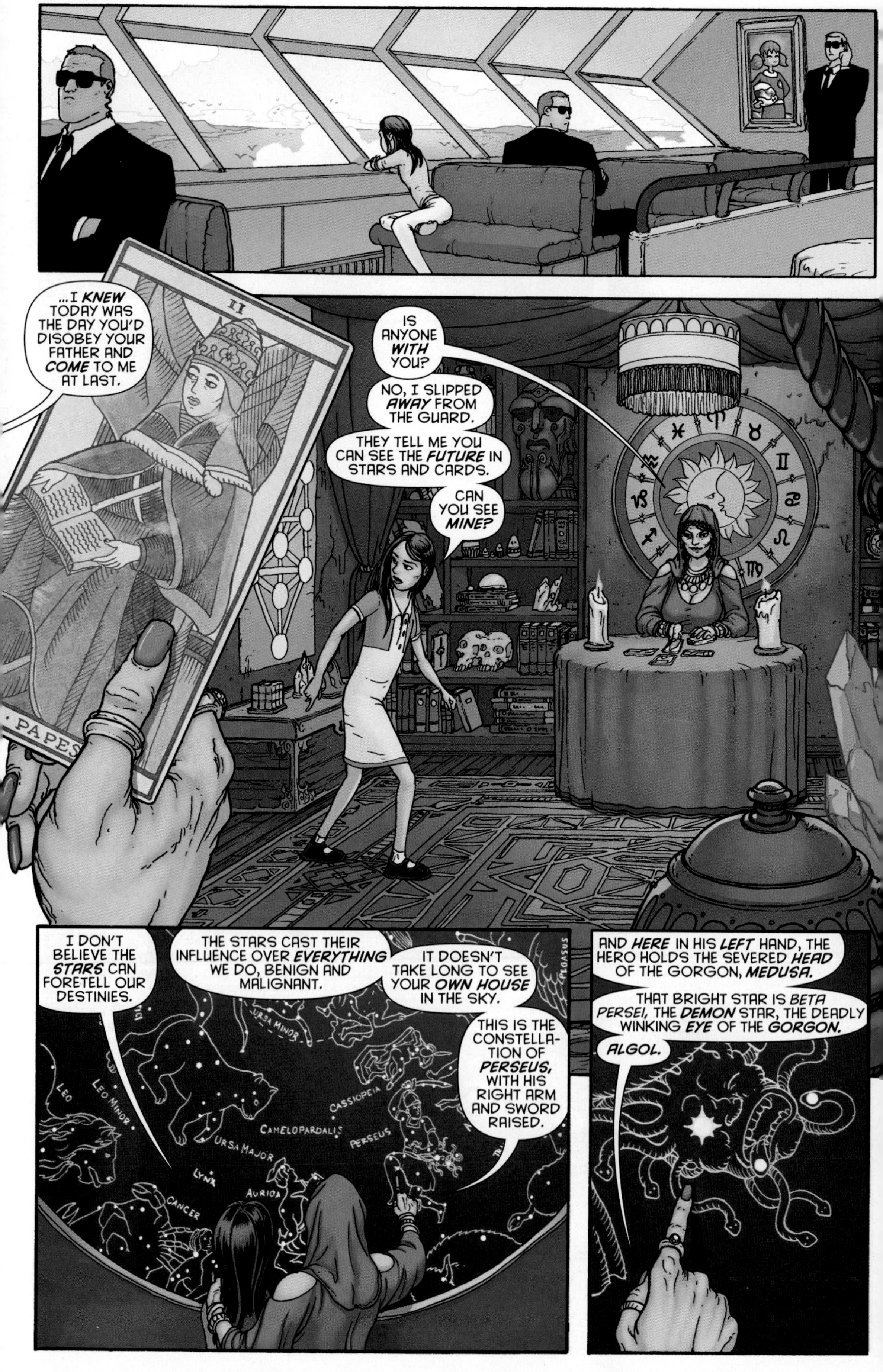
II
PAPES
...I KNEW TODAY WAS THE DAY YOU'D DISOBEY YOUR FATHER AND COME TO ME AT LAST.
IS ANYONE WITH YOU?
NO, I SLIPPED AWAY FROM THE GUARD.
THEY TELL ME YOU CAN SEE THE FUTURE IN STARS AND CARDS.
CAN YOU SEE MINE?
I DON'T BELIEVE THE STARS CAN FORETELL OUR DESTINIES.
THE STARS CAST THEIR INFLUENCE OVER EVERYTHING WE DO, BENIGN AND MALIGNANT.
IT DOESN'T TAKE LONG TO SEE YOUR OWN HOUSE IN THE SKY.
THIS IS THE CONSTELLATION OF PERSEUS, WITH HIS RIGHT ARM AND SWORD RAISED.
PEGASUS
URSA MINOR
LEO
LEO MINOR
CASSIOPEIA
CAMELOPARDALIS
PERSEUS
URSA MAJOR
LYNX
AURIGA
CANCER
AND HERE IN HIS LEFT HAND, THE HERO HOLDS THE SEVERED HEAD OF THE GORGON, MEDUSA.
THAT BRIGHT STAR IS BETA PERSEI, THE DEMON STAR, THE DEADLY WINKING EYE OF THE GORGON.
ALGOL.

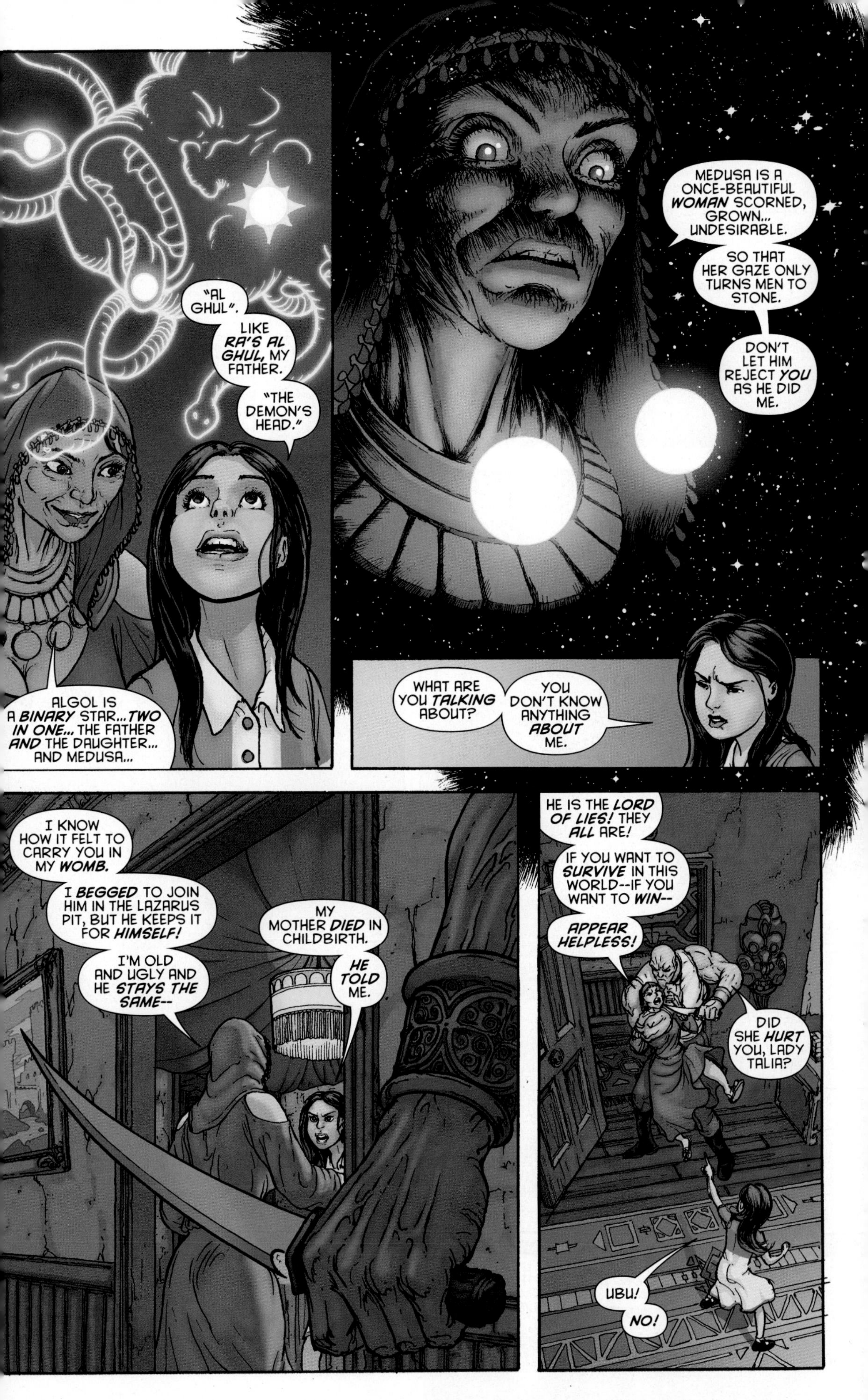
"AL GHUL".
LIKE RA'S AL GHUL, MY FATHER.
"THE DEMON'S HEAD."
ALGOL IS A BINARY STAR...TWO IN ONE... THE FATHER AND THE DAUGHTER... AND MEDUSA...
MEDUSA IS A ONCE-BEAUTIFUL WOMAN SCORNED, GROWN... UNDESIRABLE.
SO THAT HER GAZE ONLY TURNS MEN TO STONE.
DON'T LET HIM REJECT YOU AS HE DID ME.
WHAT ARE YOU TALKING ABOUT?
YOU DON'T KNOW ANYTHING ABOUT ME.
I KNOW HOW IT FELT TO CARRY YOU IN MY WOMB.
I BEGGED TO JOIN HIM IN THE LAZARUS PIT, BUT HE KEEPS IT FOR HIMSELF!
I'M OLD AND UGLY AND HE STAYS THE SAME--
MY MOTHER DIED IN CHILDBIRTH.
HE TOLD ME.
HE IS THE LORD OF LIES! THEY ALL ARE!
IF YOU WANT TO SURVIVE IN THIS WORLD--IF YOU WANT TO WIN--
APPEAR HELPLESS!
DID SHE HURT YOU, LADY TALIA?
UBU!
NO!

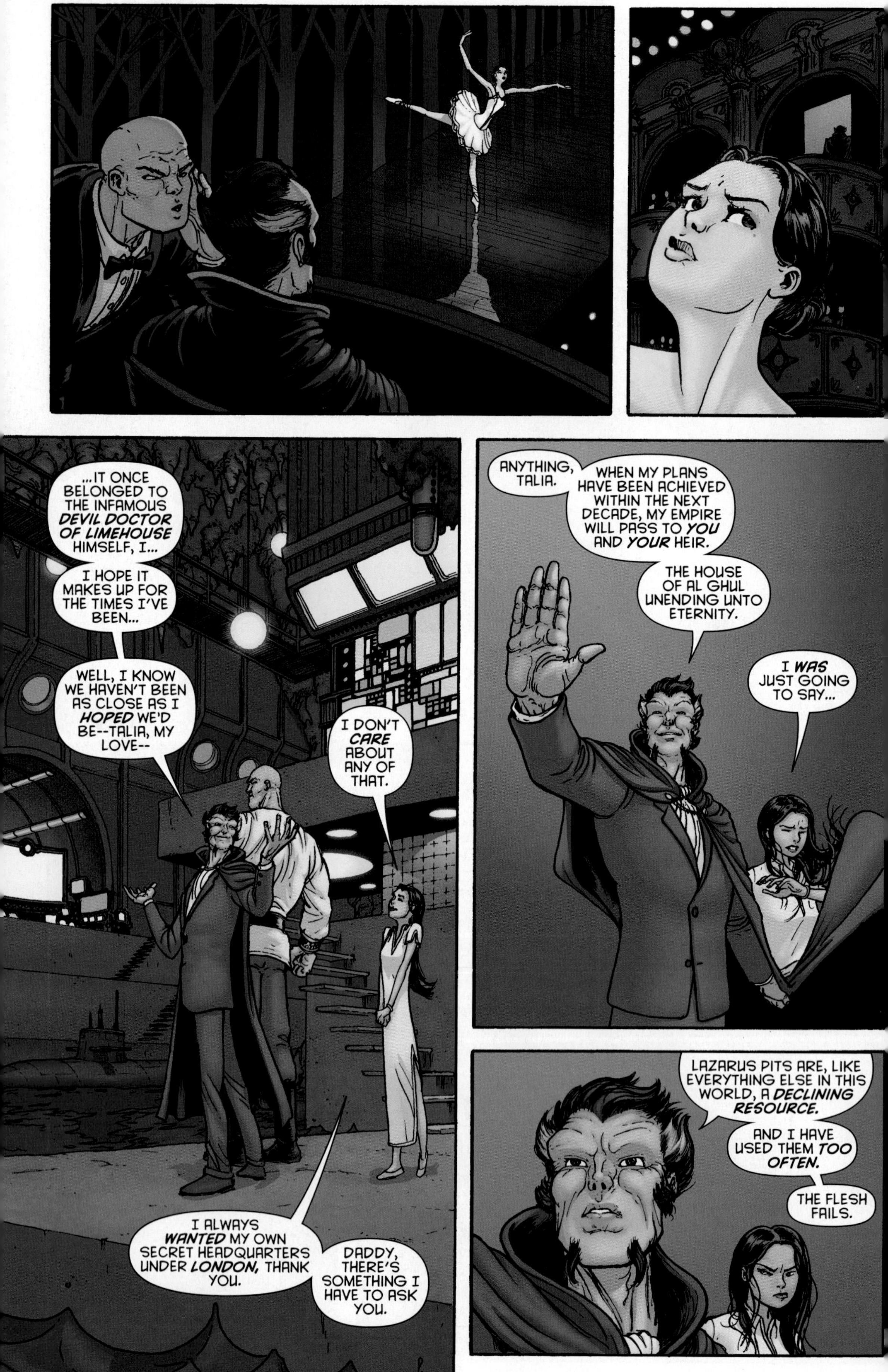
...IT ONCE BELONGED TO THE INFAMOUS DEVIL DOCTOR OF LIMEHOUSE HIMSELF, I...
I HOPE IT MAKES UP FOR THE TIMES I'VE BEEN...
WELL, I KNOW WE HAVEN'T BEEN AS CLOSE AS I HOPED WE'D BE--TALIA, MY LOVE--
I DON'T CARE ABOUT ANY OF THAT.
I ALWAYS WANTED MY OWN SECRET HEADQUARTERS UNDER LONDON, THANK YOU.
DADDY, THERE'S SOMETHING I HAVE TO ASK YOU.
ANYTHING, TALIA.
WHEN MY PLANS HAVE BEEN ACHIEVED WITHIN THE NEXT DECADE, MY EMPIRE WILL PASS TO YOU AND YOUR HEIR.
THE HOUSE OF AL GHUL UNENDING UNTO ETERNITY.
I WAS JUST GOING TO SAY...
LAZARUS PITS ARE, LIKE EVERYTHING ELSE IN THIS WORLD, A DECLINING RESOURCE.
AND I HAVE USED THEM TOO OFTEN.
THE FLESH FAILS.

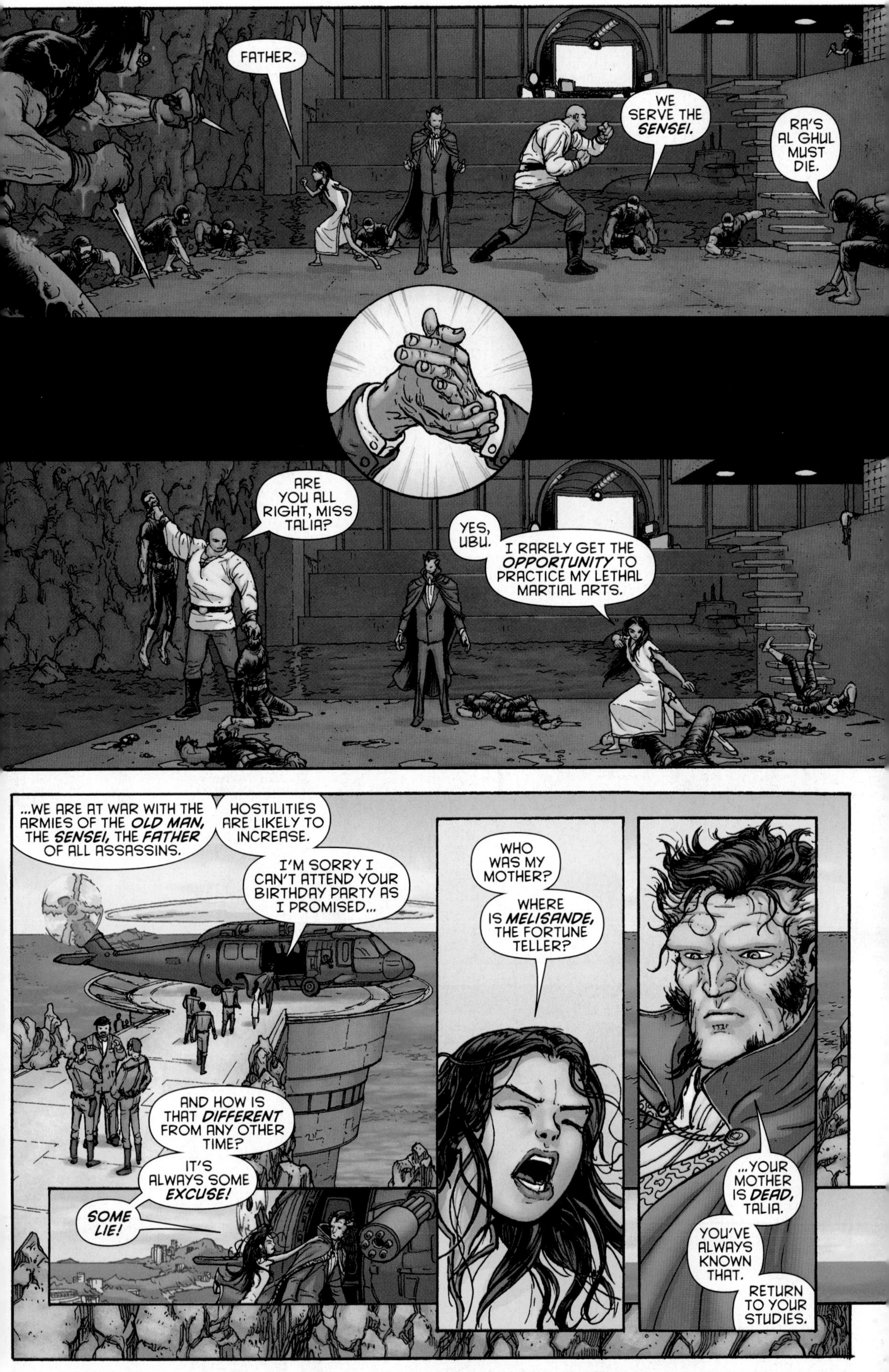

FATHER.
WE SERVE THE *SENSEI.*
RA'S AL GHUL MUST DIE.
ARE YOU ALL RIGHT, MISS TALIA?
YES, UBU.
I RARELY GET THE *OPPORTUNITY* TO PRACTICE MY LETHAL MARTIAL ARTS.
...WE ARE AT WAR WITH THE ARMIES OF THE *OLD MAN,* THE *SENSEI,* THE *FATHER* OF ALL ASSASSINS.
HOSTILITIES ARE LIKELY TO INCREASE.
I'M SORRY I CAN'T ATTEND YOUR BIRTHDAY PARTY AS I PROMISED...
AND HOW IS THAT *DIFFERENT* FROM ANY OTHER TIME?
IT'S ALWAYS SOME *EXCUSE!*
SOME LIE!
WHO WAS MY MOTHER?
WHERE IS *MELISANDE,* THE FORTUNE TELLER?
...YOUR MOTHER IS *DEAD,* TALIA.
YOU'VE ALWAYS KNOWN THAT.
RETURN TO YOUR STUDIES.

DOCTOR DARRK.

YOUR FACTION OF THE ASSASSINS LEAGUE DECLARED ITS *INDEPENDENCE* FROM MY FATHER'S LEADERSHIP.

I TAKE IT THIS IS A FORMAL *KIDNAP ATTEMPT*?

NOT SO MUCH AN *ATTEMPT*, SWEET "TALIA HEAD".

YOU ARE ALREADY *MY* PRISONER, MY HOSTAGE IN A SECRET WAR THAT SPANS THE *GLOBE*.

YOUR FATE IS SEALED.

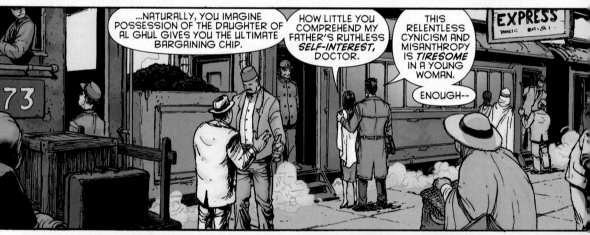

...NATURALLY, YOU IMAGINE POSSESSION OF THE DAUGHTER OF AL GHUL GIVES YOU THE ULTIMATE BARGAINING CHIP.

HOW LITTLE YOU COMPREHEND MY FATHER'S RUTHLESS *SELF-INTEREST*, DOCTOR.

THIS RELENTLESS CYNICISM AND MISANTHROPY IS *TIRESOME* IN A YOUNG WOMAN.

ENOUGH--

HAVE YOU EVEN *ONCE* ASKED YOURSELF WHY I *ALLOWED* THIS ABDUCTION TO TAKE PLACE?

I, UH...

WHAT?

YOU HAD *NO CHOICE* IN THE MATTER.

AND YOUR FATHER WILL PAY DEARLY FOR YOUR *SAFE RETURN*.

HE WILL PAY AND PAY--

AS *MANY* MEN WILL *PAY* FOR THE PLEASURE OF *YOUR* COMPANY WHEN I TIRE OF YOU.

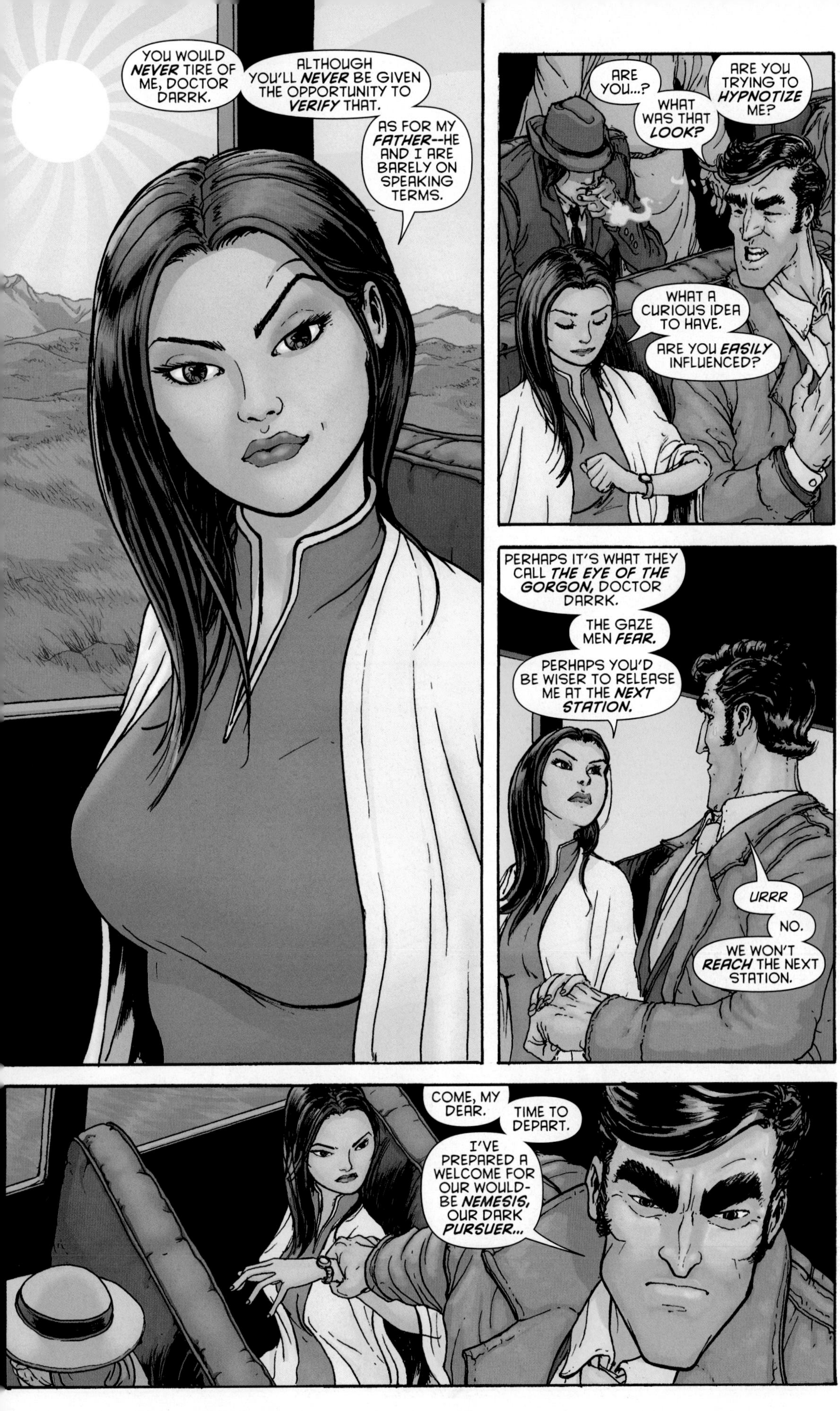
YOU WOULD NEVER TIRE OF ME, DOCTOR DARRK.
ALTHOUGH YOU'LL NEVER BE GIVEN THE OPPORTUNITY TO VERIFY THAT.
AS FOR MY FATHER--HE AND I ARE BARELY ON SPEAKING TERMS.
ARE YOU...?
WHAT WAS THAT LOOK?
ARE YOU TRYING TO HYPNOTIZE ME?
WHAT A CURIOUS IDEA TO HAVE.
ARE YOU EASILY INFLUENCED?
PERHAPS IT'S WHAT THEY CALL THE EYE OF THE GORGON, DOCTOR DARRK.
THE GAZE MEN FEAR.
PERHAPS YOU'D BE WISER TO RELEASE ME AT THE NEXT STATION.
URRR
NO.
WE WON'T REACH THE NEXT STATION.
COME, MY DEAR.
TIME TO DEPART.
I'VE PREPARED A WELCOME FOR OUR WOULD-BE NEMESIS, OUR DARK PURSUER...

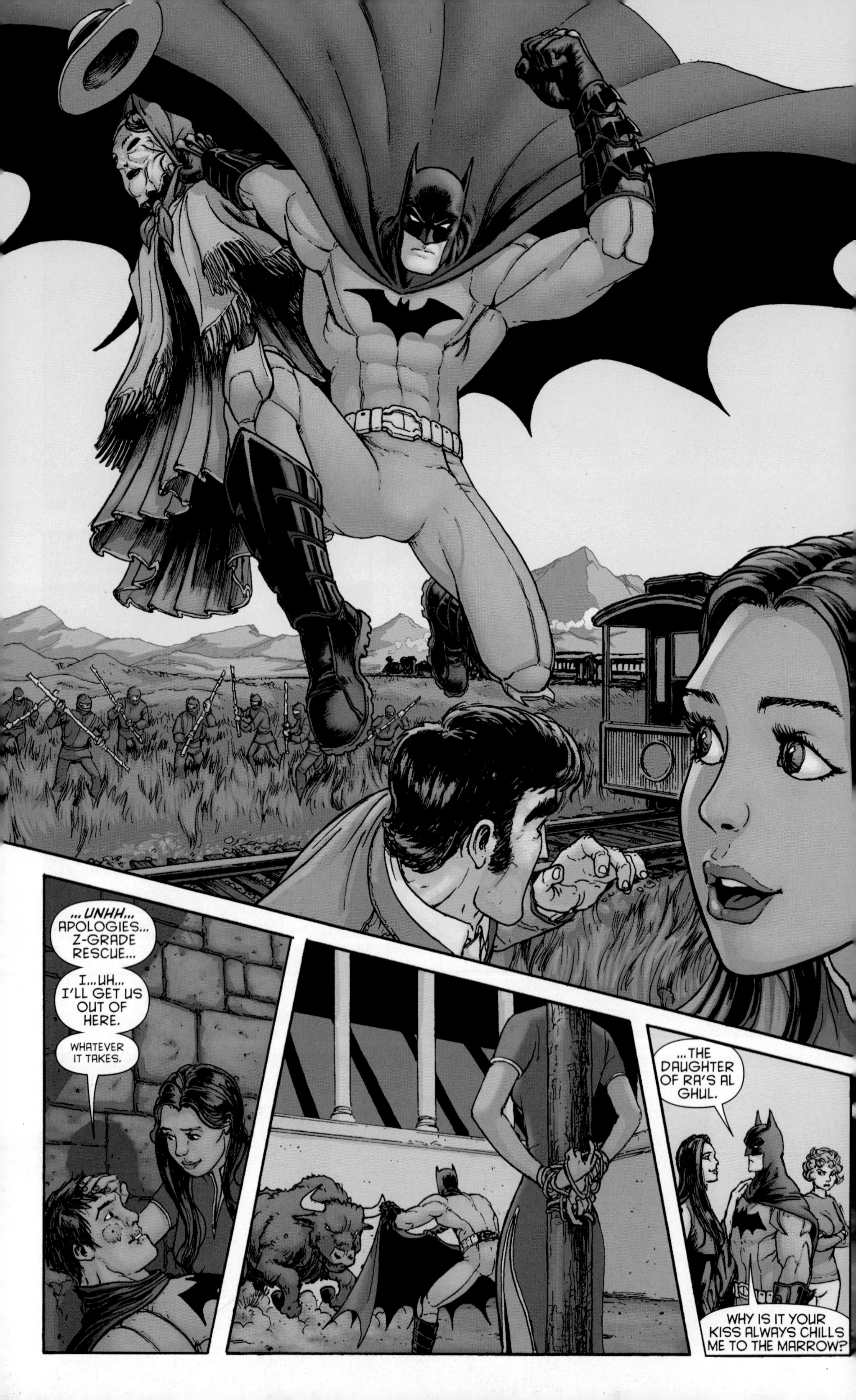
...UNHH... APOLOGIES... Z-GRADE RESCUE...
I...UH... I'LL GET US OUT OF HERE.
WHATEVER IT TAKES.
...THE DAUGHTER OF RA'S AL GHUL.
WHY IS IT YOUR KISS ALWAYS CHILLS ME TO THE MARROW?

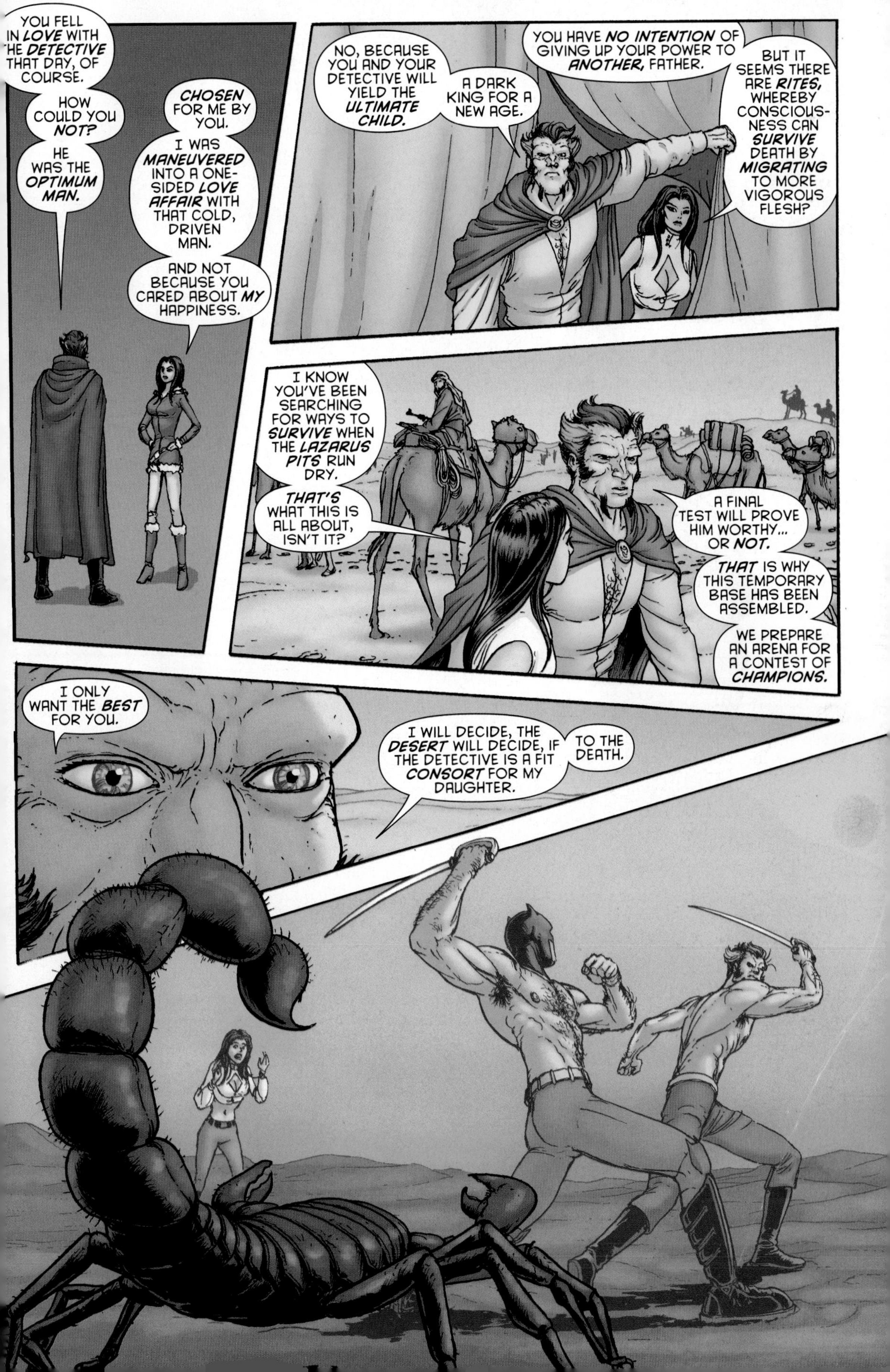
YOU FELL IN LOVE WITH THE DETECTIVE THAT DAY, OF COURSE.
HOW COULD YOU NOT?
HE WAS THE OPTIMUM MAN.
CHOSEN FOR ME BY YOU.
I WAS MANEUVERED INTO A ONE-SIDED LOVE AFFAIR WITH THAT COLD, DRIVEN MAN.
AND NOT BECAUSE YOU CARED ABOUT MY HAPPINESS.
NO, BECAUSE YOU AND YOUR DETECTIVE WILL YIELD THE ULTIMATE CHILD.
A DARK KING FOR A NEW AGE.
YOU HAVE NO INTENTION OF GIVING UP YOUR POWER TO ANOTHER, FATHER.
BUT IT SEEMS THERE ARE RITES, WHEREBY CONSCIOUSNESS CAN SURVIVE DEATH BY MIGRATING TO MORE VIGOROUS FLESH?
I KNOW YOU'VE BEEN SEARCHING FOR WAYS TO SURVIVE WHEN THE LAZARUS PITS RUN DRY.
THAT'S WHAT THIS IS ALL ABOUT, ISN'T IT?
A FINAL TEST WILL PROVE HIM WORTHY... OR NOT.
THAT IS WHY THIS TEMPORARY BASE HAS BEEN ASSEMBLED.
WE PREPARE AN ARENA FOR A CONTEST OF CHAMPIONS.
I ONLY WANT THE BEST FOR YOU.
I WILL DECIDE, THE DESERT WILL DECIDE, IF THE DETECTIVE IS A FIT CONSORT FOR MY DAUGHTER.
TO THE DEATH.

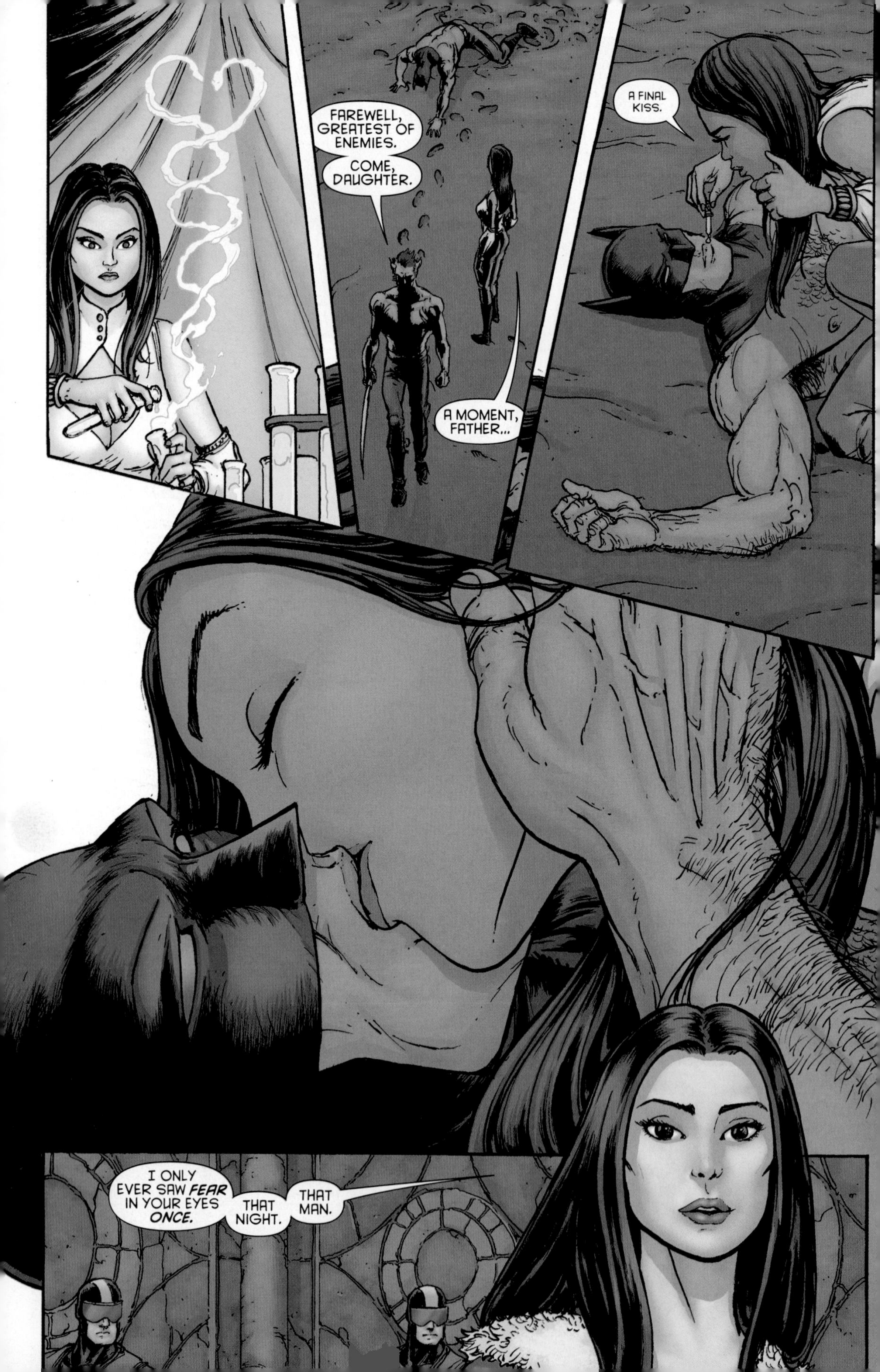
FAREWELL, GREATEST OF ENEMIES.
COME, DAUGHTER.
A MOMENT, FATHER...
A FINAL KISS.
I ONLY EVER SAW *FEAR* IN YOUR EYES *ONCE.*
THAT NIGHT.
THAT MAN.

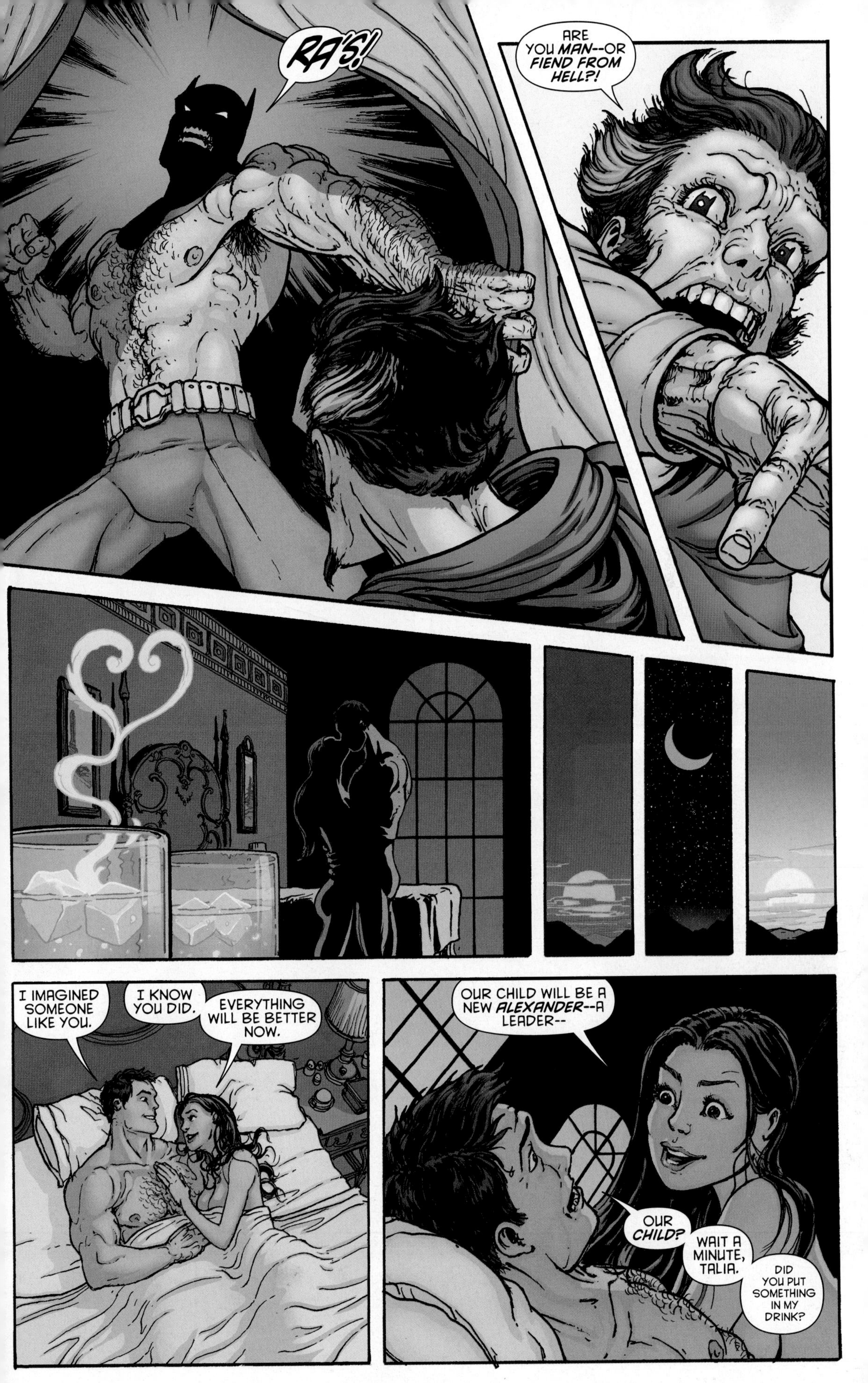
RA'S!
ARE YOU MAN--OR FIEND FROM HELL?!
I IMAGINED SOMEONE LIKE YOU.
I KNOW YOU DID.
EVERYTHING WILL BE BETTER NOW.
OUR CHILD WILL BE A NEW ALEXANDER--A LEADER--
OUR CHILD?
WAIT A MINUTE, TALIA.
DID YOU PUT SOMETHING IN MY DRINK?

I'LL CALL YOU *DAMIAN.*

ONE DAY YOU'LL RULE THE WORLD.

WHAT DO I HAVE TO *SAY,* TALIA?

NO!

WE'RE *NEVER* GOING TO BE TOGETHER!

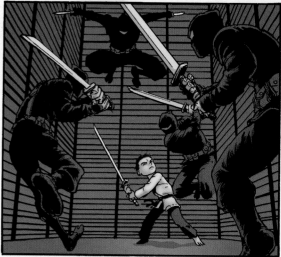

MY REPUTATION IN THE INTERNATIONAL SUPER-CRIME COMMUNITY SPEAKS FOR ITSELF, GENTLEMEN.

I INTEND TO *IMPROVE* ON MY FATHER'S WORK.

HENCE THIS *GROUP OF LIKE-MINDED INDIVIDUALS* I'M PROPOSING...

YOU'LL PAY YOUR DEBT TO ME BY INFILTRATING THE *BLACK GLOVE,* GENERAL MALENKOV.

WHILE I INTRODUCE THE DETECTIVE TO HIS *SON.*

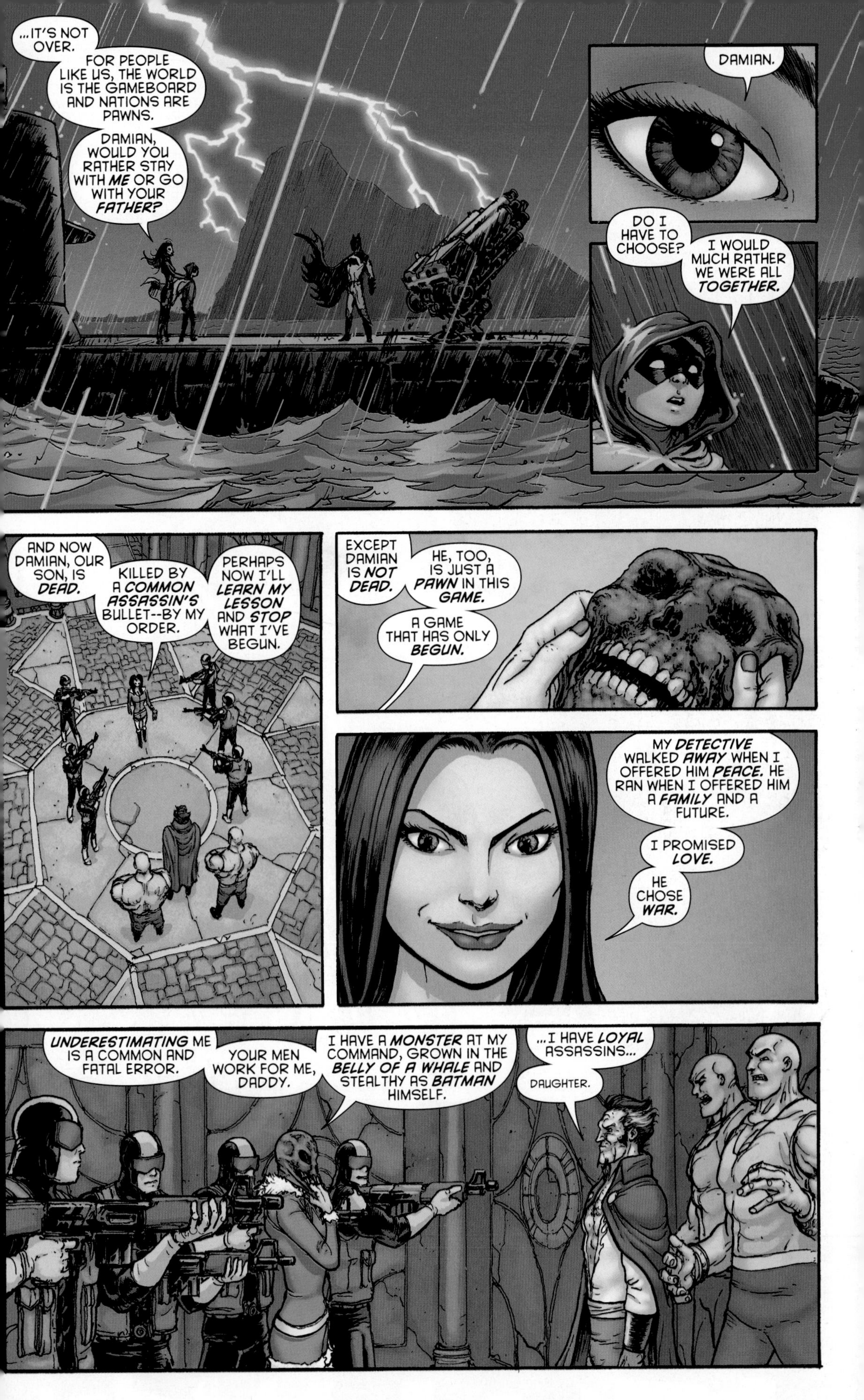
...IT'S NOT OVER.
FOR PEOPLE LIKE US, THE WORLD IS THE GAMEBOARD AND NATIONS ARE PAWNS.
DAMIAN, WOULD YOU RATHER STAY WITH ME OR GO WITH YOUR FATHER?
DAMIAN.
DO I HAVE TO CHOOSE?
I WOULD MUCH RATHER WE WERE ALL TOGETHER.
AND NOW DAMIAN, OUR SON, IS DEAD.
KILLED BY A COMMON ASSASSIN'S BULLET--BY MY ORDER.
PERHAPS NOW I'LL LEARN MY LESSON AND STOP WHAT I'VE BEGUN.
EXCEPT DAMIAN IS NOT DEAD.
HE, TOO, IS JUST A PAWN IN THIS GAME.
A GAME THAT HAS ONLY BEGUN.
MY DETECTIVE WALKED AWAY WHEN I OFFERED HIM PEACE. HE RAN WHEN I OFFERED HIM A FAMILY AND A FUTURE.
I PROMISED LOVE.
HE CHOSE WAR.
UNDERESTIMATING ME IS A COMMON AND FATAL ERROR.
YOUR MEN WORK FOR ME, DADDY.
I HAVE A MONSTER AT MY COMMAND, GROWN IN THE BELLY OF A WHALE AND STEALTHY AS BATMAN HIMSELF.
...I HAVE LOYAL ASSASSINS...
DAUGHTER.

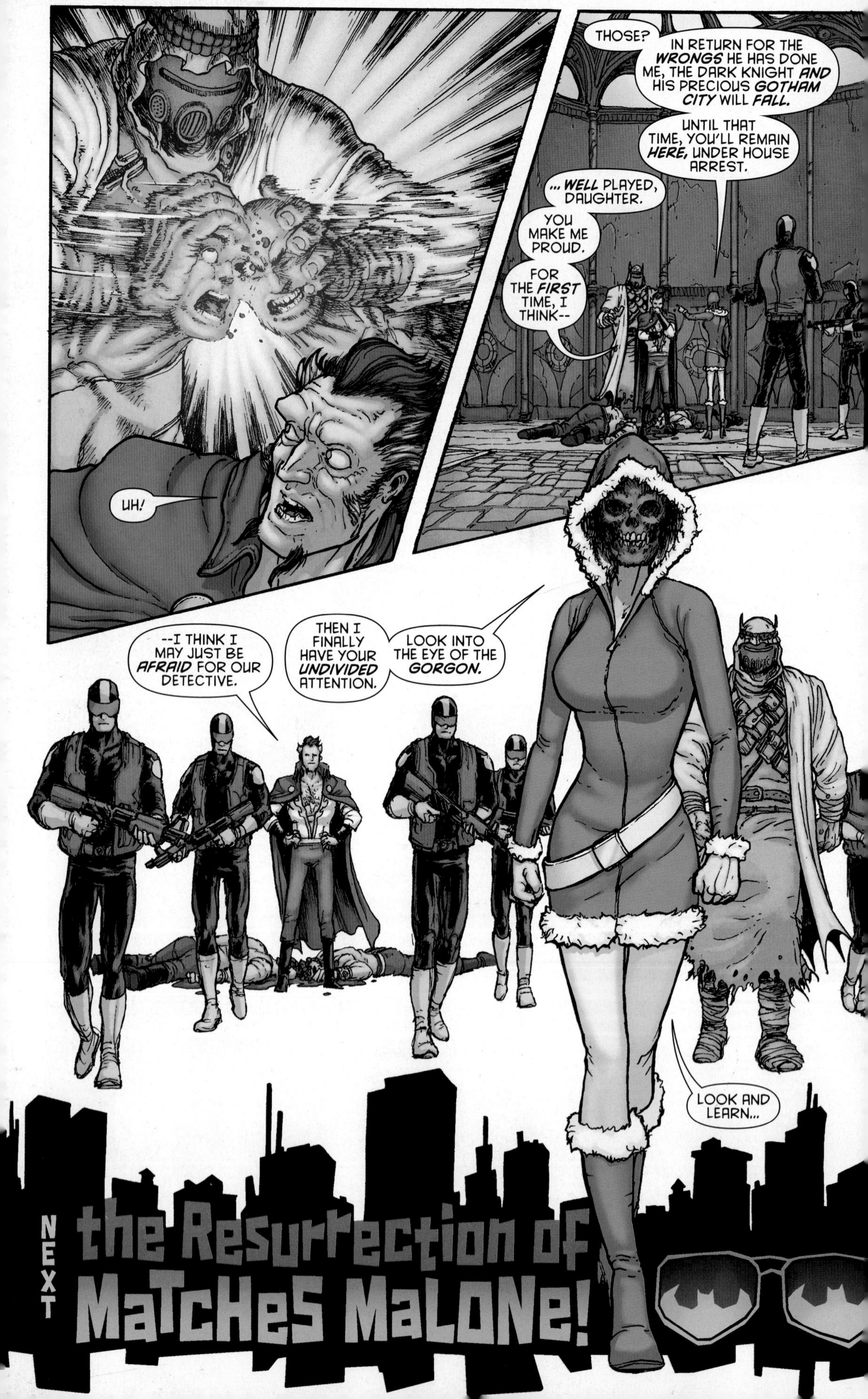
UH!
THOSE?
IN RETURN FOR THE WRONGS HE HAS DONE ME, THE DARK KNIGHT AND HIS PRECIOUS GOTHAM CITY WILL FALL.
UNTIL THAT TIME, YOU'LL REMAIN HERE, UNDER HOUSE ARREST.
...WELL PLAYED, DAUGHTER.
YOU MAKE ME PROUD.
FOR THE FIRST TIME, I THINK--
--I THINK I MAY JUST BE AFRAID FOR OUR DETECTIVE.
THEN I FINALLY HAVE YOUR UNDIVIDED ATTENTION.
LOOK INTO THE EYE OF THE GORGON.
LOOK AND LEARN...
NEXT
the Resurrection of Matches Malone!

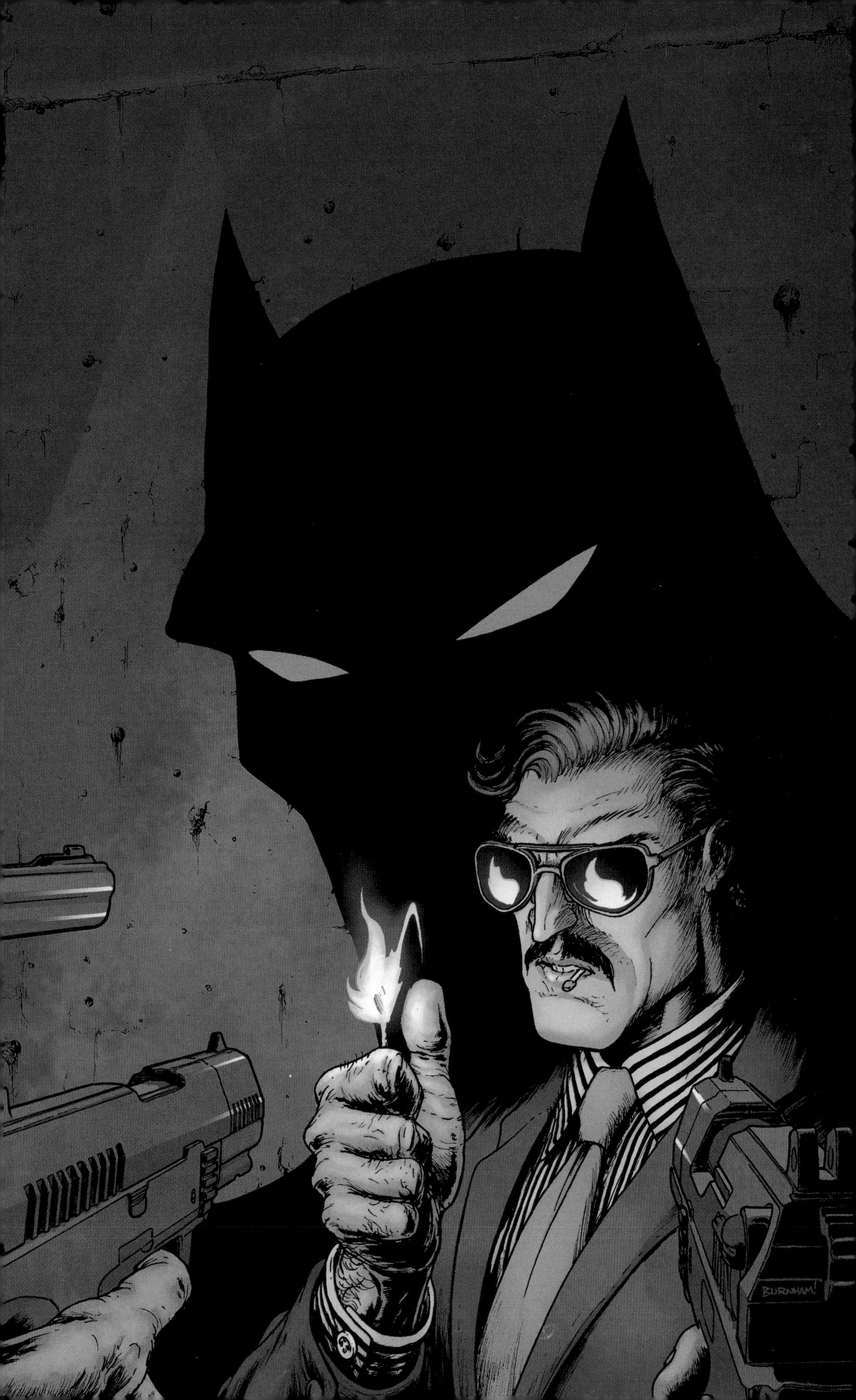
BURNHAM.

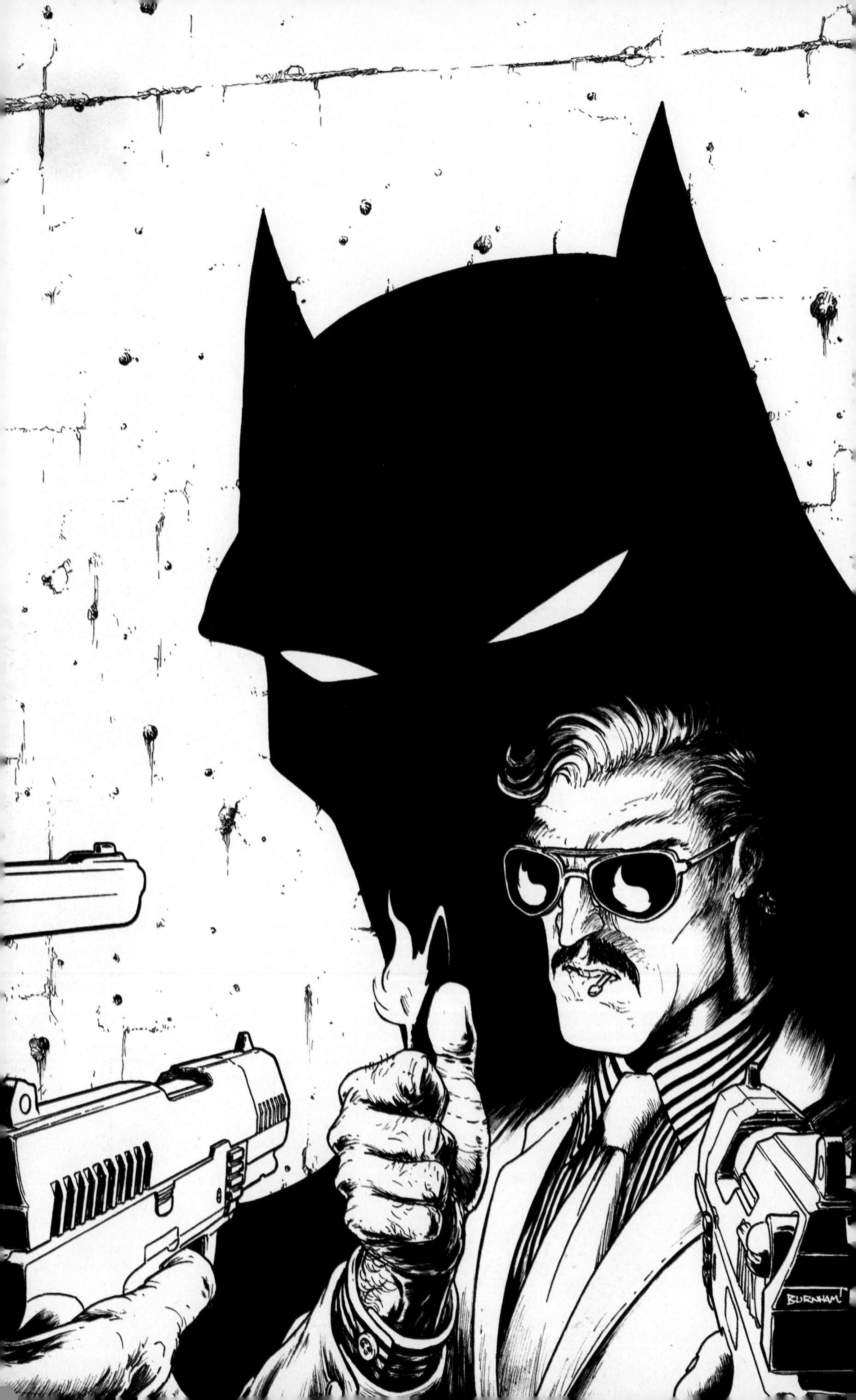
BURNHAM!

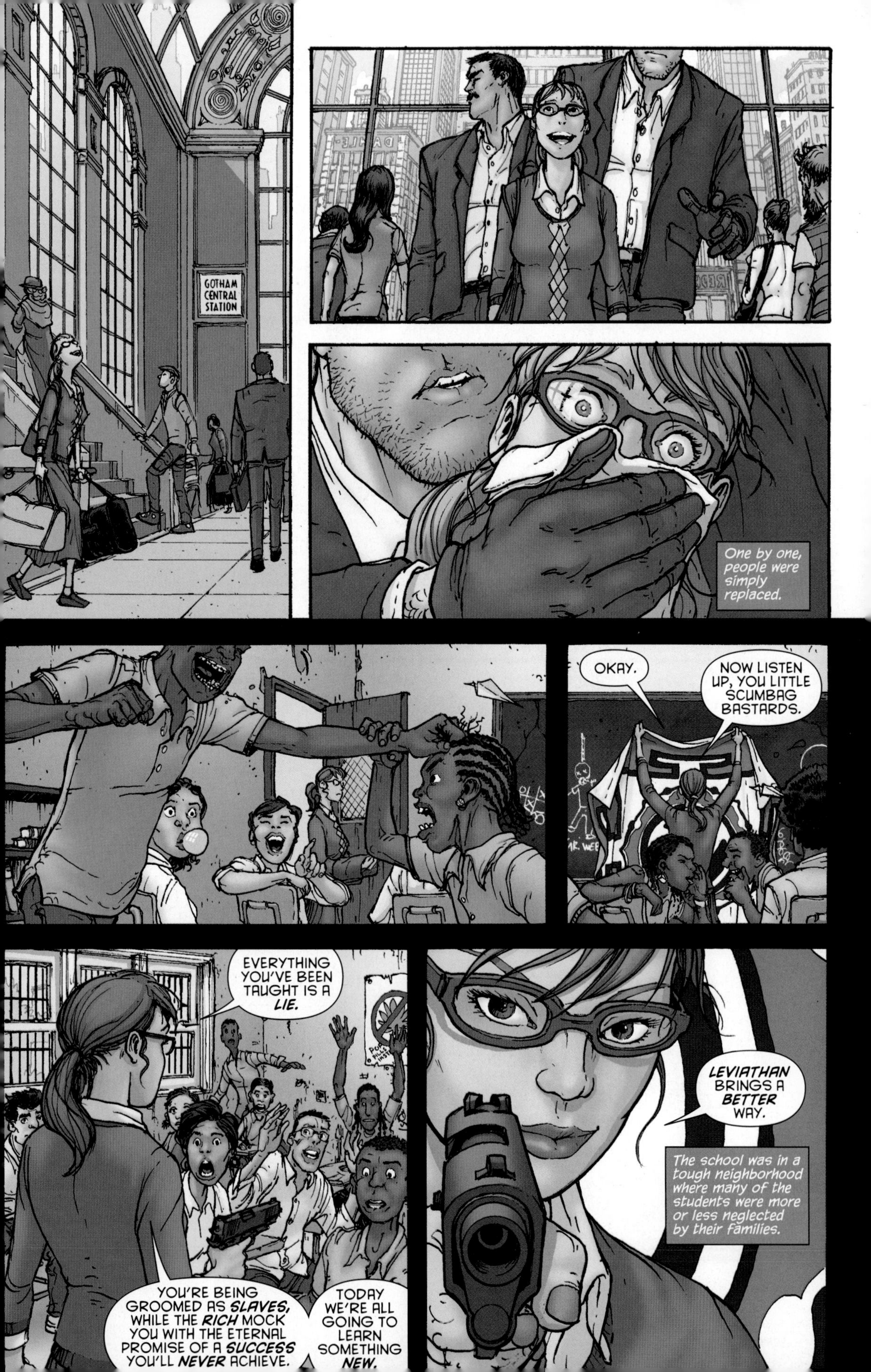
GOTHAM CENTRAL STATION
One by one, people were simply replaced.
OKAY.
NOW LISTEN UP, YOU LITTLE SCUMBAG BASTARDS.
EVERYTHING YOU'VE BEEN TAUGHT IS A *LIE.*
YOU'RE BEING GROOMED AS *SLAVES,* WHILE THE *RICH* MOCK YOU WITH THE ETERNAL PROMISE OF A *SUCCESS* YOU'LL *NEVER* ACHIEVE.
TODAY WE'RE ALL GOING TO LEARN SOMETHING *NEW.*
LEVIATHAN BRINGS A *BETTER* WAY.
The school was in a tough neighborhood where many of the students were more or less neglected by their families.

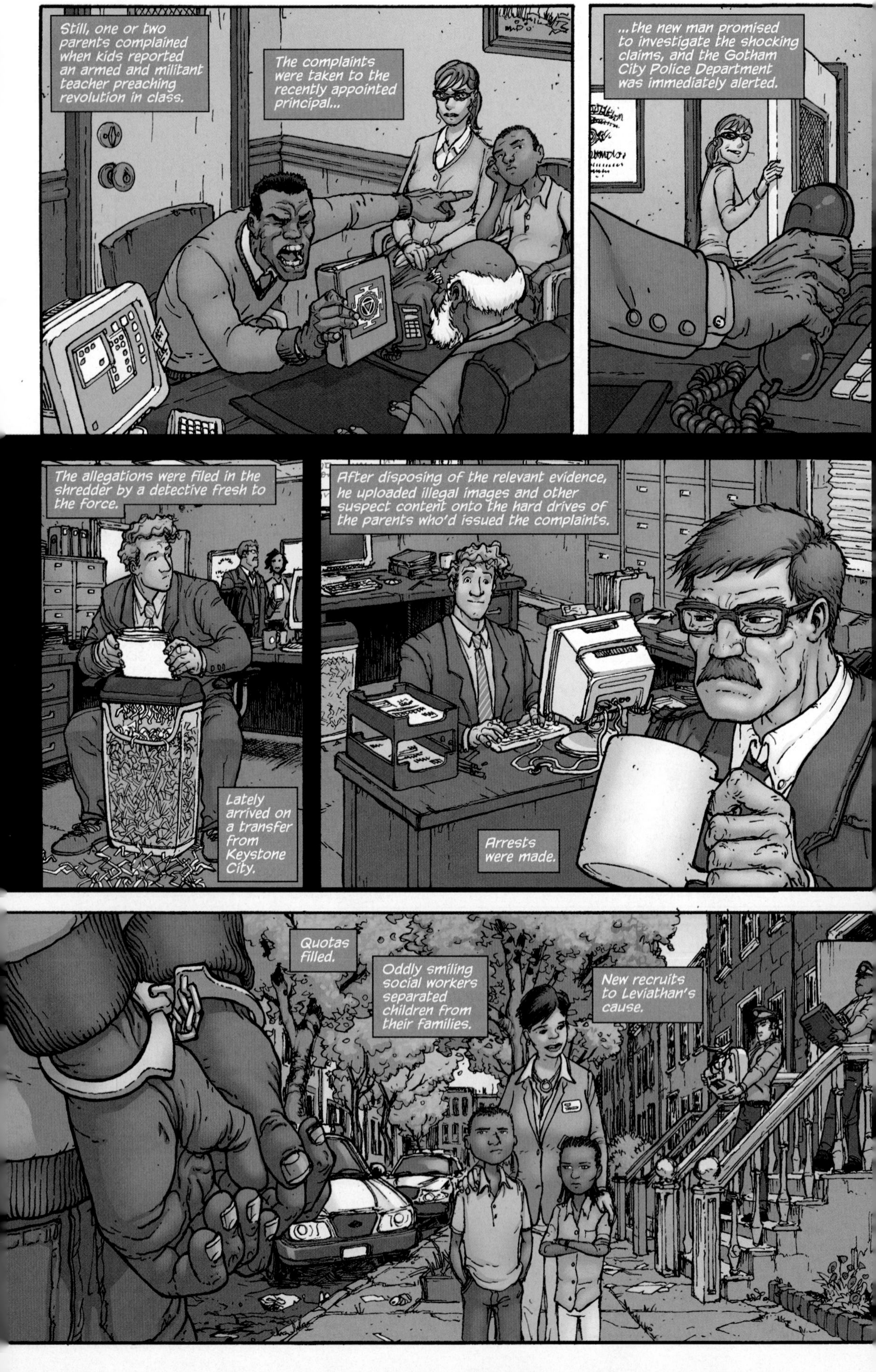
Still, one or two parents complained when kids reported an armed and militant teacher preaching revolution in class.
The complaints were taken to the recently appointed principal...
...the new man promised to investigate the shocking claims, and the Gotham City Police Department was immediately alerted.
The allegations were filed in the shredder by a detective fresh to the force.
Lately arrived on a transfer from Keystone City.
After disposing of the relevant evidence, he uploaded illegal images and other suspect content onto the hard drives of the parents who'd issued the complaints.
Arrests were made.
Quotas filled.
Oddly smiling social workers separated children from their families.
New recruits to Leviathan's cause.

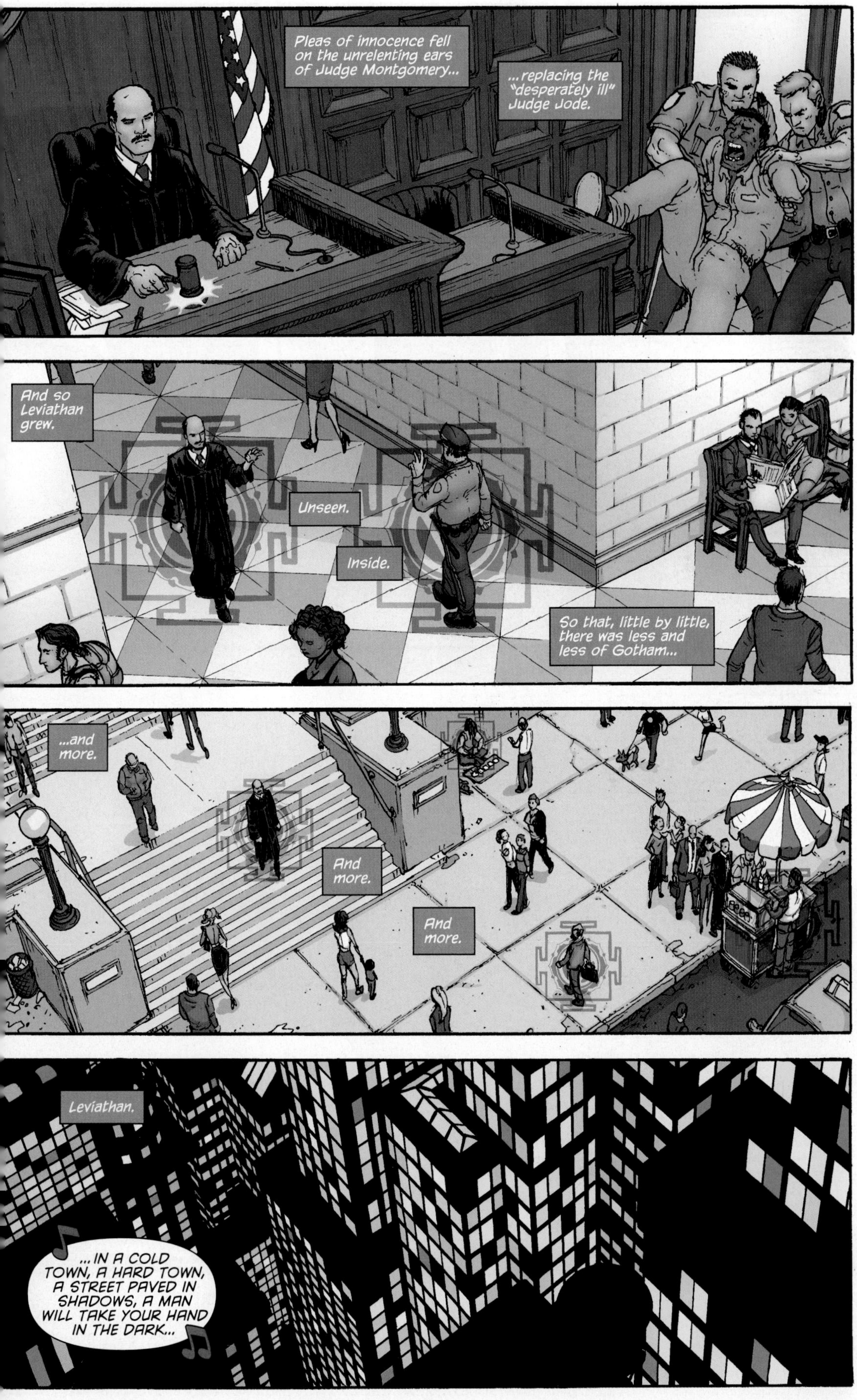
Pleas of innocence fell on the unrelenting ears of Judge Montgomery...
...replacing the "desperately ill" Judge Jode.
And so Leviathan grew.
Unseen.
Inside.
So that, little by little, there was less and less of Gotham...
...and more.
And more.
And more.
Leviathan.
...IN A COLD TOWN, A HARD TOWN, A STREET PAVED IN SHADOWS, A MAN WILL TAKE YOUR HAND IN THE DARK...

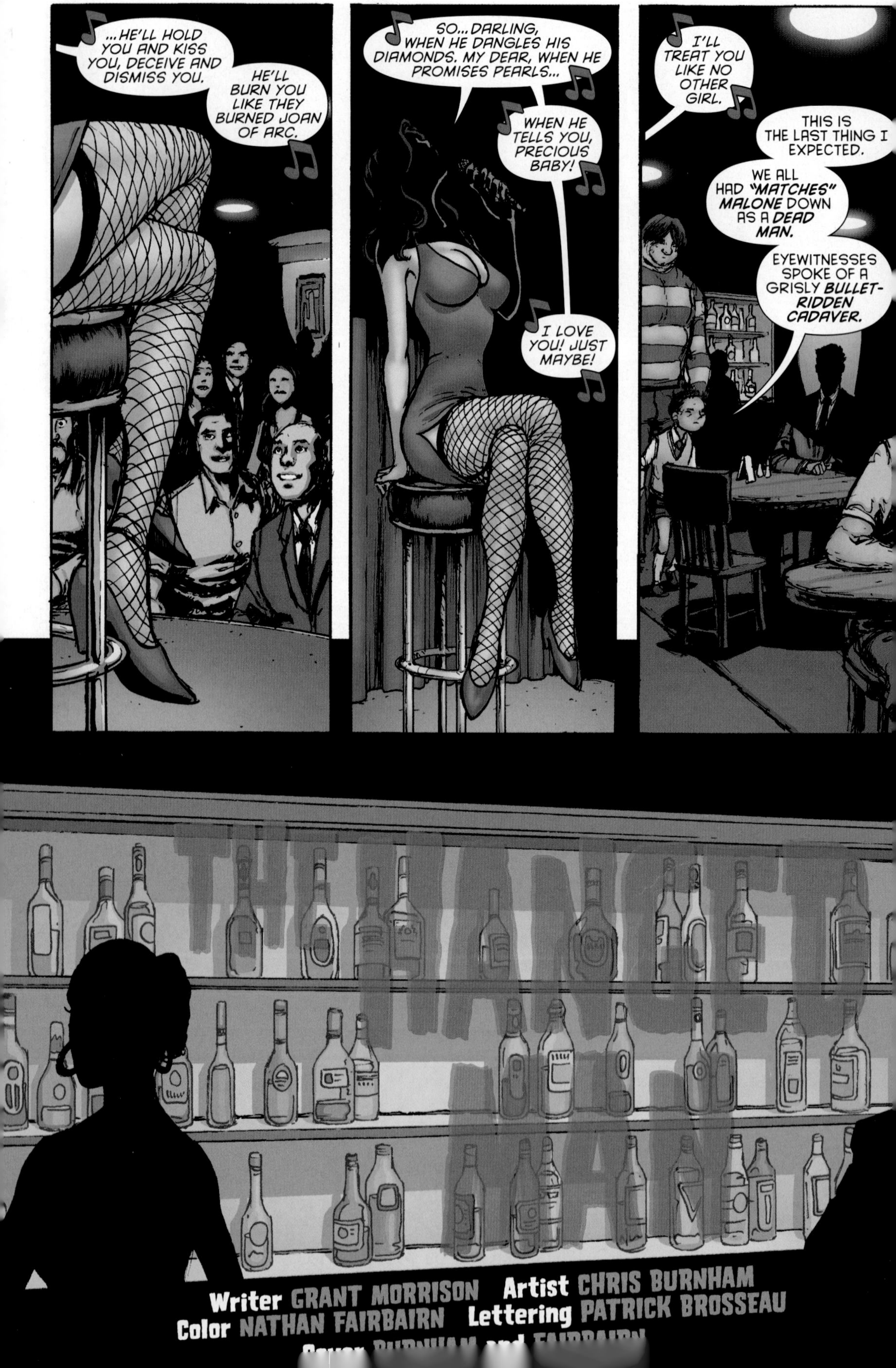
...HE'LL HOLD YOU AND KISS YOU, DECEIVE AND DISMISS YOU.
HE'LL BURN YOU LIKE THEY BURNED JOAN OF ARC.
SO... DARLING, WHEN HE DANGLES HIS DIAMONDS. MY DEAR, WHEN HE PROMISES PEARLS...
WHEN HE TELLS YOU, PRECIOUS BABY!
I LOVE YOU! JUST MAYBE!
I'LL TREAT YOU LIKE NO OTHER GIRL.
THIS IS THE LAST THING I EXPECTED.
WE ALL HAD "MATCHES" MALONE DOWN AS A DEAD MAN.
EYEWITNESSES SPOKE OF A GRISLY BULLET-RIDDEN CADAVER.
Writer GRANT MORRISON Artist CHRIS BURNHAM
Color NATHAN FAIRBAIRN Lettering PATRICK BROSSEAU

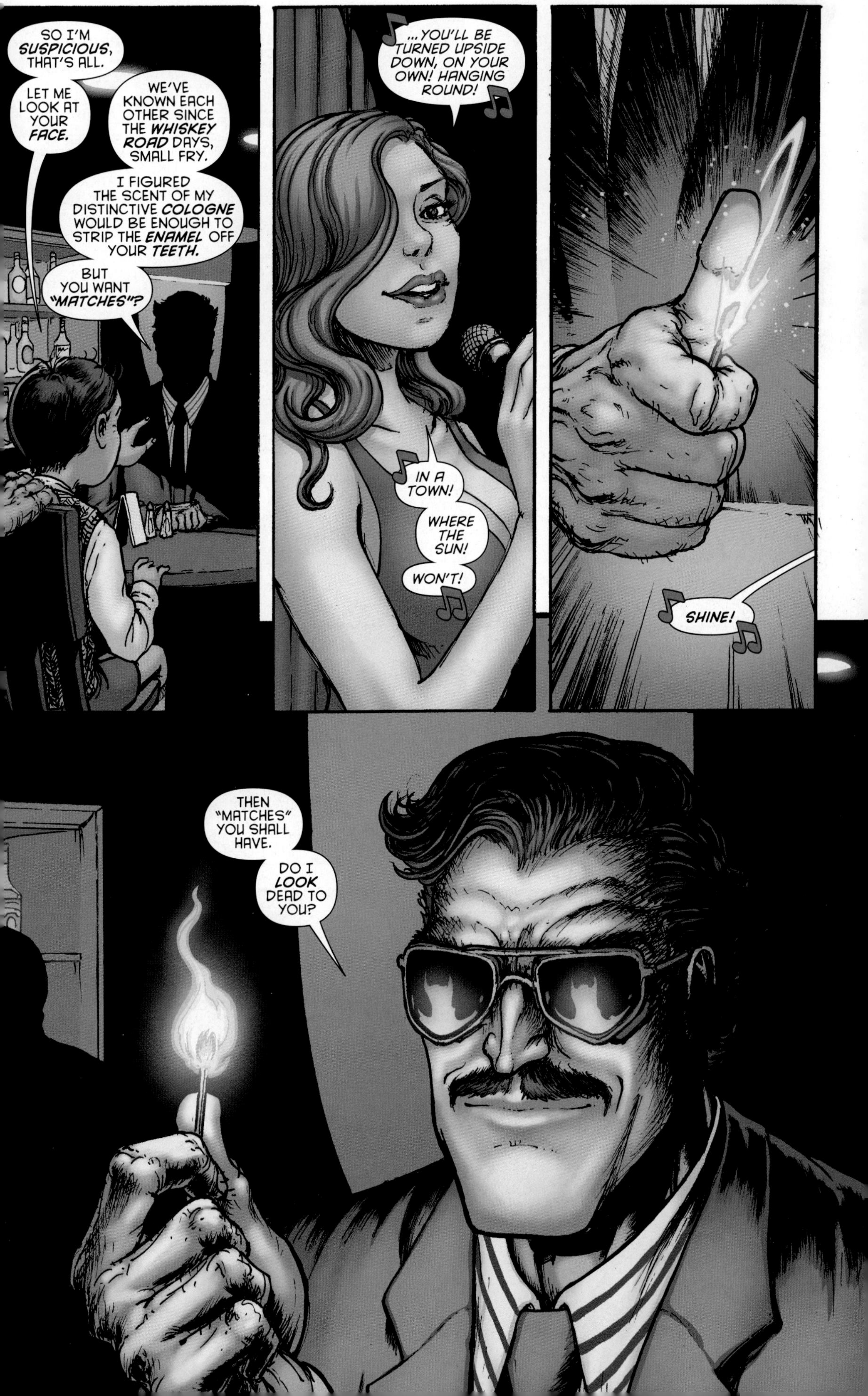
SO I'M SUSPICIOUS, THAT'S ALL.
LET ME LOOK AT YOUR FACE.
WE'VE KNOWN EACH OTHER SINCE THE WHISKEY ROAD DAYS, SMALL FRY.
I FIGURED THE SCENT OF MY DISTINCTIVE COLOGNE WOULD BE ENOUGH TO STRIP THE ENAMEL OFF YOUR TEETH.
BUT YOU WANT "MATCHES"?
...YOU'LL BE TURNED UPSIDE DOWN, ON YOUR OWN! HANGING ROUND!
IN A TOWN!
WHERE THE SUN!
WON'T!
SHINE!
THEN "MATCHES" YOU SHALL HAVE.
DO I LOOK DEAD TO YOU?

I DROPPED THE "SMALL." IT'S "FRY."

SO ALL THEM STORIES ABOUT HOW SCARFACE HAD YOU WHACKED OLD SCHOOL...

...THAT WAS ALL JUST...MISINFORMATION?

YOU'D TAKE THE WORD OF A VENTRILOQUIST DUMMY OVER THE EVIDENCE OF YOUR OWN EYES?

YOU MIDGETS ARE ALL IN THIS TOGETHER.

I HAD TO DISAPPEAR BEFORE I GOT DISAPPEARED, AND NOW I'M BACK.

AND WHAT'S WITH SHADES INDOORS, MATCHES?

WHAT ARE YOU, GEORGE MICHAEL?

PEOPLE TALK.

PORPHYRIA.

ONE MORE FACT ABOUT ME YOU NEVER KNEW, HUH?

MY EYES WATER IN THE LIGHT, MY SKIN BURNS LIKE A VAMPIRE ON VACATION.

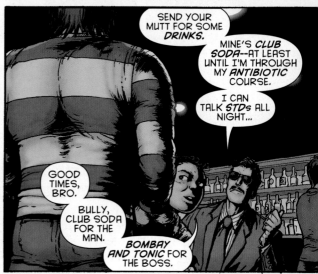

SEND YOUR MUTT FOR SOME DRINKS.

MINE'S CLUB SODA--AT LEAST UNTIL I'M THROUGH MY ANTIBIOTIC COURSE.

I CAN TALK STDS ALL NIGHT...

GOOD TIMES, BRO.

BULLY, CLUB SODA FOR THE MAN. BOMBAY AND TONIC FOR THE BOSS.

...THIS ONE'S FOR FREE, MY LITTLE ACTION FIGURE.

YOU'VE BEEN WONDERIN' WHY YOUR RIVERSIDE BUSINESS INTERESTS ARE LEAKING REVENUE, AM I RIGHT?

THE BOY BULLY MOONLIGHTS ON BOSS PENGUIN'S PAYROLL.

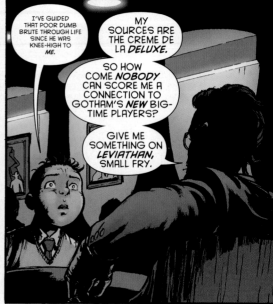

I'VE GUIDED THAT POOR DUMB BRUTE THROUGH LIFE SINCE HE WAS KNEE-HIGH TO ME.

MY SOURCES ARE THE CREME DE LA DELUXE.

SO HOW COME NOBODY CAN SCORE ME A CONNECTION TO GOTHAM'S NEW BIG-TIME PLAYERS?

GIVE ME SOMETHING ON LEVIATHAN, SMALL FRY.

"FRY."

MATCHES, WE'RE HERE TO PAY OUR RESPECTS TO *TONY AND JOE GRIMM.*

THAT'S *IT.*

THEY CALLED YOU *"RUMPELSTILTSKIN"* WHEN YOU RAN WITH THE *BROTHERS GRIMM.*

I FIGURED YOU AND *RESPECT* HAD AGREED TO A TRIAL *SEPARATION.*

I NEED A CONTACT IN *LEVIATHAN.*

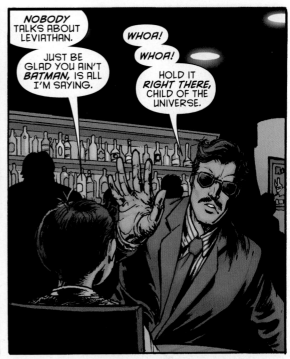

NOBODY TALKS ABOUT LEVIATHAN.

JUST BE GLAD YOU AIN'T *BATMAN,* IS ALL I'M SAYING.

WHOA!

WHOA!

HOLD IT *RIGHT THERE,* CHILD OF THE UNIVERSE.

WHAT IS IT?

WHAT YOU *LOOKING* AT?

YOU LOST INTEREST IN ME AND MY LIFE *ALREADY?*

...*LEAVE* IT, MALONE!

YOU DON'T KNOW WHAT YOU'RE *DEALING* WITH!

I'LL *ARRANGE* YOUR CONTACT, OKAY...?

NOBODY EVER CALLED MATCHES MALONE A KNIGHT IN SHINING ARMOR, BUT GIMME A *BREAK* HERE!

A *DAMSEL IN DISTRESS* AND NO ONE'S STEPPING UP?

BACK OFF, *MUCHACHOS.*

YOU'RE TANGLING WITH A MASTER OF *KARATE.*

AND JUST IN CASE YOU THINK MY LIFELONG DEDICATION TO *NON-VIOLENCE* GIVES YOU BOYS AN UNFAIR *ADVANTAGE...*

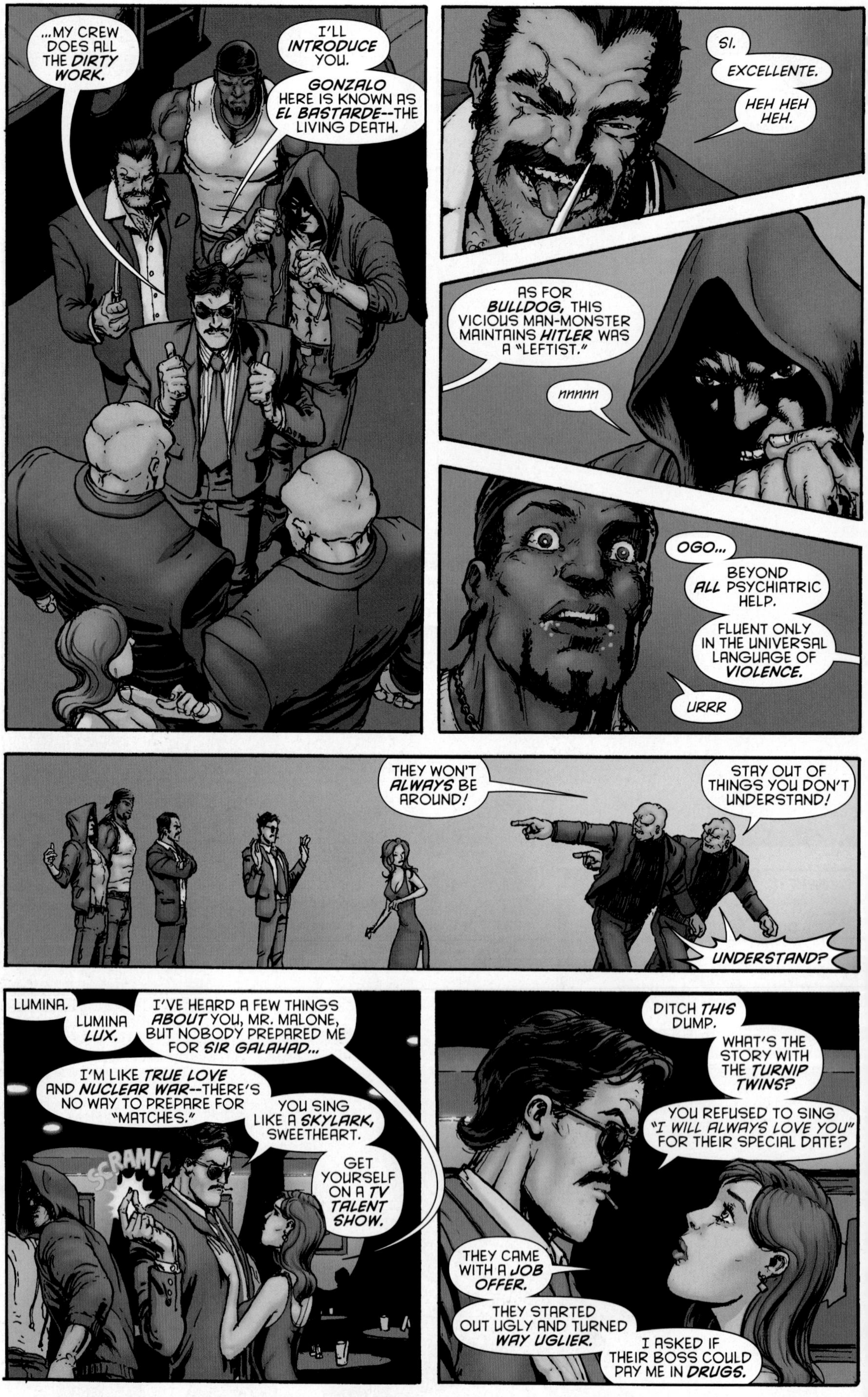
...MY CREW DOES ALL THE DIRTY WORK.
I'LL INTRODUCE YOU.
GONZALO HERE IS KNOWN AS EL BASTARDE--THE LIVING DEATH.
SI.
EXCELLENTE.
HEH HEH HEH.
AS FOR BULLDOG, THIS VICIOUS MAN-MONSTER MAINTAINS HITLER WAS A "LEFTIST."
nnnnn
OGO...
BEYOND ALL PSYCHIATRIC HELP.
FLUENT ONLY IN THE UNIVERSAL LANGUAGE OF VIOLENCE.
URRR
THEY WON'T ALWAYS BE AROUND!
STAY OUT OF THINGS YOU DON'T UNDERSTAND!
UNDERSTAND?
LUMINA.
LUMINA LUX.
I'VE HEARD A FEW THINGS ABOUT YOU, MR. MALONE, BUT NOBODY PREPARED ME FOR SIR GALAHAD...
I'M LIKE TRUE LOVE AND NUCLEAR WAR--THERE'S NO WAY TO PREPARE FOR "MATCHES."
YOU SING LIKE A SKYLARK, SWEETHEART.
GET YOURSELF ON A TV TALENT SHOW.
SCRAM!
DITCH THIS DUMP.
WHAT'S THE STORY WITH THE TURNIP TWINS?
YOU REFUSED TO SING "I WILL ALWAYS LOVE YOU" FOR THEIR SPECIAL DATE?
THEY CAME WITH A JOB OFFER.
THEY STARTED OUT UGLY AND TURNED WAY UGLIER.
I ASKED IF THEIR BOSS COULD PAY ME IN DRUGS.

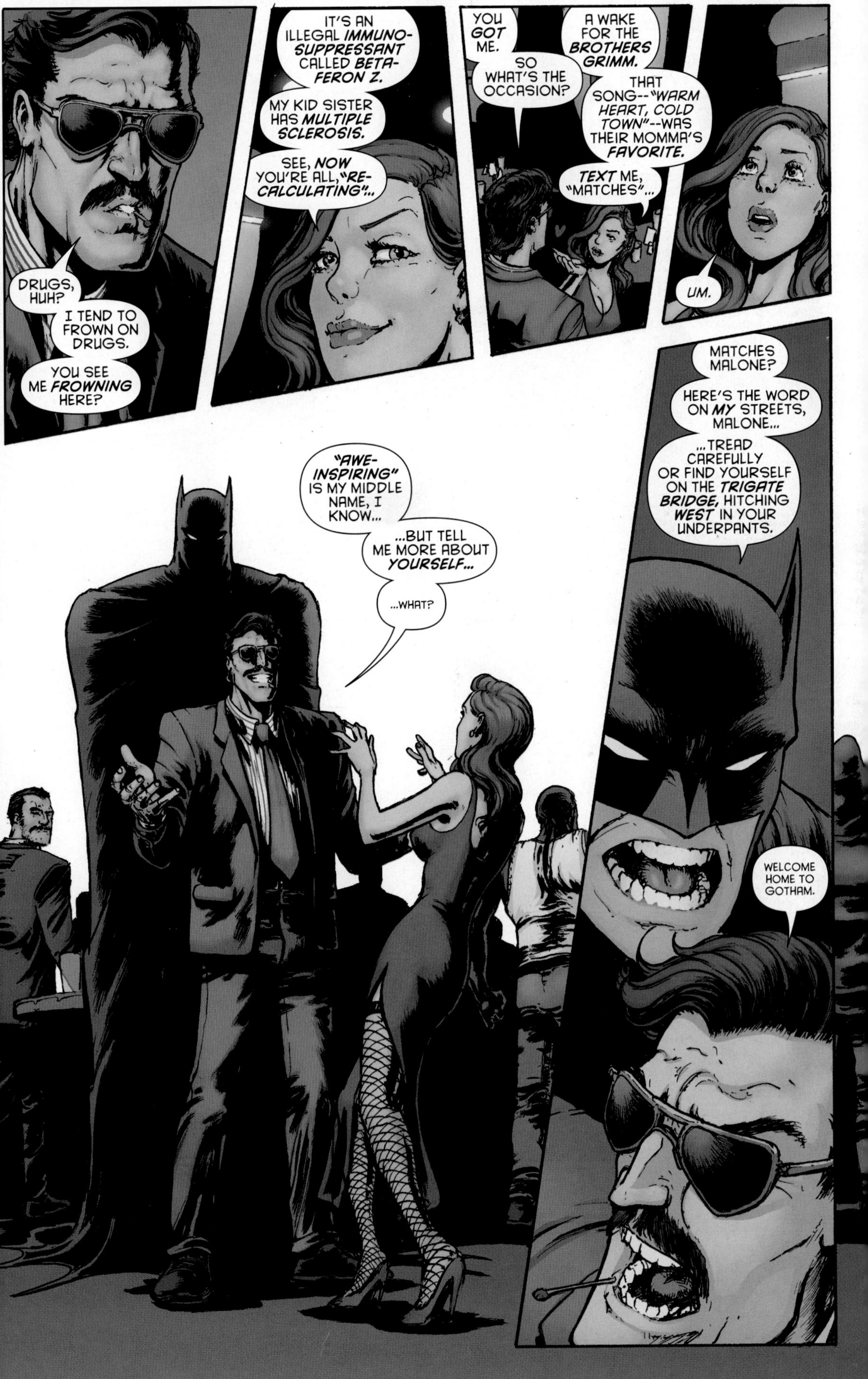
DRUGS, HUH?
I TEND TO FROWN ON DRUGS.
YOU SEE ME FROWNING HERE?
IT'S AN ILLEGAL IMMUNO-SUPPRESSANT CALLED BETA-FERON Z.
MY KID SISTER HAS MULTIPLE SCLEROSIS.
SEE, NOW YOU'RE ALL, "RE-CALCULATING"...
YOU GOT ME.
SO WHAT'S THE OCCASION?
A WAKE FOR THE BROTHERS GRIMM.
THAT SONG--"WARM HEART, COLD TOWN"--WAS THEIR MOMMA'S FAVORITE.
TEXT ME, "MATCHES"...
UM.
"AWE-INSPIRING" IS MY MIDDLE NAME, I KNOW...
...BUT TELL ME MORE ABOUT YOURSELF...
...WHAT?
MATCHES MALONE?
HERE'S THE WORD ON MY STREETS, MALONE...
...TREAD CAREFULLY OR FIND YOURSELF ON THE TRIGATE BRIDGE, HITCHING WEST IN YOUR UNDERPANTS.
WELCOME HOME TO GOTHAM.

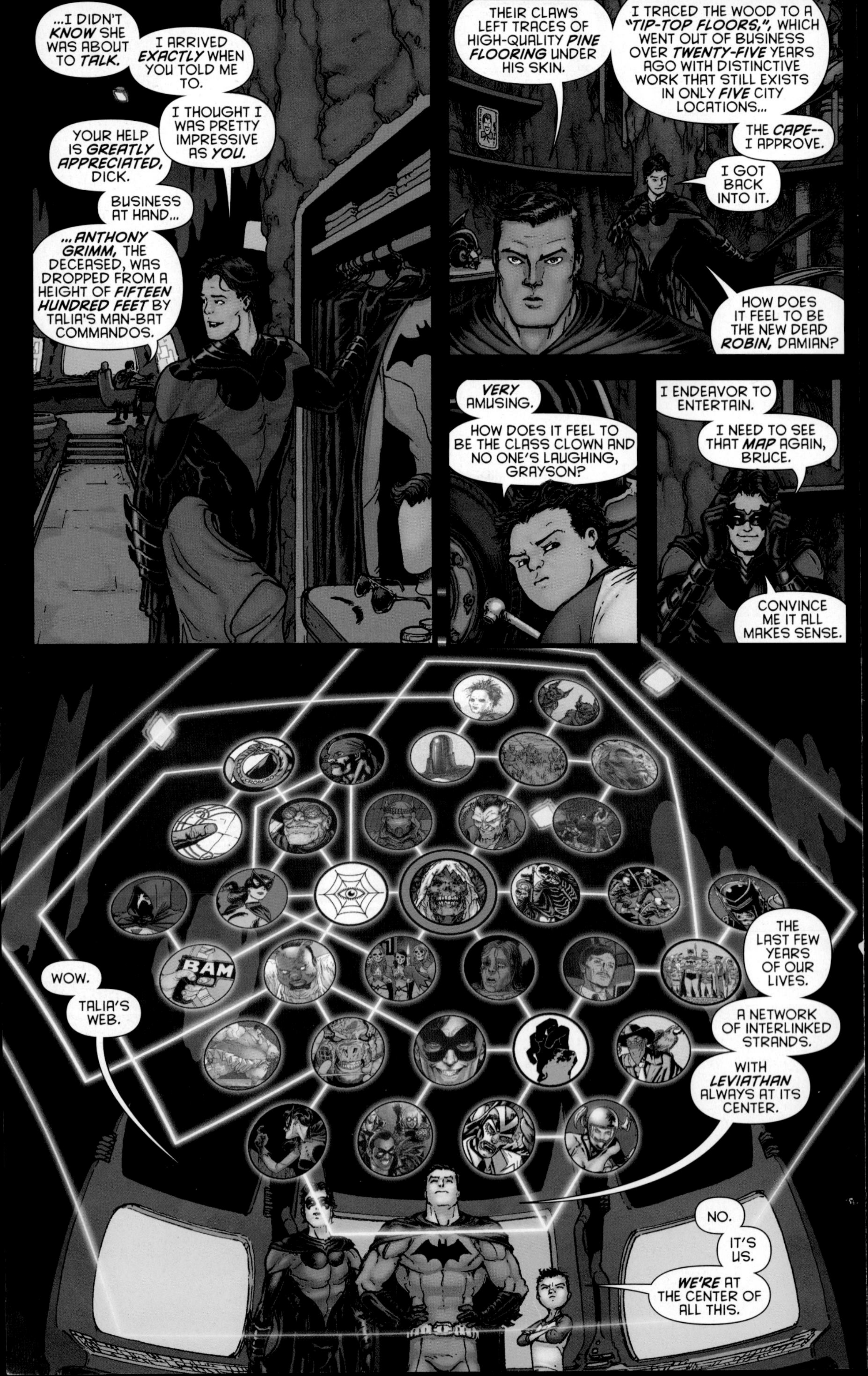
...I DIDN'T KNOW SHE WAS ABOUT TO TALK.
I ARRIVED EXACTLY WHEN YOU TOLD ME TO.
I THOUGHT I WAS PRETTY IMPRESSIVE AS YOU.
YOUR HELP IS GREATLY APPRECIATED, DICK.
BUSINESS AT HAND...
...ANTHONY GRIMM, THE DECEASED, WAS DROPPED FROM A HEIGHT OF FIFTEEN HUNDRED FEET BY TALIA'S MAN-BAT COMMANDOS.
THEIR CLAWS LEFT TRACES OF HIGH-QUALITY PINE FLOORING UNDER HIS SKIN.
I TRACED THE WOOD TO A "TIP-TOP FLOORS,", WHICH WENT OUT OF BUSINESS OVER TWENTY-FIVE YEARS AGO WITH DISTINCTIVE WORK THAT STILL EXISTS IN ONLY FIVE CITY LOCATIONS...
THE CAPE-- I APPROVE.
I GOT BACK INTO IT.
HOW DOES IT FEEL TO BE THE NEW DEAD ROBIN, DAMIAN?
VERY AMUSING.
HOW DOES IT FEEL TO BE THE CLASS CLOWN AND NO ONE'S LAUGHING, GRAYSON?
I ENDEAVOR TO ENTERTAIN.
I NEED TO SEE THAT MAP AGAIN, BRUCE.
CONVINCE ME IT ALL MAKES SENSE.
BAM
WOW.
TALIA'S WEB.
THE LAST FEW YEARS OF OUR LIVES.
A NETWORK OF INTERLINKED STRANDS.
WITH LEVIATHAN ALWAYS AT ITS CENTER.
NO.
IT'S US.
WE'RE AT THE CENTER OF ALL THIS.

...IF I MAY INTRUDE, MASTER BRUCE, THE ANIMAL DOES INDEED CARRY A SYNTHETIC *HORMONE*, AS SUSPECTED.

DERIVED FROM *PROFESSOR PYG'S* PHARMACEUTICAL BREAKTHROUGHS, IT SEEMS.

PYG!

HAMBURGERS FOR SALE IN *DARK TOWER* OUTLETS CONCEAL A *MIND CONTROL DRUG* PRECURSOR.

DON'T MAKE ME DEAL WITH *THAT* FREAK AGAIN.

HE'S STILL TUCKED UP IN ARKHAM, RIGHT?

TALIA'S HACKING INTO THE GOTHAM *FOODCHAIN*.

THE *ASSASSINS LEAGUE* IS HERE.

THEY'RE *ALL* HERE, SOMEWHERE IN THE CITY...

DON'T LET HIM GIVE YOU A HARD TIME. *I* LEFT ROBIN BEHIND TO BECOME *NIGHTWING*.

ROBIN IS *GROUNDED*.

HE SAYS IT'S BECAUSE MOTHER SENT THE WORLD'S GREATEST ASSASSINS TO GOTHAM TO *KILL* ME.

THE *REAL* TRUTH IS HE'S *ANGRY* BECAUSE I KILLED SOME GENOCIDAL *MADMAN*.

I'M NOT ANGRY-- ROBIN WAS A FLASHING *TARGET*.

YOU'LL STAY RIGHT *HERE*, DAMIAN, FOR YOUR OWN SAFETY AND UNTIL OPERATION *"KILL BOX"* IS *COMPLETE*.

RIGHT NOW, THE WORLD THINKS ROBIN IS *DEAD*, AND THAT'S EXACTLY WHAT WE WANT.

YES, FATHER.

BUT MOTHER *WILL* KNOW IT'S A *RUSE*.

SHE'S DOING THIS TO *SEPARATE* ME FROM YOU.

WHY WOULD SHE DO *THAT*, DAMIAN?

WHY *ELSE*? TO LEAVE *YOU* UNPROTECTED.

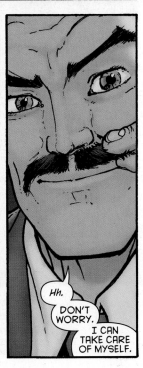

Hh. DON'T WORRY. I CAN TAKE CARE OF MYSELF.

...IT'S LIKE A NEW *RELIGION*.

TUESDAYS AND THURSDAYS, THEY SACRIFICE A *GOAT* TO KALI.

THREE EYED JACKS

BATMAN?

GOATS?

HOW THE HELL DO *GOATS* FIGURE INTO THIS?

LILITH, KALI, THE *DARK MOTHER*, TIAMAT... *LEVIATHAN*...IT'S SYMBOLISM AND IMAGERY...

COMPUTER GAMES, MYTHOLOGY.

THIS IS CREEPY STUFF YOU LOOK UP ON THE *INTERNET*.

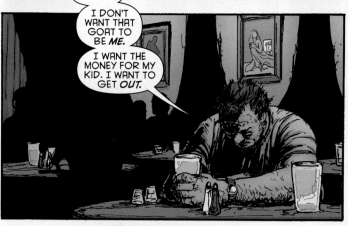

A *GOAT*.

I DON'T WANT THAT GOAT TO BE *ME*.

I WANT THE MONEY FOR MY KID. I WANT TO GET *OUT*.

I NEED THE GOSSIP ON THE *STREETS*, GOATBOY.

THE INTERNET'S TOO SLOW FOR HOW I DO BUSINESS.

YOU SAY YOU KILLED ROBIN THE BOY WONDER, SO WHERE DO YOU COLLECT YOUR HALF BILLION-DOLLAR REWARD?

LADIES AND GENTLEMEN, THE VOICE OF AN ANGEL HERSELF, IT'S TIPPY TREESIDE!

I WAS *BLINDFOLDED*-- TAKEN FOR A RIDE--

--I WASN'T SUPPOSED TO *KNOW* WHERE I WOUND UP, BUT *NOBODY* KNOWS THIS CITY LIKE I DO.

I COULD *FEEL* EVERY TWIST AND TURN AND CORNER, LIKE *MUSCLE MEMORY*.

THEN I *SMELLED* THAT--*SMELL*-- THAT *THING*.

I HEARD THE RUMOR THEY USED BATMAN'S *DNA* TO BUILD A *FRANKENSTEIN MONSTER*.

I SAW IT *KILL* A GUY...

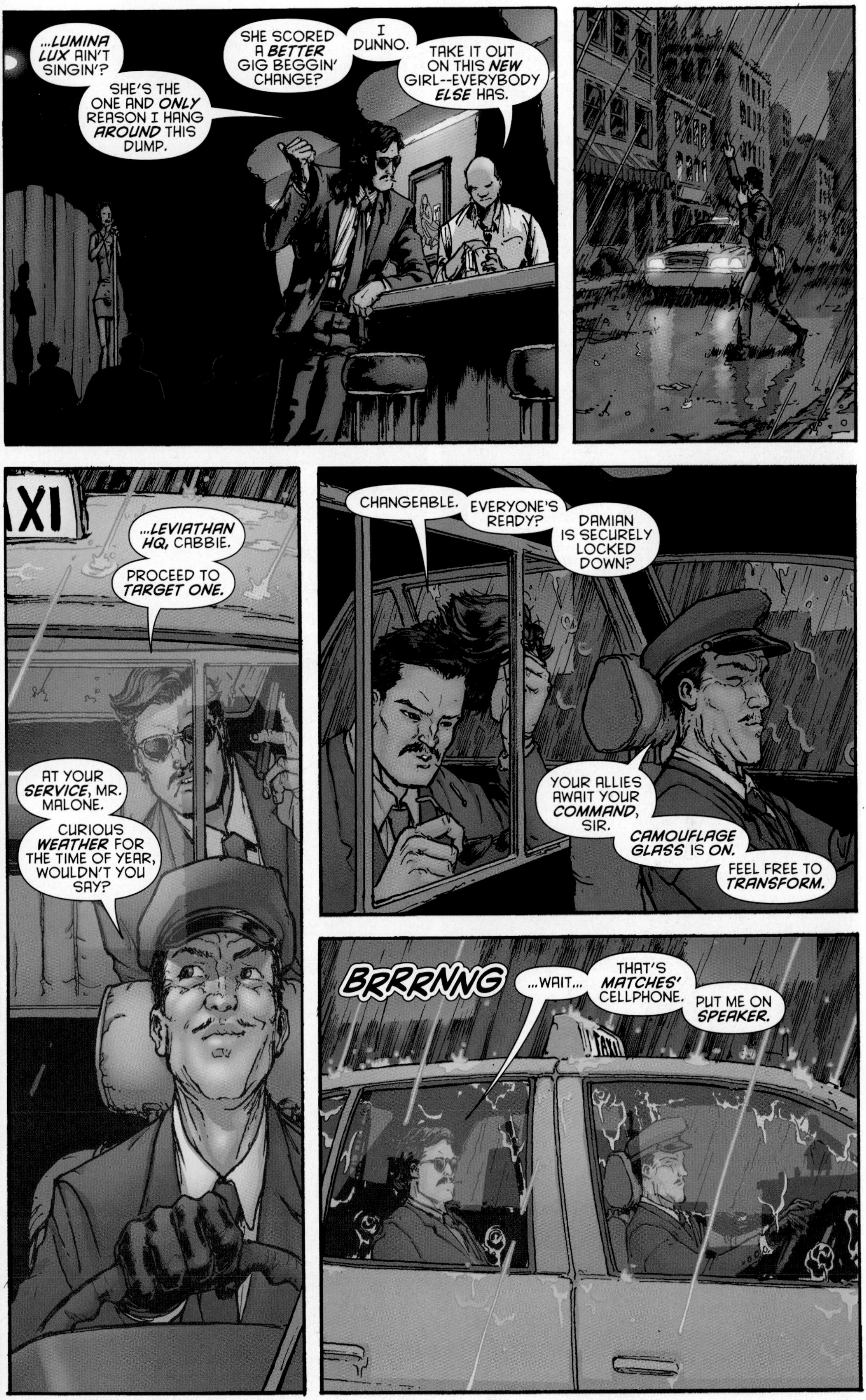
...LUMINA LUX AIN'T SINGIN'?
SHE'S THE ONE AND ONLY REASON I HANG AROUND THIS DUMP.
SHE SCORED A BETTER GIG BEGGIN' CHANGE?
I DUNNO.
TAKE IT OUT ON THIS NEW GIRL--EVERYBODY ELSE HAS.
TAXI
...LEVIATHAN HQ, CABBIE.
PROCEED TO TARGET ONE.
AT YOUR SERVICE, MR. MALONE.
CURIOUS WEATHER FOR THE TIME OF YEAR, WOULDN'T YOU SAY?
CHANGEABLE.
EVERYONE'S READY?
DAMIAN IS SECURELY LOCKED DOWN?
YOUR ALLIES AWAIT YOUR COMMAND, SIR.
CAMOUFLAGE GLASS IS ON.
FEEL FREE TO TRANSFORM.
BRRRNNG
...WAIT...
THAT'S MATCHES' CELLPHONE.
PUT ME ON SPEAKER.

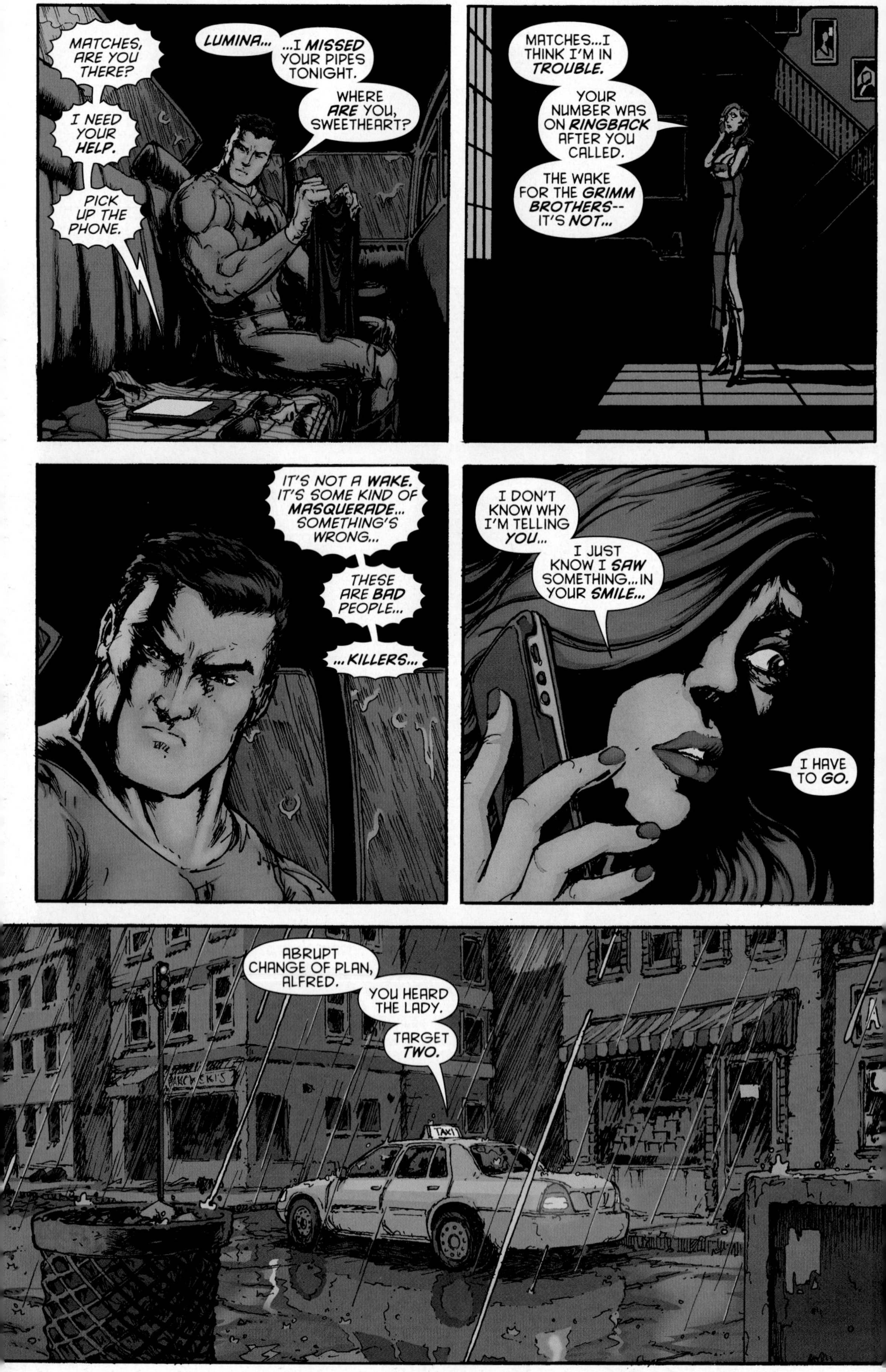

MATCHES, ARE YOU THERE?
I NEED YOUR HELP.
PICK UP THE PHONE.
LUMINA...
...I MISSED YOUR PIPES TONIGHT.
WHERE ARE YOU, SWEETHEART?
MATCHES...I THINK I'M IN TROUBLE.
YOUR NUMBER WAS ON RINGBACK AFTER YOU CALLED.
THE WAKE FOR THE GRIMM BROTHERS-- IT'S NOT...
IT'S NOT A WAKE. IT'S SOME KIND OF MASQUERADE... SOMETHING'S WRONG...
THESE ARE BAD PEOPLE...
...KILLERS...
I DON'T KNOW WHY I'M TELLING YOU...
I JUST KNOW I SAW SOMETHING...IN YOUR SMILE...
I HAVE TO GO.
ABRUPT CHANGE OF PLAN, ALFRED.
YOU HEARD THE LADY.
TARGET TWO.
TAXI

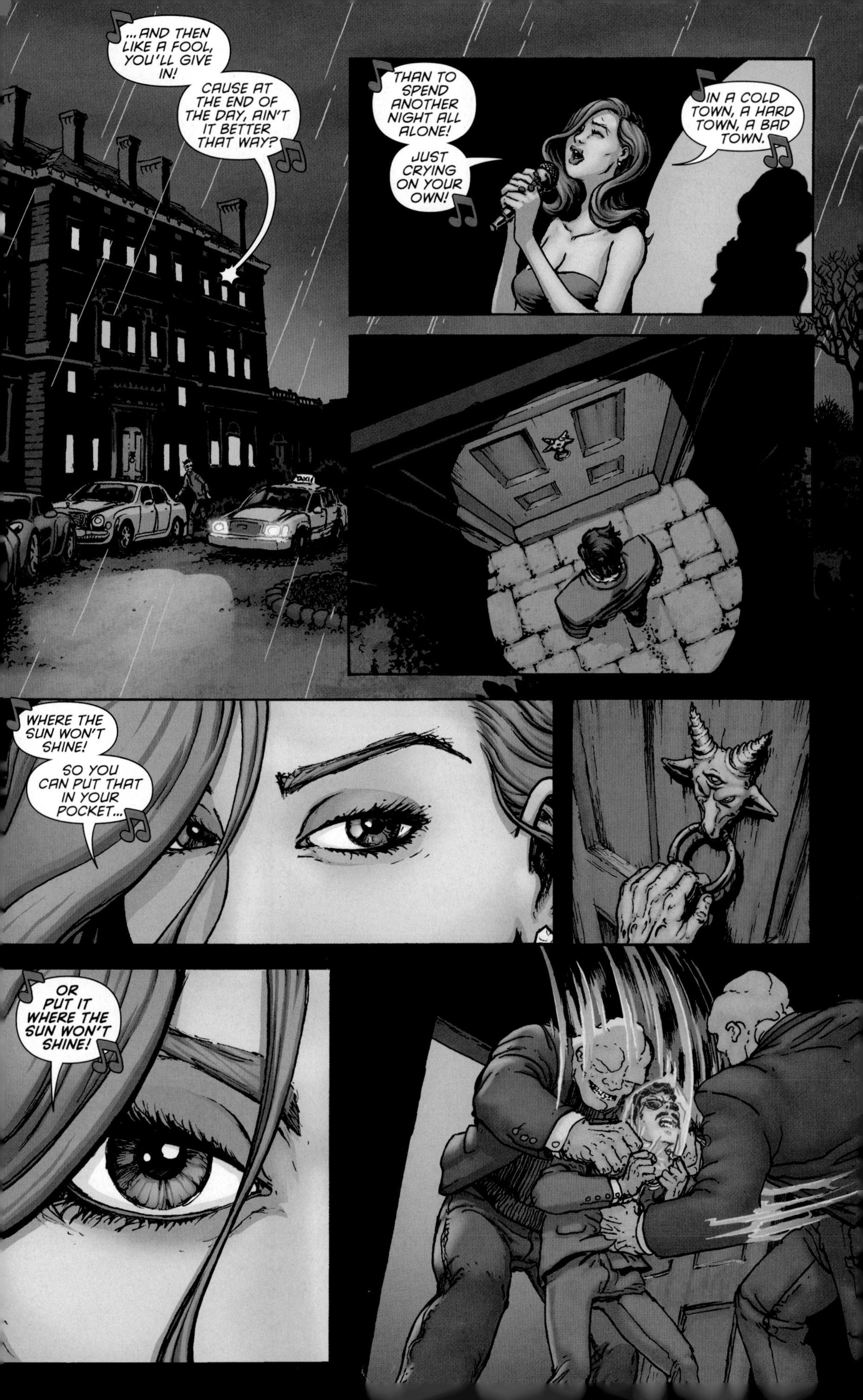
...AND THEN LIKE A FOOL, YOU'LL GIVE IN!
CAUSE AT THE END OF THE DAY, AIN'T IT BETTER THAT WAY?
THAN TO SPEND ANOTHER NIGHT ALL ALONE!
JUST CRYING ON YOUR OWN!
IN A COLD TOWN, A HARD TOWN, A BAD TOWN.
WHERE THE SUN WON'T SHINE!
SO YOU CAN PUT THAT IN YOUR POCKET...
OR PUT IT WHERE THE SUN WON'T SHINE!

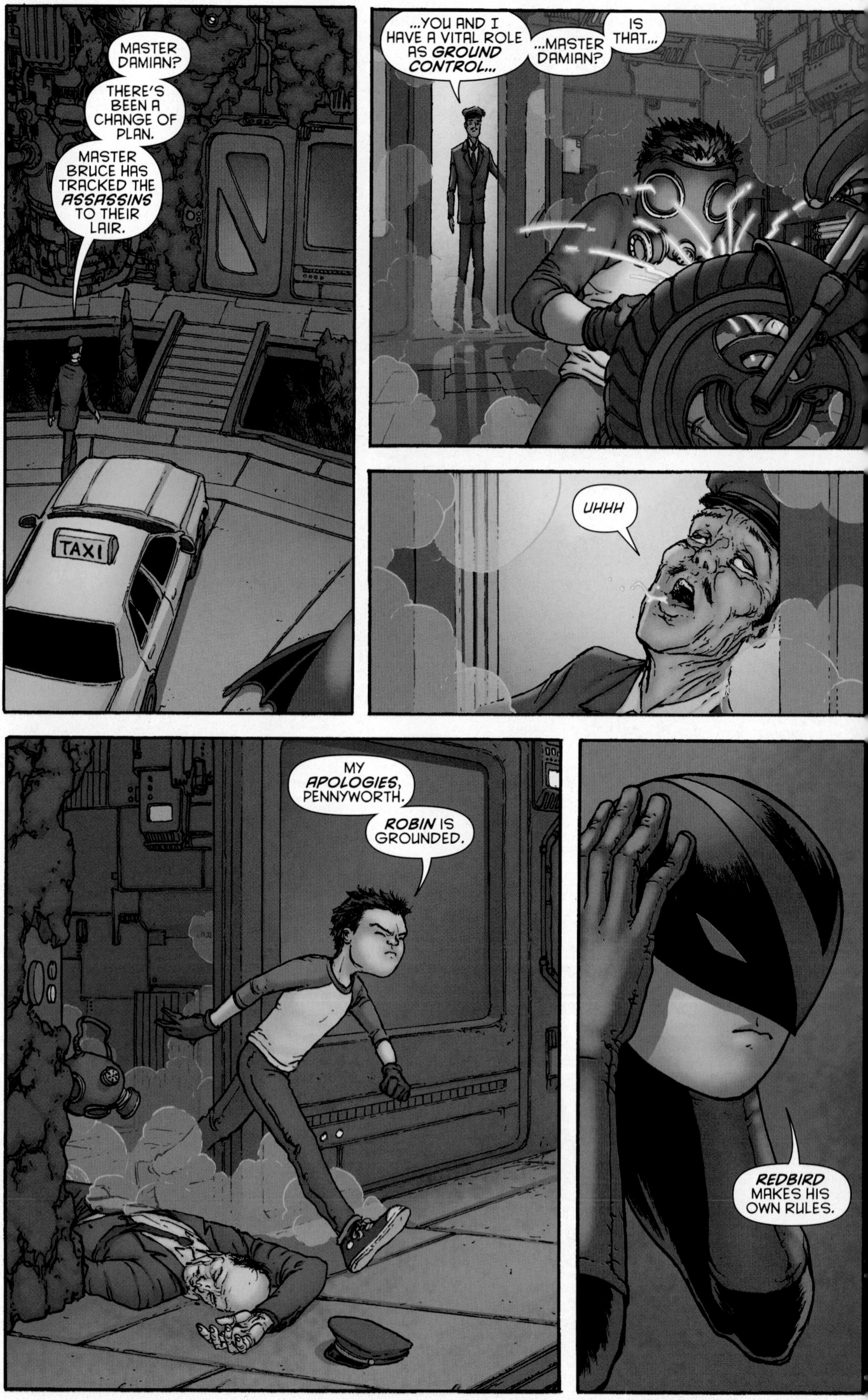
MASTER DAMIAN?
THERE'S BEEN A CHANGE OF PLAN.
MASTER BRUCE HAS TRACKED THE ASSASSINS TO THEIR LAIR.
TAXI
...YOU AND I HAVE A VITAL ROLE AS GROUND CONTROL...
IS THAT...
...MASTER DAMIAN?
UHHH
MY APOLOGIES, PENNYWORTH.
ROBIN IS GROUNDED.
REDBIRD MAKES HIS OWN RULES.

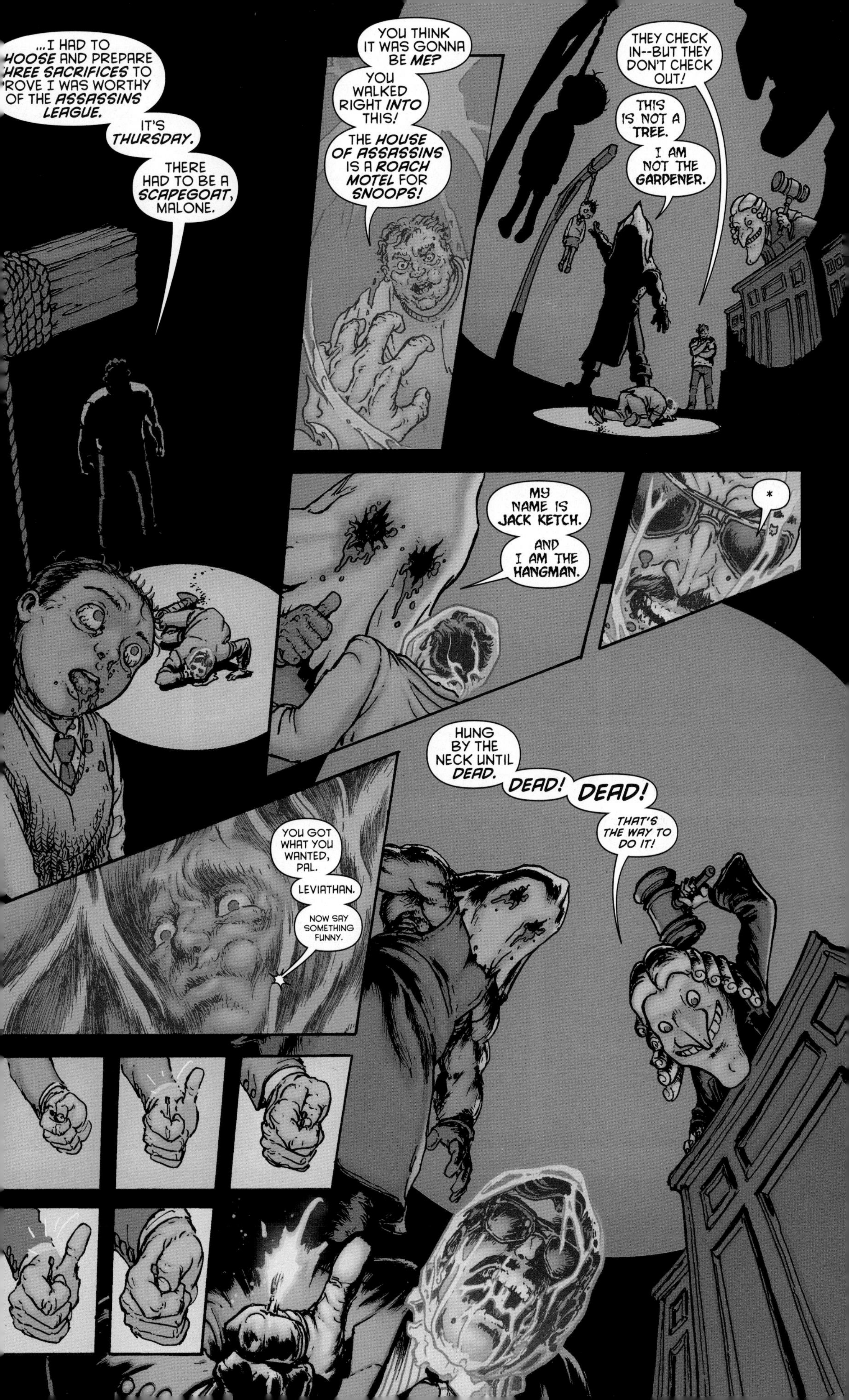
...I HAD TO
HOOSE AND PREPARE THREE SACRIFICES TO ROVE I WAS WORTHY OF THE ASSASSINS LEAGUE.
IT'S THURSDAY.
THERE HAD TO BE A SCAPEGOAT, MALONE.
YOU THINK IT WAS GONNA BE ME?
YOU WALKED RIGHT INTO THIS!
THE HOUSE OF ASSASSINS IS A ROACH MOTEL FOR SNOOPS!
THEY CHECK IN--BUT THEY DON'T CHECK OUT!
THIS IS NOT A TREE.
I AM NOT THE GARDENER.
MY NAME IS JACK KETCH.
AND I AM THE HANGMAN.
*
HUNG BY THE NECK UNTIL DEAD.
DEAD!
DEAD!
THAT'S THE WAY TO DO IT!
YOU GOT WHAT YOU WANTED, PAL.
LEVIATHAN.
NOW SAY SOMETHING FUNNY.

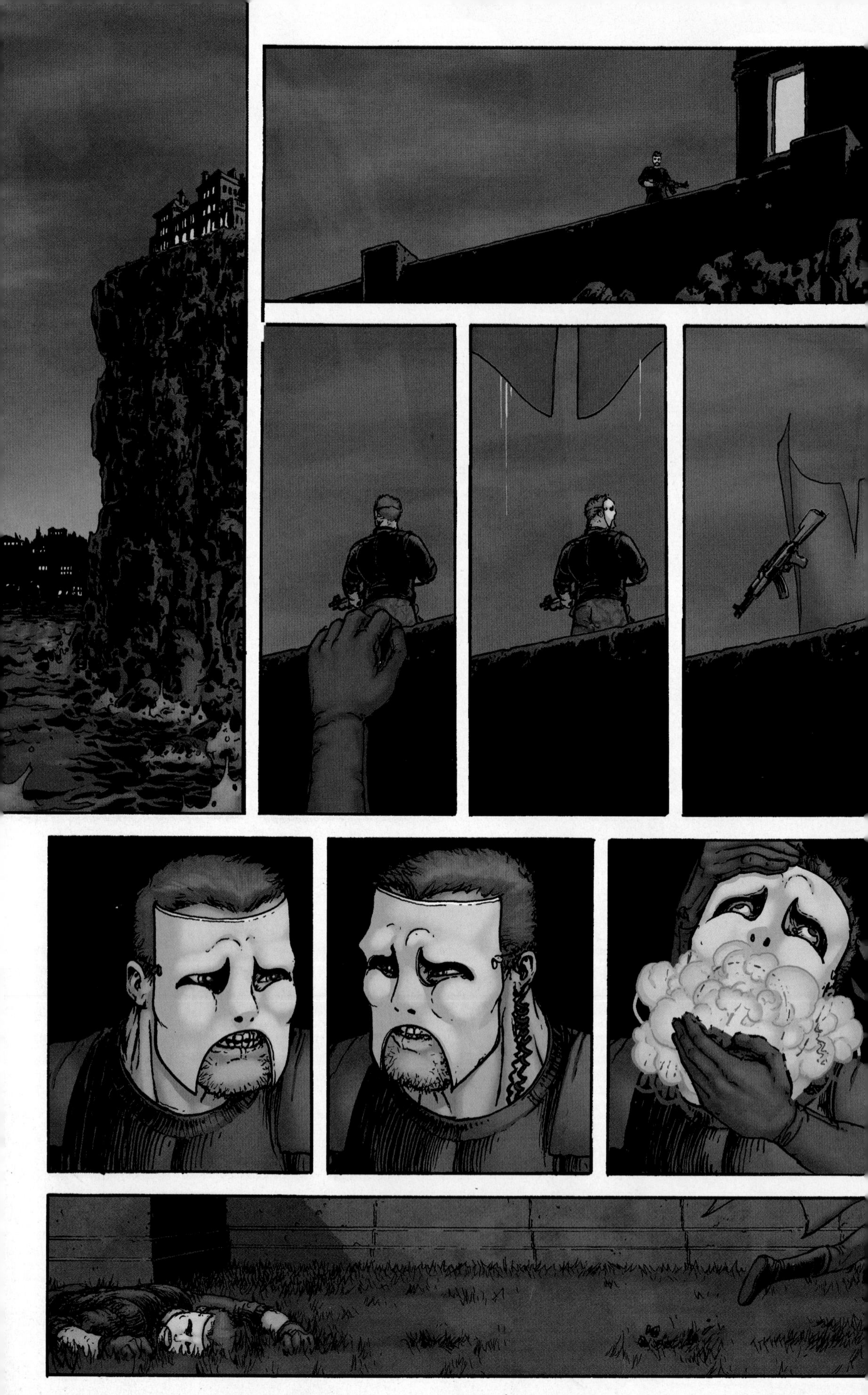

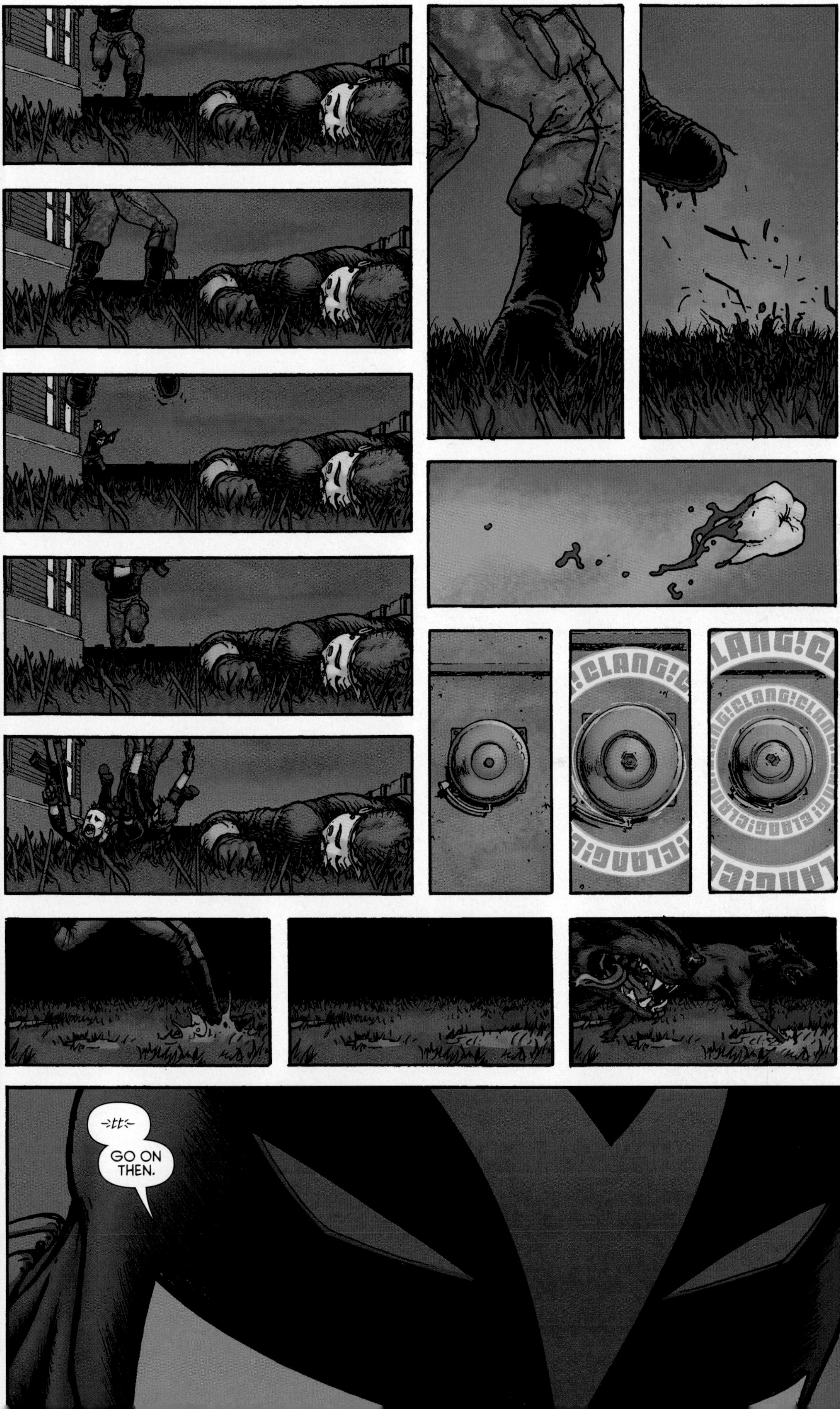

CLANG! CLANG! CLANG! CLANG!
-tt-
GO ON THEN.

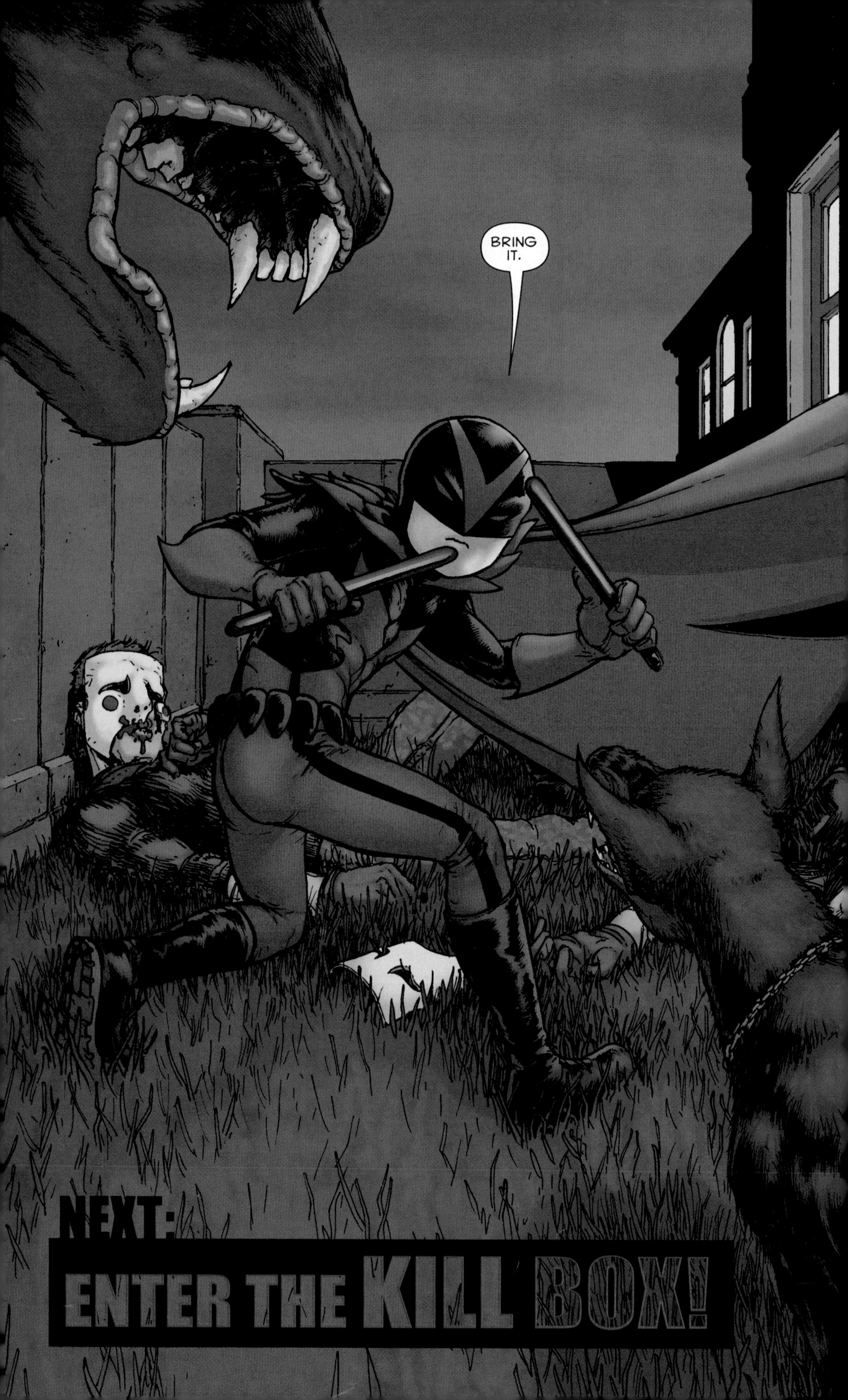

BRING IT.
NEXT:
ENTER THE KILL BOX!

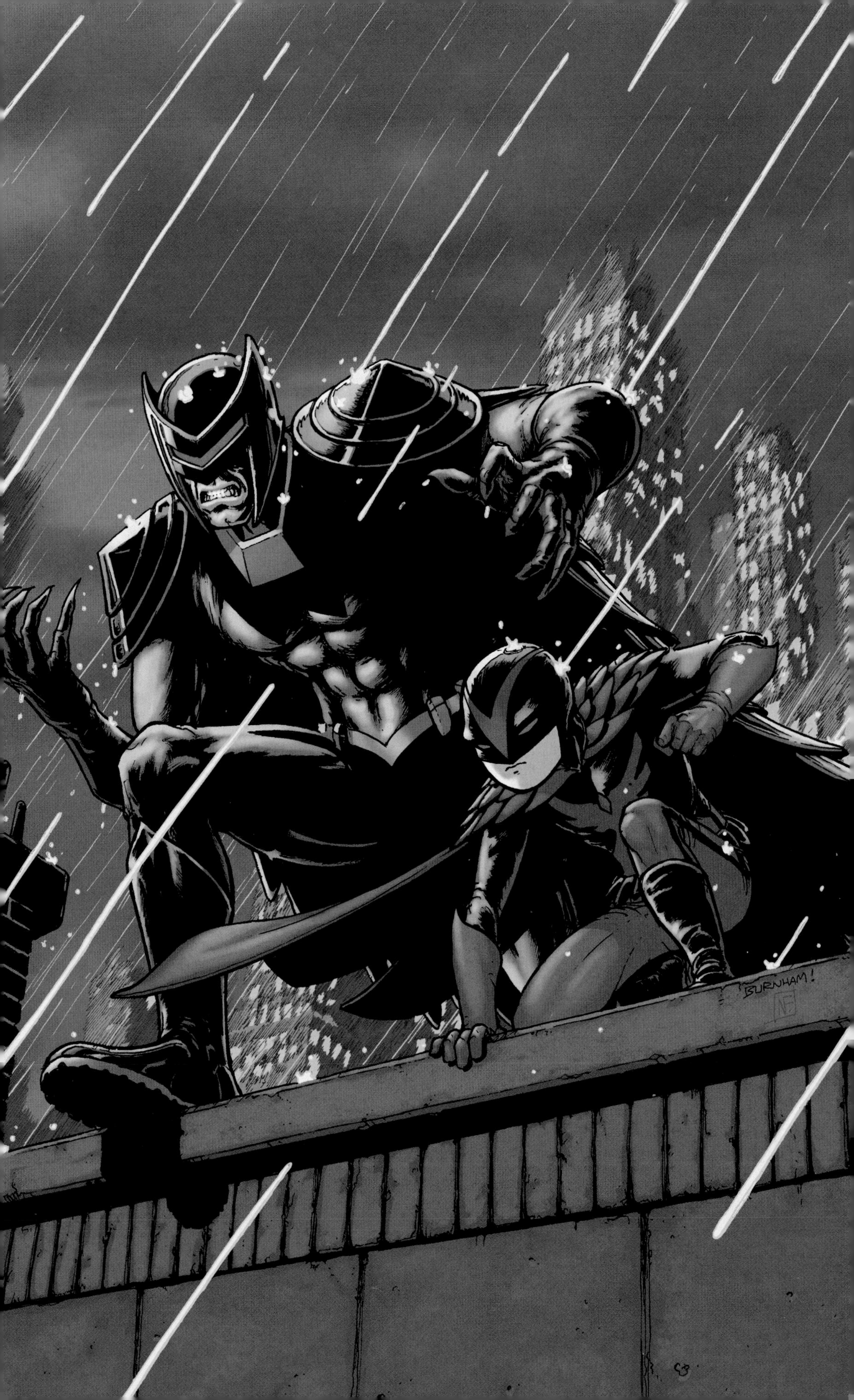
BURNHAM!

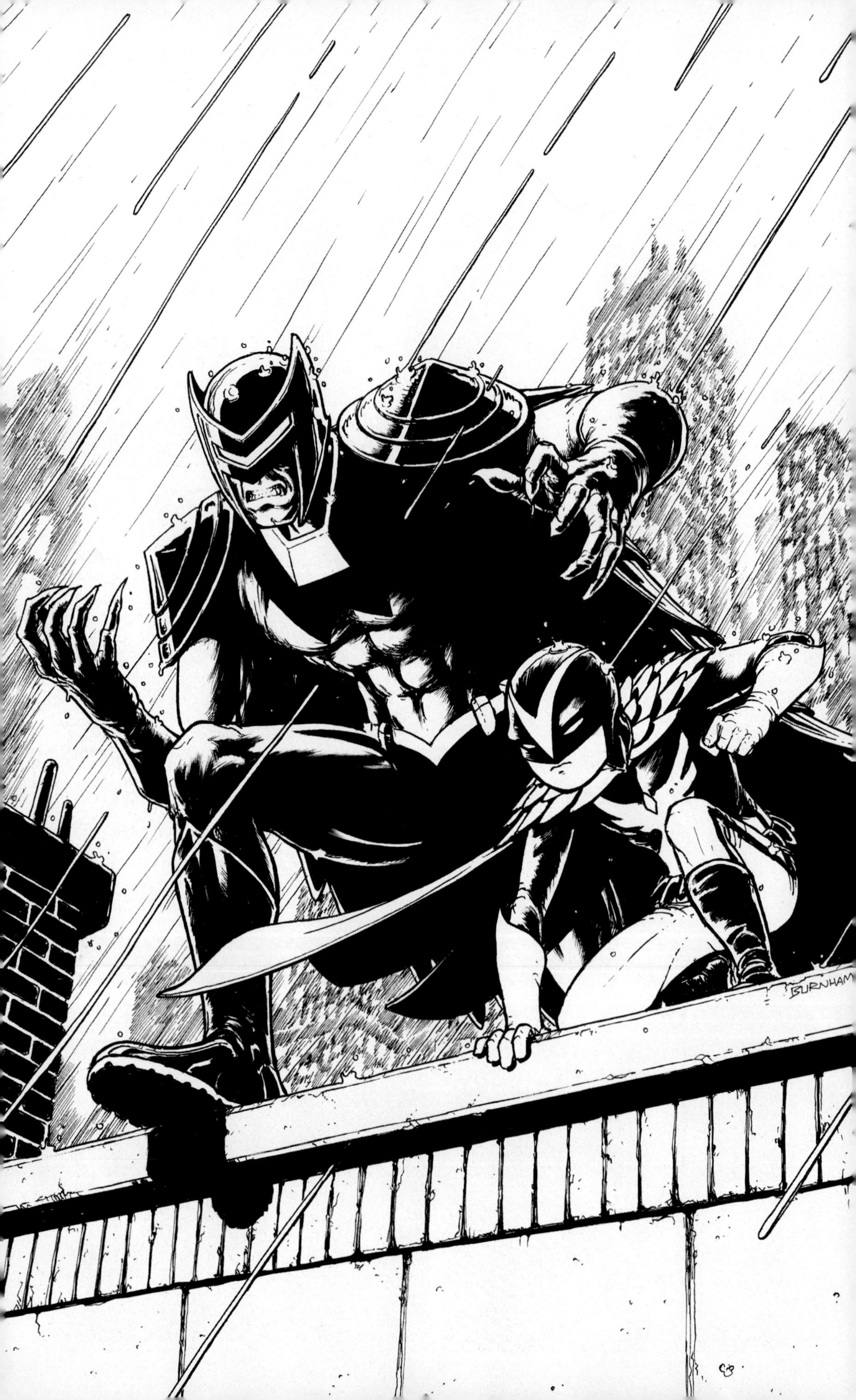
BURNHAM

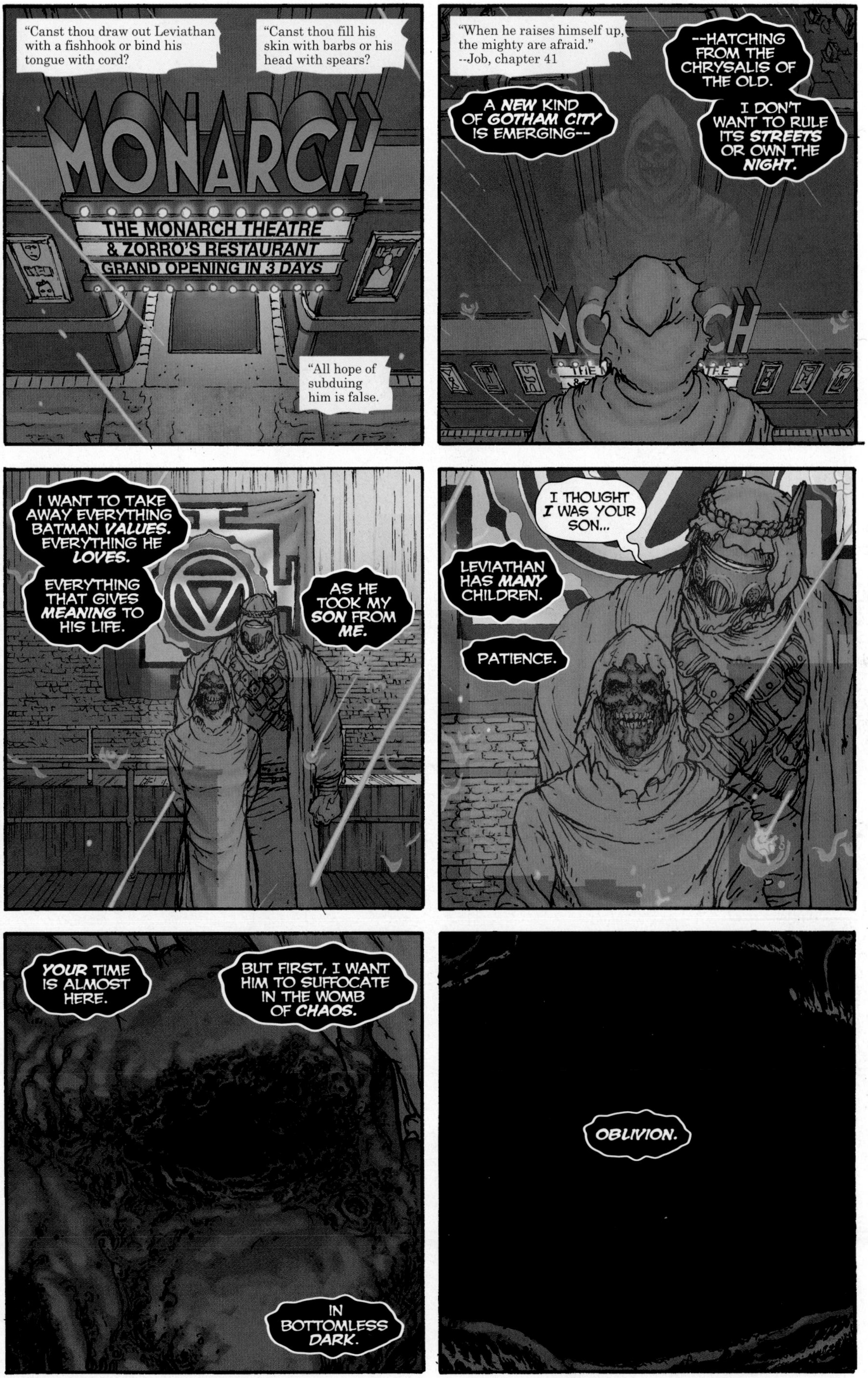
"Canst thou draw out Leviathan with a fishhook or bind his tongue with cord?
"Canst thou fill his skin with barbs or his head with spears?
MONARCH
THE MONARCH THEATRE
& ZORRO'S RESTAURANT
GRAND OPENING IN 3 DAYS
"All hope of subduing him is false.
"When he raises himself up, the mighty are afraid." --Job, chapter 41
A NEW KIND OF GOTHAM CITY IS EMERGING--
--HATCHING FROM THE CHRYSALIS OF THE OLD.
I DON'T WANT TO RULE ITS STREETS OR OWN THE NIGHT.
I WANT TO TAKE AWAY EVERYTHING BATMAN VALUES. EVERYTHING HE LOVES.
EVERYTHING THAT GIVES MEANING TO HIS LIFE.
AS HE TOOK MY SON FROM ME.
I THOUGHT I WAS YOUR SON...
LEVIATHAN HAS MANY CHILDREN.
PATIENCE.
YOUR TIME IS ALMOST HERE.
BUT FIRST, I WANT HIM TO SUFFOCATE IN THE WOMB OF CHAOS.
IN BOTTOMLESS DARK.
OBLIVION.

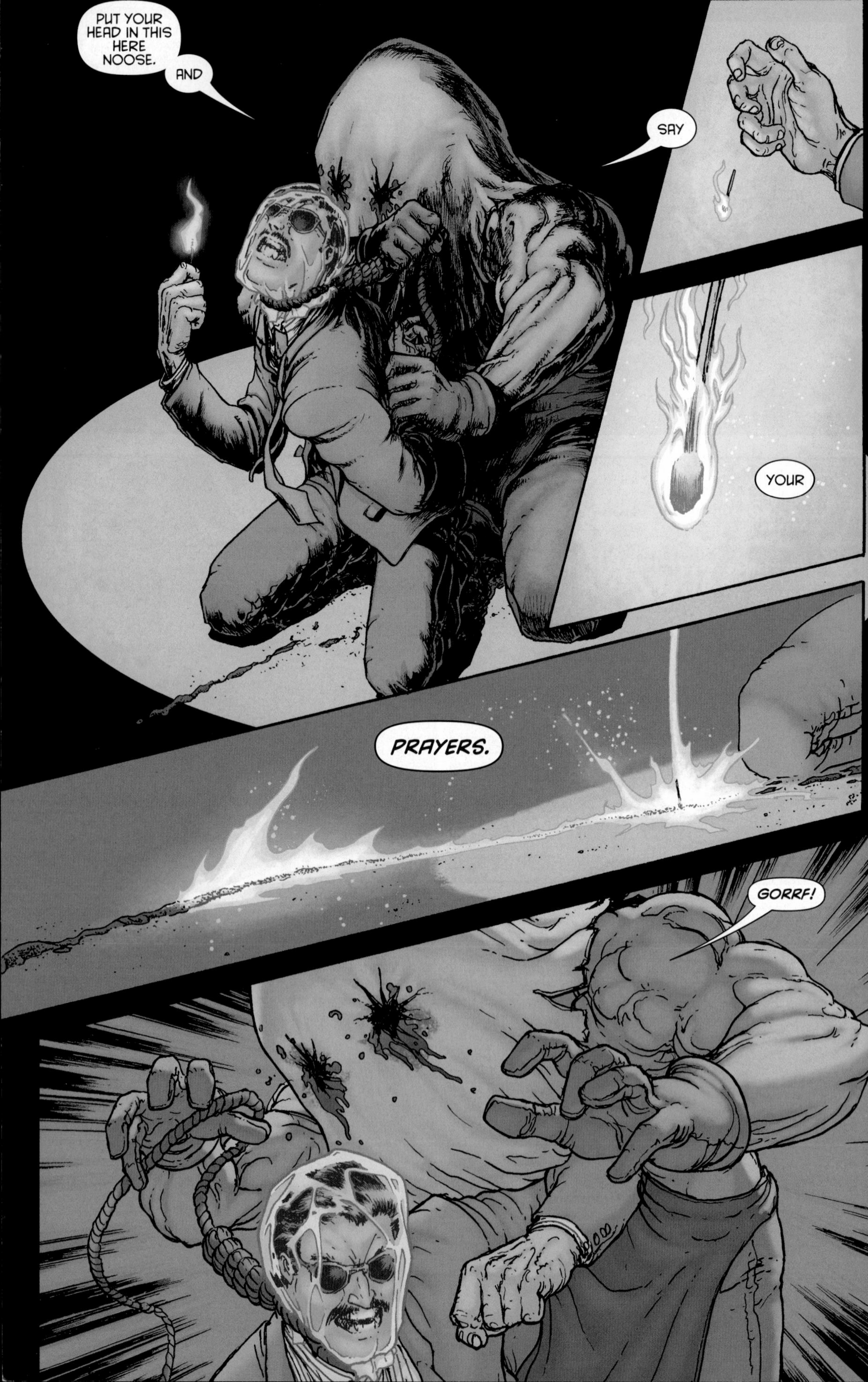

PUT YOUR HEAD IN THIS HERE NOOSE.
AND
SAY
YOUR
PRAYERS.
GORRF!

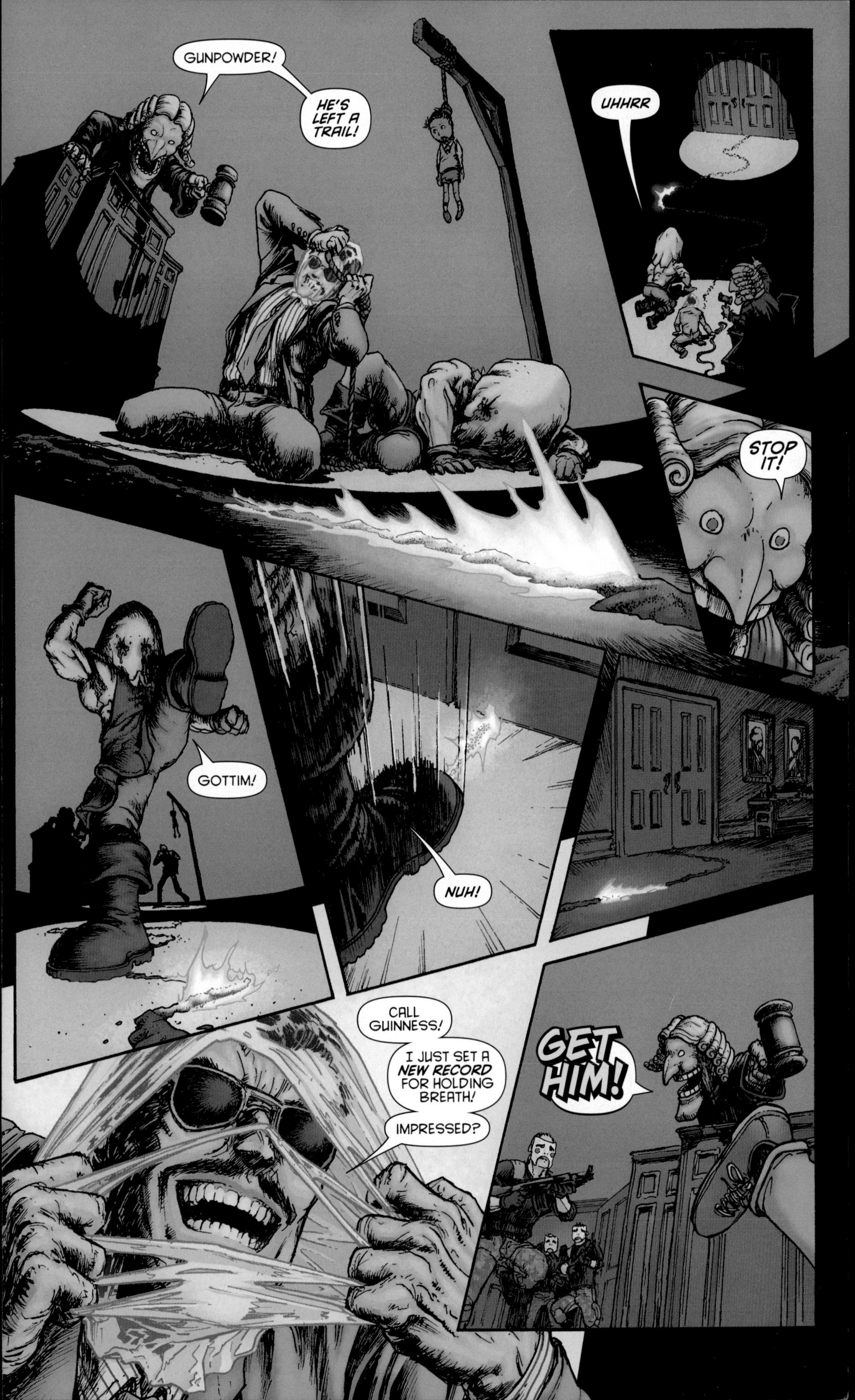
GUNPOWDER!
HE'S LEFT A TRAIL!
UHHRR
STOP IT!
GOTTIM!
NUH!
CALL GUINNESS!
I JUST SET A NEW RECORD FOR HOLDING BREATH!
IMPRESSED?
GET HIM!

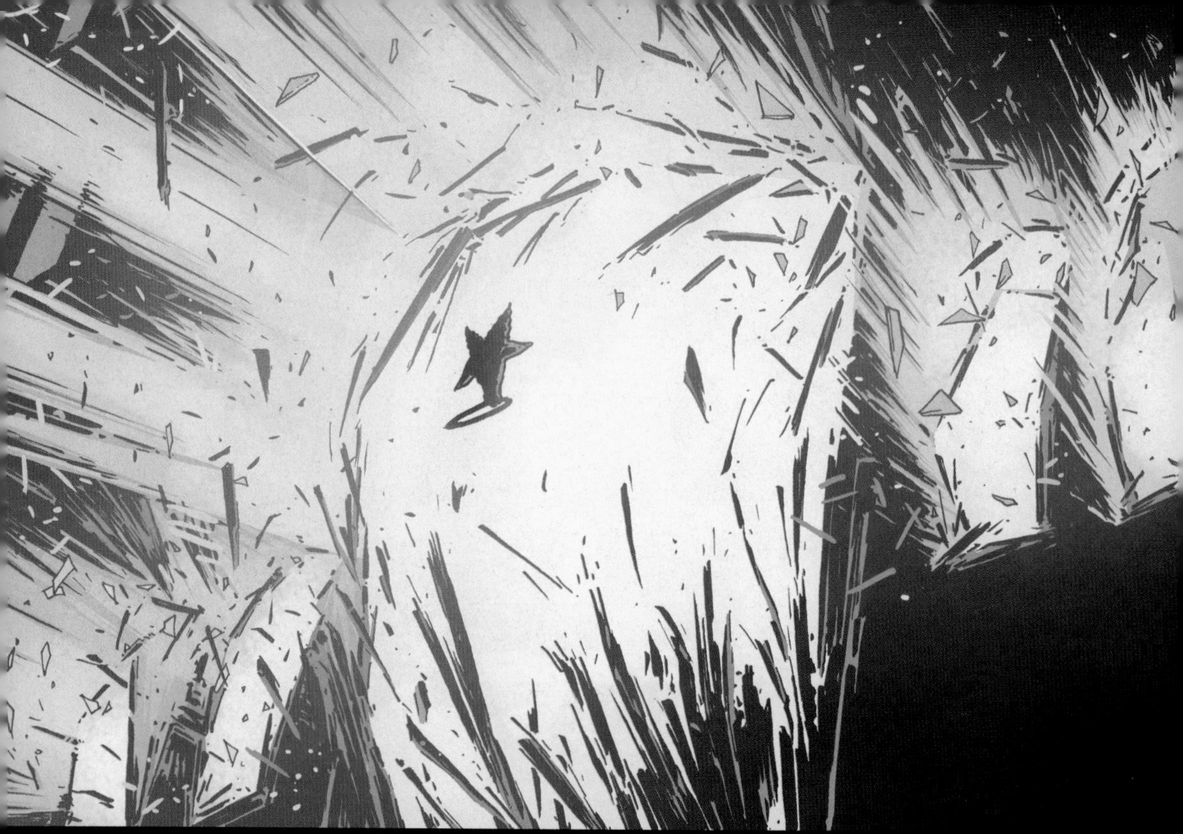

writer GRANT MORRISON artist CHRIS BURNHAM
color NATHAN FAIRBAIRN lettering DAVE SHARPE
cover BURNHAM and FAIRBAIRN

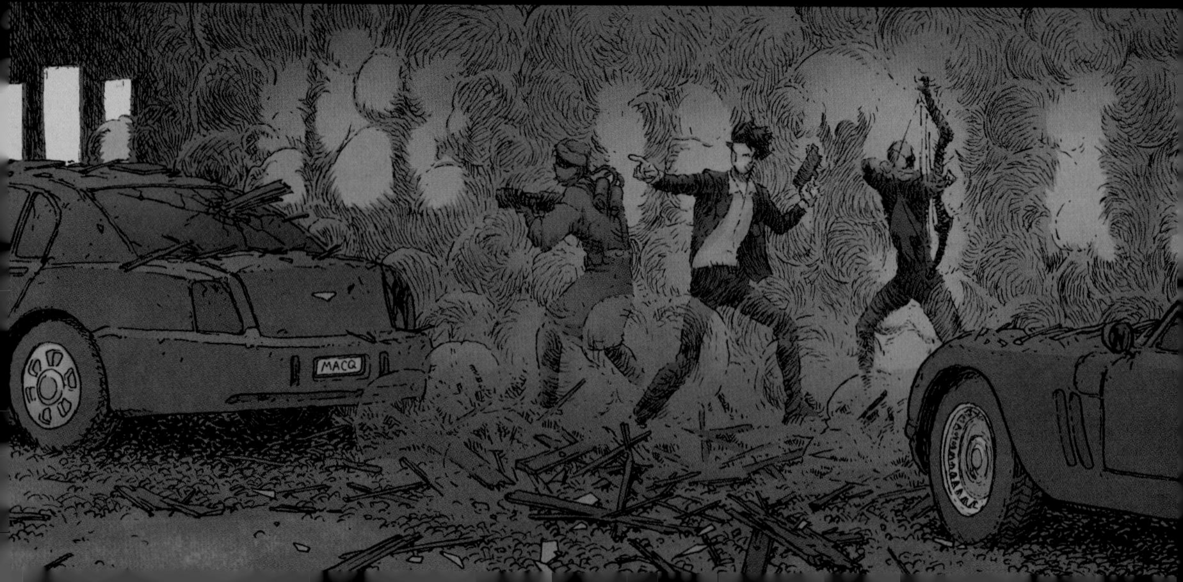
MACQ

KILL

BOX

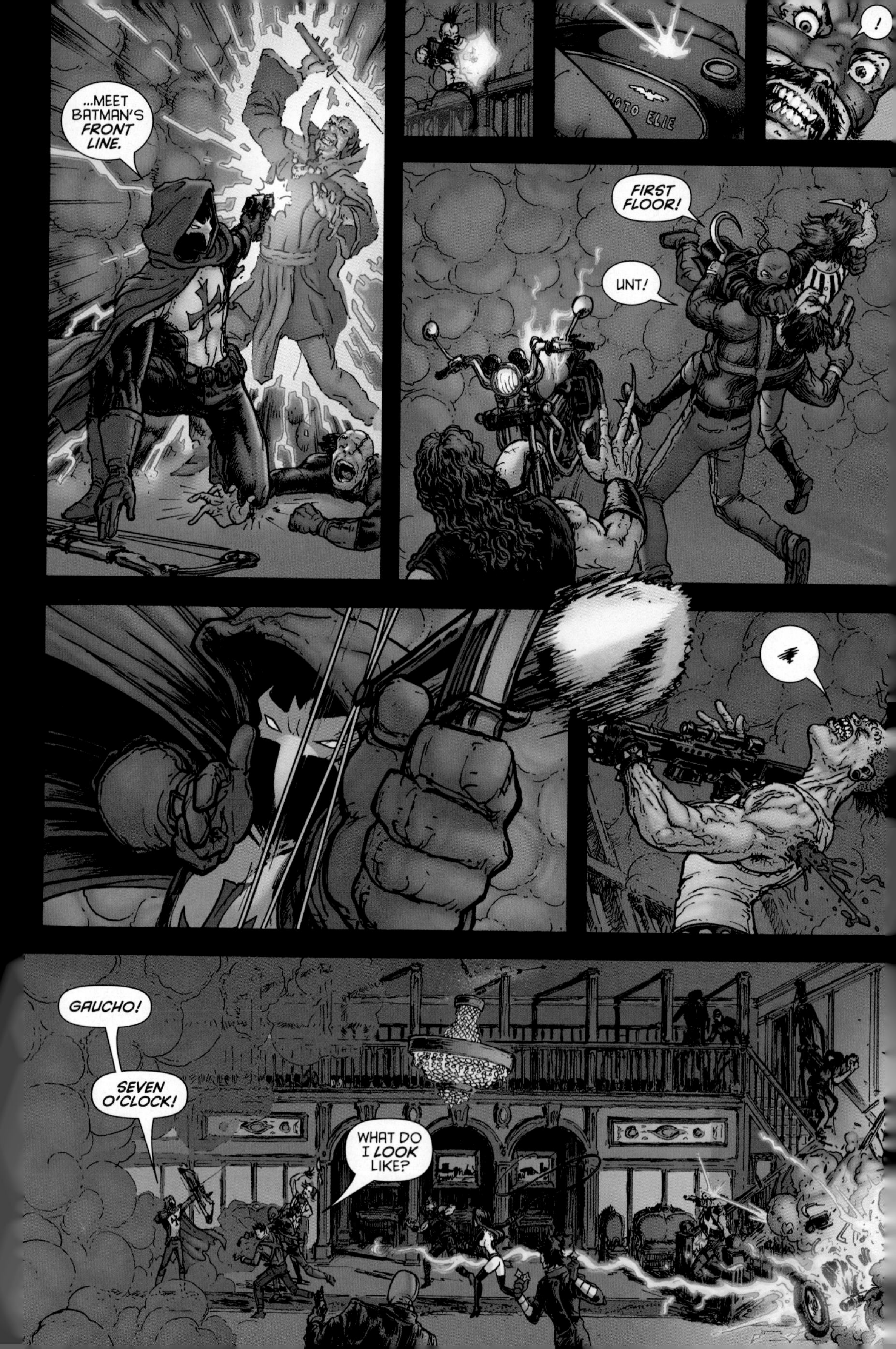
...MEET BATMAN'S FRONT LINE.
!
FIRST FLOOR!
UNT!
GAUCHO!
SEVEN O'CLOCK!
WHAT DO I LOOK LIKE?
MOTO ELIE

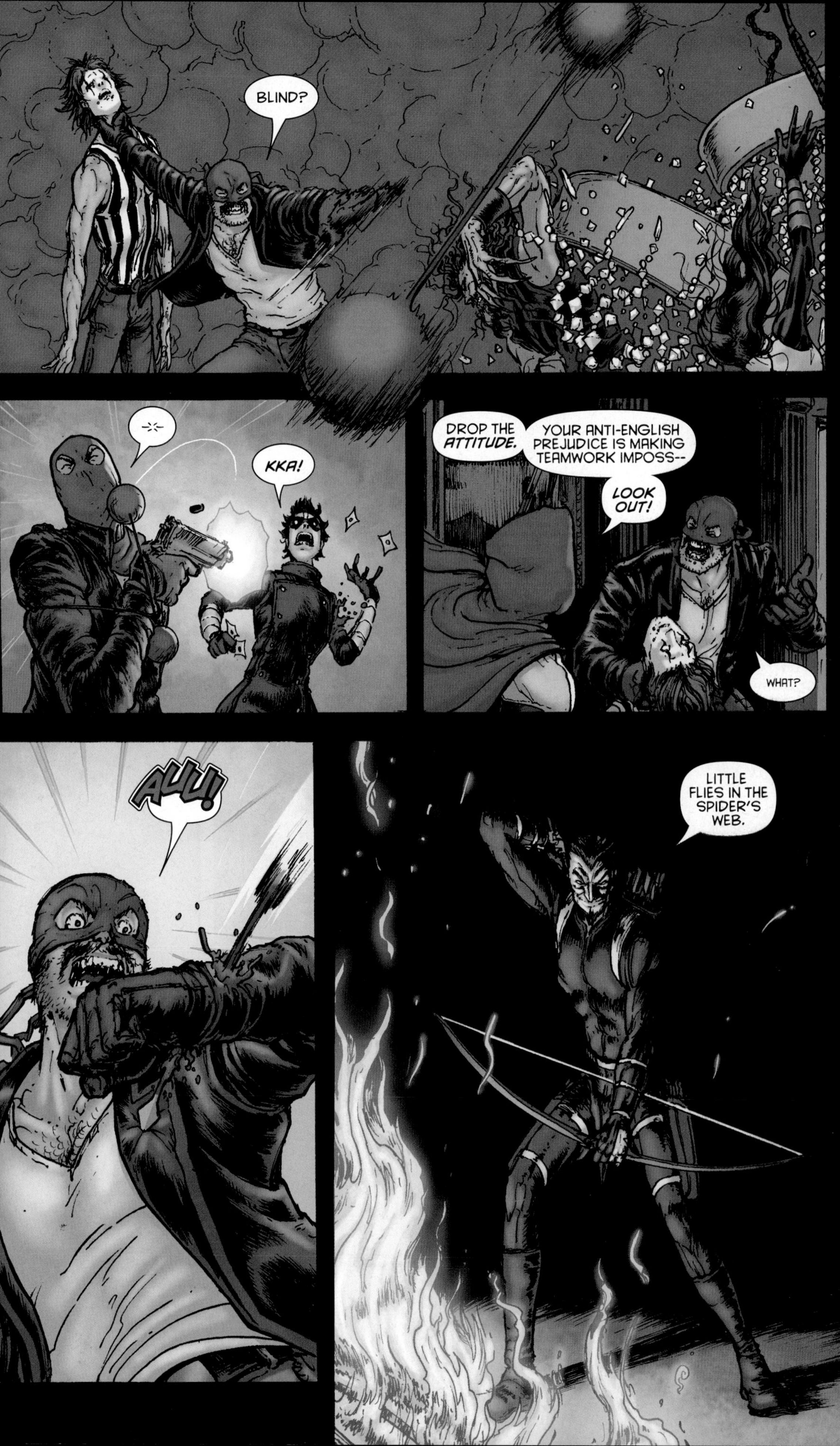
BLIND?
-!-
KKA!
DROP THE ATTITUDE.
YOUR ANTI-ENGLISH PREJUDICE IS MAKING TEAMWORK IMPOSS--
LOOK OUT!
WHAT?
AUU!
LITTLE FLIES IN THE SPIDER'S WEB.

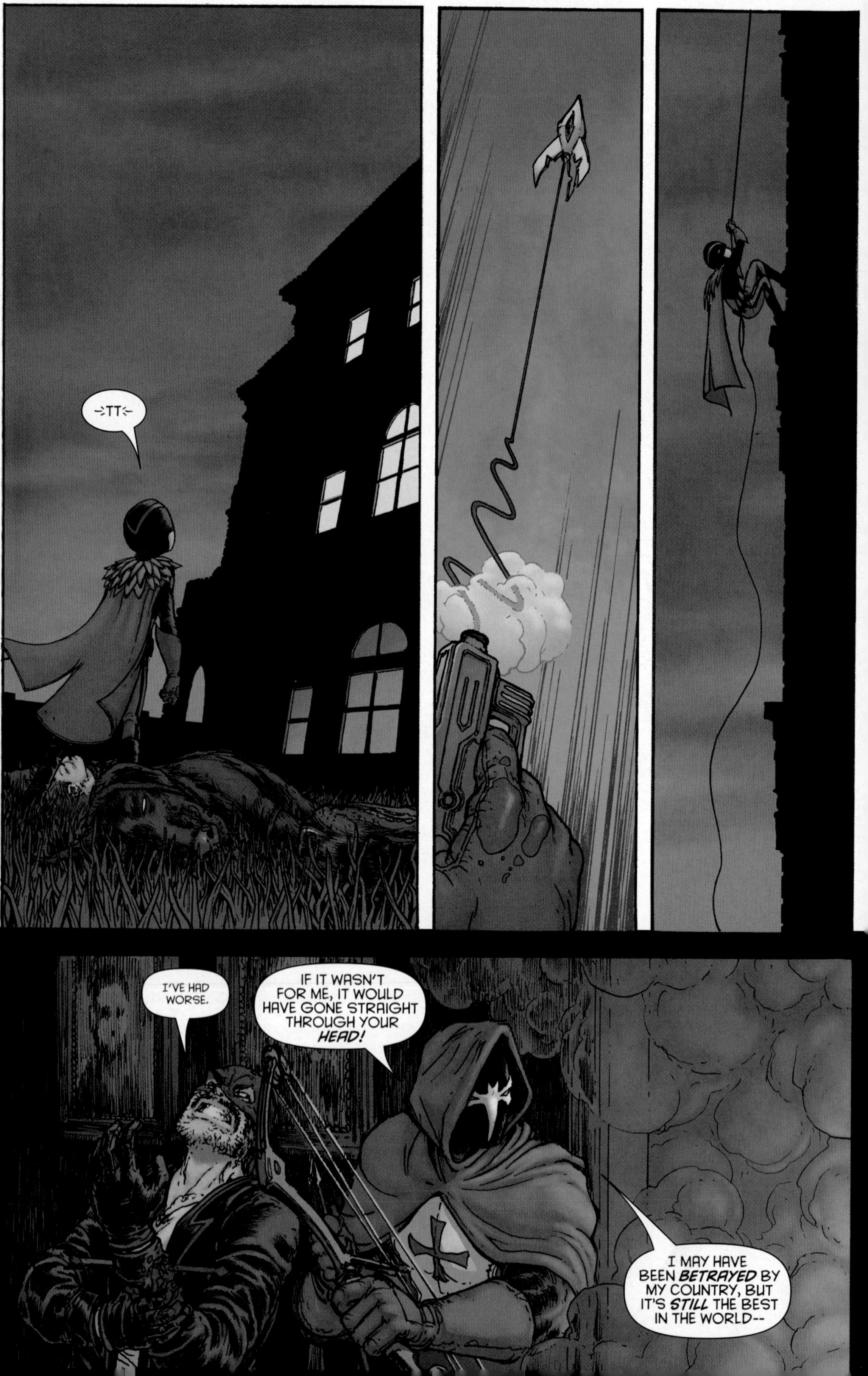
-TT-
I'VE HAD WORSE.
IF IT WASN'T FOR ME, IT WOULD HAVE GONE STRAIGHT THROUGH YOUR HEAD!
I MAY HAVE BEEN BETRAYED BY MY COUNTRY, BUT IT'S STILL THE BEST IN THE WORLD--

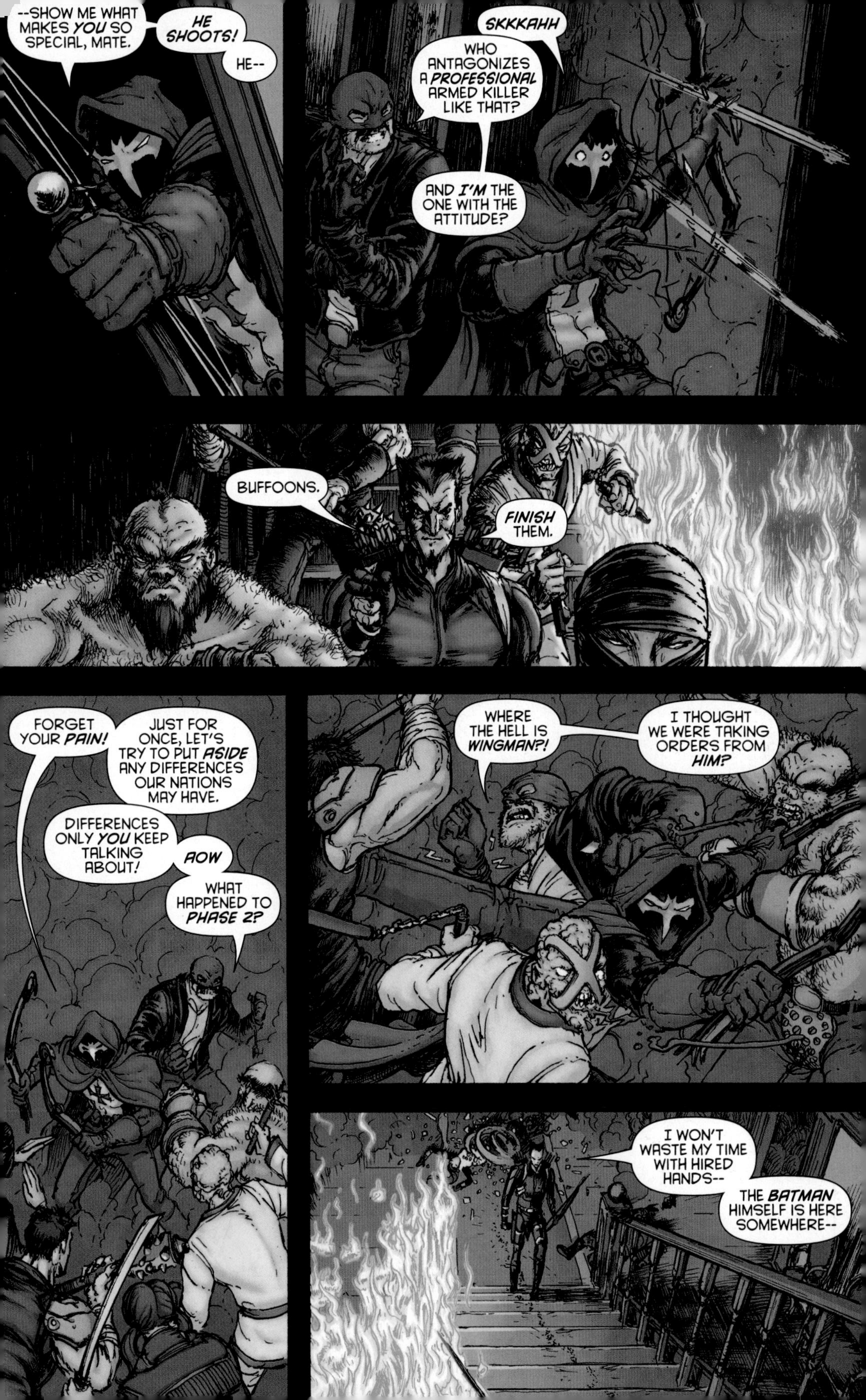
--SHOW ME WHAT MAKES YOU SO SPECIAL, MATE.
HE SHOOTS!
HE--
SKKKAHH
WHO ANTAGONIZES A PROFESSIONAL ARMED KILLER LIKE THAT?
AND I'M THE ONE WITH THE ATTITUDE?
BUFFOONS.
FINISH THEM.
FORGET YOUR PAIN!
JUST FOR ONCE, LET'S TRY TO PUT ASIDE ANY DIFFERENCES OUR NATIONS MAY HAVE.
DIFFERENCES ONLY YOU KEEP TALKING ABOUT!
AOW
WHAT HAPPENED TO PHASE 2?
WHERE THE HELL IS WINGMAN?!
I THOUGHT WE WERE TAKING ORDERS FROM HIM?
I WON'T WASTE MY TIME WITH HIRED HANDS--
THE BATMAN HIMSELF IS HERE SOMEWHERE--

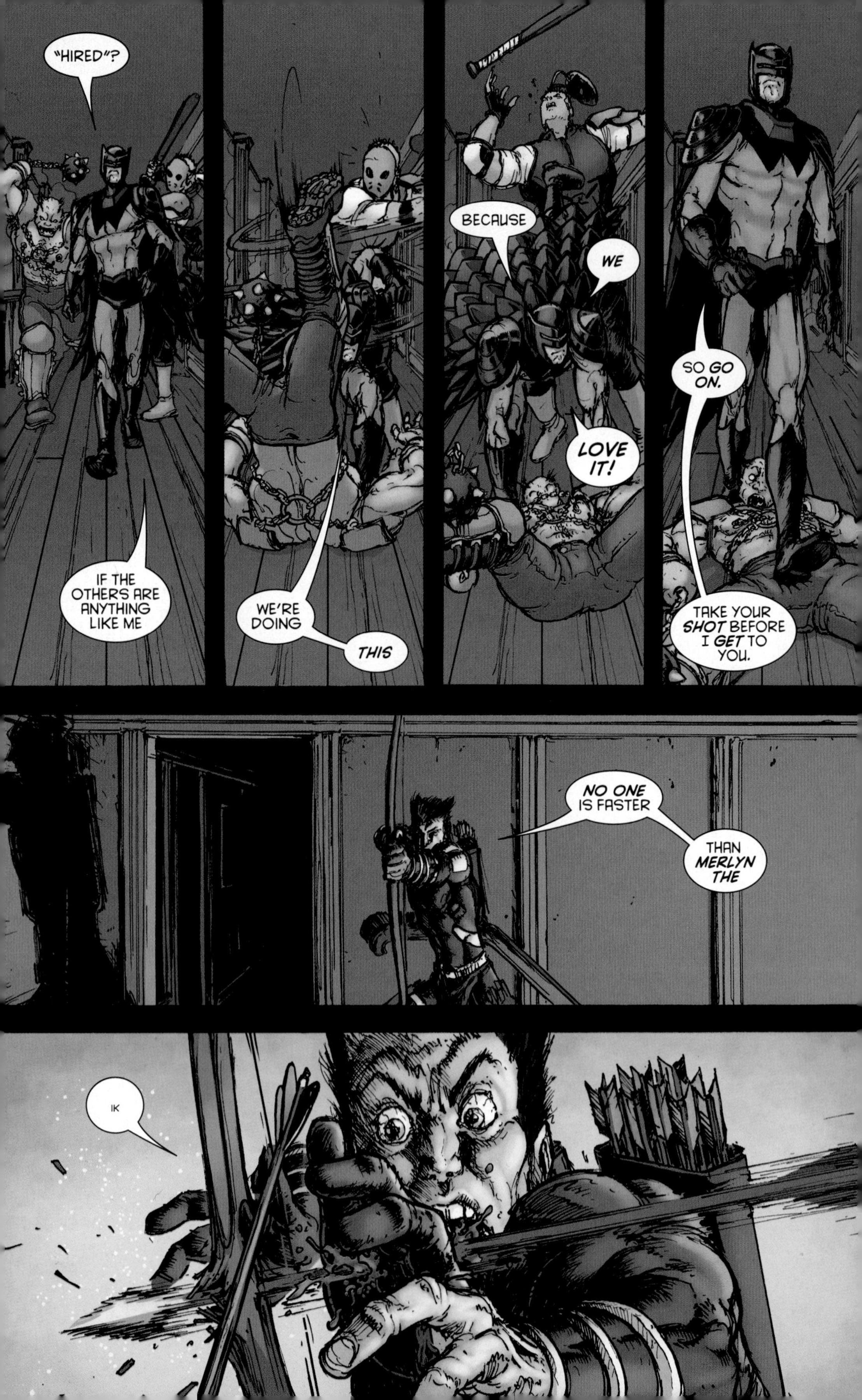
"HIRED"?
IF THE OTHERS ARE ANYTHING LIKE ME
WE'RE DOING
THIS
BECAUSE
WE
LOVE IT!
SO GO ON.
TAKE YOUR SHOT BEFORE I GET TO YOU.
NO ONE IS FASTER
THAN MERLYN THE
IK

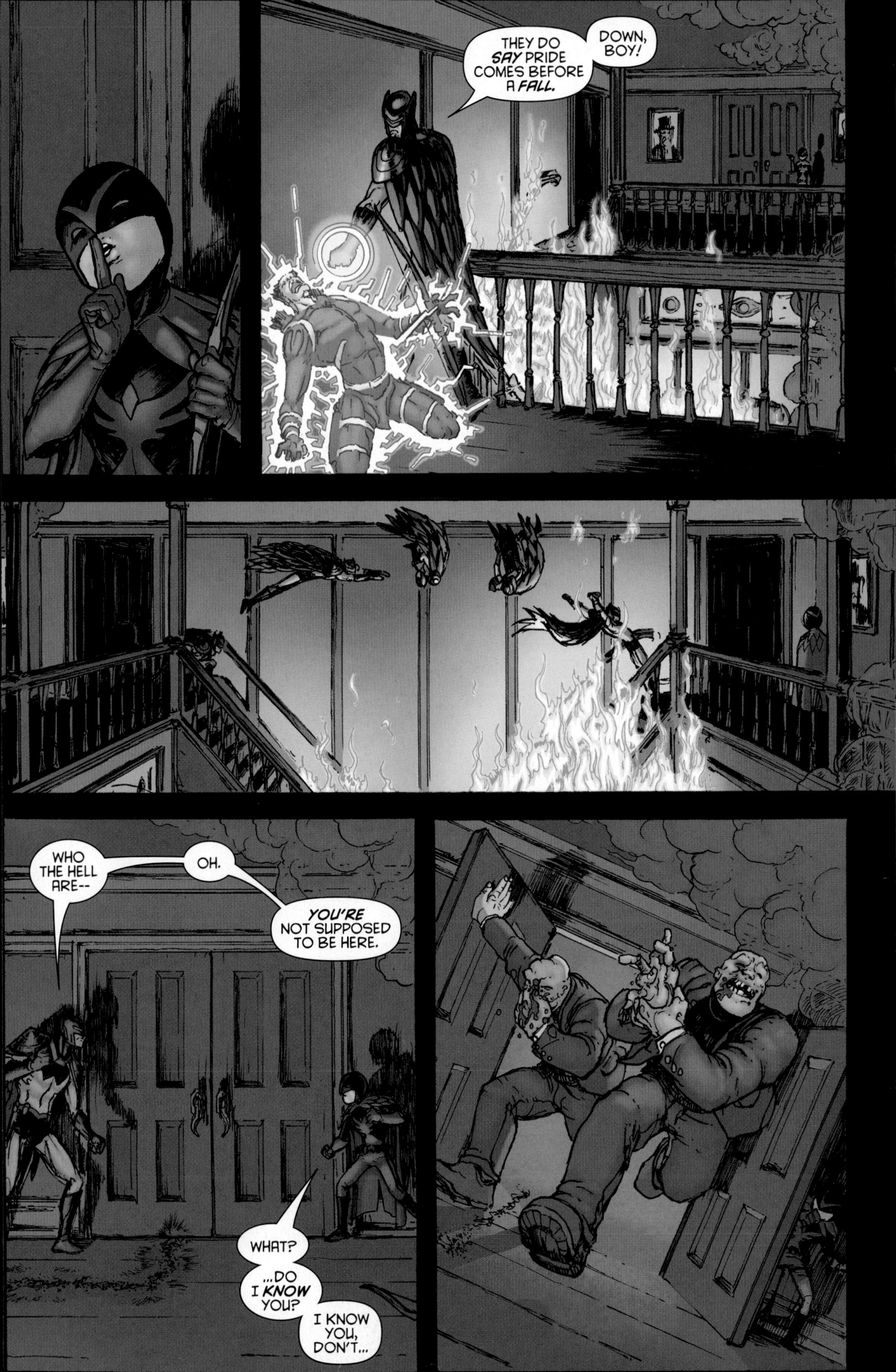
THEY DO SAY PRIDE COMES BEFORE A FALL.
DOWN, BOY!
WHO THE HELL ARE--
OH.
YOU'RE NOT SUPPOSED TO BE HERE.
WHAT?
...DO I KNOW YOU?
I KNOW YOU, DON'T...

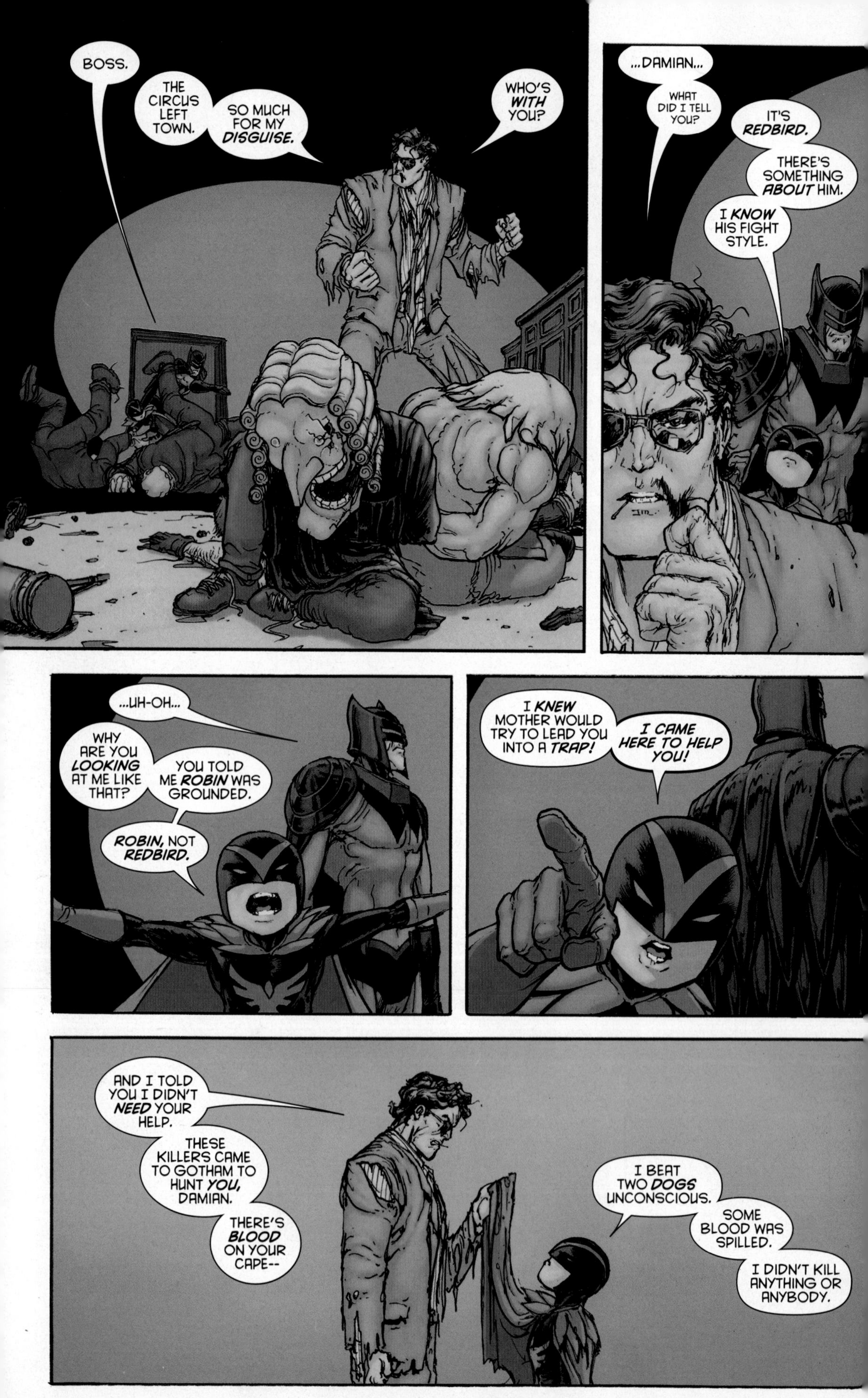
BOSS.
THE CIRCUS LEFT TOWN.
SO MUCH FOR MY DISGUISE.
WHO'S WITH YOU?
...DAMIAN...
WHAT DID I TELL YOU?
IT'S REDBIRD.
THERE'S SOMETHING ABOUT HIM.
I KNOW HIS FIGHT STYLE.
...UH-OH...
WHY ARE YOU LOOKING AT ME LIKE THAT?
YOU TOLD ME ROBIN WAS GROUNDED.
ROBIN, NOT REDBIRD.
I KNEW MOTHER WOULD TRY TO LEAD YOU INTO A TRAP!
I CAME HERE TO HELP YOU!
AND I TOLD YOU I DIDN'T NEED YOUR HELP.
THESE KILLERS CAME TO GOTHAM TO HUNT YOU, DAMIAN.
THERE'S BLOOD ON YOUR CAPE--
I BEAT TWO DOGS UNCONSCIOUS.
SOME BLOOD WAS SPILLED.
I DIDN'T KILL ANYTHING OR ANYBODY.

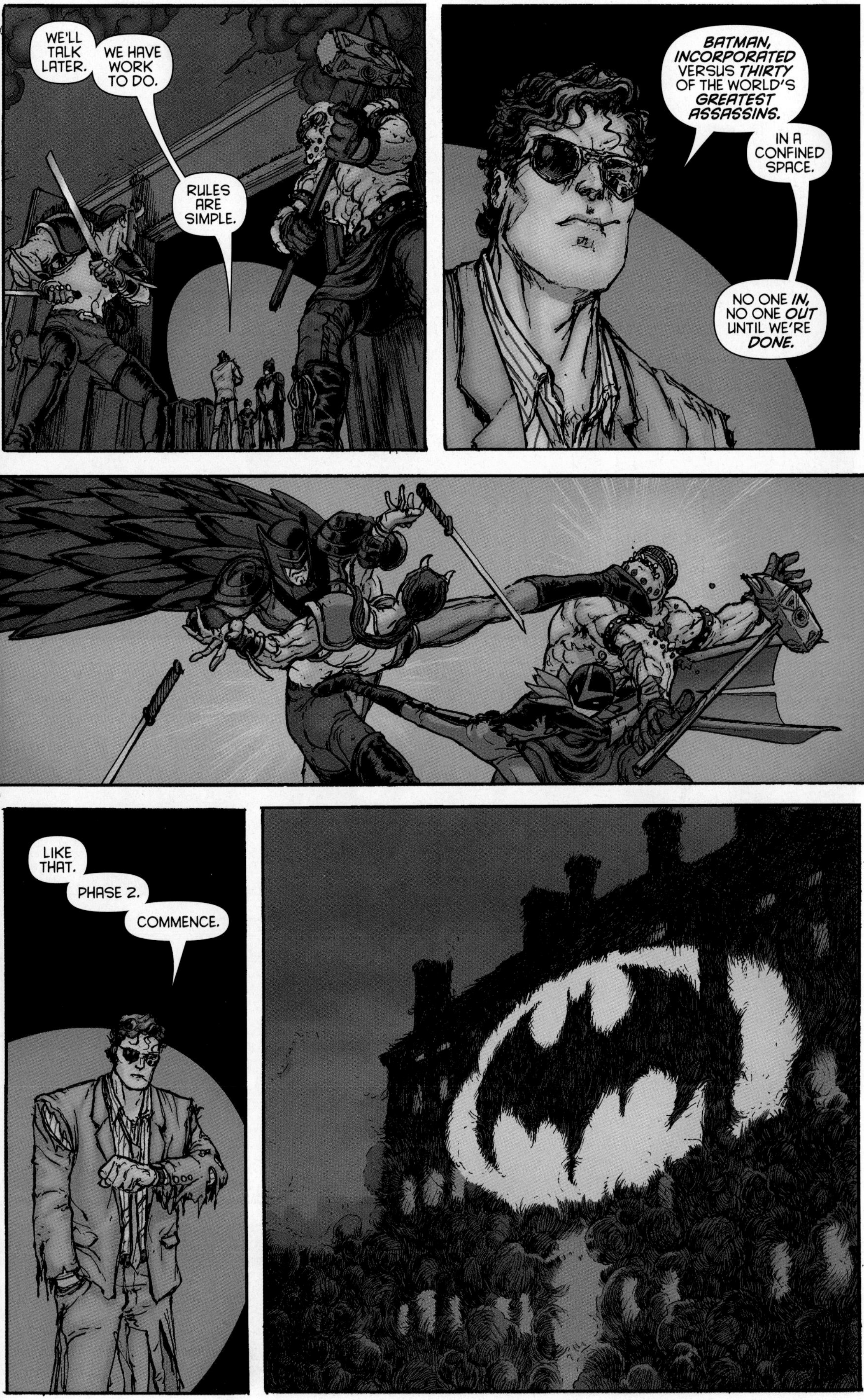
WE'LL TALK LATER.
WE HAVE WORK TO DO.
RULES ARE SIMPLE.
BATMAN, INCORPORATED VERSUS THIRTY OF THE WORLD'S GREATEST ASSASSINS.
IN A CONFINED SPACE.
NO ONE IN, NO ONE OUT UNTIL WE'RE DONE.
LIKE THAT.
PHASE 2.
COMMENCE.

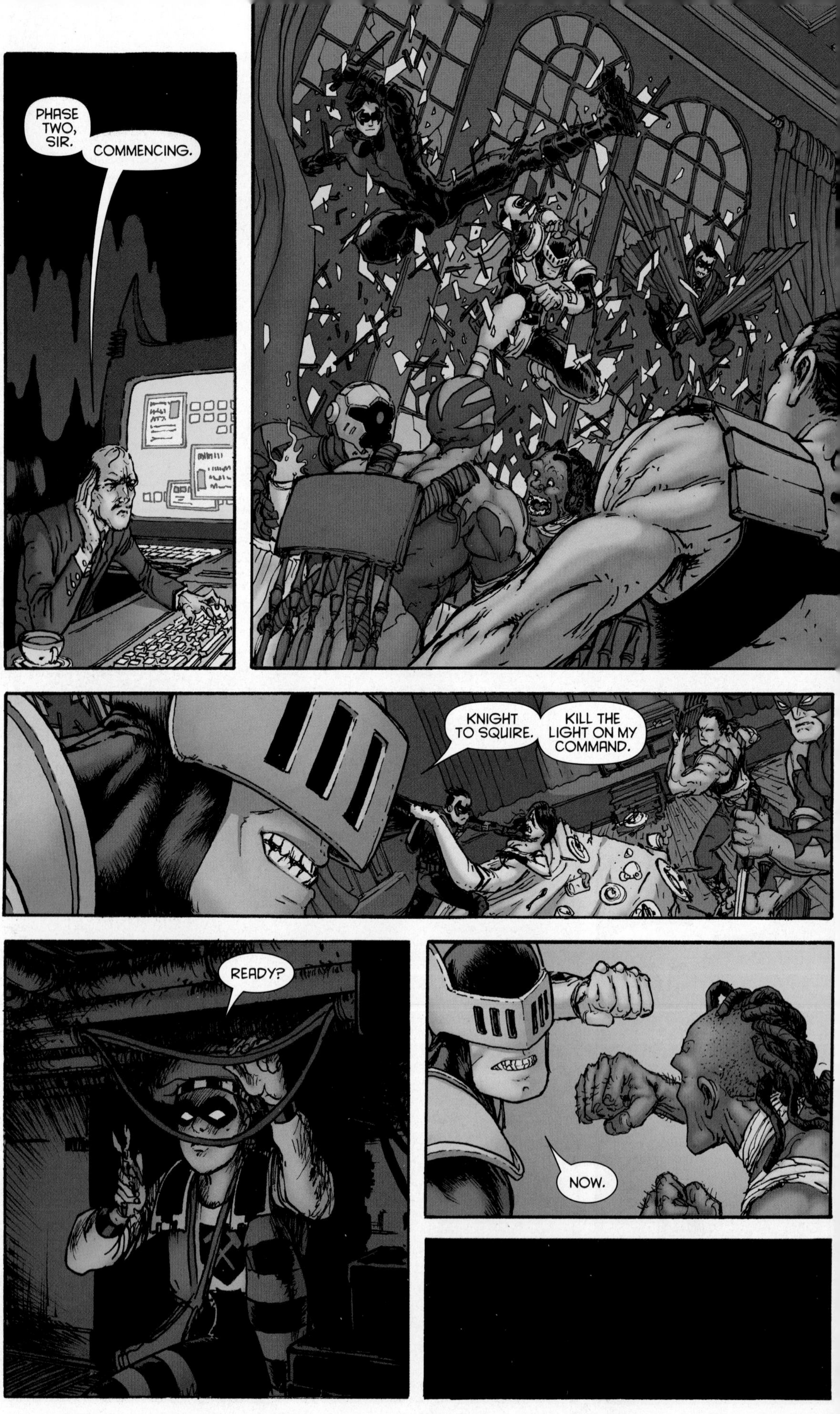
PHASE TWO, SIR.
COMMENCING.
KNIGHT TO SQUIRE.
KILL THE LIGHT ON MY COMMAND.
READY?
NOW.

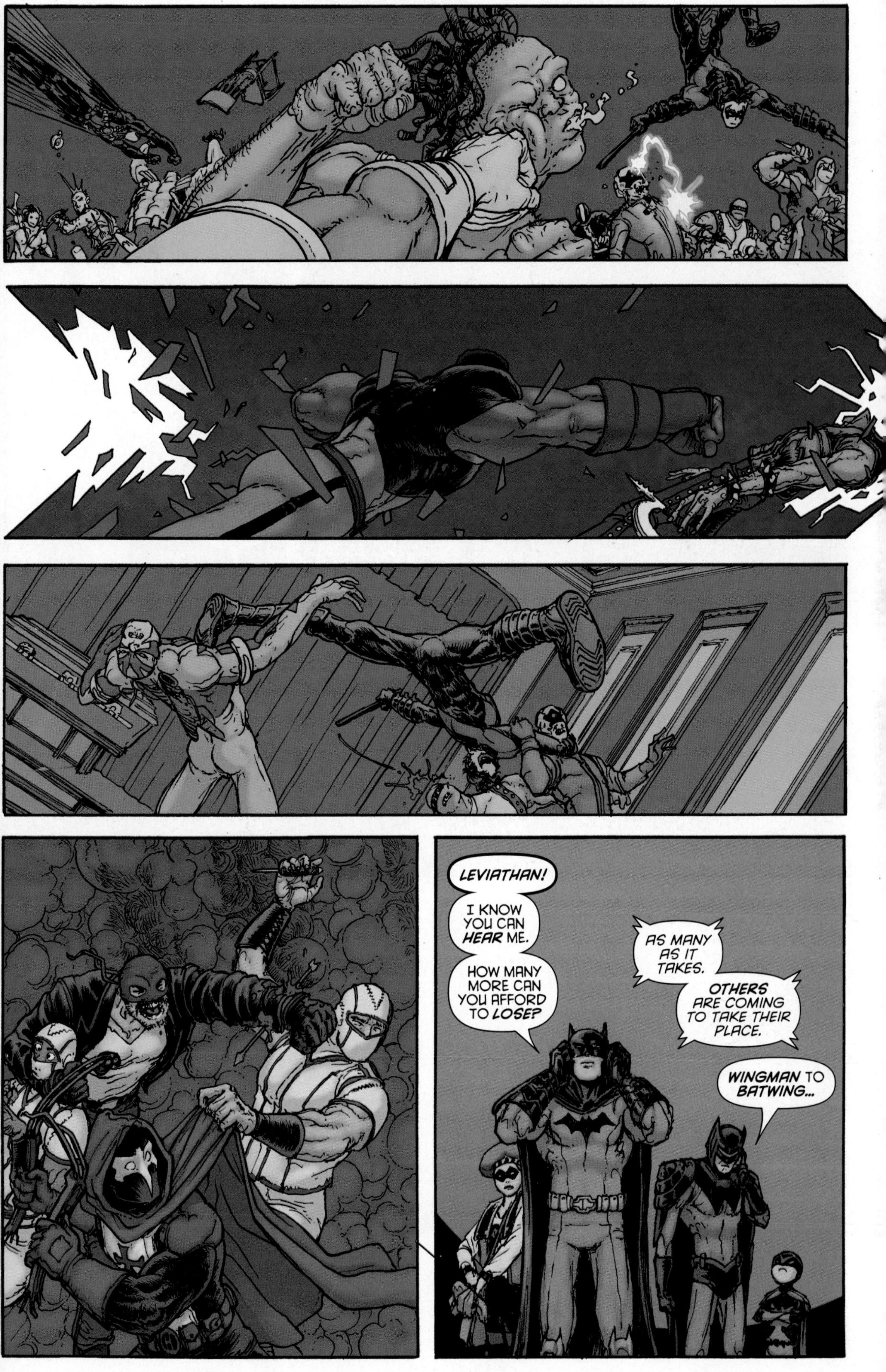
LEVIATHAN!
I KNOW YOU CAN HEAR ME.
HOW MANY MORE CAN YOU AFFORD TO LOSE?
AS MANY AS IT TAKES.
OTHERS ARE COMING TO TAKE THEIR PLACE.
WINGMAN TO BATWING...

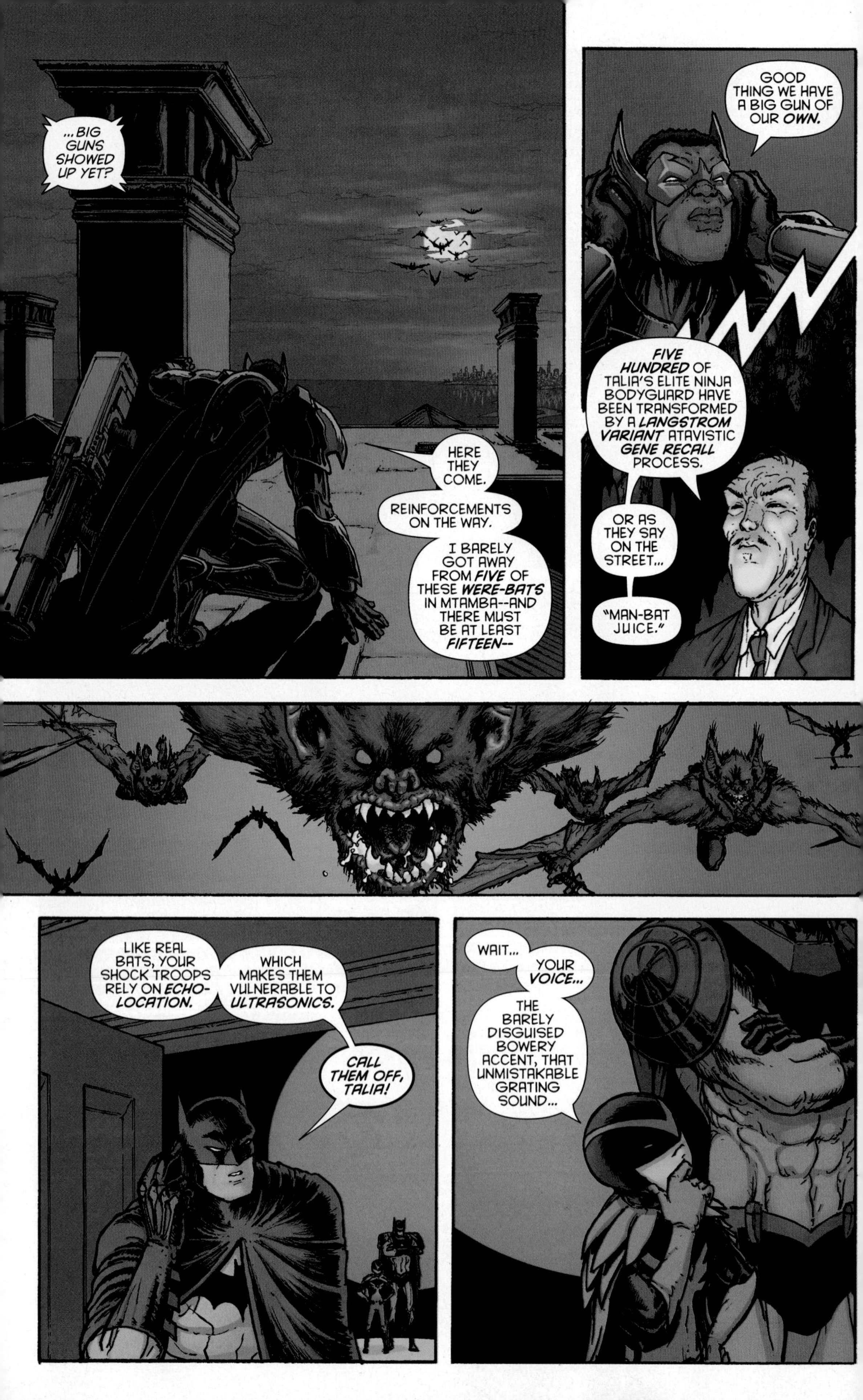

...BIG GUNS SHOWED UP YET?
GOOD THING WE HAVE A BIG GUN OF OUR *OWN.*
HERE THEY COME.
REINFORCEMENTS ON THE WAY.
I BARELY GOT AWAY FROM *FIVE* OF THESE *WERE-BATS* IN MTAMBA--AND THERE MUST BE AT LEAST *FIFTEEN--*
FIVE HUNDRED OF TALIA'S ELITE NINJA BODYGUARD HAVE BEEN TRANSFORMED BY A *LANGSTROM VARIANT* ATAVISTIC *GENE RECALL* PROCESS.
OR AS THEY SAY ON THE STREET...
"MAN-BAT JUICE."
LIKE REAL BATS, YOUR SHOCK TROOPS RELY ON *ECHO-LOCATION.*
WHICH MAKES THEM VULNERABLE TO *ULTRASONICS.*
CALL THEM OFF, TALIA!
WAIT...
YOUR *VOICE...*
THE BARELY DISGUISED BOWERY ACCENT, THAT UNMISTAKABLE GRATING SOUND...

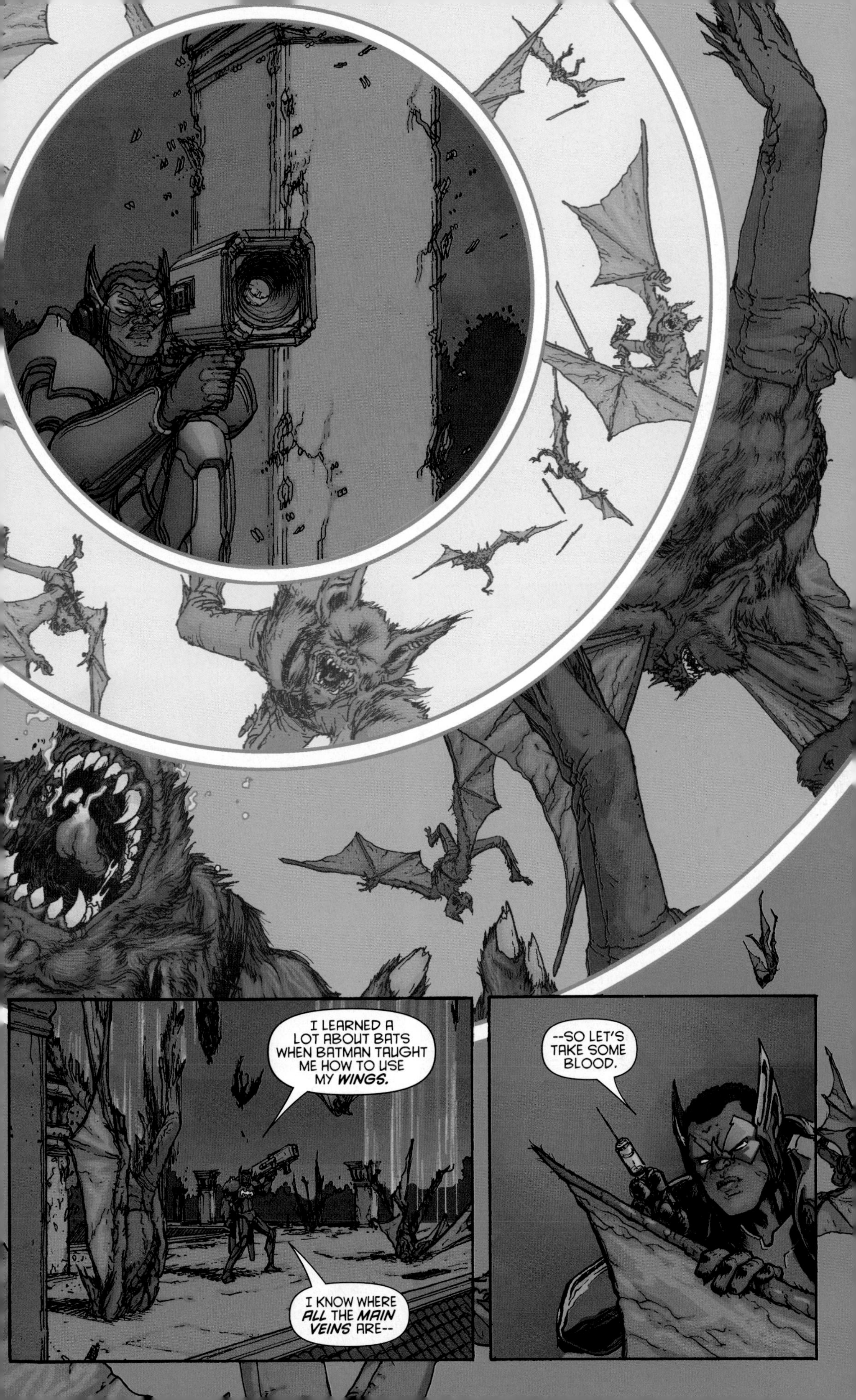
I LEARNED A LOT ABOUT BATS WHEN BATMAN TAUGHT ME HOW TO USE MY WINGS.
I KNOW WHERE ALL THE MAIN VEINS ARE--
--SO LET'S TAKE SOME BLOOD.

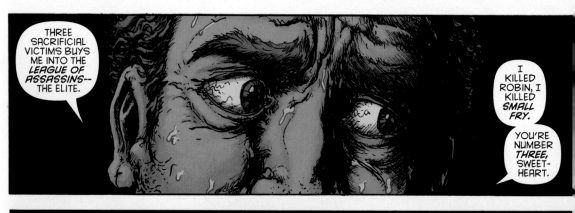

THREE SACRIFICIAL VICTIMS BUYS ME INTO THE *LEAGUE OF ASSASSINS*-- THE ELITE.

I KILLED ROBIN, I KILLED *SMALL FRY.*

YOU'RE NUMBER *THREE,* SWEETHEART.

YOU HAVE A GREAT VOICE, I'M SORRY.

BUT I DO *THIS,* I MAKE THE *BIG TIME.*

I DON'T NEED TO RUN ERRANDS FOR *BATMAN* OR *ANYBODY* ELSE.

...LEMME GO...

...WHATEVER THIS IS...IT'S NOT...

I DID THIS FOR MY *CHILD,* SO YOU SHUT YOUR FACE!

YOU DON'T LOOK AT ME!

YOU DON'T GET TO *JUDGE* ME.

GAHH--

YOU'RE *CHOKING* ME.

WHO'S THERE?

NOW YOU'RE IN TROUBLE.

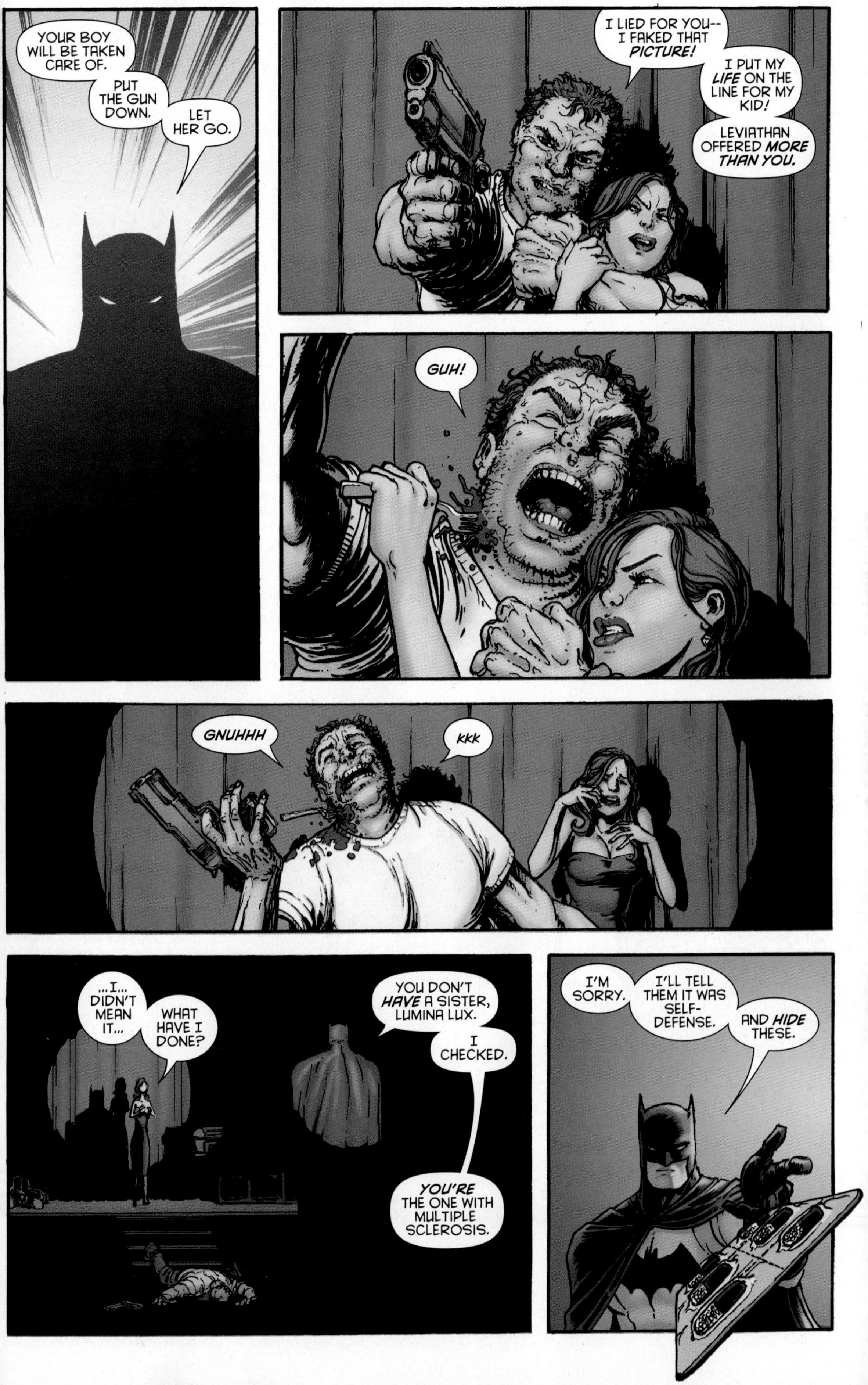
YOUR BOY WILL BE TAKEN CARE OF.
PUT THE GUN DOWN.
LET HER GO.
I LIED FOR YOU-- I FAKED THAT PICTURE!
I PUT MY LIFE ON THE LINE FOR MY KID!
LEVIATHAN OFFERED MORE THAN YOU.
GUH!
GNUHHH
kkk
...I... DIDN'T MEAN IT...
WHAT HAVE I DONE?
YOU DON'T HAVE A SISTER, LUMINA LUX.
I CHECKED.
YOU'RE THE ONE WITH MULTIPLE SCLEROSIS.
I'M SORRY.
I'LL TELL THEM IT WAS SELF-DEFENSE.
AND HIDE THESE.

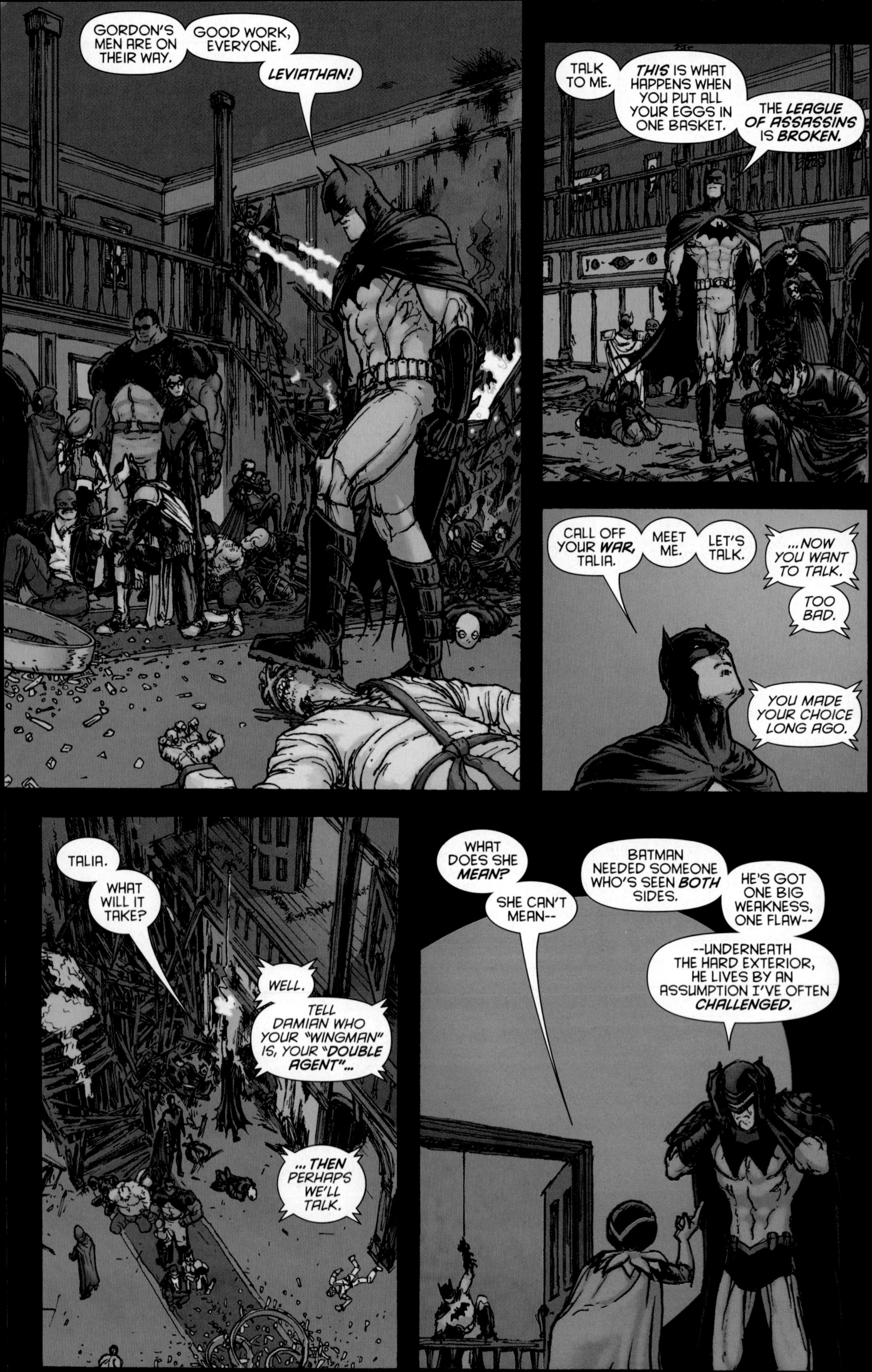
GORDON'S MEN ARE ON THEIR WAY.
GOOD WORK, EVERYONE.
LEVIATHAN!
TALK TO ME.
THIS IS WHAT HAPPENS WHEN YOU PUT ALL YOUR EGGS IN ONE BASKET.
THE LEAGUE OF ASSASSINS IS BROKEN.
CALL OFF YOUR WAR, TALIA.
MEET ME.
LET'S TALK.
...NOW YOU WANT TO TALK.
TOO BAD.
YOU MADE YOUR CHOICE LONG AGO.
TALIA.
WHAT WILL IT TAKE?
WELL.
TELL DAMIAN WHO YOUR "WINGMAN" IS, YOUR "DOUBLE AGENT"...
...THEN PERHAPS WE'LL TALK.
WHAT DOES SHE MEAN?
SHE CAN'T MEAN--
BATMAN NEEDED SOMEONE WHO'S SEEN BOTH SIDES.
HE'S GOT ONE BIG WEAKNESS, ONE FLAW--
--UNDERNEATH THE HARD EXTERIOR, HE LIVES BY AN ASSUMPTION I'VE OFTEN CHALLENGED.

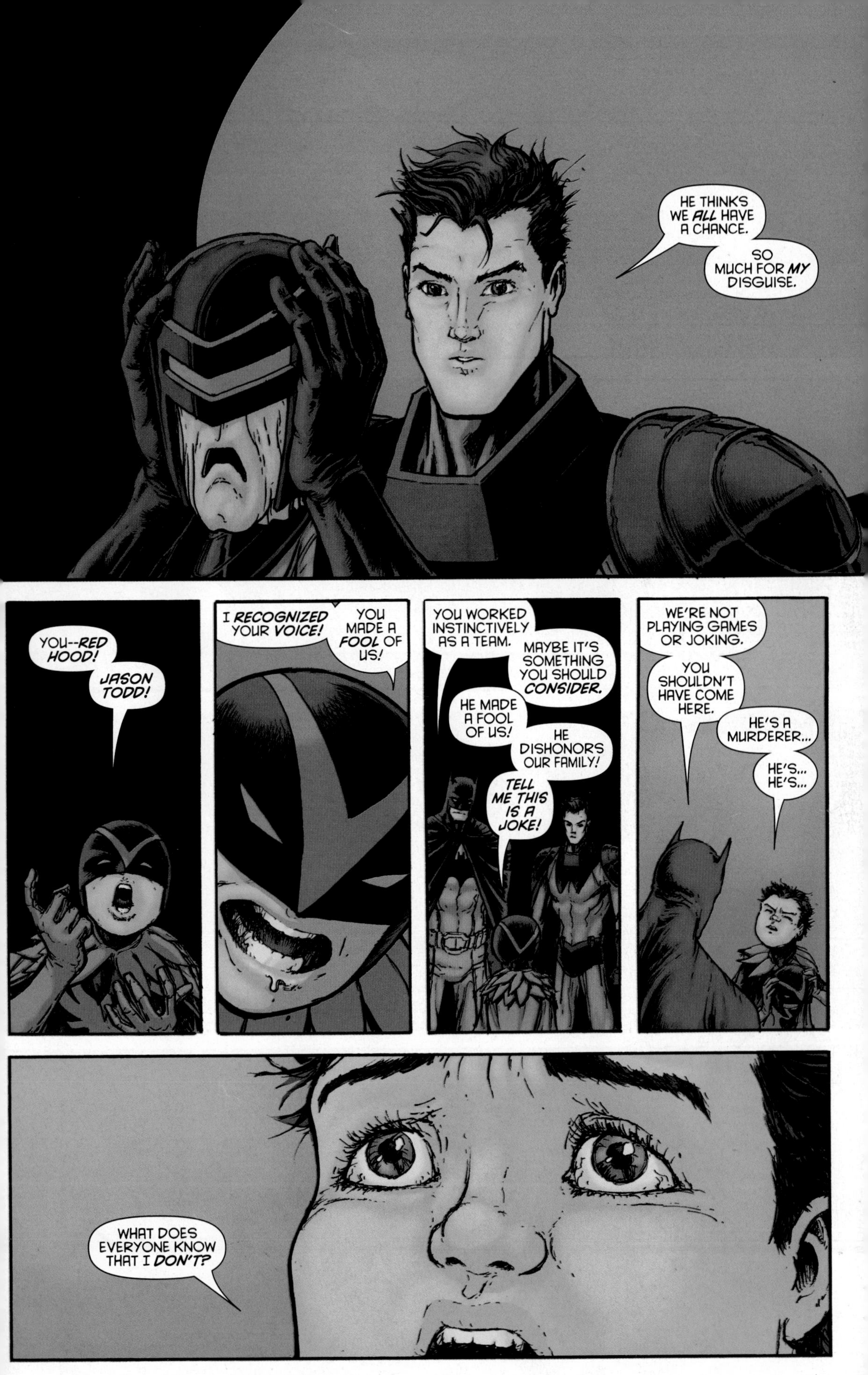

HE THINKS WE ALL HAVE A CHANCE.
SO MUCH FOR MY DISGUISE.
YOU--RED HOOD!
JASON TODD!
I RECOGNIZED YOUR VOICE!
YOU MADE A FOOL OF US!
YOU WORKED INSTINCTIVELY AS A TEAM.
MAYBE IT'S SOMETHING YOU SHOULD CONSIDER.
HE MADE A FOOL OF US!
HE DISHONORS OUR FAMILY!
TELL ME THIS IS A JOKE!
WE'RE NOT PLAYING GAMES OR JOKING.
YOU SHOULDN'T HAVE COME HERE.
HE'S A MURDERER...
HE'S... HE'S...
WHAT DOES EVERYONE KNOW THAT I DON'T?

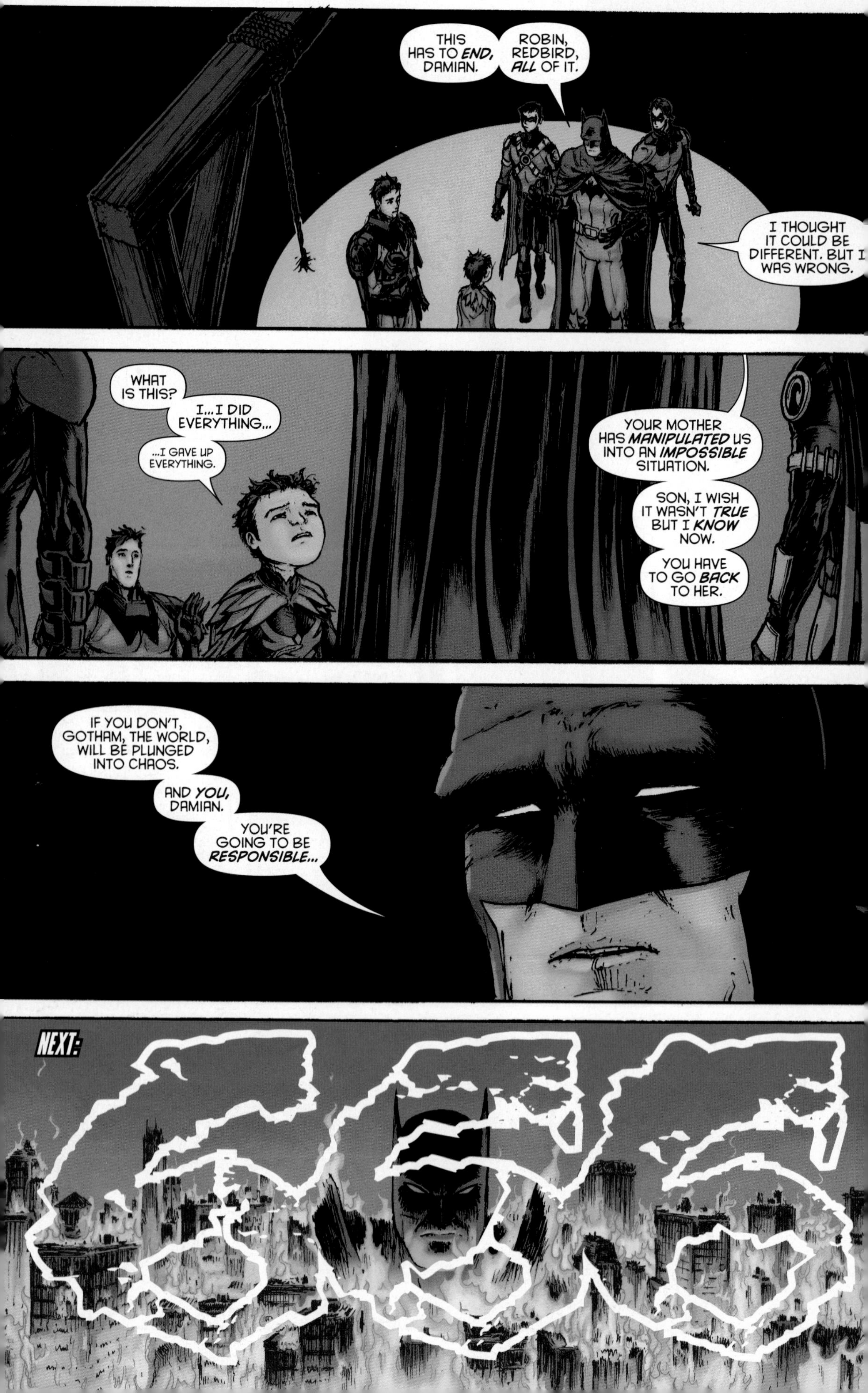
THIS HAS TO END, DAMIAN.
ROBIN, REDBIRD, ALL OF IT.
I THOUGHT IT COULD BE DIFFERENT. BUT I WAS WRONG.
WHAT IS THIS?
I...I DID EVERYTHING...
...I GAVE UP EVERYTHING.
YOUR MOTHER HAS MANIPULATED US INTO AN IMPOSSIBLE SITUATION.
SON, I WISH IT WASN'T TRUE BUT I KNOW NOW.
YOU HAVE TO GO BACK TO HER.
IF YOU DON'T, GOTHAM, THE WORLD, WILL BE PLUNGED INTO CHAOS.
AND YOU, DAMIAN.
YOU'RE GOING TO BE RESPONSIBLE...
NEXT:

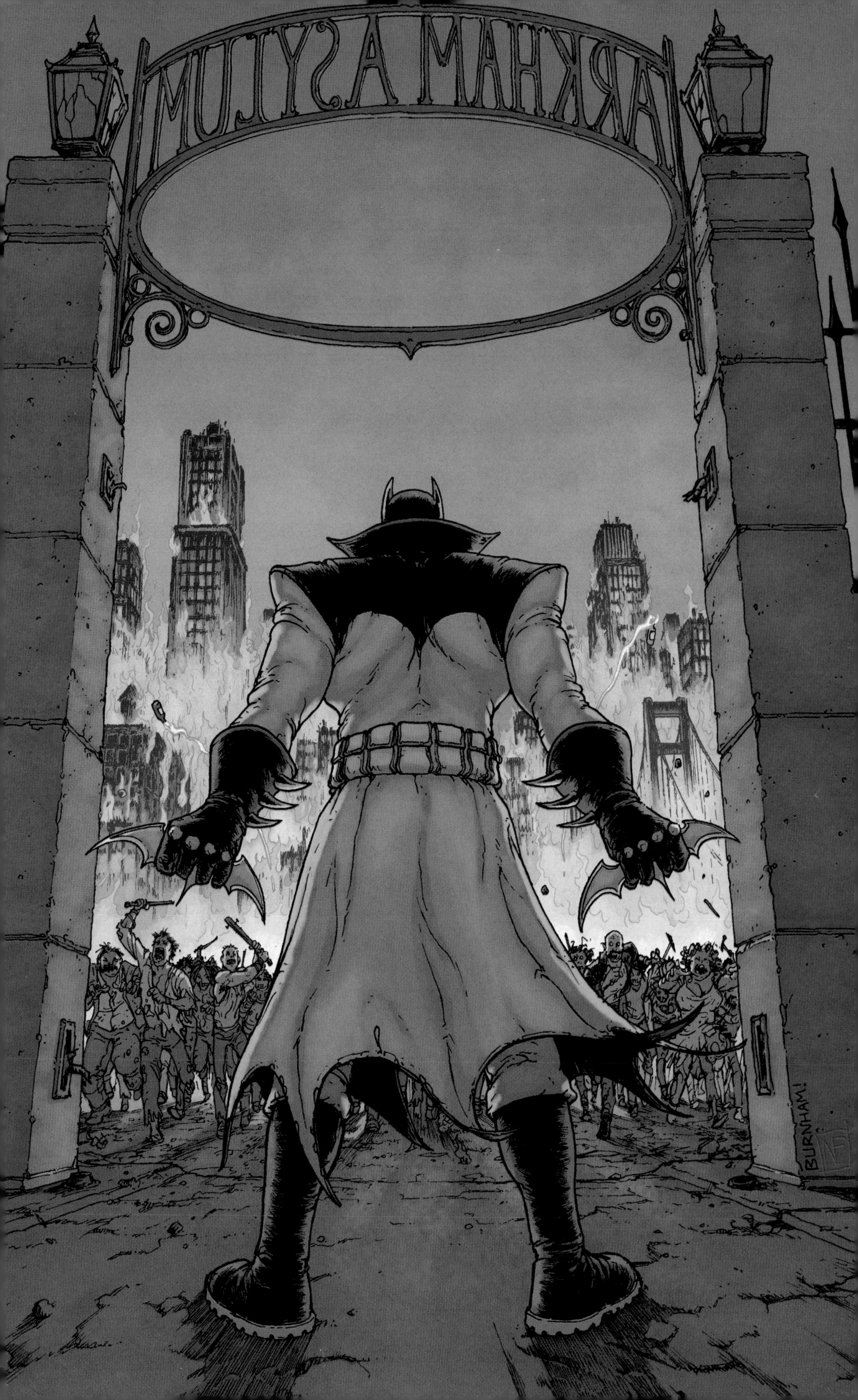
ARKHAM ASYLUM
BURNHAM!

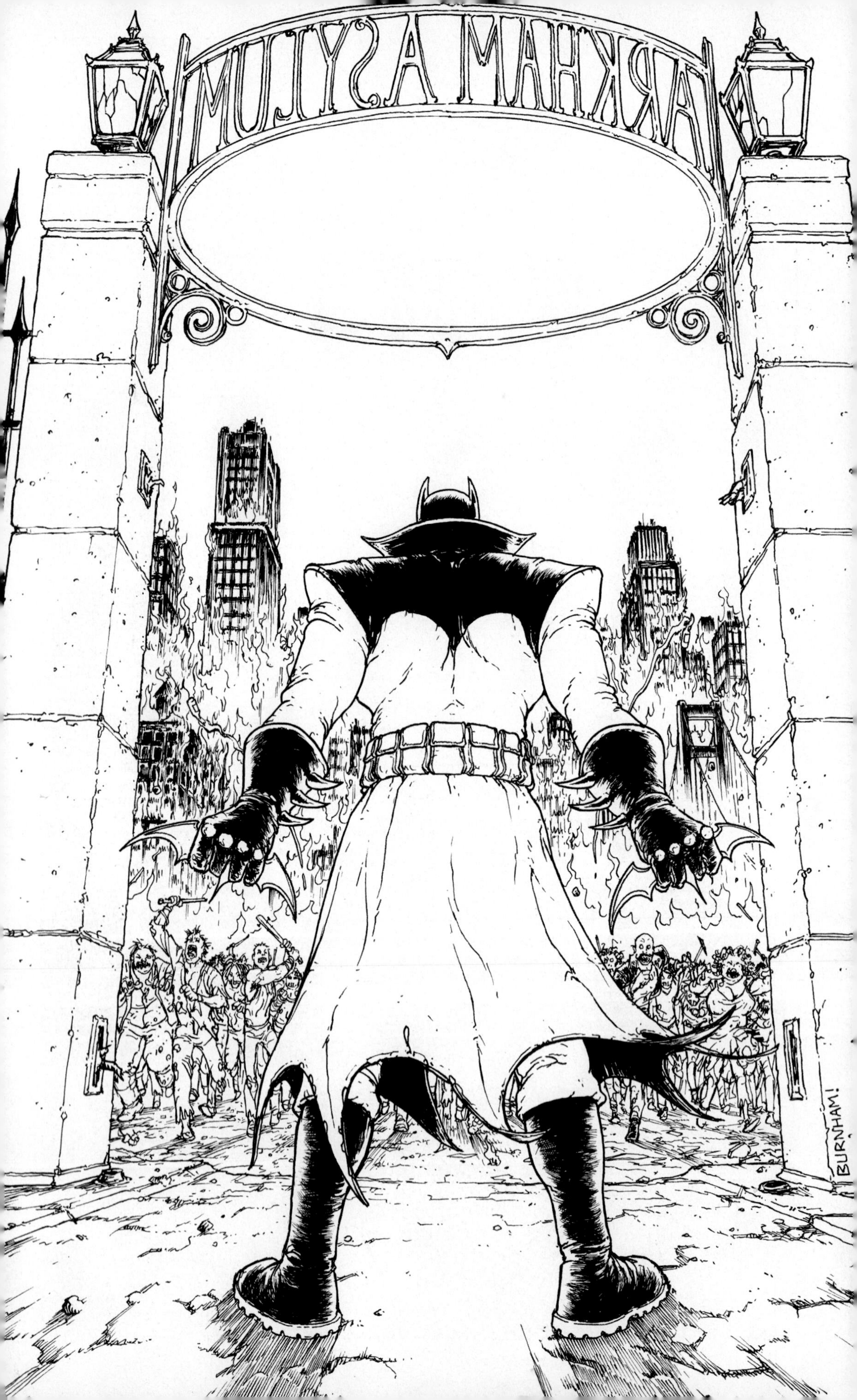
ARKHAM ASYLUM
BURNHAM!

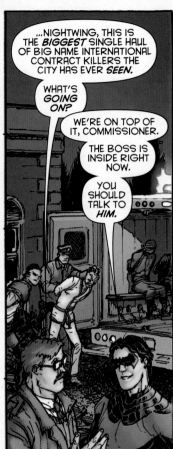

...NIGHTWING, THIS IS THE *BIGGEST* SINGLE HAUL OF BIG NAME INTERNATIONAL CONTRACT KILLER'S THE CITY HAS EVER *SEEN.*

WHAT'S *GOING ON?*

WE'RE ON TOP OF IT, COMMISSIONER.

THE BOSS IS INSIDE RIGHT NOW.

YOU SHOULD TALK TO *HIM.*

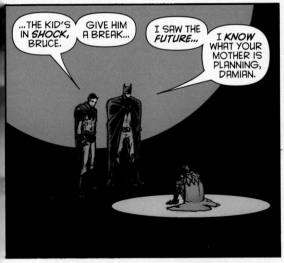

...THE KID'S IN *SHOCK,* BRUCE.

GIVE HIM A BREAK...

I SAW THE *FUTURE...*

I *KNOW* WHAT YOUR MOTHER IS PLANNING, DAMIAN.

SHE *WANTED* YOU TO JOIN ME AS *ROBIN.*

SHE INTENDS FOR YOU TO *REPLACE* ME, AND THAT CAN'T HAPPEN.

BECAUSE... IF *YOU* BECOME *BATMAN...*

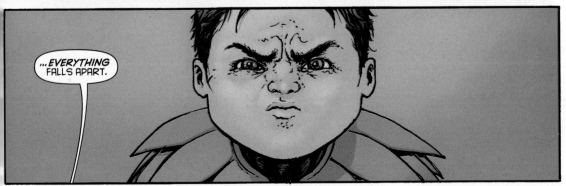

...*EVERYTHING* FALLS APART.

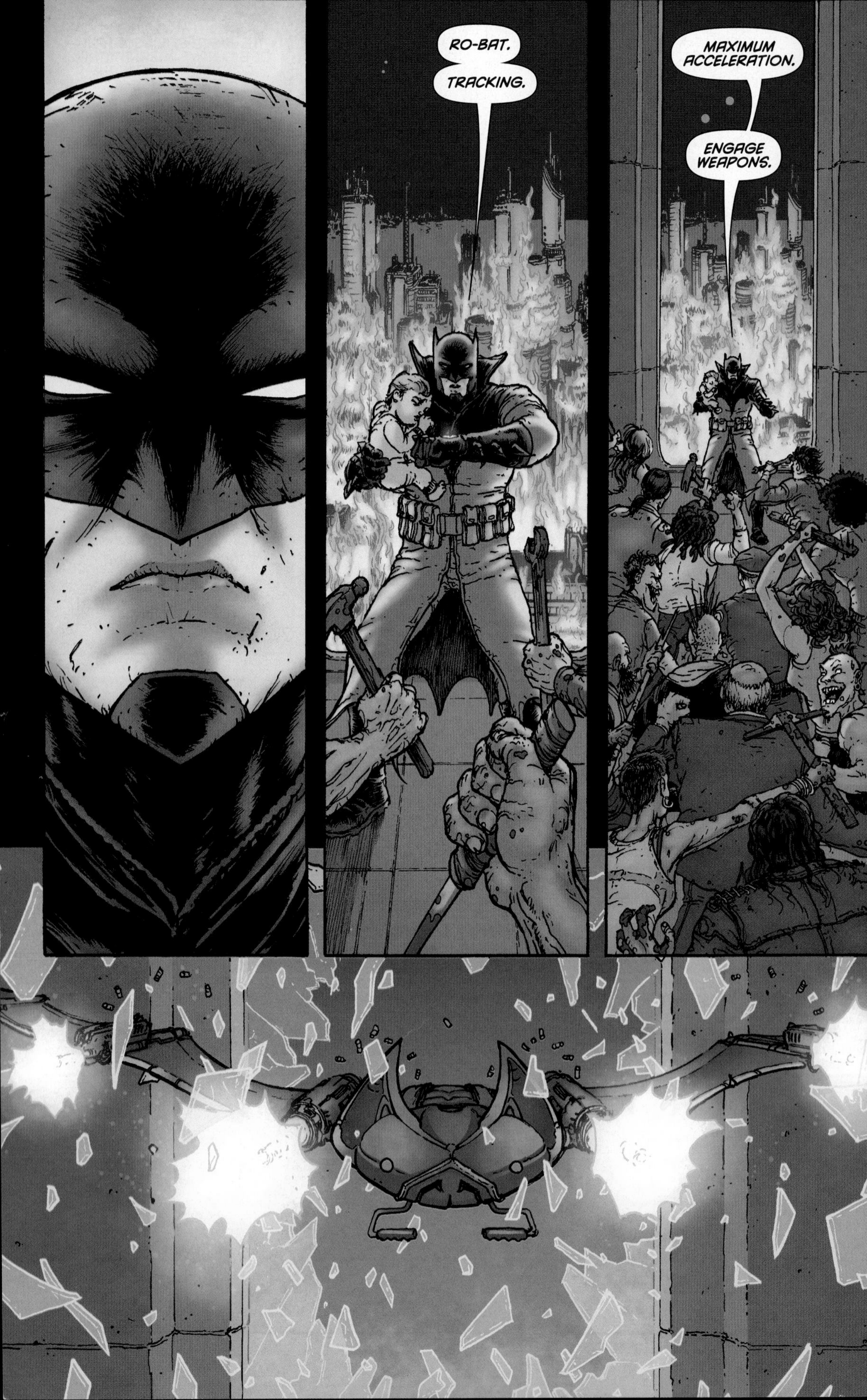
RO-BAT.
TRACKING.
MAXIMUM ACCELERATION.
ENGAGE WEAPONS.

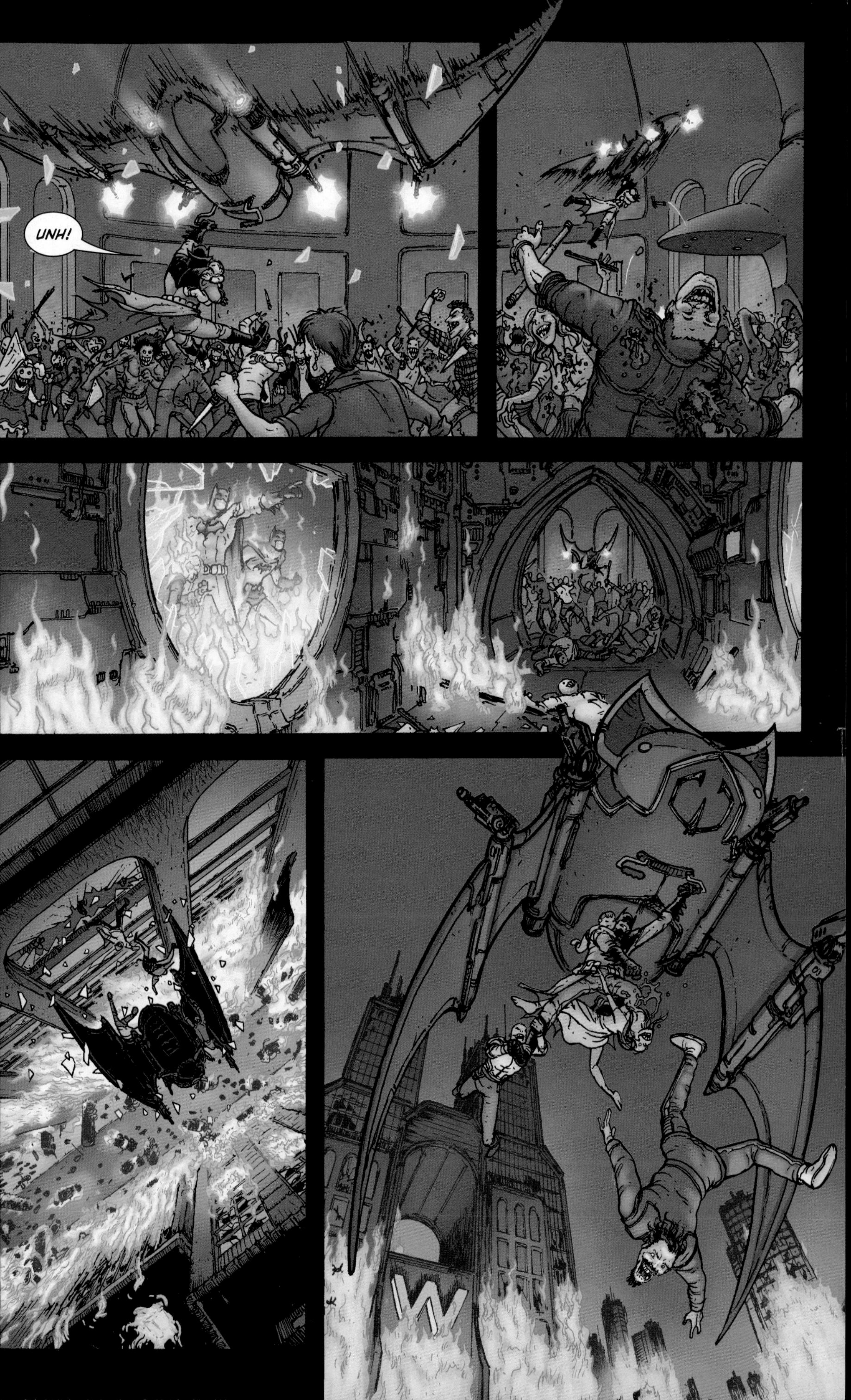
UNH!

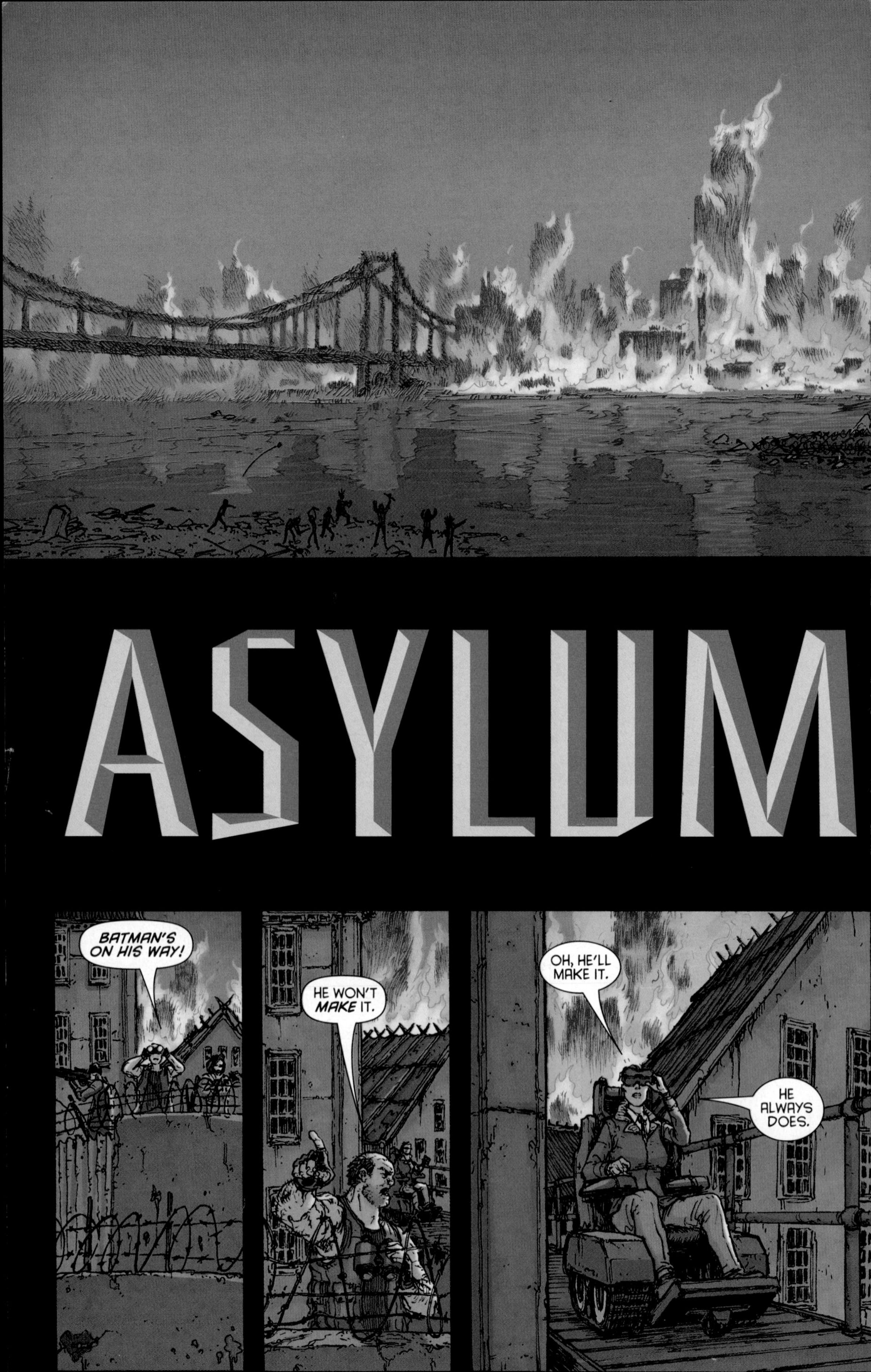
ASYLUM
BATMAN'S ON HIS WAY!
HE WON'T MAKE IT.
OH, HE'LL MAKE IT.
HE ALWAYS DOES.

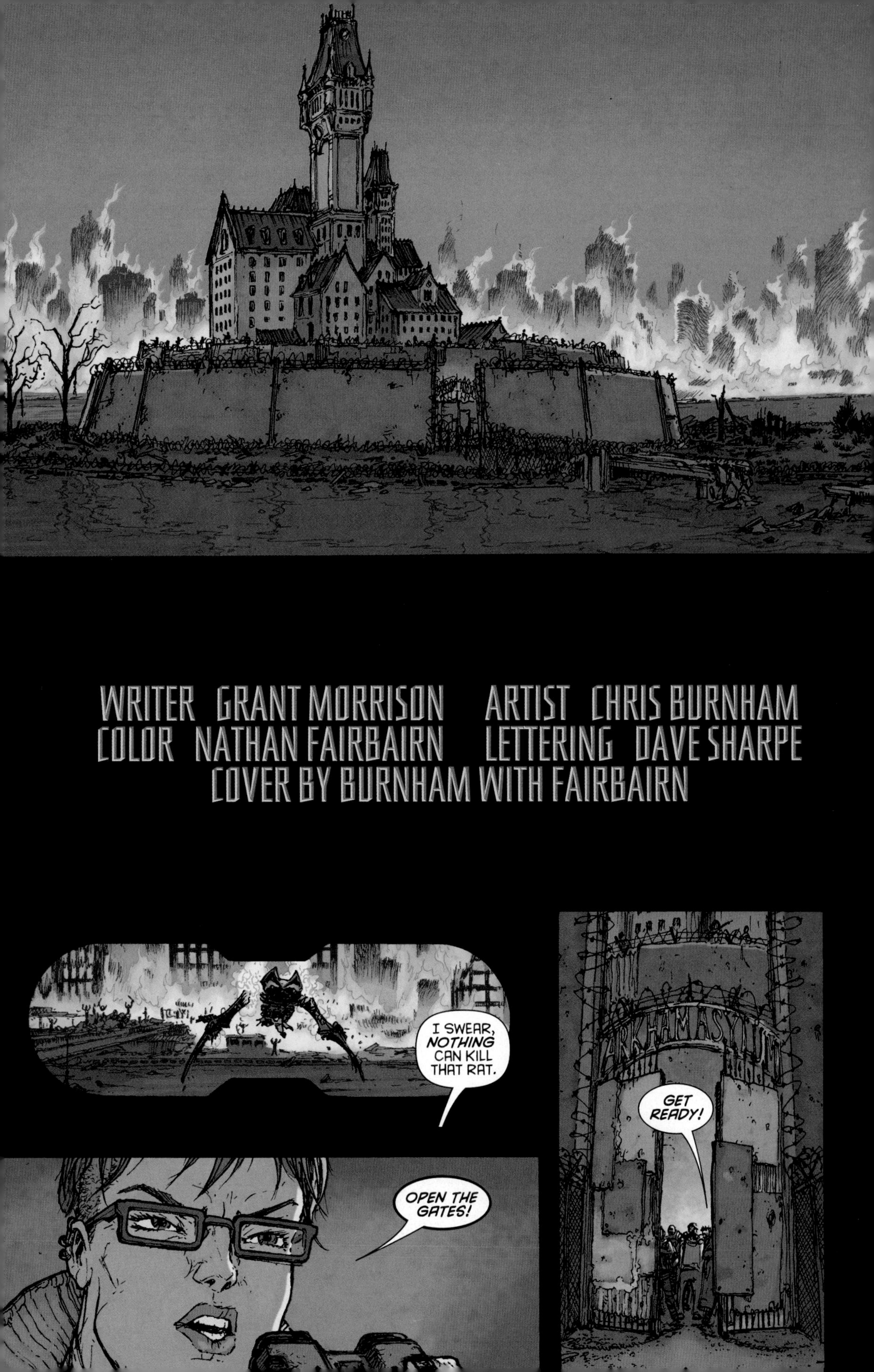
WRITER GRANT MORRISON ARTIST CHRIS BURNHAM
COLOR NATHAN FAIRBAIRN LETTERING DAVE SHARPE
COVER BY BURNHAM WITH FAIRBAIRN
I SWEAR, NOTHING CAN KILL THAT RAT.
OPEN THE GATES!
ARKHAM ASYLUM
GET READY!

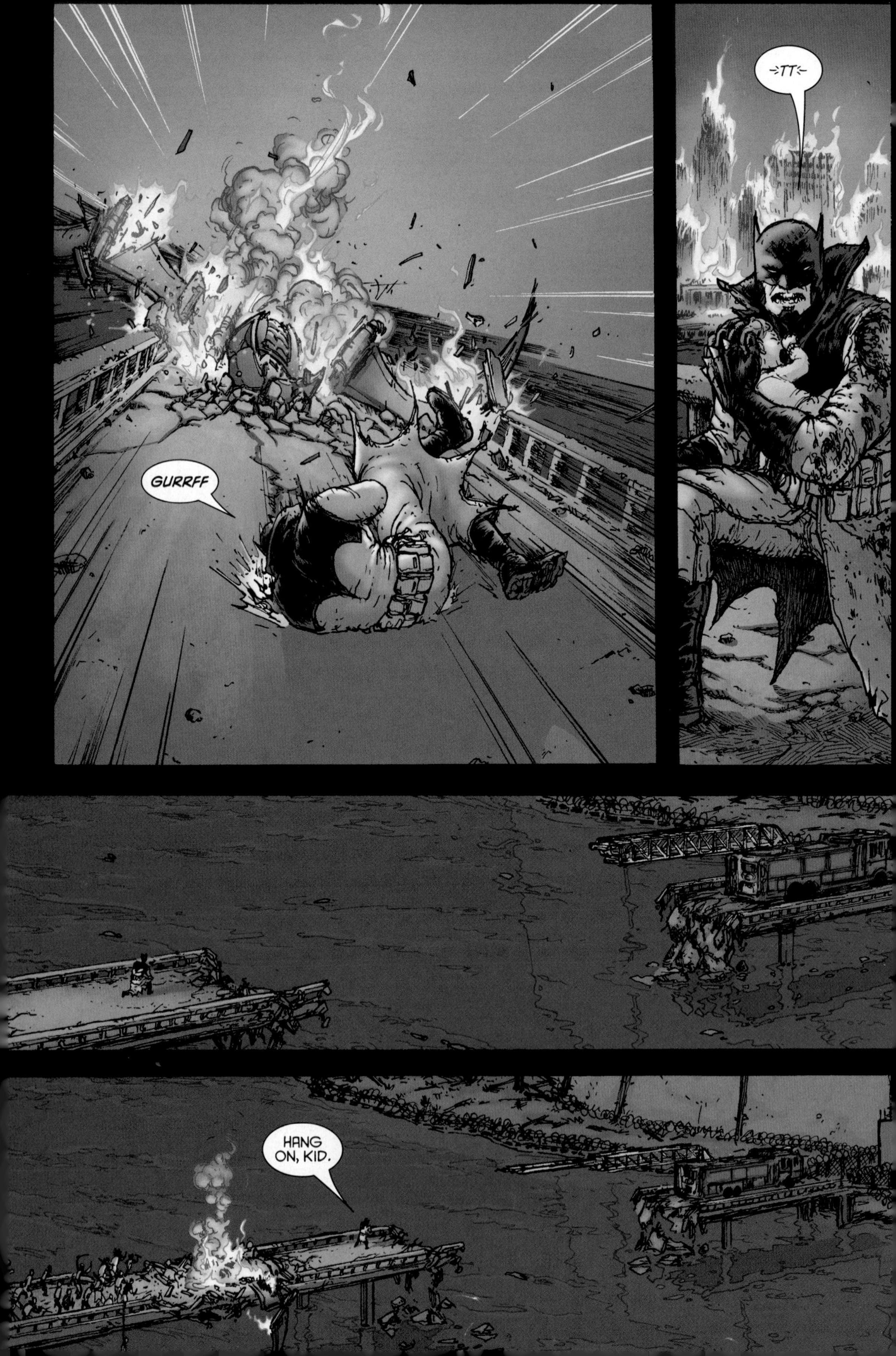
GURRFF
=TT=
HANG ON, KID.

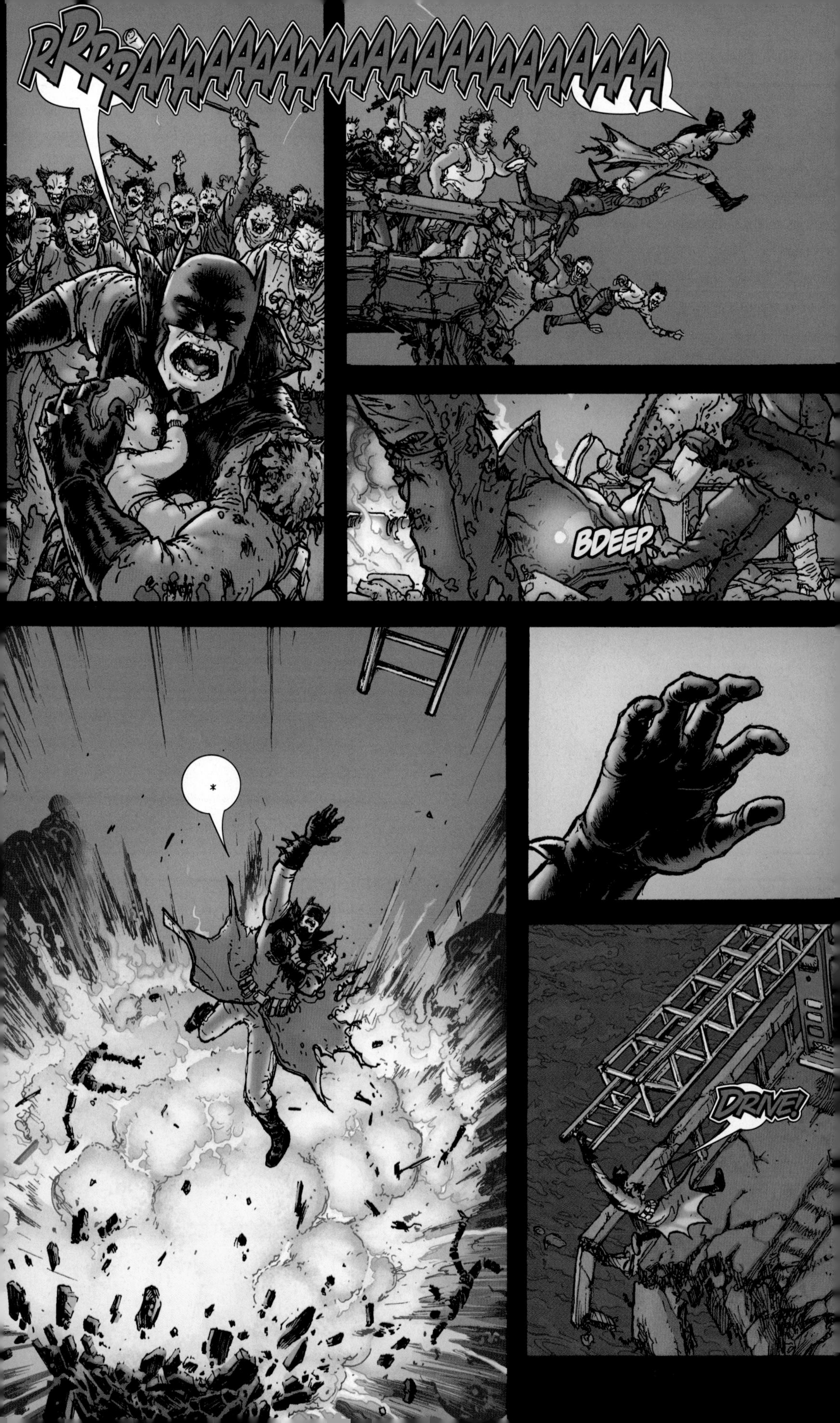
RRRRAAAAAAAAAAAAAAAAAAAAAAA
BDEEP
*
DRNE!

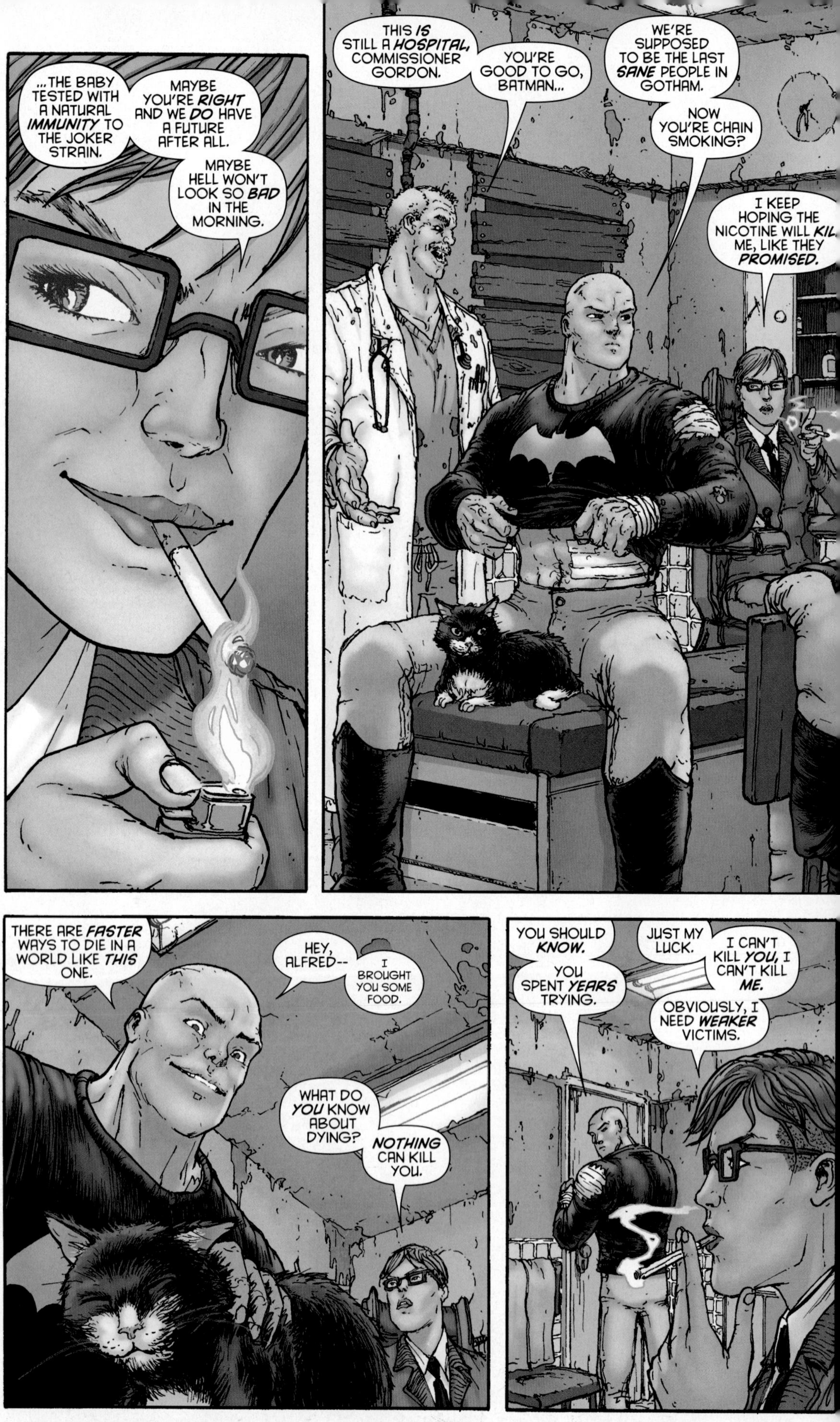
...THE BABY TESTED WITH A NATURAL *IMMUNITY* TO THE JOKER STRAIN.
MAYBE YOU'RE *RIGHT* AND WE *DO* HAVE A FUTURE AFTER ALL.
MAYBE HELL WON'T LOOK SO *BAD* IN THE MORNING.
THIS *IS* STILL A *HOSPITAL,* COMMISSIONER GORDON.
YOU'RE GOOD TO GO, BATMAN...
WE'RE SUPPOSED TO BE THE LAST *SANE* PEOPLE IN GOTHAM.
NOW YOU'RE CHAIN SMOKING?
I KEEP HOPING THE NICOTINE WILL *KIL* ME, LIKE THEY *PROMISED.*
THERE ARE *FASTER* WAYS TO DIE IN A WORLD LIKE *THIS* ONE.
HEY, ALFRED--
I BROUGHT YOU SOME FOOD.
WHAT DO *YOU* KNOW ABOUT DYING?
NOTHING CAN KILL YOU.
YOU SHOULD *KNOW.*
YOU SPENT *YEARS* TRYING.
JUST MY LUCK.
I CAN'T KILL *YOU,* I CAN'T KILL *ME.*
OBVIOUSLY, I NEED *WEAKER* VICTIMS.

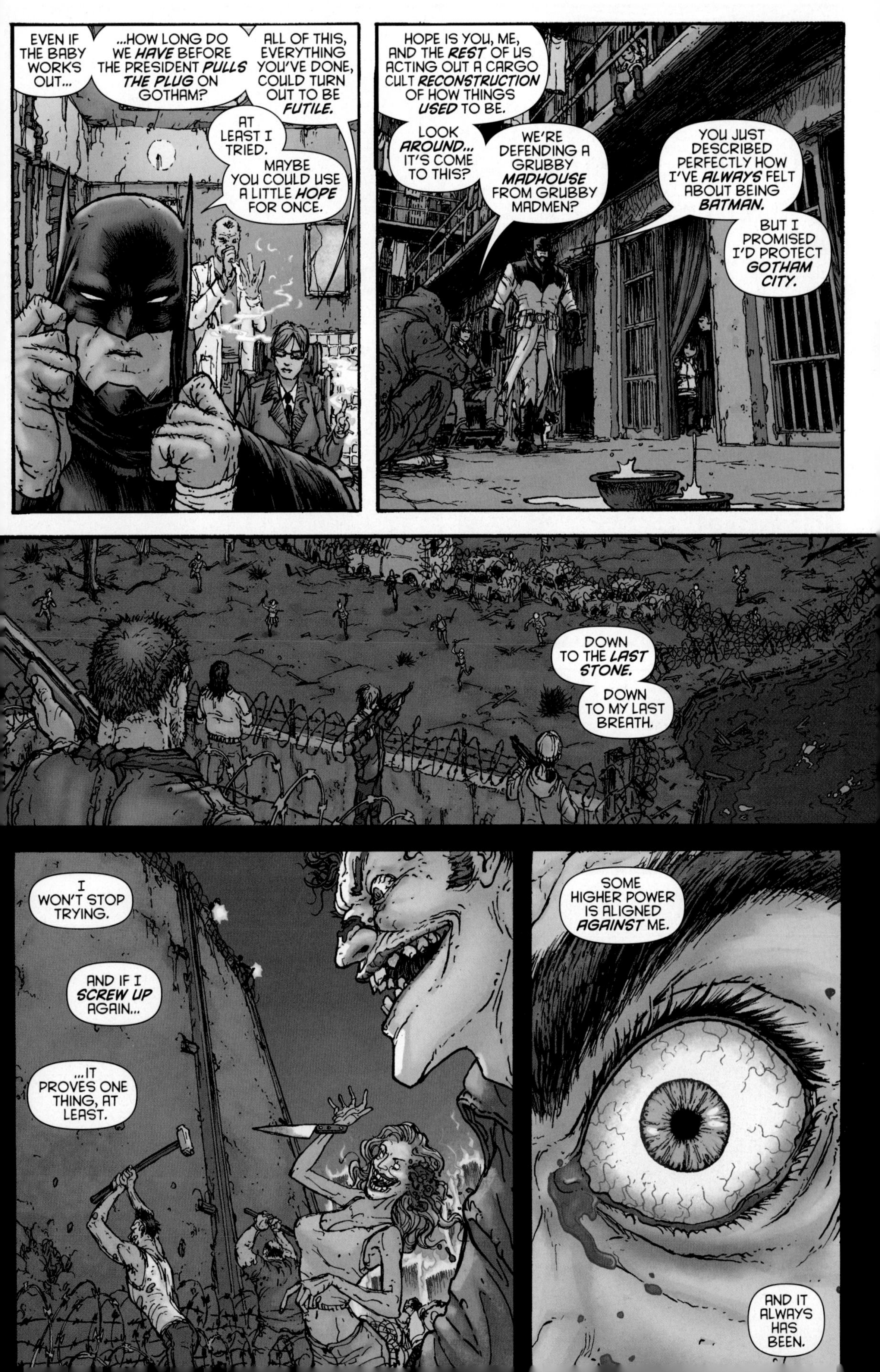
EVEN IF THE BABY WORKS OUT...
...HOW LONG DO WE HAVE BEFORE THE PRESIDENT PULLS THE PLUG ON GOTHAM?
ALL OF THIS, EVERYTHING YOU'VE DONE, COULD TURN OUT TO BE FUTILE.
AT LEAST I TRIED.
MAYBE YOU COULD USE A LITTLE HOPE FOR ONCE.
HOPE IS YOU, ME, AND THE REST OF US ACTING OUT A CARGO CULT RECONSTRUCTION OF HOW THINGS USED TO BE.
LOOK AROUND... IT'S COME TO THIS?
WE'RE DEFENDING A GRUBBY MADHOUSE FROM GRUBBY MADMEN?
YOU JUST DESCRIBED PERFECTLY HOW I'VE ALWAYS FELT ABOUT BEING BATMAN.
BUT I PROMISED I'D PROTECT GOTHAM CITY.
DOWN TO THE LAST STONE.
DOWN TO MY LAST BREATH.
I WON'T STOP TRYING.
AND IF I SCREW UP AGAIN...
...IT PROVES ONE THING, AT LEAST.
SOME HIGHER POWER IS ALIGNED AGAINST ME.
AND IT ALWAYS HAS BEEN.

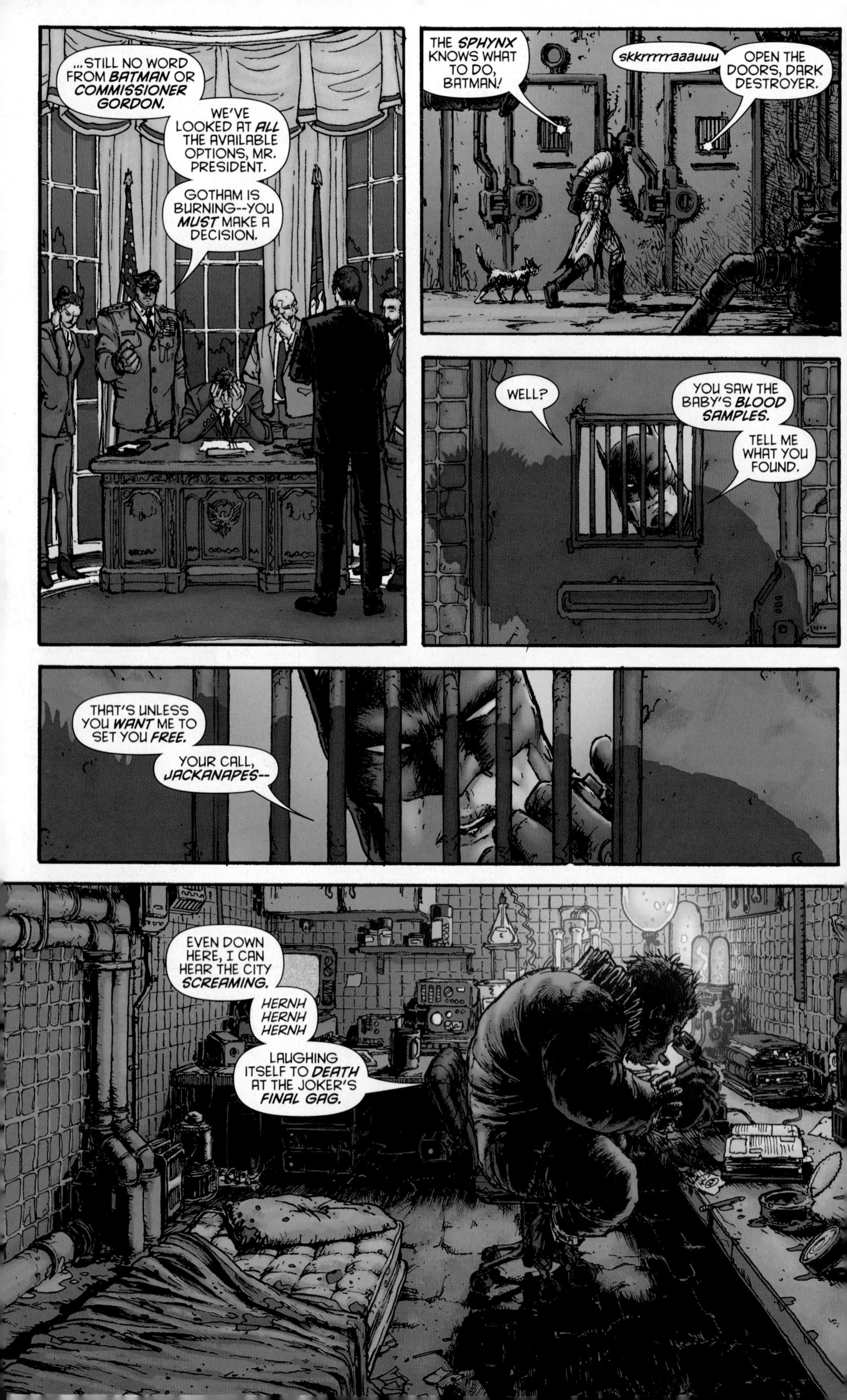
...STILL NO WORD FROM BATMAN OR COMMISSIONER GORDON.
WE'VE LOOKED AT ALL THE AVAILABLE OPTIONS, MR. PRESIDENT.
GOTHAM IS BURNING--YOU MUST MAKE A DECISION.
THE SPHYNX KNOWS WHAT TO DO, BATMAN!
skkrrrrraaauuu
OPEN THE DOORS, DARK DESTROYER.
WELL?
YOU SAW THE BABY'S BLOOD SAMPLES.
TELL ME WHAT YOU FOUND.
THAT'S UNLESS YOU WANT ME TO SET YOU FREE.
YOUR CALL, JACKANAPES--
EVEN DOWN HERE, I CAN HEAR THE CITY SCREAMING.
HERNH HERNH HERNH
LAUGHING ITSELF TO DEATH AT THE JOKER'S FINAL GAG.

IT'S A **MADHOUSE** OUT THERE.

THIS IS THE **END**, BATMAN. THE PLAGUE HORSE FORETOLD IN **REVELATIONS.**

I'M SAFE **HERE**, FOR NOW.

BABYLON **FALLS!**

THE **VALUES** YOU DEFENDED ARE **MEANINGLESS!**

YOU COME BEGGING TO ME!

AND I'M A **MONSTER** IN A WORLD **MADE** FOR MONSTERS.

YOU WON'T LAST **LONG** UNLESS WE GET OUT.

SUPERMARKETS ARE **LOW** ON BANANAS.

AND CIGARS.

I'LL GROW FAT ON ALL YOUR FLESH.

HERNH HERNH HERNH

BATMAN BEGS FOR HELP FROM HIS ENEMIES!

GURKK

YOU'RE A **MONSTER**, BUT YOU'RE THE BEST **MOLECULAR BIOLOGIST** THIS DUMP HAS TO OFFER!

I'LL TAKE WHAT I CAN GET TO **END** THIS.

CAN WE MAKE AN **ANTIDOTE**, YOU BASTARD?

END IT? THE **DEVIL** IS PREPARING HIS ARENA FOR THE **FINAL BATTLE.**

GOTHAM IS **HELL'S** CAPITAL ON EARTH!

THERE'S A **REASON** THE CHILD HAS **NO** SYMPTOMS!

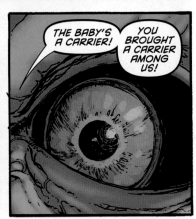

THE BABY'S A CARRIER!

YOU BROUGHT A CARRIER AMONG US!

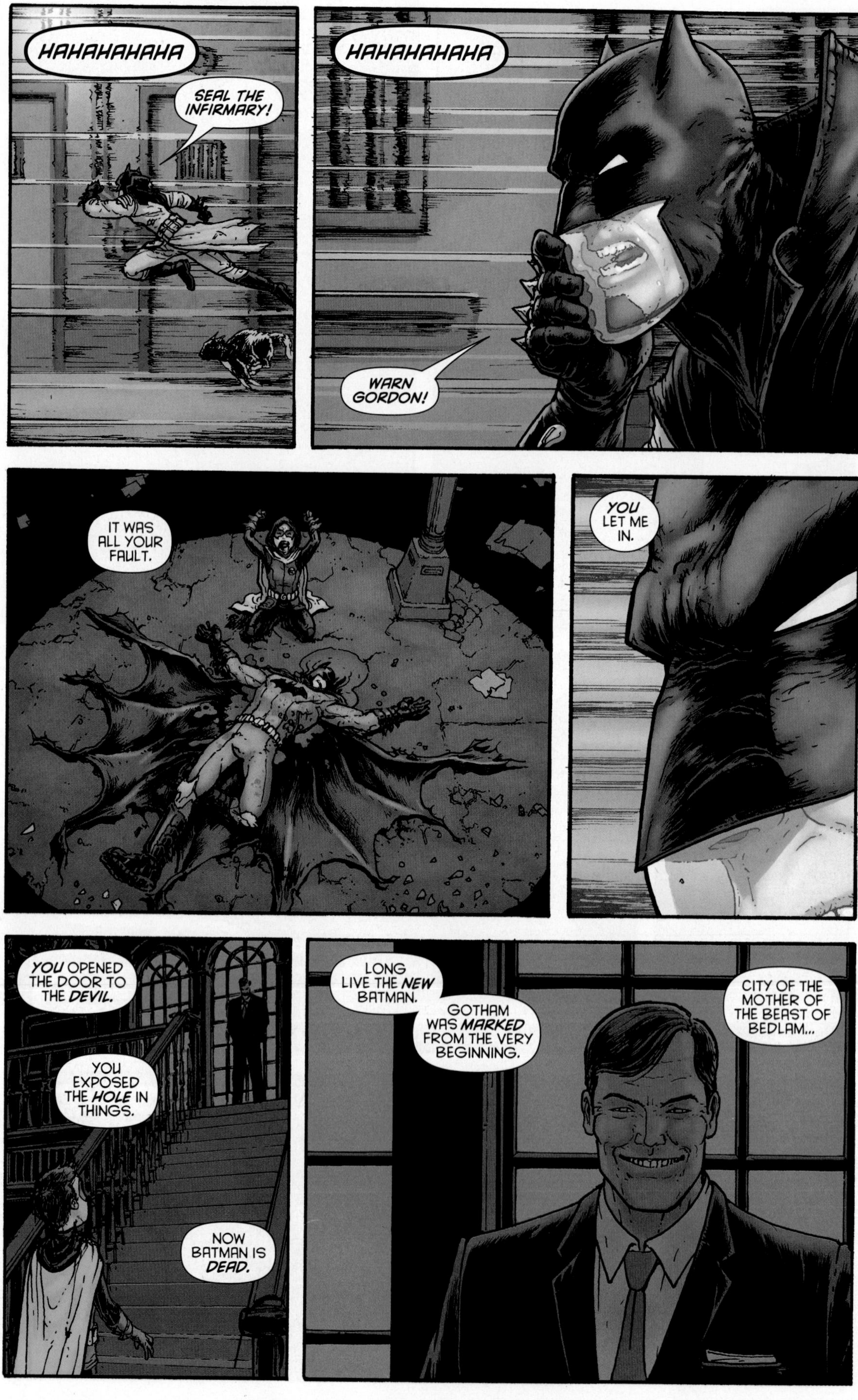
HAHAHAHAHA
SEAL THE INFIRMARY!
HAHAHAHAHA
WARN GORDON!
IT WAS ALL YOUR FAULT.
YOU LET ME IN.
YOU OPENED THE DOOR TO THE DEVIL.
YOU EXPOSED THE HOLE IN THINGS.
NOW BATMAN IS DEAD.
LONG LIVE THE NEW BATMAN.
GOTHAM WAS MARKED FROM THE VERY BEGINNING.
CITY OF THE MOTHER OF THE BEAST OF BEDLAM...

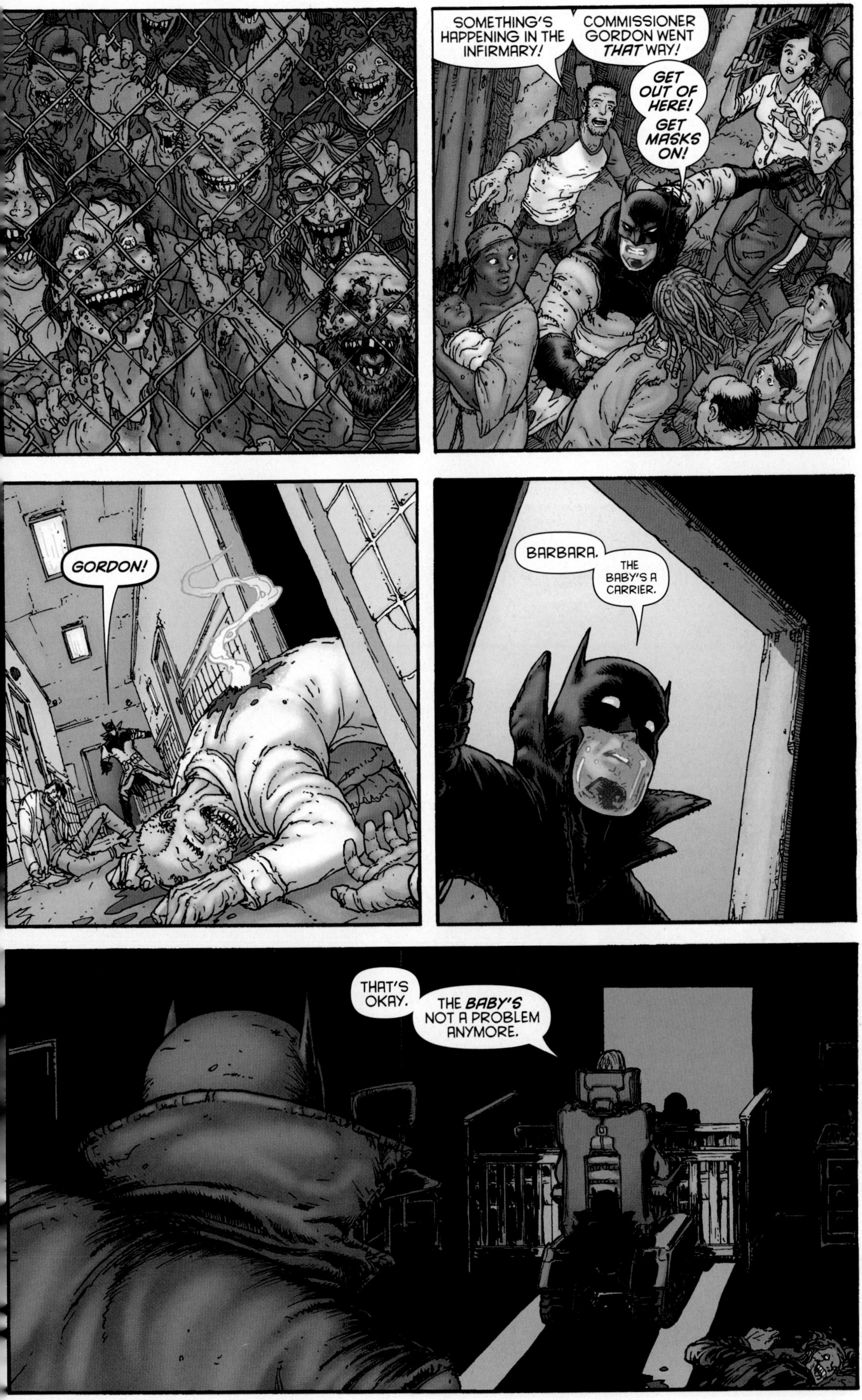
SOMETHING'S HAPPENING IN THE INFIRMARY!
COMMISSIONER GORDON WENT THAT WAY!
GET OUT OF HERE! GET MASKS ON!
GORDON!
BARBARA.
THE BABY'S A CARRIER.
THAT'S OKAY.
THE BABY'S NOT A PROBLEM ANYMORE.

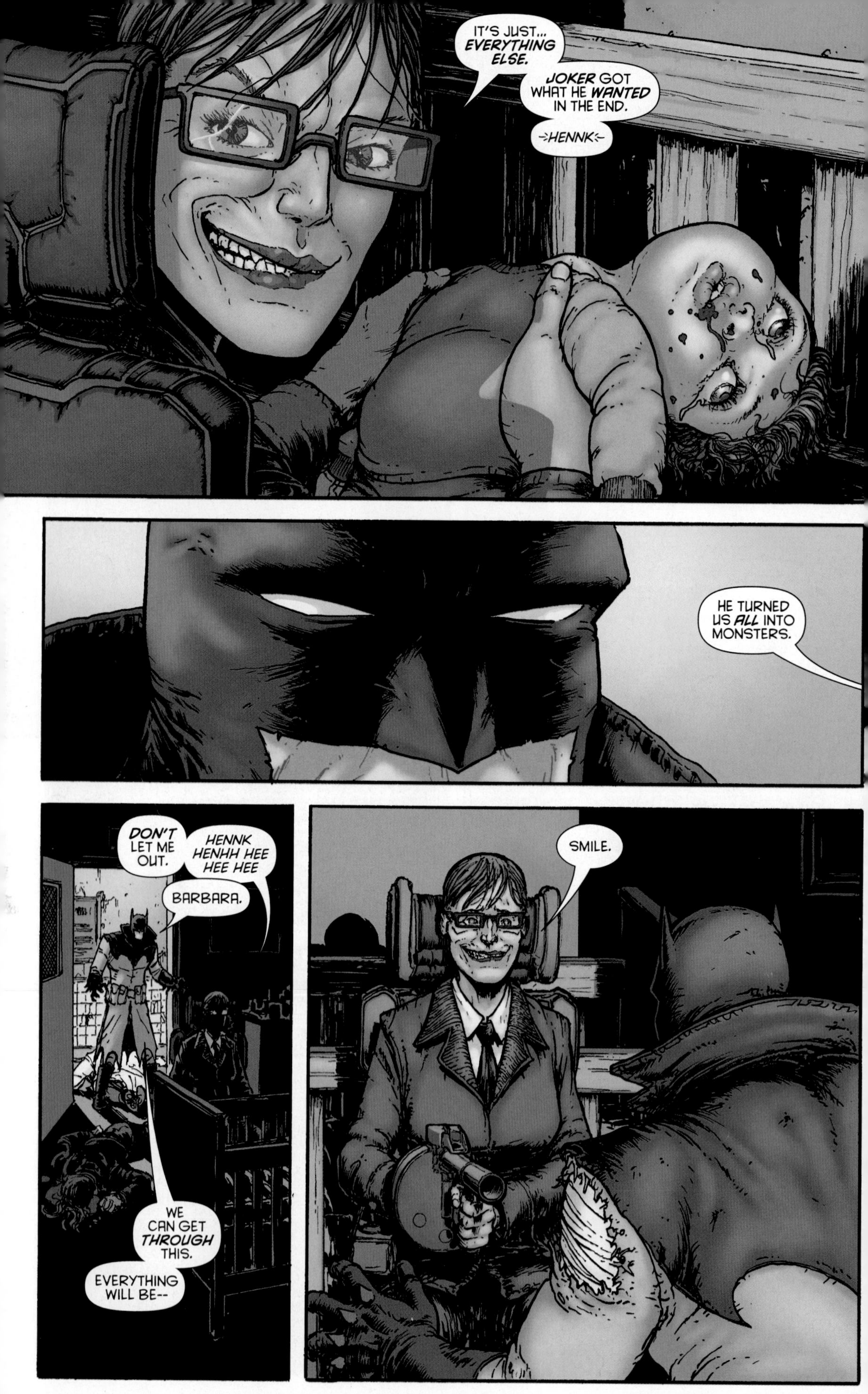
IT'S JUST... EVERYTHING ELSE.
JOKER GOT WHAT HE WANTED IN THE END.
-HENNK-
HE TURNED US ALL INTO MONSTERS.
DON'T LET ME OUT.
HENNK HENHH HEE HEE HEE
BARBARA.
WE CAN GET THROUGH THIS.
EVERYTHING WILL BE--
SMILE.

IT'S DONE.

YOU'VE DONE THE RIGHT THING, MR. PRESIDENT.

THERE IS ONLY *ONE SURE WAY* TO CONTAIN THE GOTHAM PANDEMIC.

MAKE AN *END* OF IT.

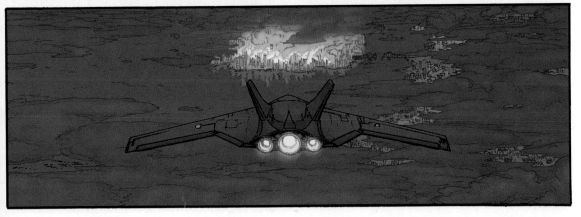

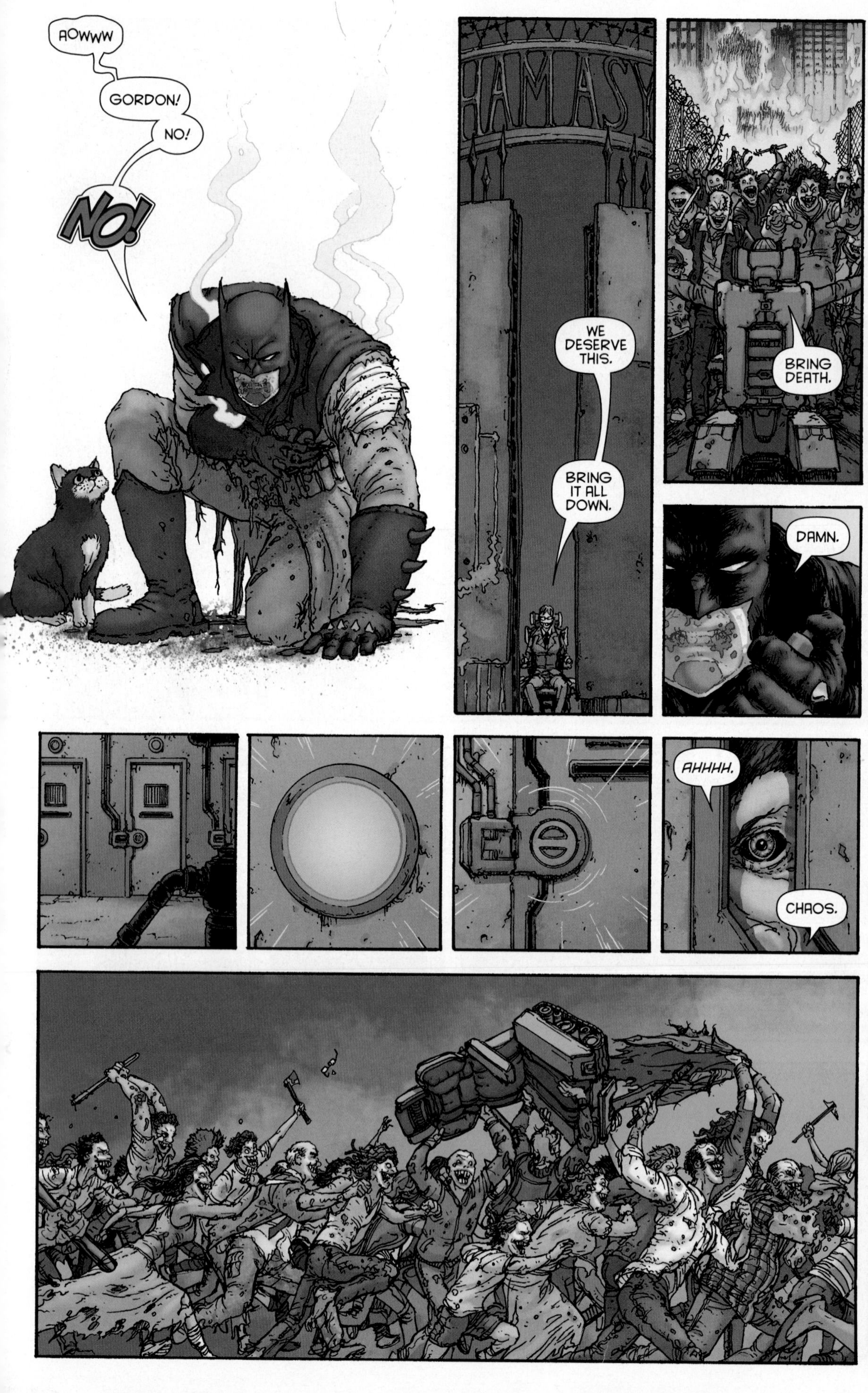
AOWWW
GORDON!
NO!
NO!
HAM ASY
WE DESERVE THIS.
BRING IT ALL DOWN.
BRING DEATH.
DAMN.
AHHHH.
CHAOS.

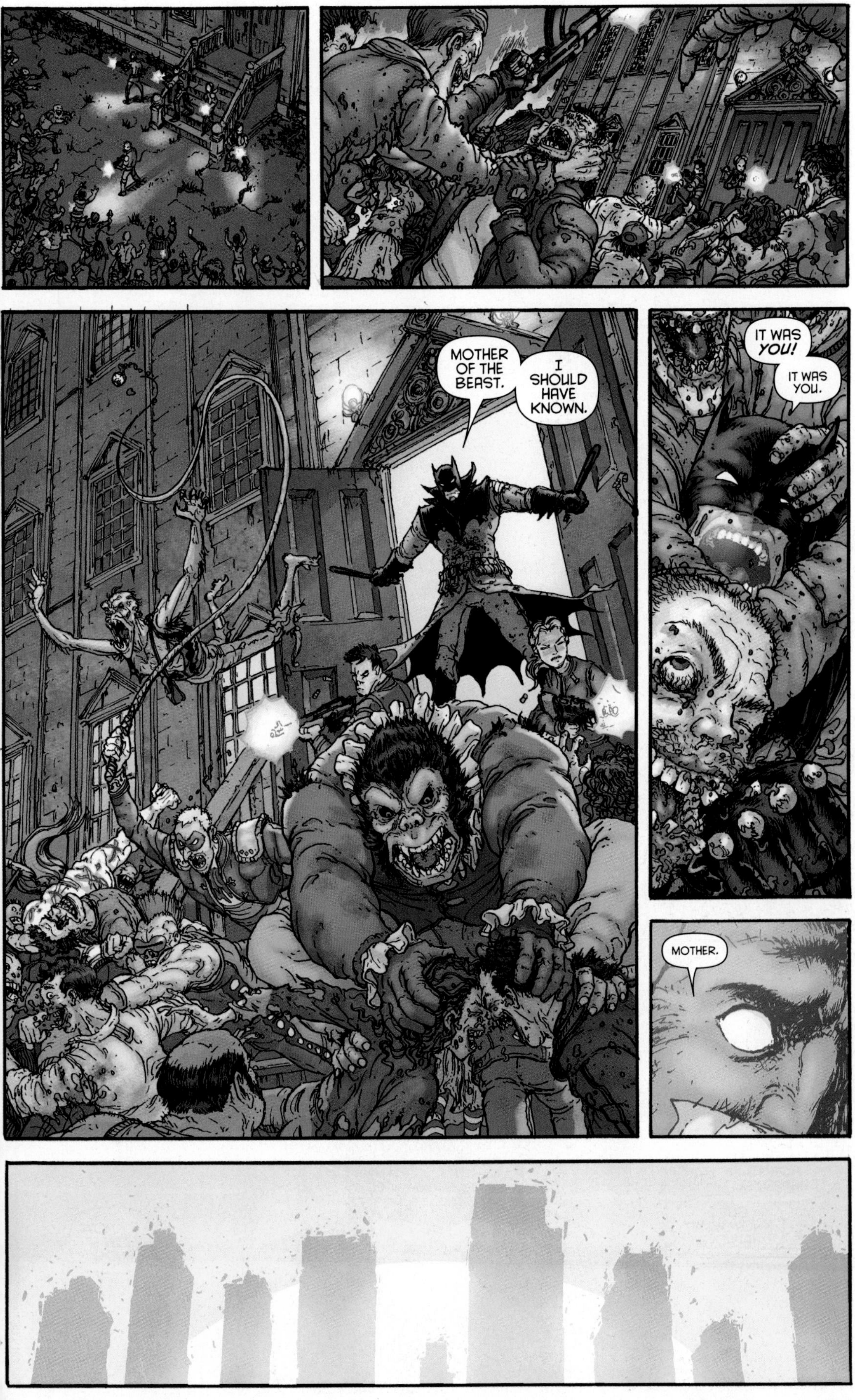
MOTHER OF THE BEAST.
I SHOULD HAVE KNOWN.
IT WAS YOU!
IT WAS YOU.
MOTHER.

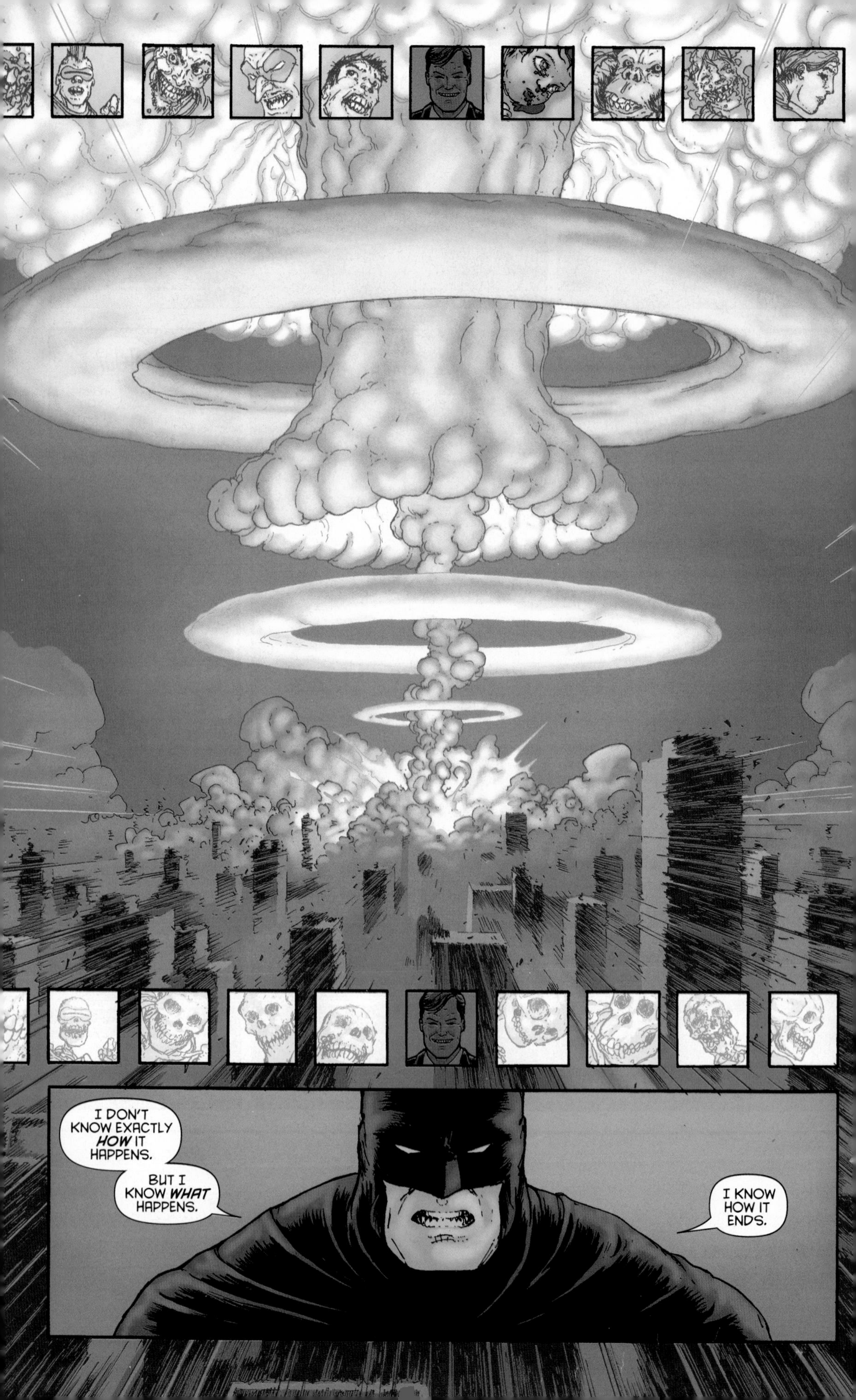

I DON'T KNOW EXACTLY *HOW* IT HAPPENS.
BUT I KNOW *WHAT* HAPPENS.
I KNOW HOW IT ENDS.

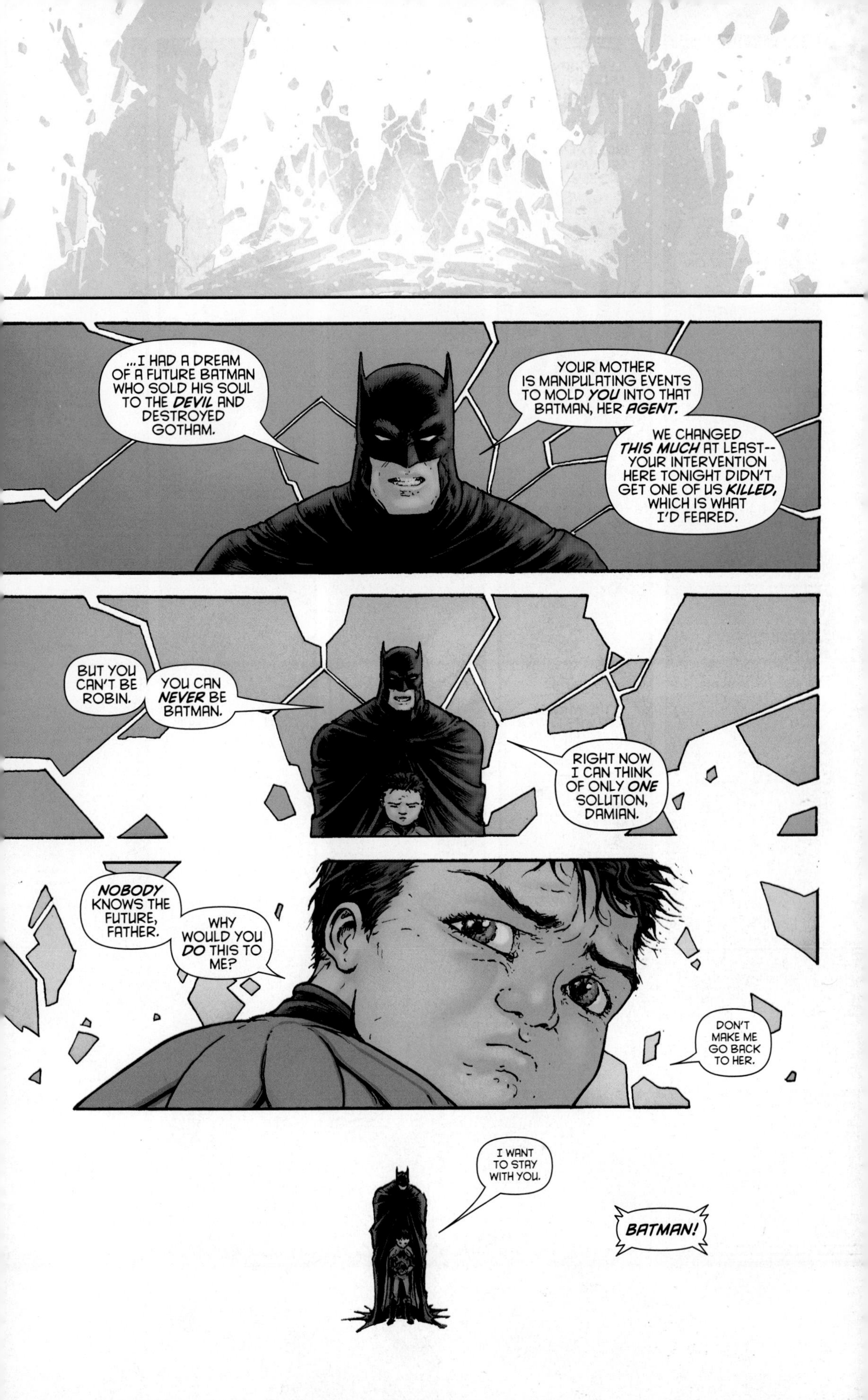
...I HAD A DREAM OF A FUTURE BATMAN WHO SOLD HIS SOUL TO THE DEVIL AND DESTROYED GOTHAM.
YOUR MOTHER IS MANIPULATING EVENTS TO MOLD YOU INTO THAT BATMAN, HER AGENT.
WE CHANGED THIS MUCH AT LEAST-- YOUR INTERVENTION HERE TONIGHT DIDN'T GET ONE OF US KILLED, WHICH IS WHAT I'D FEARED.
BUT YOU CAN'T BE ROBIN.
YOU CAN NEVER BE BATMAN.
RIGHT NOW I CAN THINK OF ONLY ONE SOLUTION, DAMIAN.
NOBODY KNOWS THE FUTURE, FATHER.
WHY WOULD YOU DO THIS TO ME?
DON'T MAKE ME GO BACK TO HER.
I WANT TO STAY WITH YOU.
BATMAN!

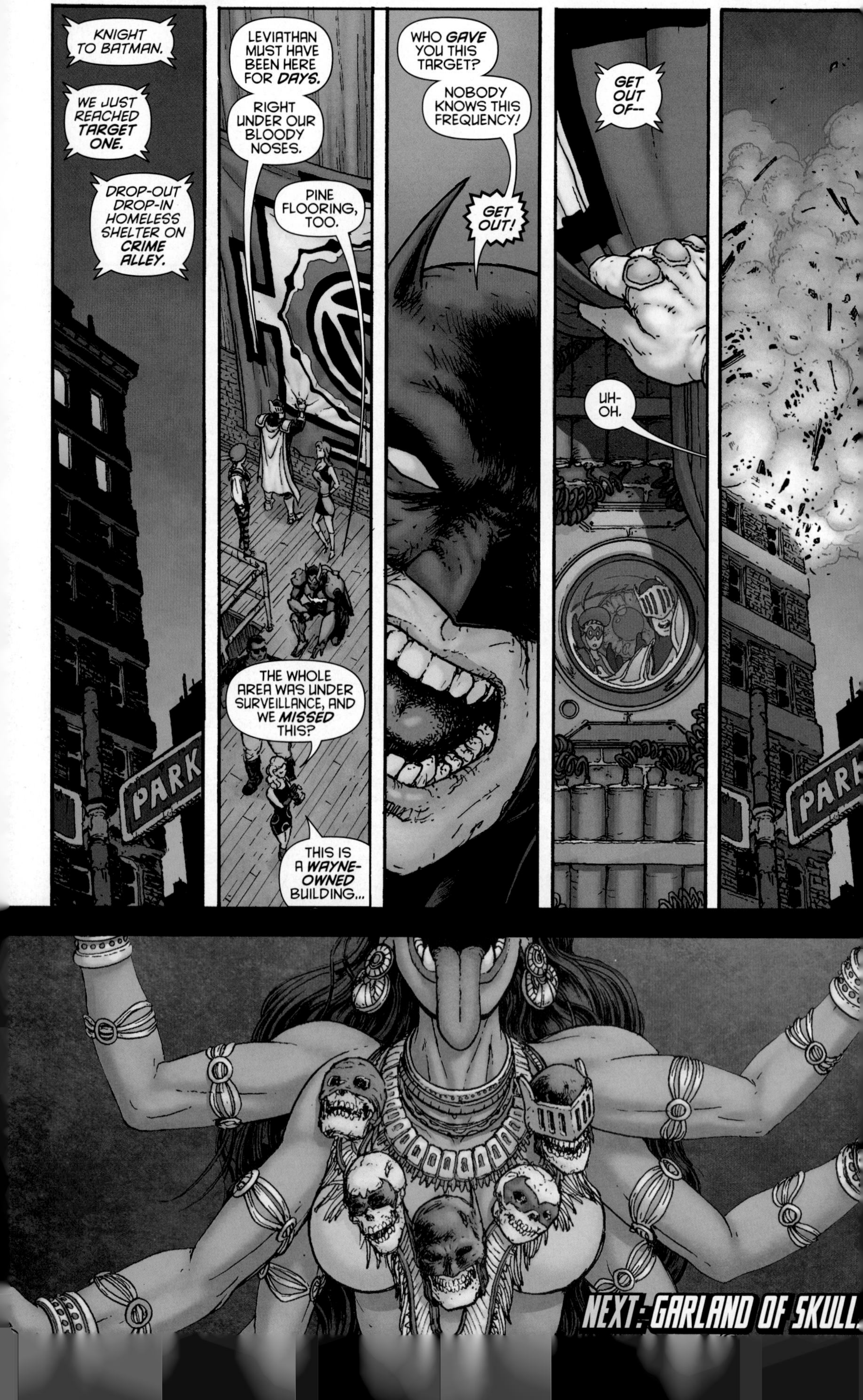
KNIGHT TO BATMAN.
WE JUST REACHED TARGET ONE.
DROP-OUT DROP-IN HOMELESS SHELTER ON CRIME ALLEY.
PARK
LEVIATHAN MUST HAVE BEEN HERE FOR DAYS.
RIGHT UNDER OUR BLOODY NOSES.
PINE FLOORING, TOO.
THE WHOLE AREA WAS UNDER SURVEILLANCE, AND WE MISSED THIS?
THIS IS A WAYNE-OWNED BUILDING...
WHO GAVE YOU THIS TARGET?
NOBODY KNOWS THIS FREQUENCY!
GET OUT!
GET OUT OF--
UH-OH.
PARK
NEXT: GARLAND OF SKULL.

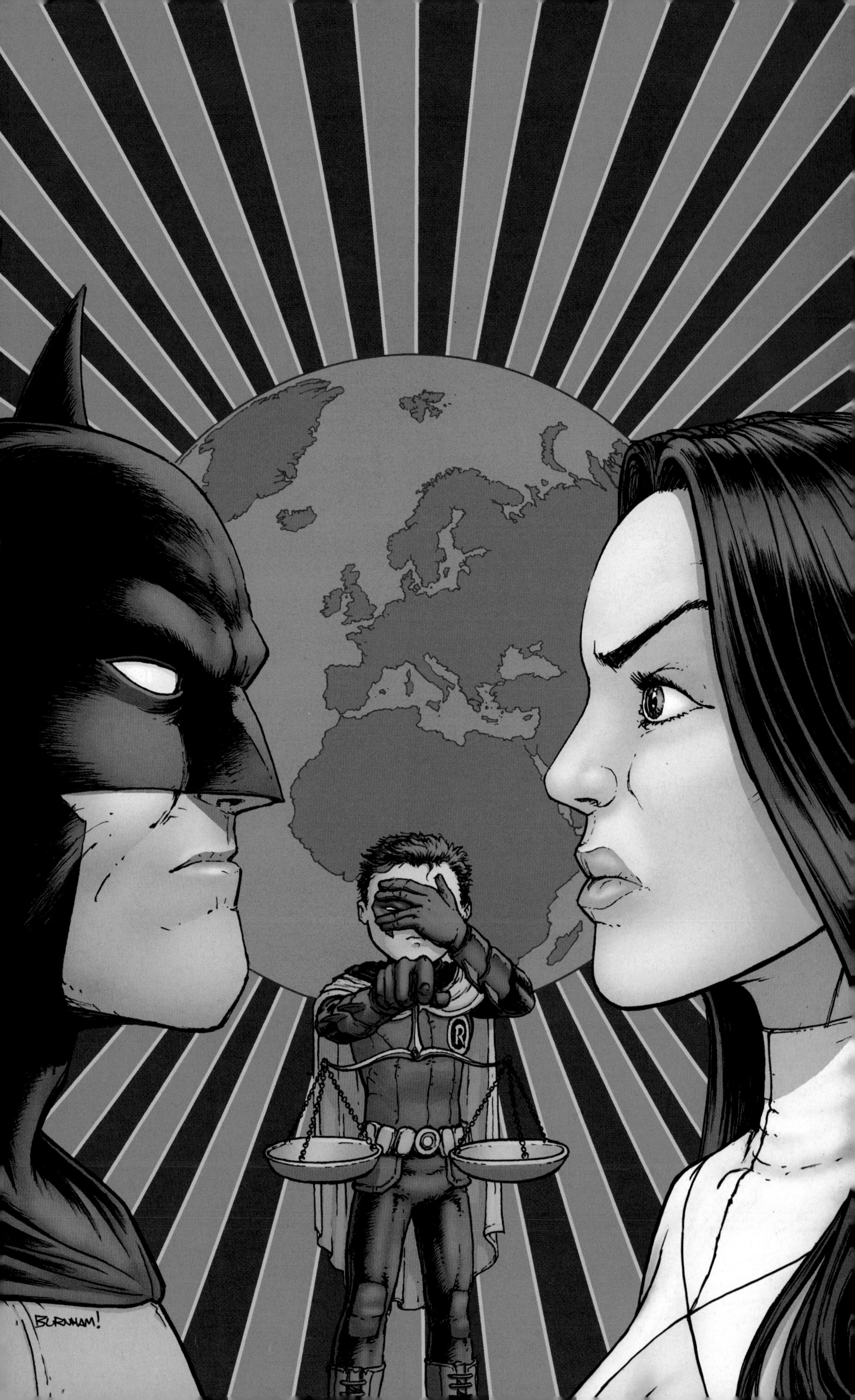
BURNHAM!

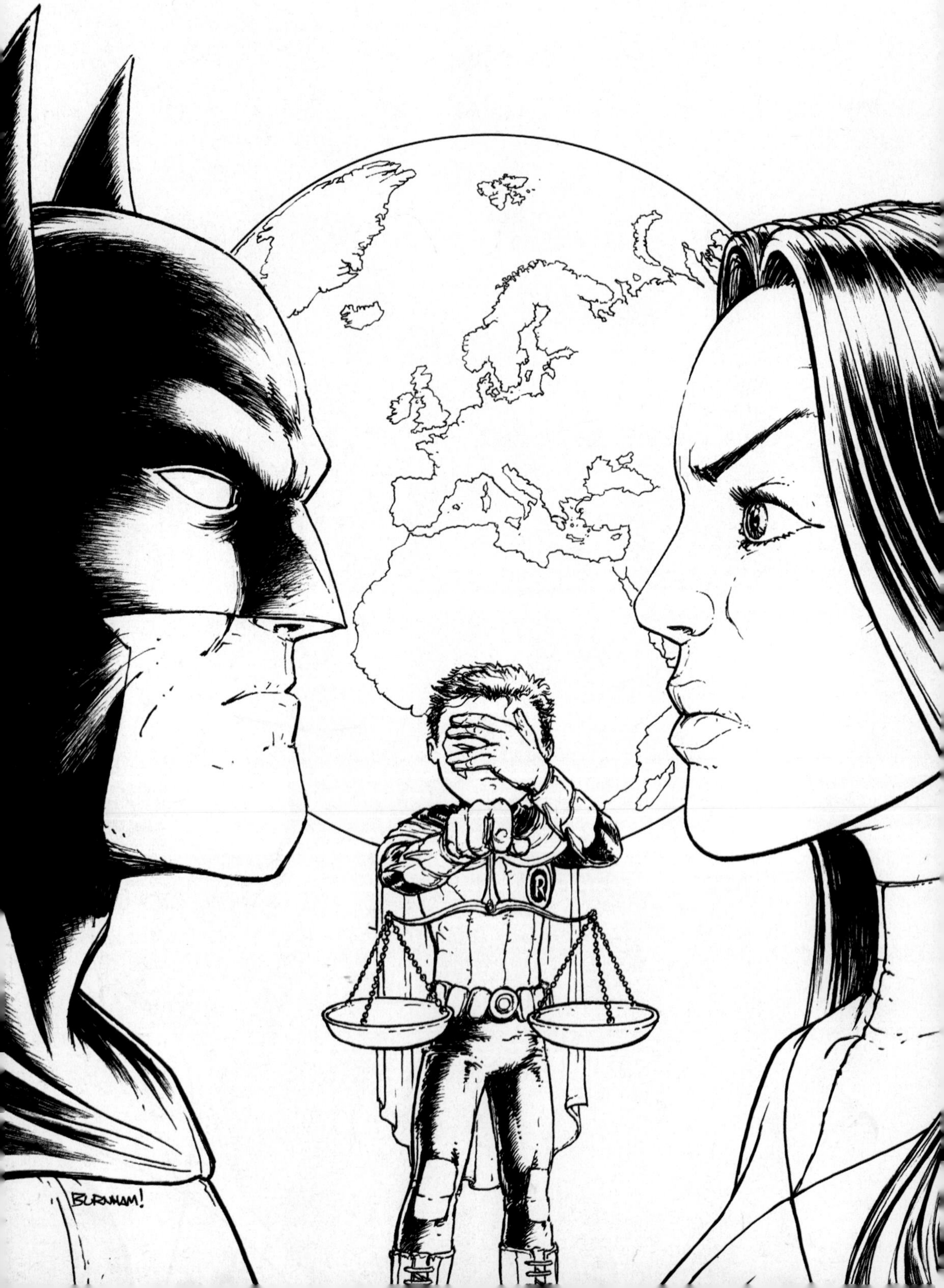
BURNHAM!

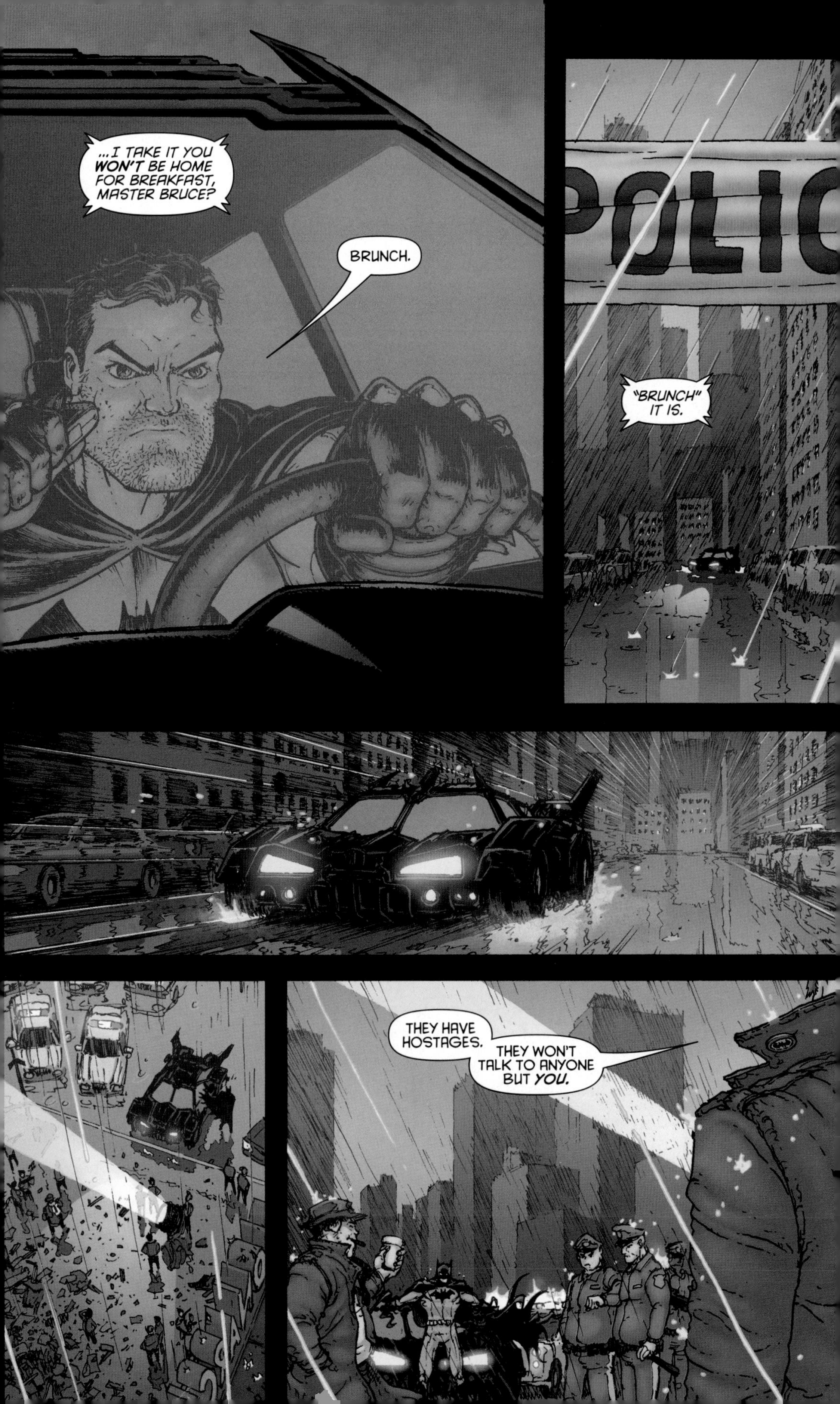
...I TAKE IT YOU WON'T BE HOME FOR BREAKFAST, MASTER BRUCE?
BRUNCH.
POLIC
"BRUNCH" IT IS.
THEY HAVE HOSTAGES.
THEY WON'T TALK TO ANYONE BUT YOU.

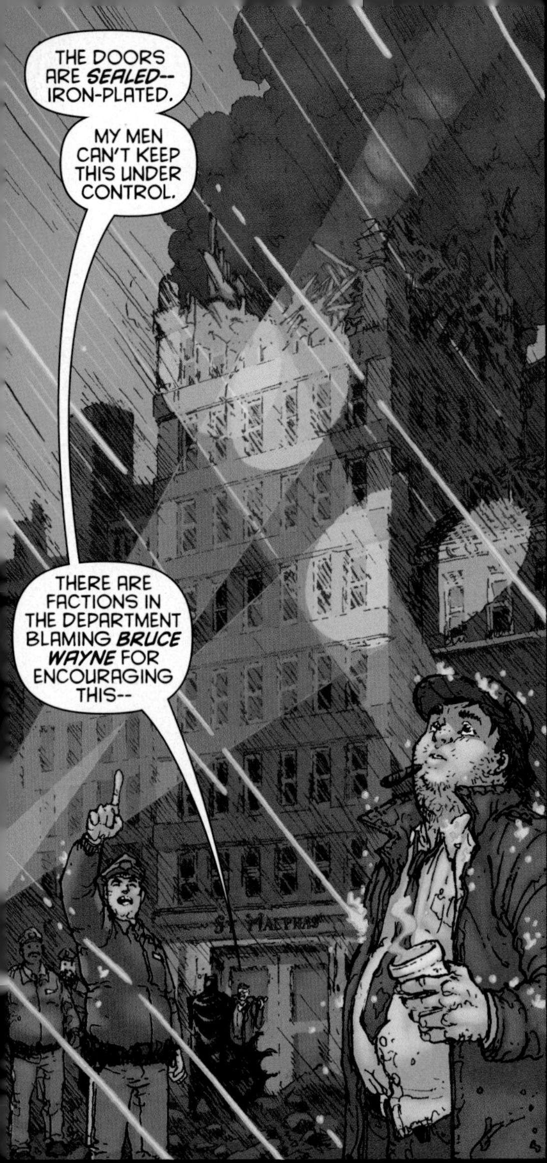
THE DOORS ARE *SEALED*-- IRON-PLATED.
MY MEN CAN'T KEEP THIS UNDER CONTROL.
THERE ARE FACTIONS IN THE DEPARTMENT BLAMING *BRUCE WAYNE* FOR ENCOURAGING THIS--

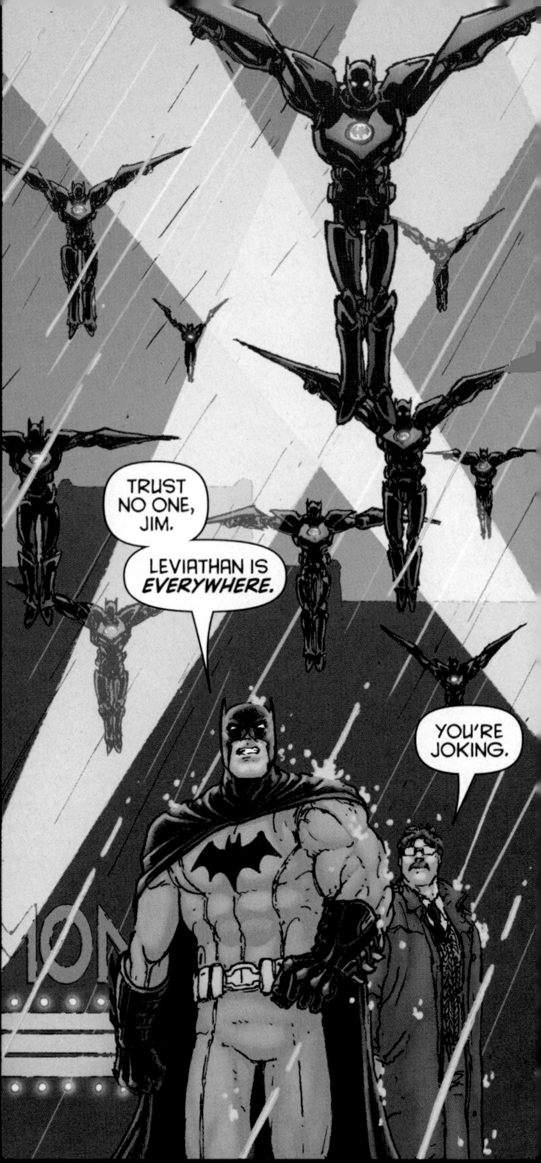
TRUST NO ONE, JIM.
LEVIATHAN IS *EVERYWHERE.*
YOU'RE JOKING.

GARLAND OF SKULLS

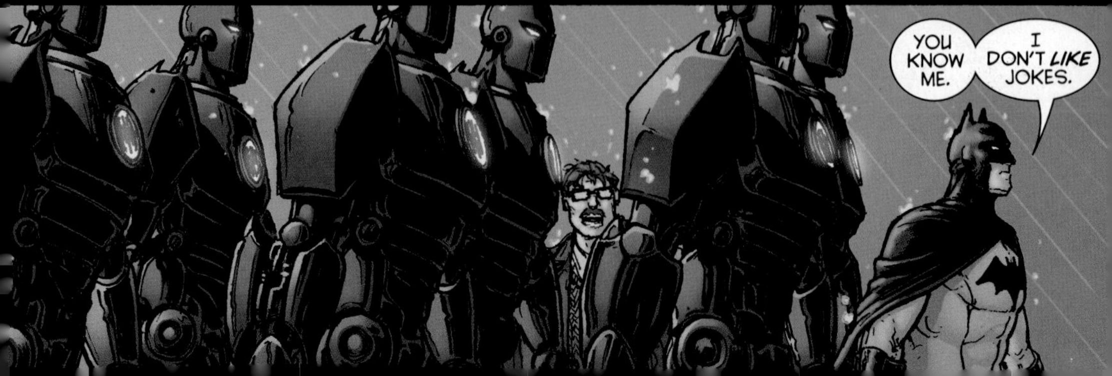
YOU KNOW ME.
I DON'T *LIKE* JOKES.

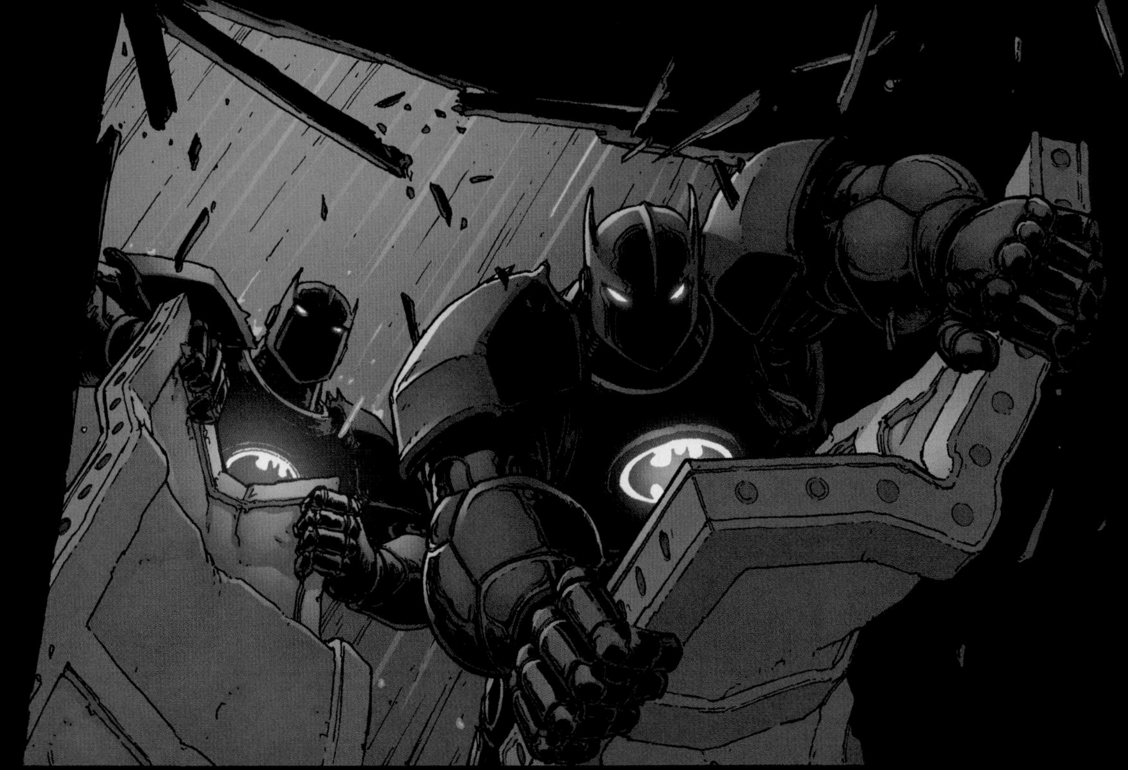

GRANT MORRISON WRITER CHRIS BURNHAM ARTIST

ANDRES GUINALDO AND BIT ADDITIONAL ART PGS 13-16

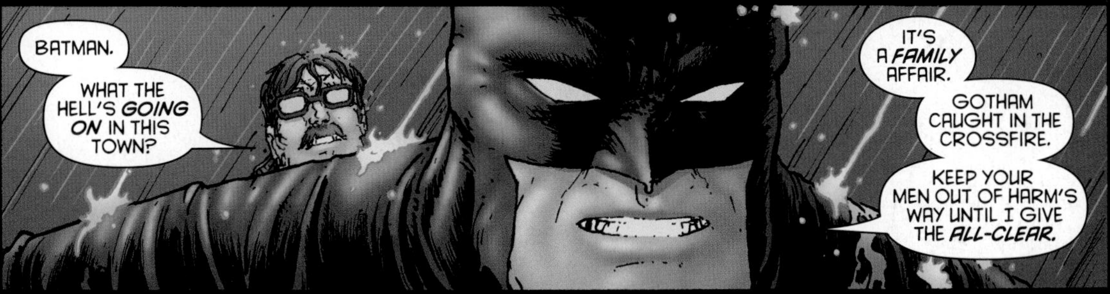

BATMAN.
WHAT THE HELL'S *GOING ON* IN THIS TOWN?
IT'S A *FAMILY* AFFAIR.
GOTHAM CAUGHT IN THE CROSSFIRE.
KEEP YOUR MEN OUT OF HARM'S WAY UNTIL I GIVE THE *ALL-CLEAR.*

NATHAN FAIRBAIRN COLORS DAVE SHARPE LETTERS

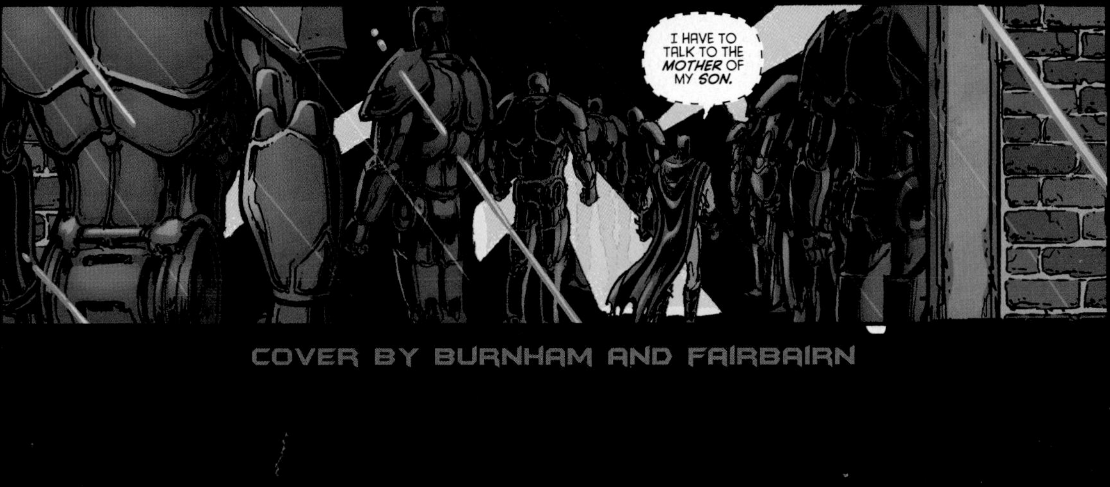

I HAVE TO TALK TO THE *MOTHER* OF MY *SON.*

COVER BY BURNHAM AND FAIRBAIRN

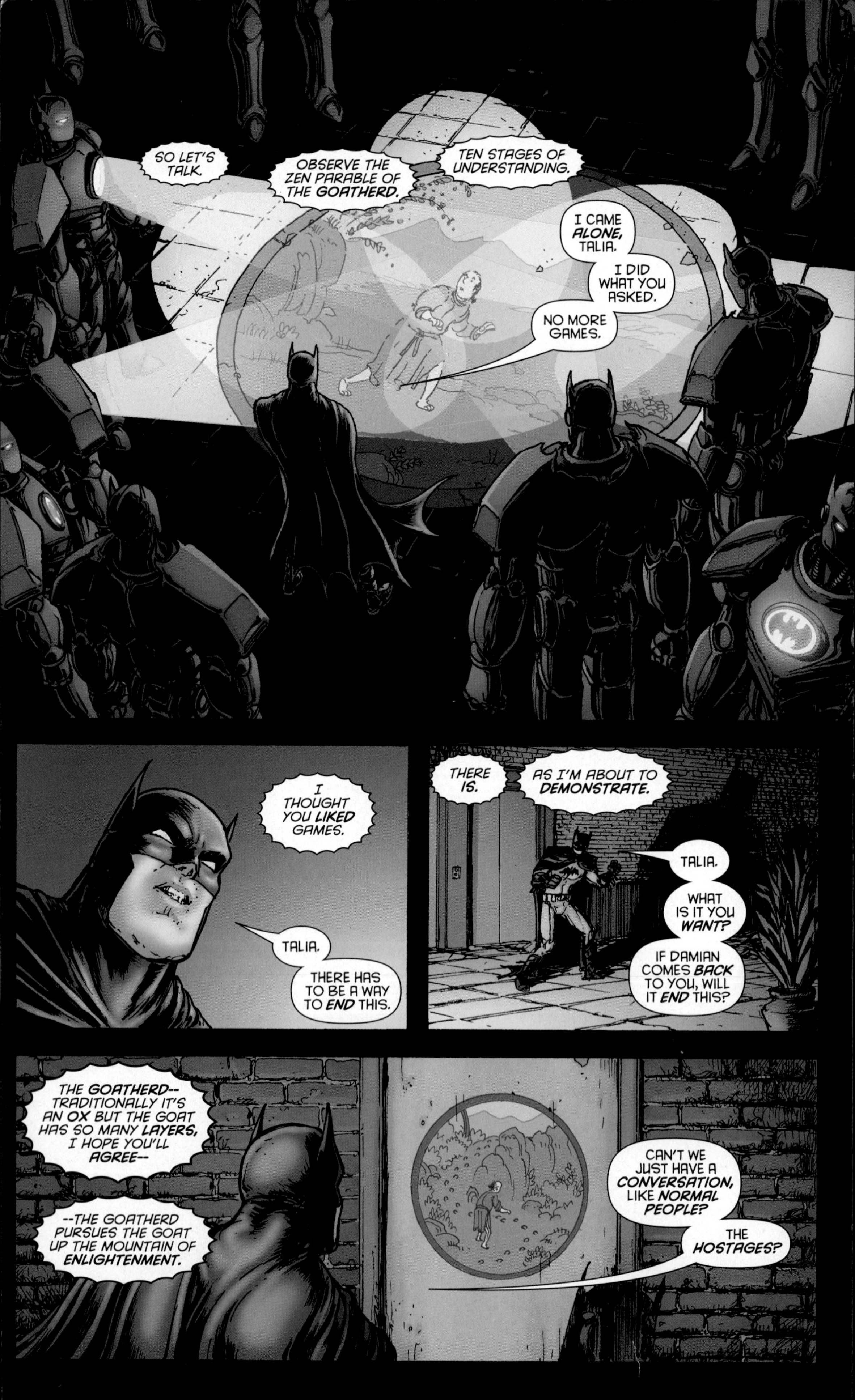
SO LET'S TALK.
OBSERVE THE ZEN PARABLE OF THE GOATHERD.
TEN STAGES OF UNDERSTANDING.
I CAME ALONE, TALIA.
I DID WHAT YOU ASKED.
NO MORE GAMES.
I THOUGHT YOU LIKED GAMES.
TALIA.
THERE HAS TO BE A WAY TO END THIS.
THERE IS.
AS I'M ABOUT TO DEMONSTRATE.
TALIA.
WHAT IS IT YOU WANT?
IF DAMIAN COMES BACK TO YOU, WILL IT END THIS?
THE GOATHERD-- TRADITIONALLY IT'S AN OX BUT THE GOAT HAS SO MANY LAYERS, I HOPE YOU'LL AGREE--
--THE GOATHERD PURSUES THE GOAT UP THE MOUNTAIN OF ENLIGHTENMENT.
CAN'T WE JUST HAVE A CONVERSATION, LIKE NORMAL PEOPLE?
THE HOSTAGES?

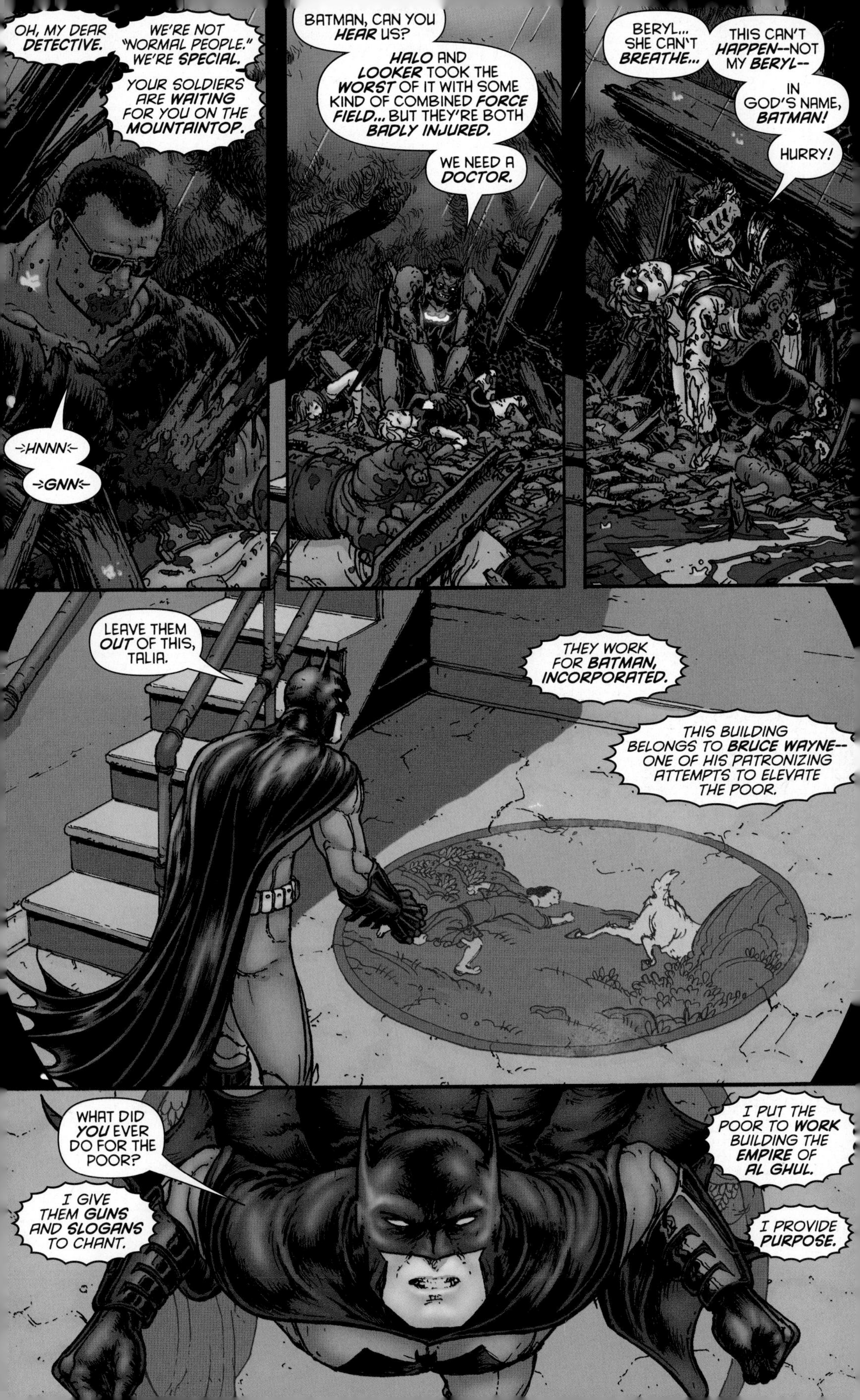
OH, MY DEAR DETECTIVE.
WE'RE NOT "NORMAL PEOPLE." WE'RE SPECIAL.
YOUR SOLDIERS ARE WAITING FOR YOU ON THE MOUNTAINTOP.
HNNN
GNN
BATMAN, CAN YOU HEAR US?
HALO AND LOOKER TOOK THE WORST OF IT WITH SOME KIND OF COMBINED FORCE FIELD... BUT THEY'RE BOTH BADLY INJURED.
WE NEED A DOCTOR.
BERYL... SHE CAN'T BREATHE...
THIS CAN'T HAPPEN--NOT MY BERYL--
IN GOD'S NAME, BATMAN!
HURRY!
LEAVE THEM OUT OF THIS, TALIA.
THEY WORK FOR BATMAN, INCORPORATED.
THIS BUILDING BELONGS TO BRUCE WAYNE-- ONE OF HIS PATRONIZING ATTEMPTS TO ELEVATE THE POOR.
WHAT DID YOU EVER DO FOR THE POOR?
I GIVE THEM GUNS AND SLOGANS TO CHANT.
I PUT THE POOR TO WORK BUILDING THE EMPIRE OF AL GHUL.
I PROVIDE PURPOSE.

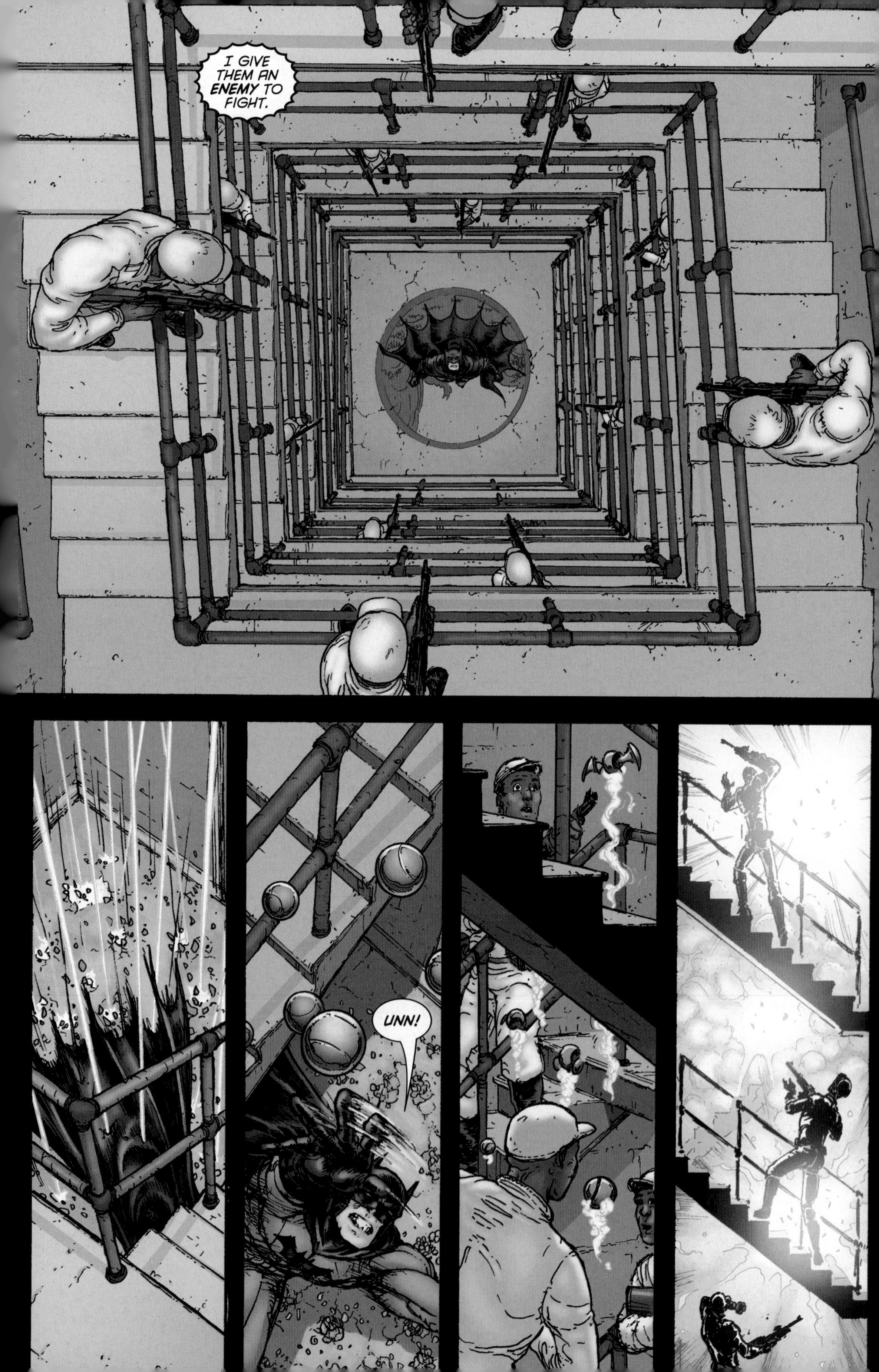
I GIVE THEM AN ENEMY TO FIGHT.
UNN!

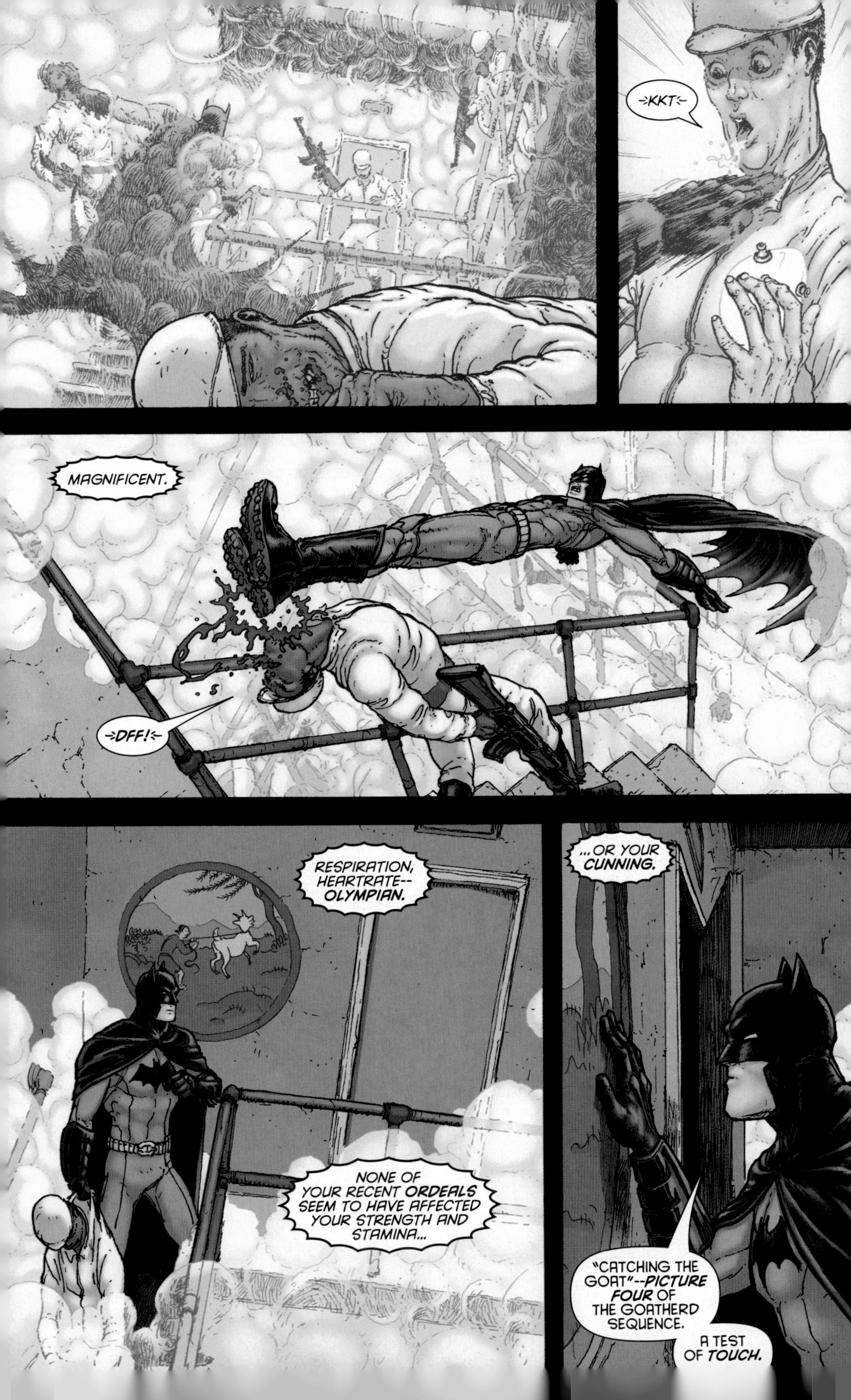

-KKT-
MAGNIFICENT.
-DFF!-
RESPIRATION, HEARTRATE-- OLYMPIAN.
NONE OF YOUR RECENT ORDEALS SEEM TO HAVE AFFECTED YOUR STRENGTH AND STAMINA...
...OR YOUR CUNNING.
"CATCHING THE GOAT"--PICTURE FOUR OF THE GOATHERD SEQUENCE.
A TEST OF TOUCH.

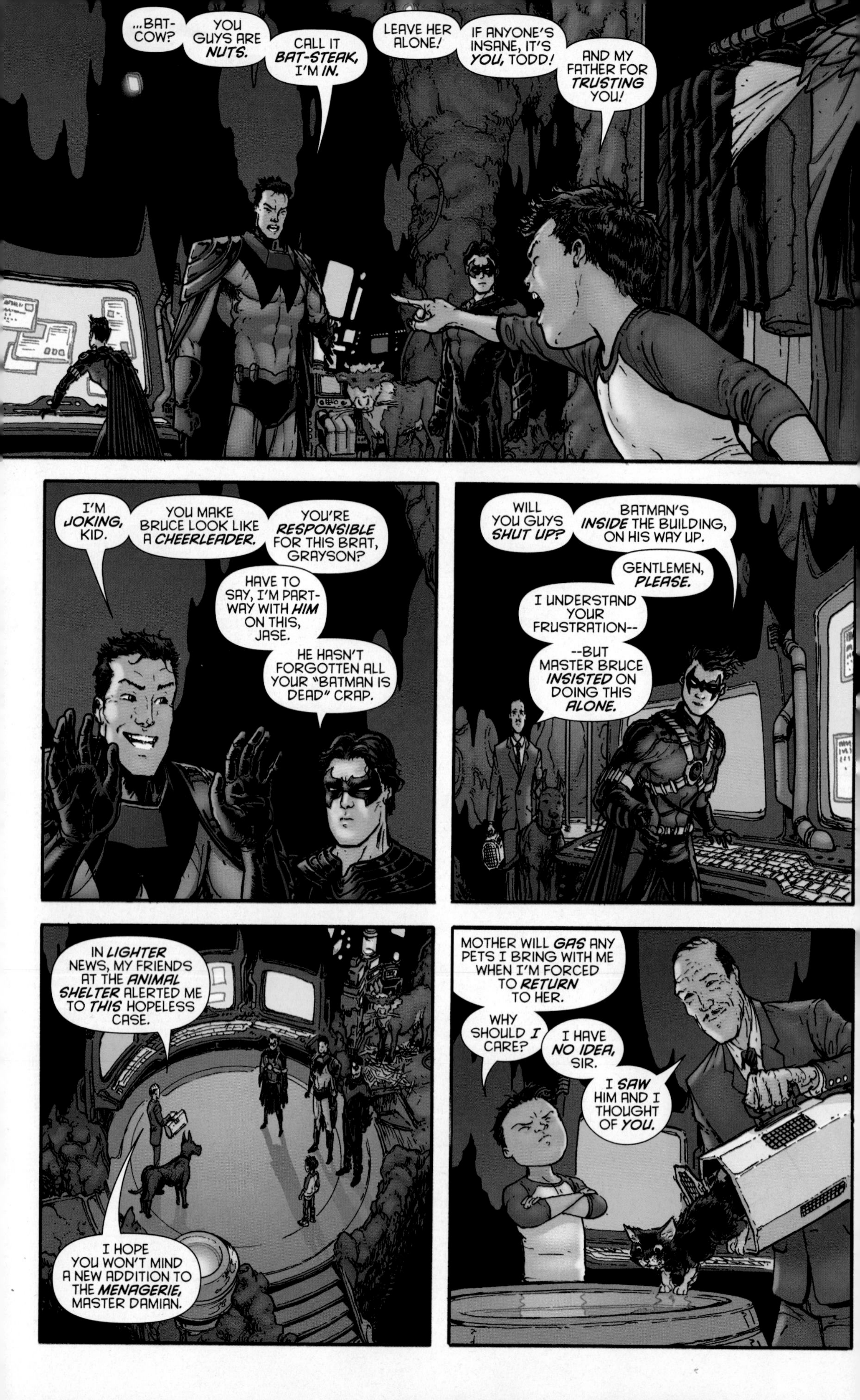
...BAT-COW?
YOU GUYS ARE NUTS.
CALL IT BAT-STEAK, I'M IN.
LEAVE HER ALONE!
IF ANYONE'S INSANE, IT'S YOU, TODD!
AND MY FATHER FOR TRUSTING YOU!
I'M JOKING, KID.
YOU MAKE BRUCE LOOK LIKE A CHEERLEADER.
YOU'RE RESPONSIBLE FOR THIS BRAT, GRAYSON?
HAVE TO SAY, I'M PART-WAY WITH HIM ON THIS, JASE.
HE HASN'T FORGOTTEN ALL YOUR "BATMAN IS DEAD" CRAP.
WILL YOU GUYS SHUT UP?
BATMAN'S INSIDE THE BUILDING, ON HIS WAY UP.
GENTLEMEN, PLEASE.
I UNDERSTAND YOUR FRUSTRATION--
--BUT MASTER BRUCE INSISTED ON DOING THIS ALONE.
IN LIGHTER NEWS, MY FRIENDS AT THE ANIMAL SHELTER ALERTED ME TO THIS HOPELESS CASE.
I HOPE YOU WON'T MIND A NEW ADDITION TO THE MENAGERIE, MASTER DAMIAN.
MOTHER WILL GAS ANY PETS I BRING WITH ME WHEN I'M FORCED TO RETURN TO HER.
WHY SHOULD I CARE?
I HAVE NO IDEA, SIR.
I SAW HIM AND I THOUGHT OF YOU.

WHAT DOES...

!

SFFT!

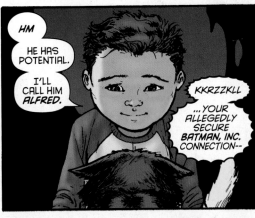

HM

HE HAS POTENTIAL.

I'LL CALL HIM ALFRED.

KKRZZKLL

...YOUR ALLEGEDLY SECURE BATMAN, INC. CONNECTION--

--I KNOW EVERYTHING.

THAT'S MOTHER'S VOICE.

AND FATHER.

DAMIAN WAS BORN TO PROVIDE SPARE PARTS FOR RA'S AL GHUL...

...IS IT ANY WONDER HE CHOSE TO REJECT EVERYTHING YOU AND YOUR FATHER STAND FOR?

MOOOO

HOW LONG HAVE YOU *BEEN* IN THIS BUILDING?

MY PEOPLE CAN ERECT AND DISMANTLE A FULLY FUNCTIONING *HEADQUARTERS* IN EIGHTEEN HOURS.

WE'VE ALREADY MOVED ON TO THE *NEW* PLACE.

TOK

TIK

TOK

TIK

OK

OK

TIK

TOK

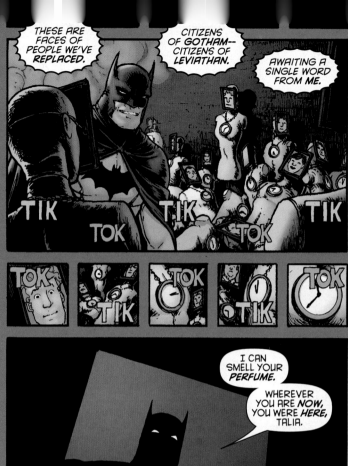

THESE ARE FACES OF PEOPLE WE'VE *REPLACED.*

CITIZENS OF *GOTHAM--* CITIZENS OF *LEVIATHAN.*

AWAITING A SINGLE WORD FROM *ME.*

TIK

TOK

TIK

TOK

TIK

TOK

TIK

TOK

TIK

I CAN SMELL YOUR *PERFUME.*

WHEREVER YOU ARE *NOW,* YOU WERE *HERE,* TALIA.

TIK

YOU *REMEMBER* MY PERFUME?

IT SMELLS OF THE DESERT BY MOONLIGHT.

TALIA.

REMEMBER--

DID YOU *EVER* LOVE ME?

THE DEVIL'S DAUGHTER.

YOU WERE *EVERYTHING* I EVER *DREAMED* ABOUT.

BUT THIS ISN'T *YOU,* TALIA...

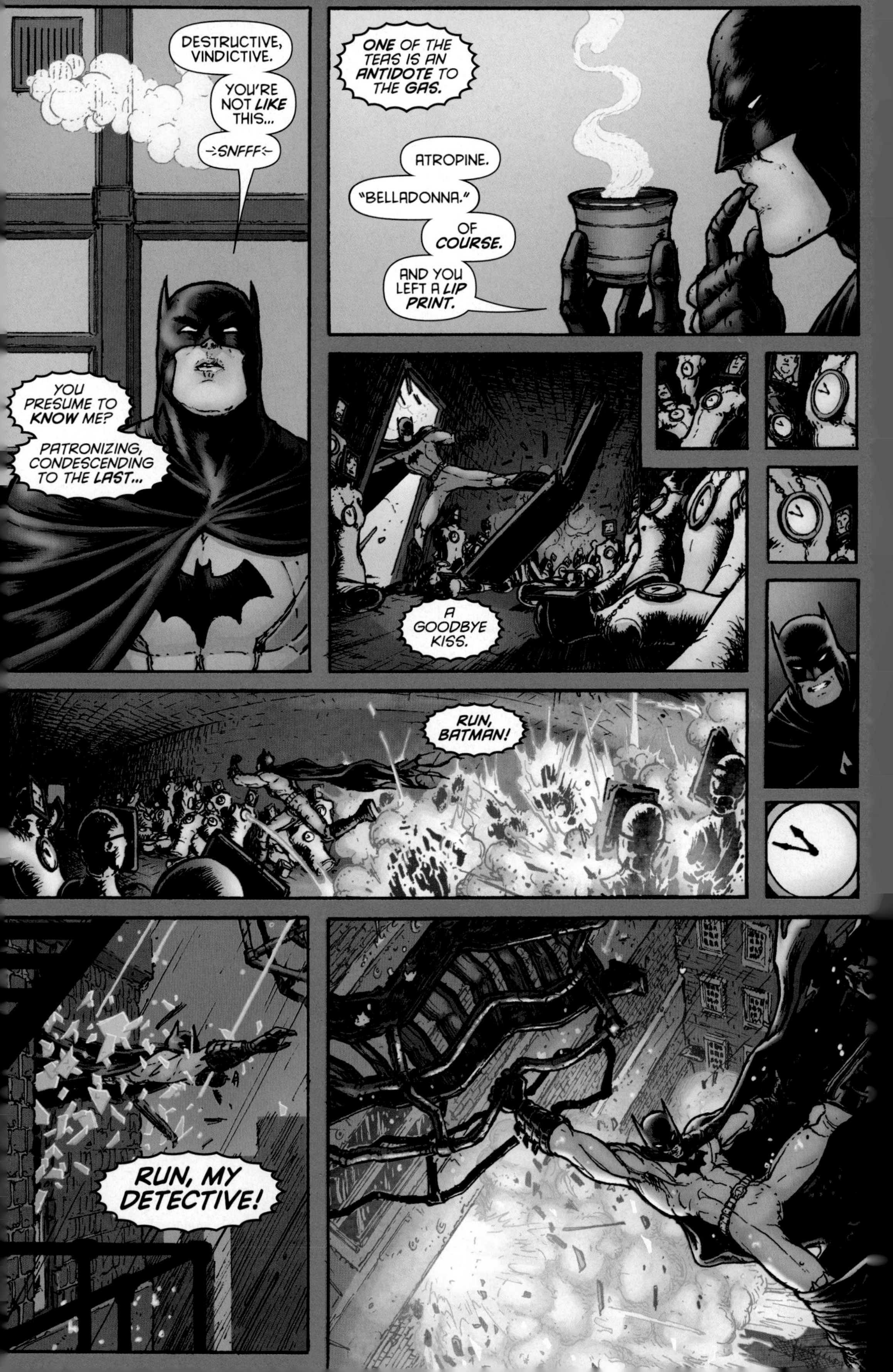
DESTRUCTIVE, VINDICTIVE.
YOU'RE NOT LIKE THIS...
-SNFFF-
YOU PRESUME TO KNOW ME?
PATRONIZING, CONDESCENDING TO THE LAST...
ONE OF THE TEAS IS AN ANTIDOTE TO THE GAS.
ATROPINE.
"BELLADONNA."
OF COURSE.
AND YOU LEFT A LIP PRINT.
A GOODBYE KISS.
RUN, BATMAN!
RUN, MY DETECTIVE!

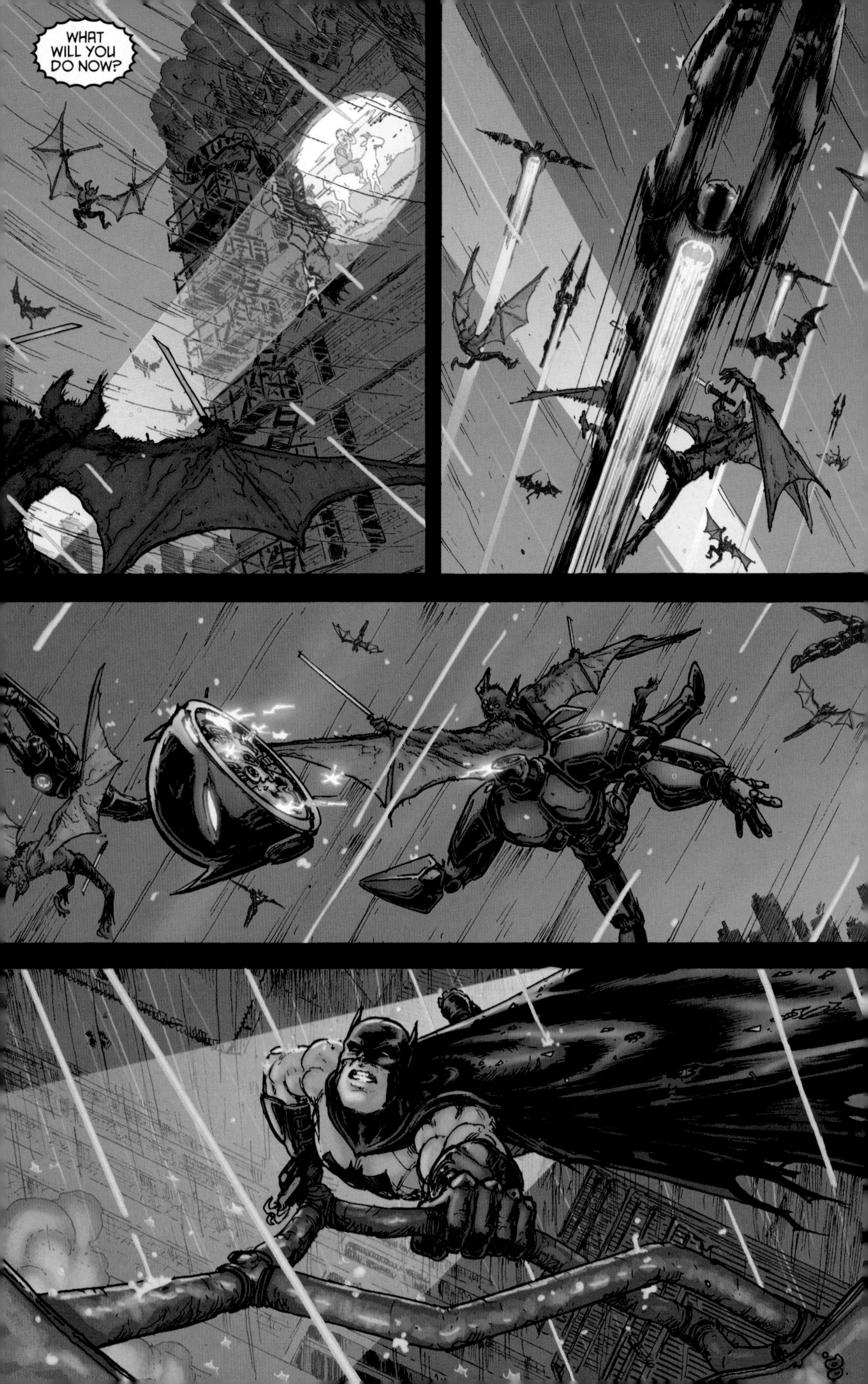
WHAT WILL YOU DO NOW?

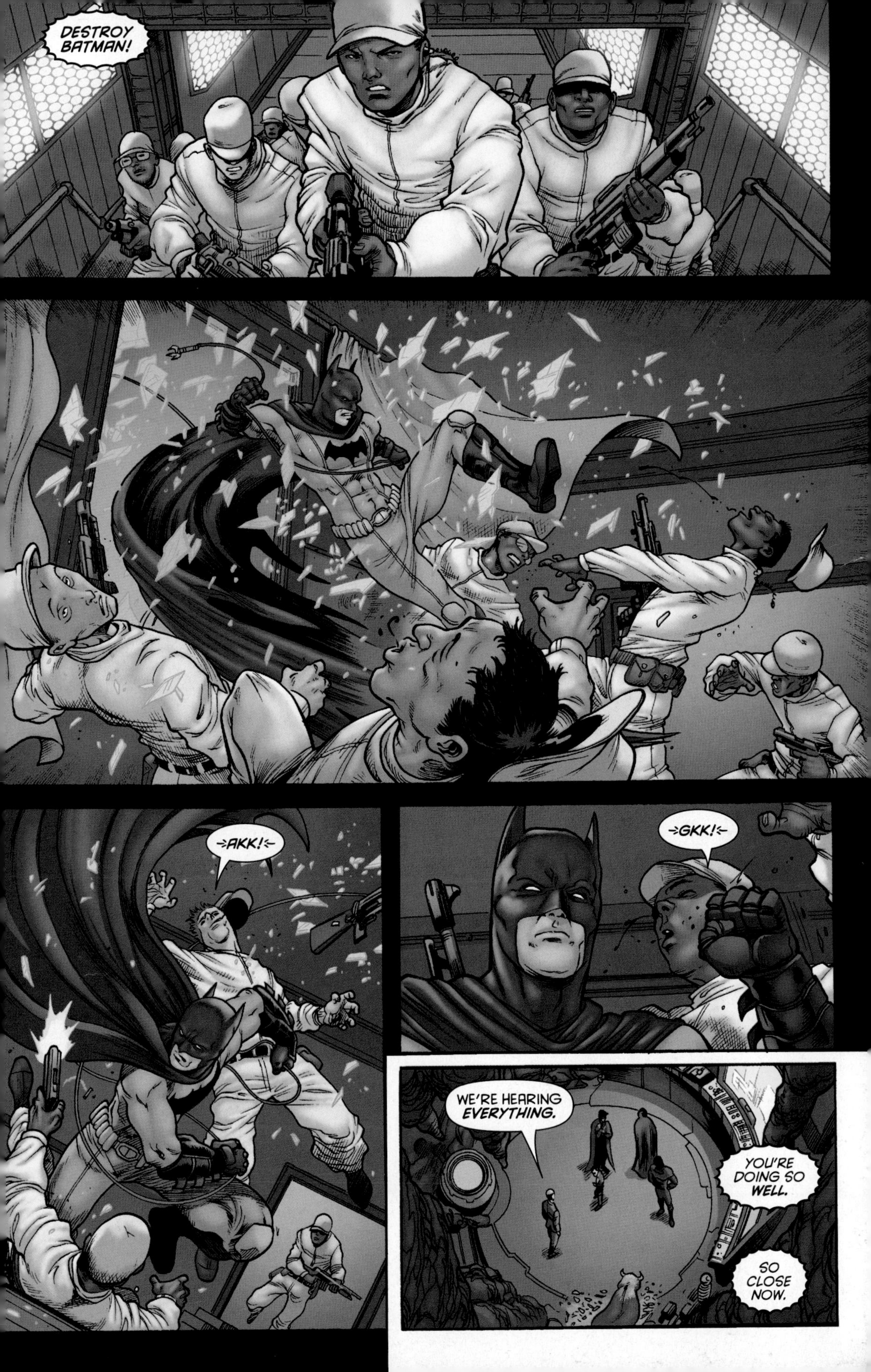
DESTROY BATMAN!
AKK!
GKK!
WE'RE HEARING EVERYTHING.
YOU'RE DOING SO WELL.
SO CLOSE NOW.

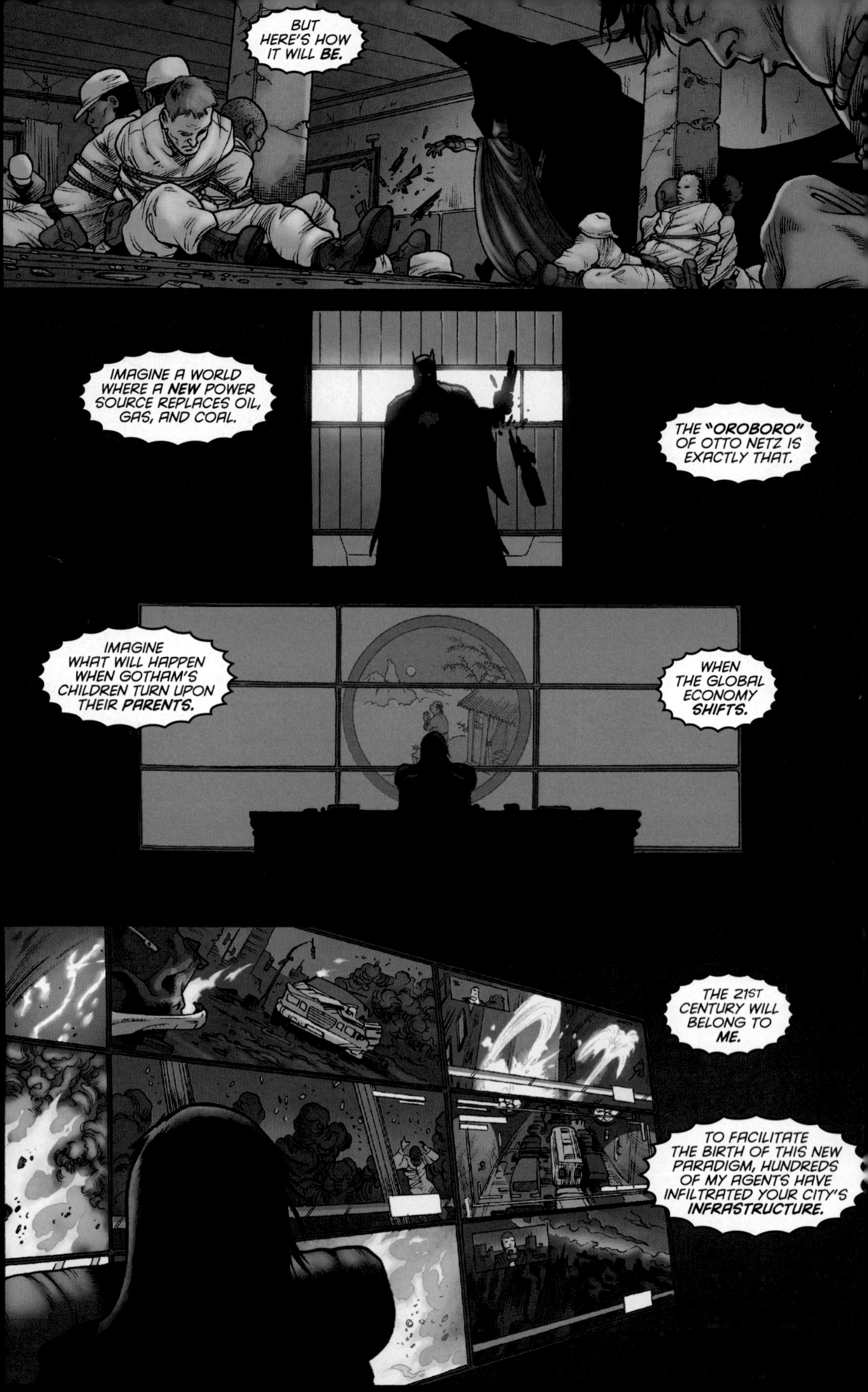
BUT HERE'S HOW IT WILL BE.
IMAGINE A WORLD WHERE A NEW POWER SOURCE REPLACES OIL, GAS, AND COAL.
THE "OROBORO" OF OTTO NETZ IS EXACTLY THAT.
IMAGINE WHAT WILL HAPPEN WHEN GOTHAM'S CHILDREN TURN UPON THEIR PARENTS.
WHEN THE GLOBAL ECONOMY SHIFTS.
THE 21ST CENTURY WILL BELONG TO ME.
TO FACILITATE THE BIRTH OF THIS NEW PARADIGM, HUNDREDS OF MY AGENTS HAVE INFILTRATED YOUR CITY'S INFRASTRUCTURE.

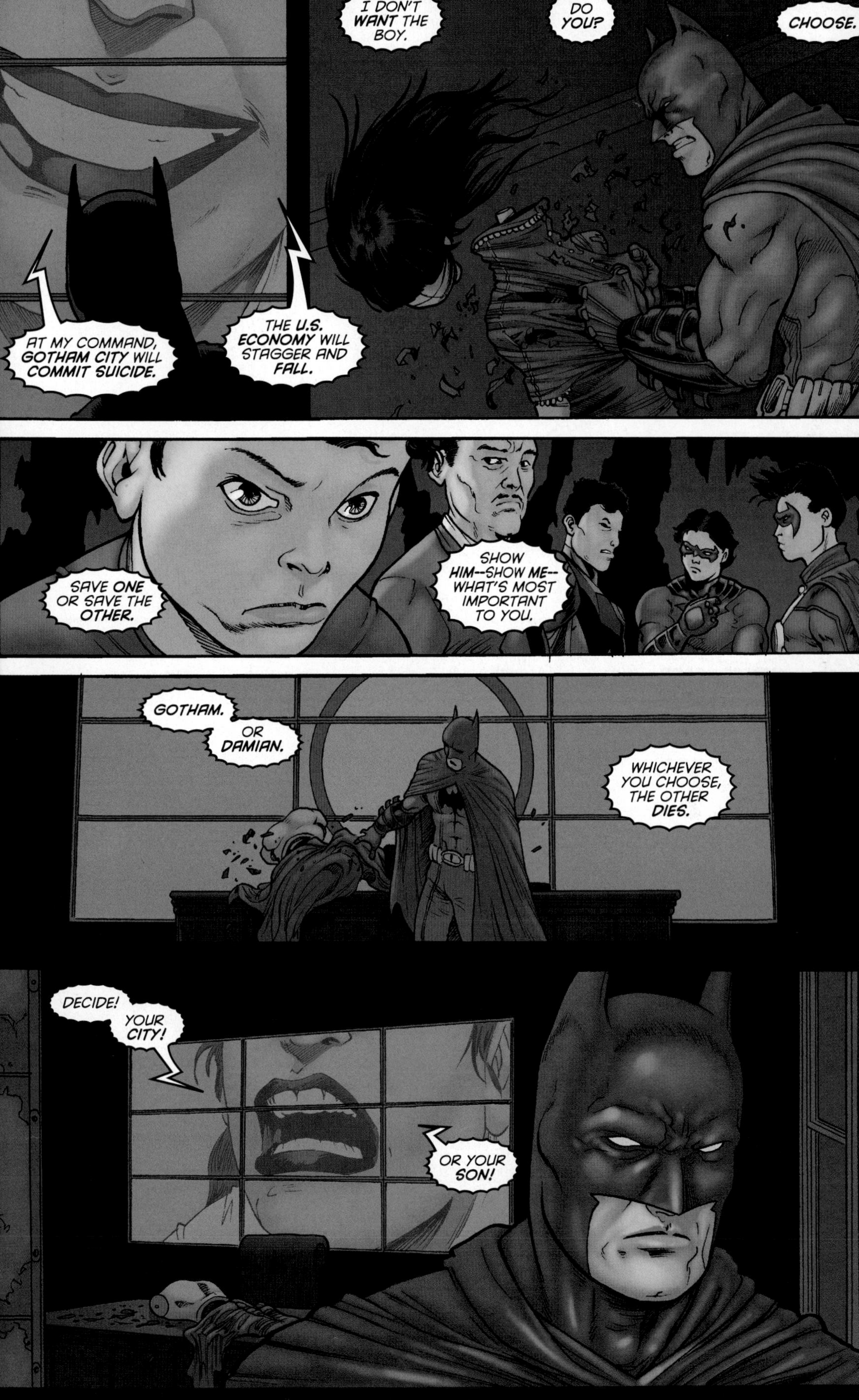

I DON'T WANT THE BOY.
DO YOU?
CHOOSE.
AT MY COMMAND, GOTHAM CITY WILL COMMIT SUICIDE.
THE U.S. ECONOMY WILL STAGGER AND FALL.
SAVE ONE OR SAVE THE OTHER.
SHOW HIM--SHOW ME--WHAT'S MOST IMPORTANT TO YOU.
GOTHAM.
OR DAMIAN.
WHICHEVER YOU CHOOSE, THE OTHER DIES.
DECIDE!
YOUR CITY!
OR YOUR SON!

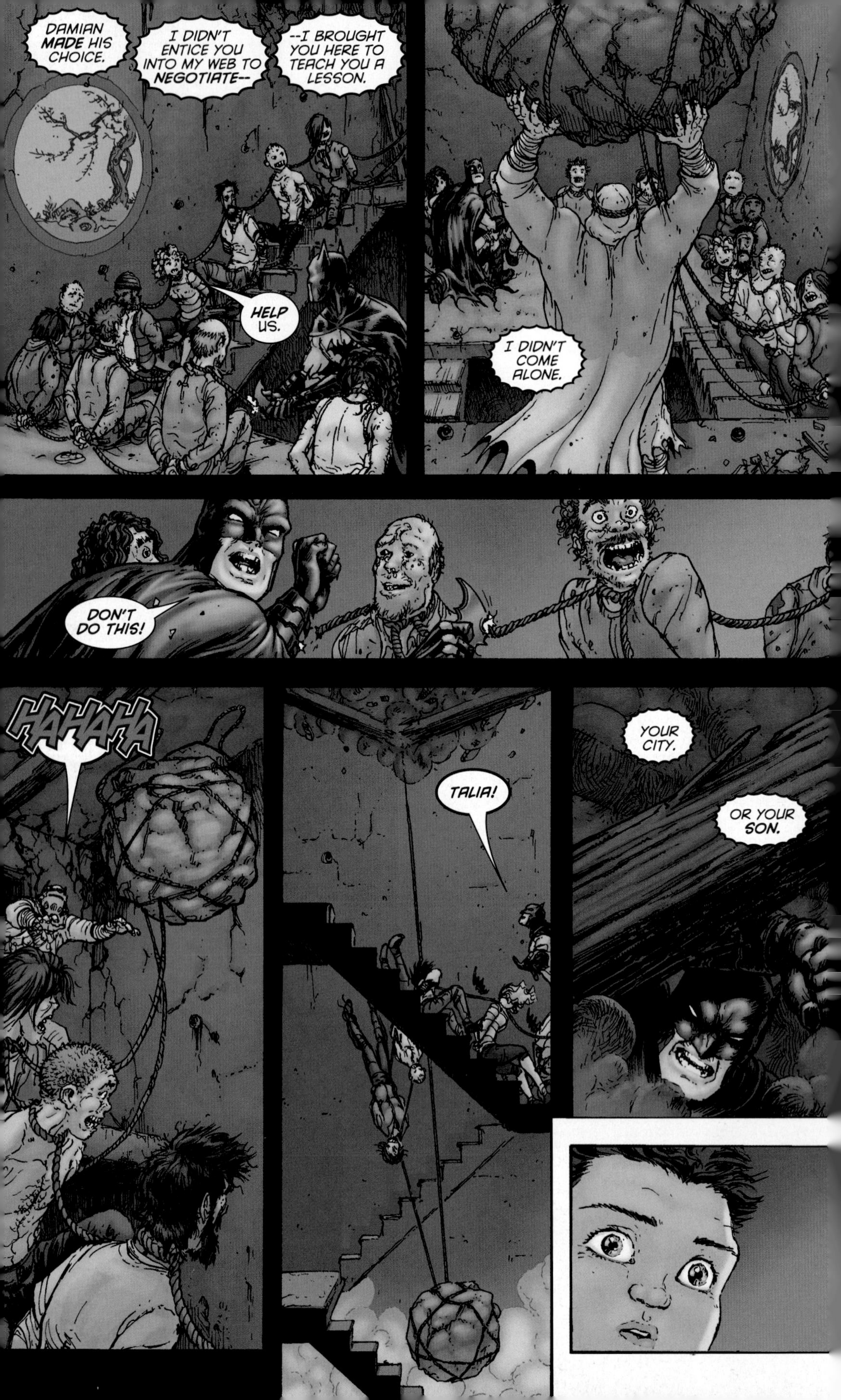
DAMIAN MADE HIS CHOICE.
I DIDN'T ENTICE YOU INTO MY WEB TO NEGOTIATE--
--I BROUGHT YOU HERE TO TEACH YOU A LESSON.
HELP US.
I DIDN'T COME ALONE.
DON'T DO THIS!
HAHAHA
TALIA!
YOUR CITY.
OR YOUR SON.

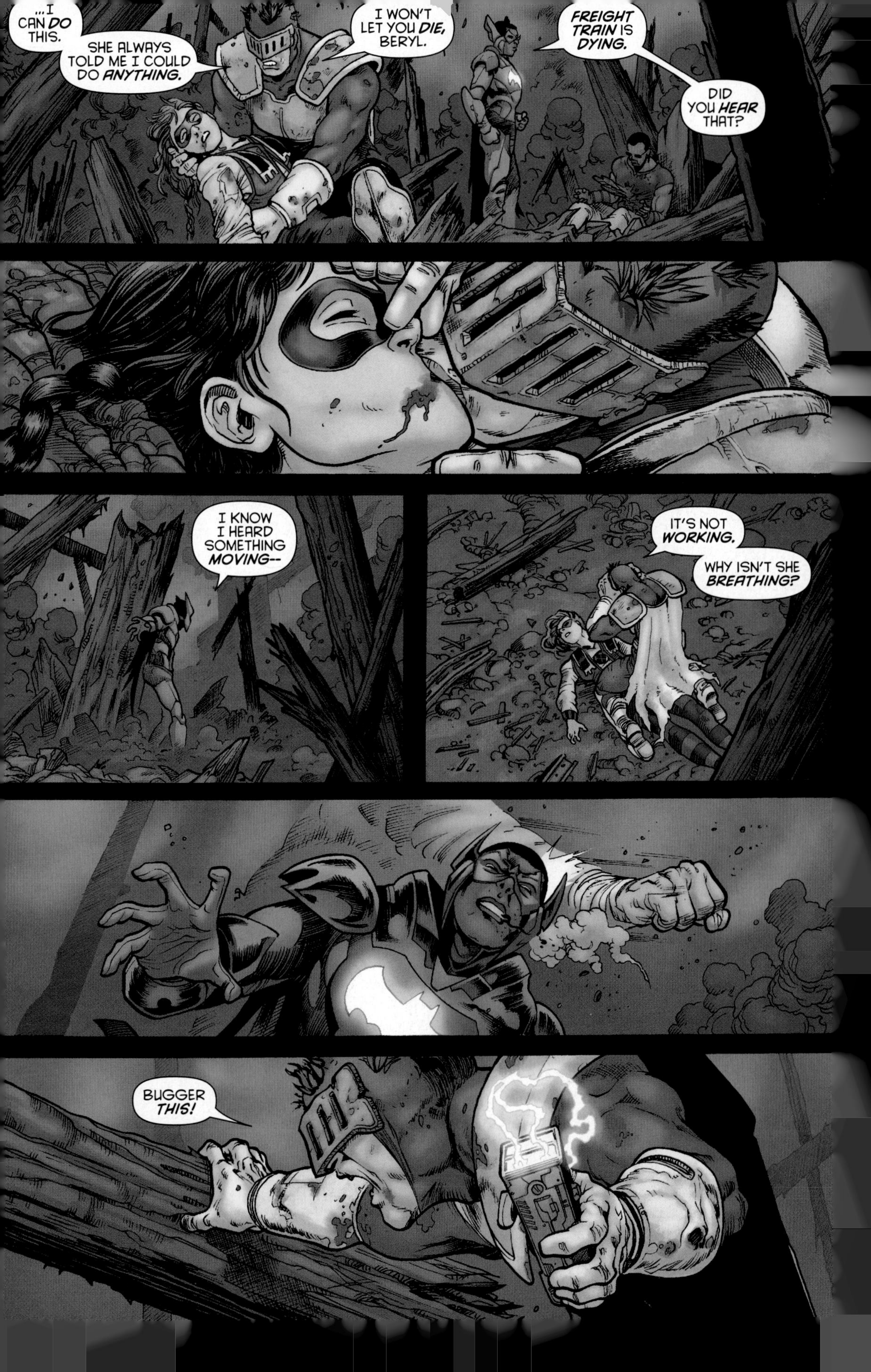
...I CAN DO THIS.
SHE ALWAYS TOLD ME I COULD DO ANYTHING.
I WON'T LET YOU DIE, BERYL.
FREIGHT TRAIN IS DYING.
DID YOU HEAR THAT?
I KNOW I HEARD SOMETHING MOVING--
IT'S NOT WORKING.
WHY ISN'T SHE BREATHING?
BUGGER THIS!

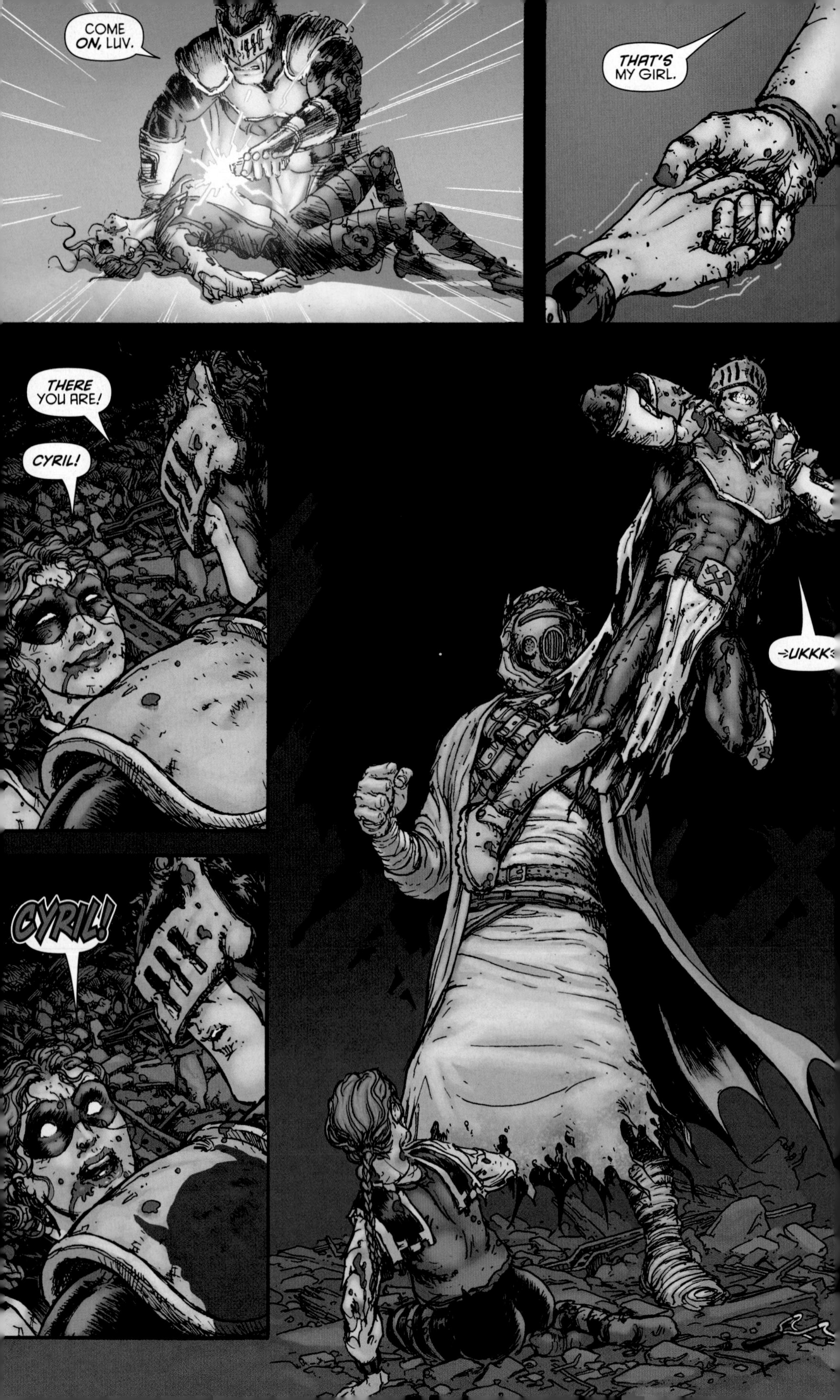
COME ON, LUV.
THAT'S MY GIRL.
THERE YOU ARE!
CYRIL!
CYRIL!
UKKK

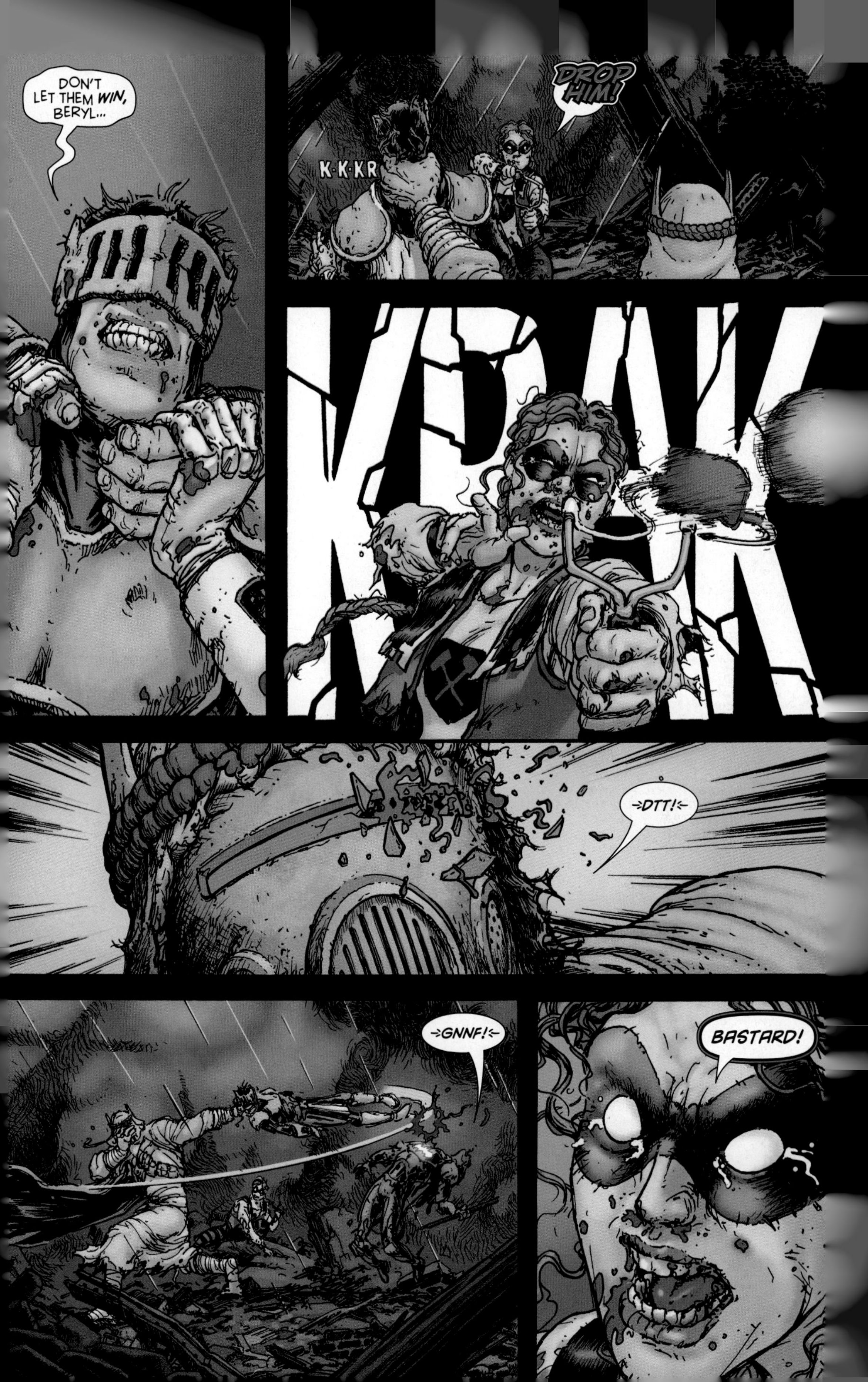
DON'T LET THEM WIN, BERYL...
DROP HIM!
K-K-KR
KRAK
-DTT!-
-GNNF!-
BASTARD!

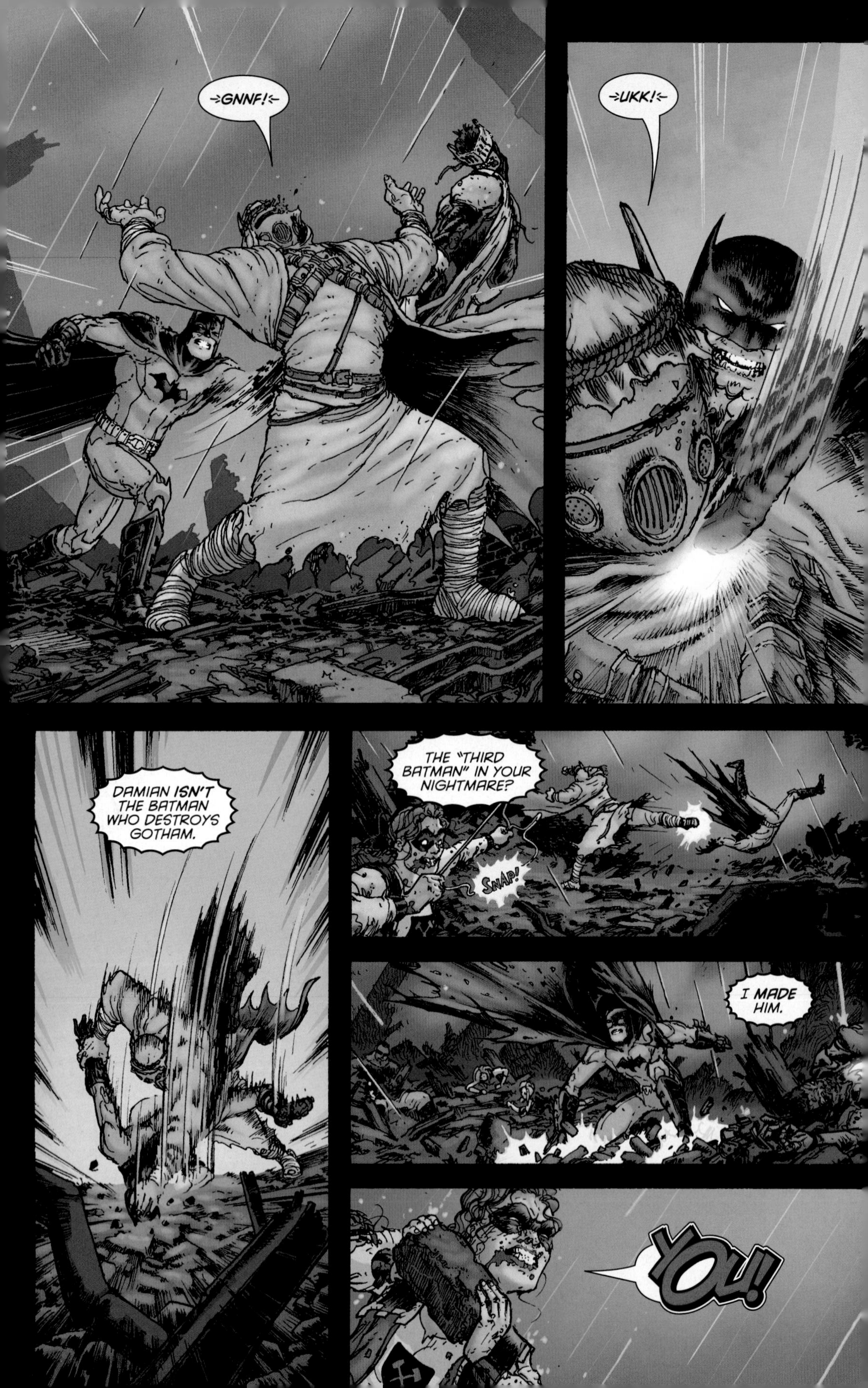

-GNNF!-
-UKK!-
DAMIAN ISN'T THE BATMAN WHO DESTROYS GOTHAM.
THE "THIRD BATMAN" IN YOUR NIGHTMARE?
SNAP!
I MADE HIM.
YOU!

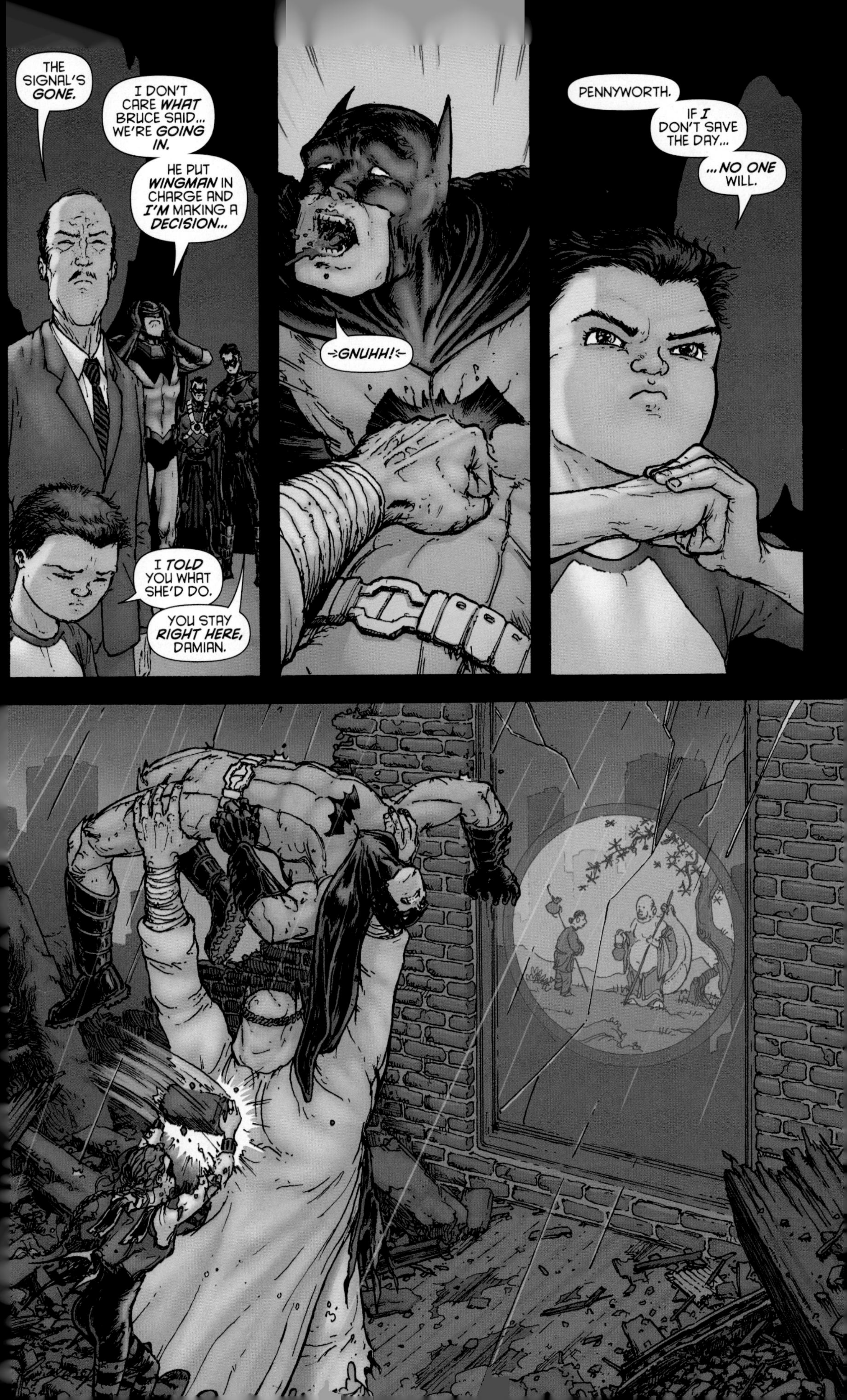
THE SIGNAL'S GONE.
I DON'T CARE WHAT BRUCE SAID... WE'RE GOING IN.
HE PUT WINGMAN IN CHARGE AND I'M MAKING A DECISION...
I TOLD YOU WHAT SHE'D DO.
YOU STAY RIGHT HERE, DAMIAN.
GNUHH!
PENNYWORTH.
IF I DON'T SAVE THE DAY...
...NO ONE WILL.

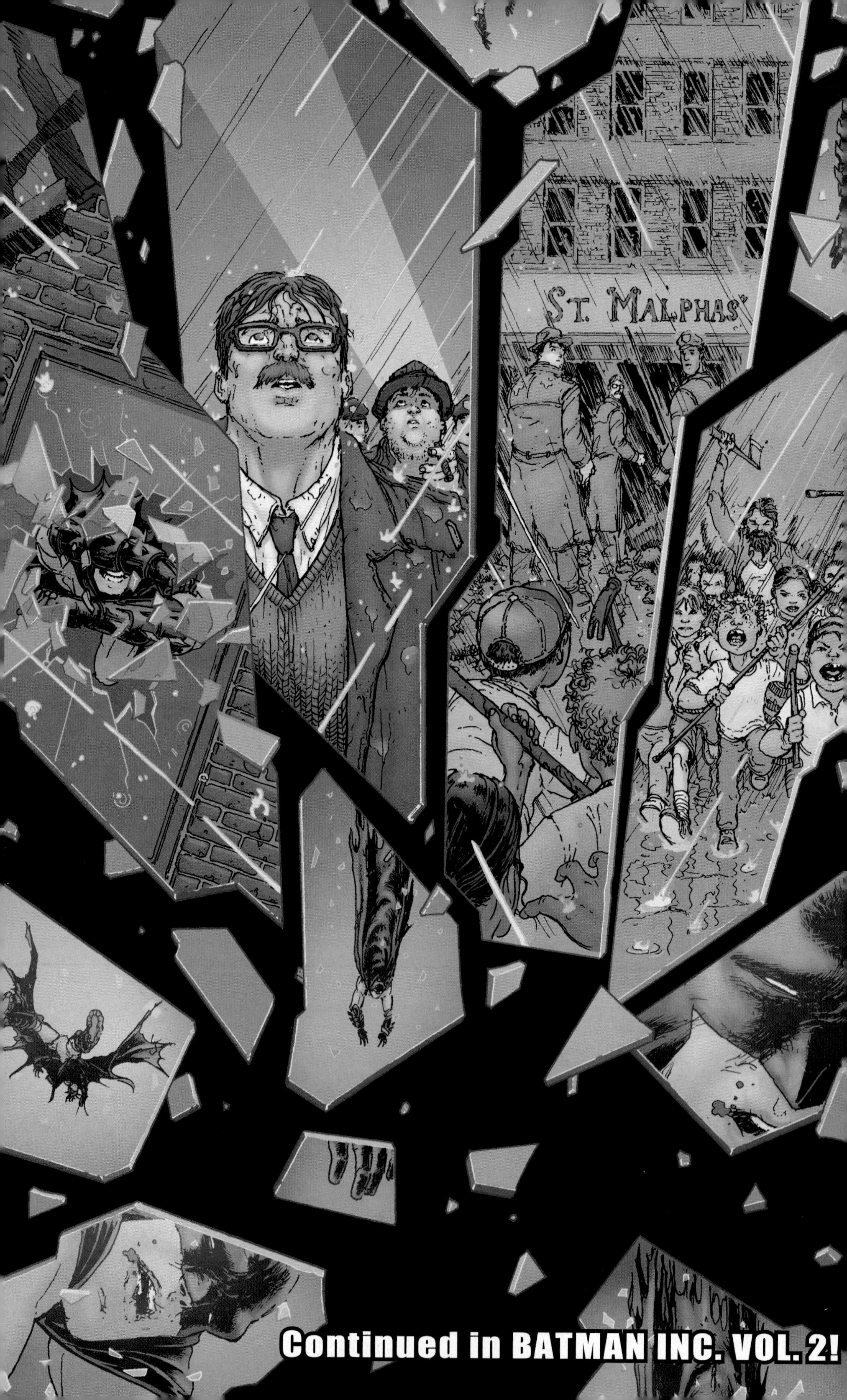
ST. MALPHAS'

Continued in BATMAN INC. VOL. 2!

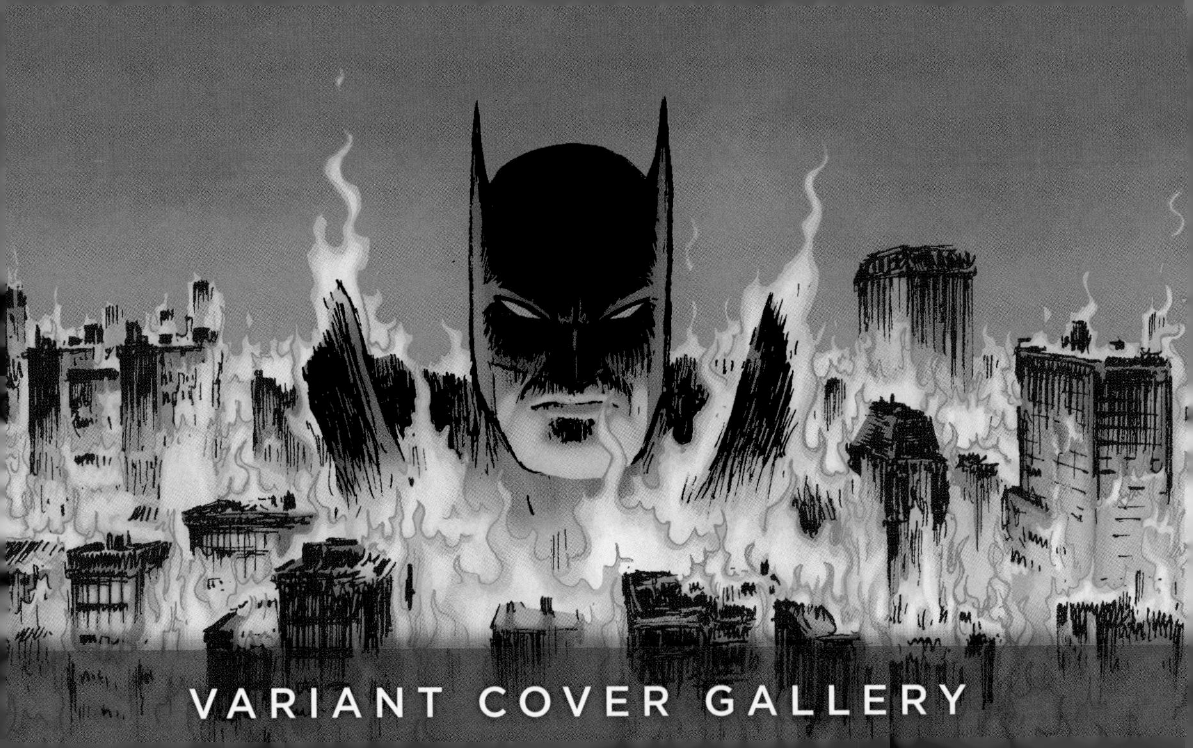

VARIANT COVER GALLERY

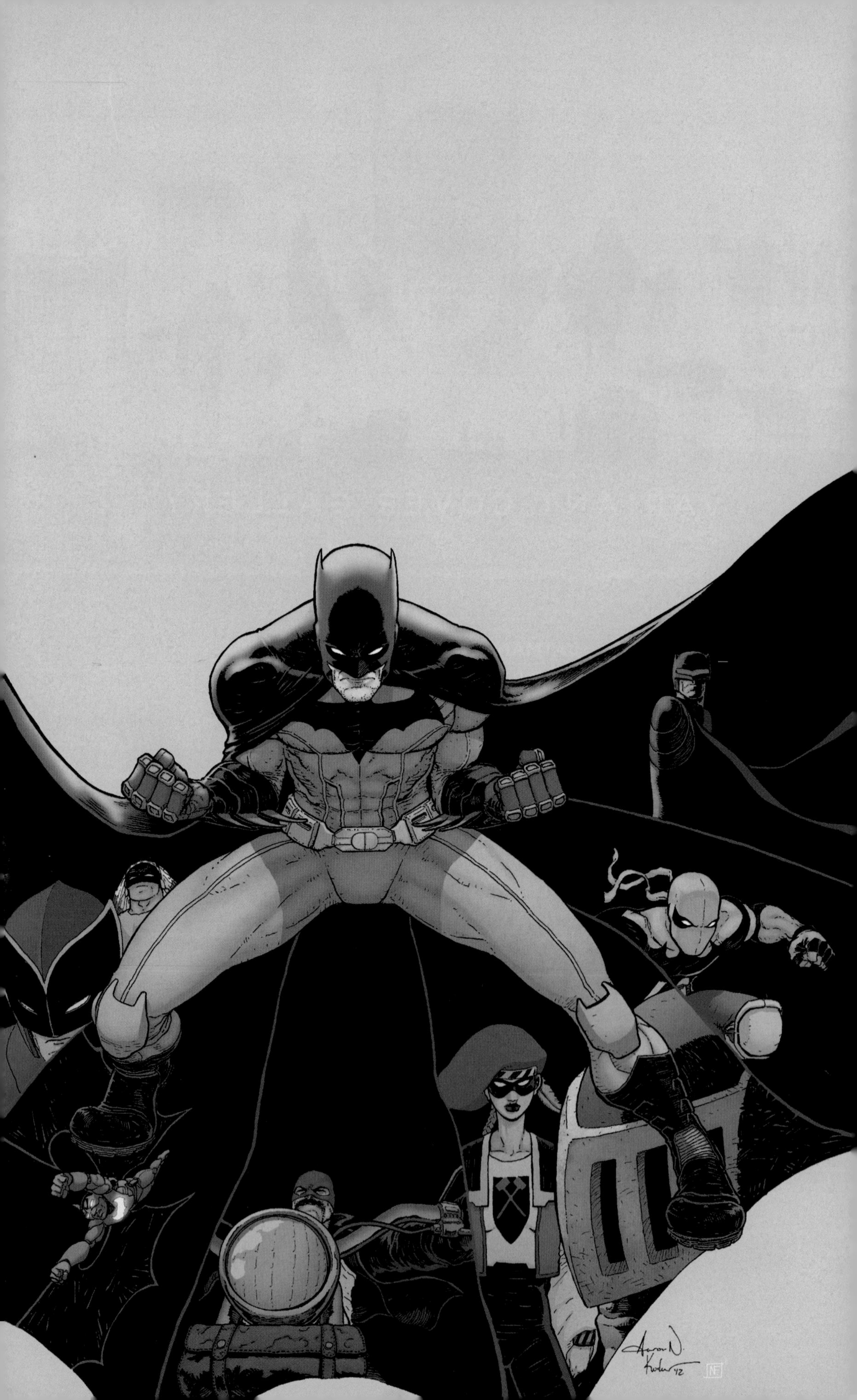

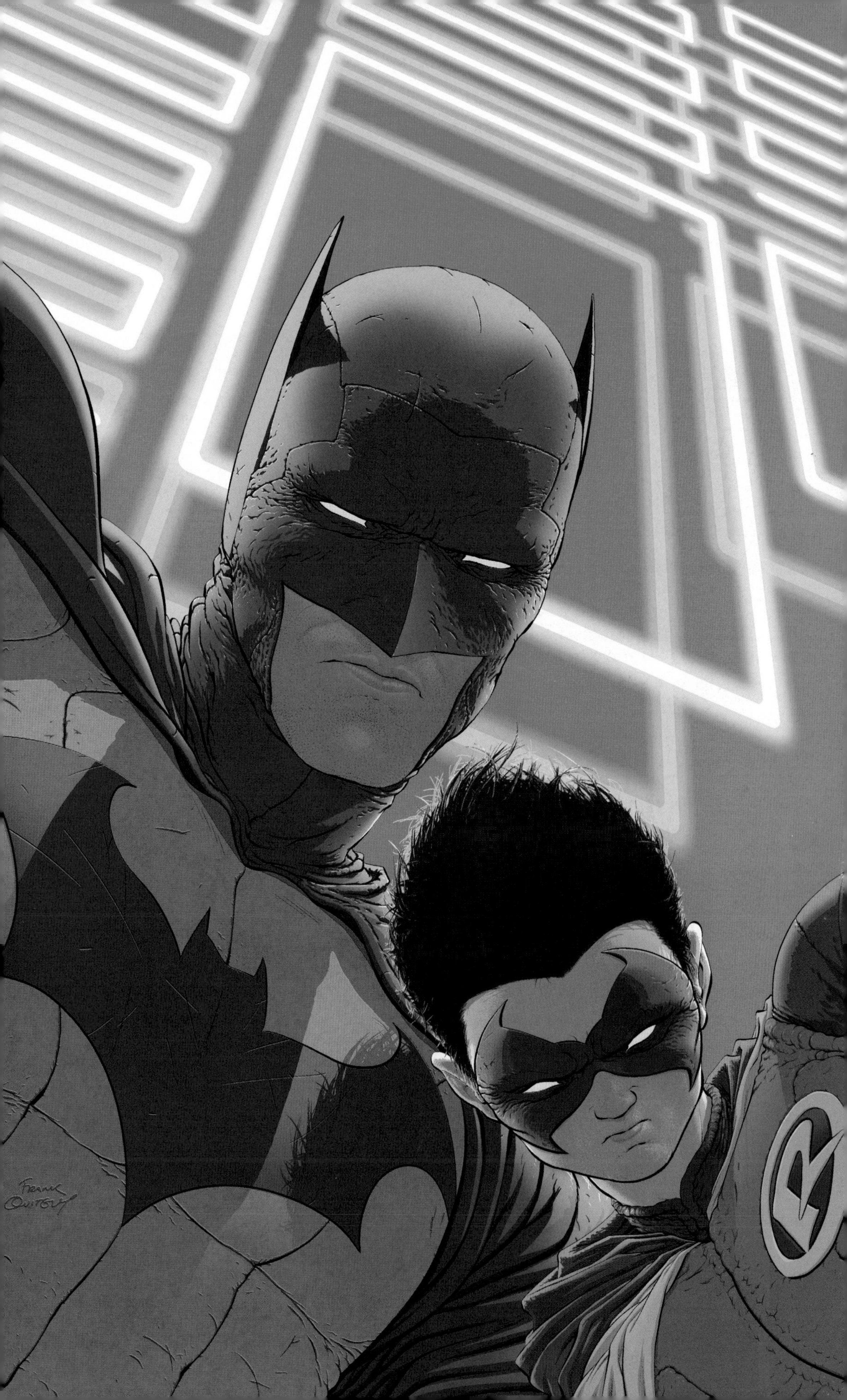

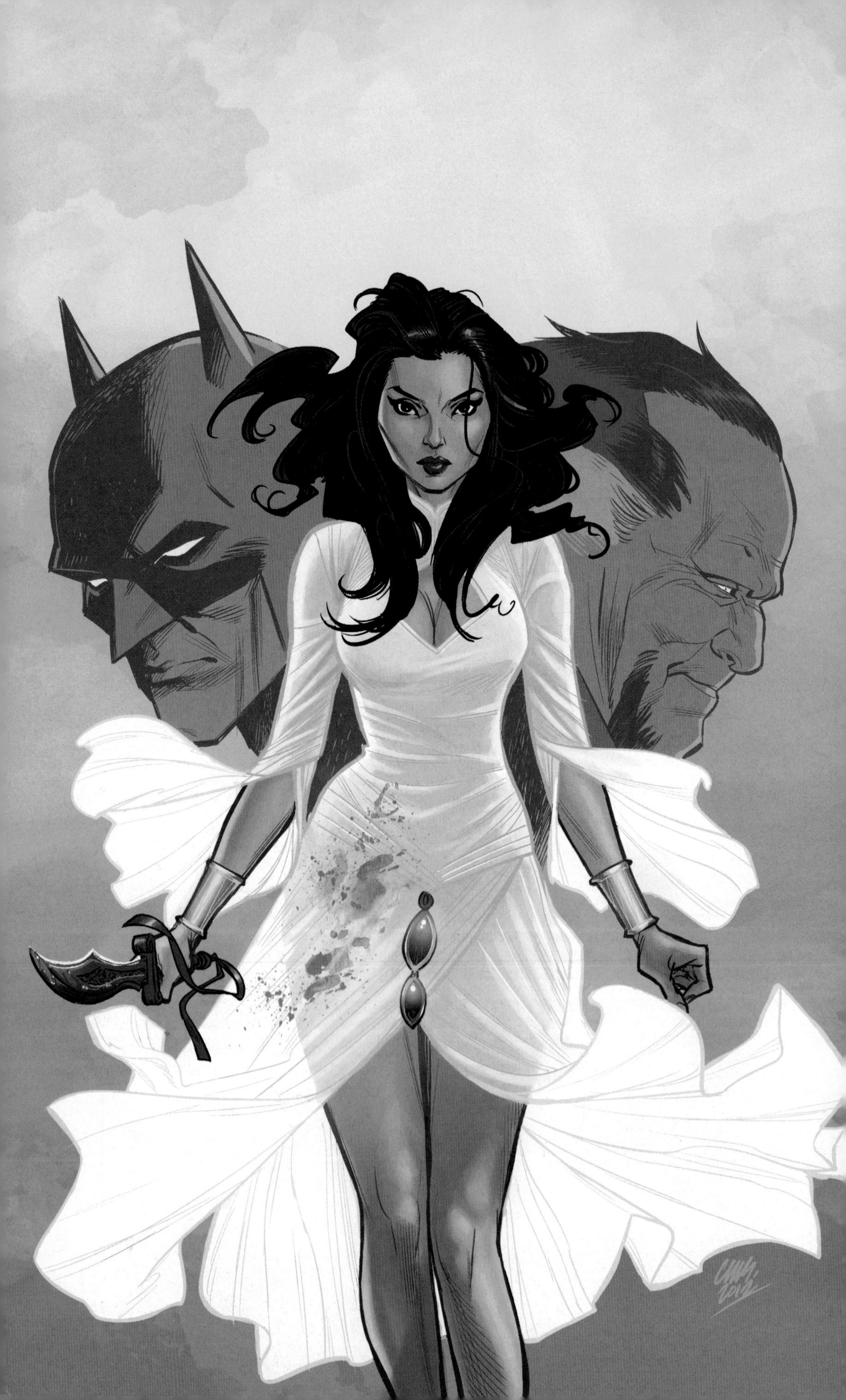